Complete
WOODWORKING
HANDBOOK

by

JEANNETTE T. ADAMS

and

EMANUELE STIERI

Drawings by
JOHN G. MARINAC

ARCO PUBLISHING COMPANY, INC.   New York

Published by Arco Publishing Company, Inc.

219 Park Avenue South, New York, N. Y. 10003

Eighth Printing, 1974

Library of Congress

Catalog Card Number: 60-8584

ISBN 0-668-00718-4

Printed in the United States of America

Preface

THIS BOOK has been produced to satisfy a demand for a complete handbook on woodworking, and covers every phase of this important subject.

Emphasis has been placed on providing complete directions for using and maintaining every hand- and power-driven woodworking tool used in the workshop.

Instructions for making new woodworking projects or for making repairs, and finishing and polishing furniture are fully illustrated with detailed and dimensional drawings, diagrams, and photographs. Lists of required tools and materials are also given.

Every effort has been made by the author to give the worker authoritative information on all up-to-date materials; as well as information that will enable him to select the requisite tools wisely, keep them in good condition, and choose the correct material for any object he may desire to construct. This information can be of inestimable value to the worker.

All projects and procedures described are well within the abilities of the average worker who has the inclination to use tools intelligently. Practicability has been the main consideration.

This book comprises descriptions of different kinds of wood and wood products. A complete chapter on glues and gluing methods; a chapter on painting tools and equipment; and a chapter on paints, painting, and finishing procedures. To facilitate quick reference several tables have been included.

The COMPLETE WOODWORKING HANDBOOK has been planned with the conviction that it will be a welcome and valued aid to those who have long desired a complete handbook on the subject.

J. T. A.

iii

Acknowledgments

THE AUTHOR desires to acknowledge with thanks the assistance of the following national organizations and branches of the government that have co-operated in the production of this book:

American Steel & Wire Co., American Brush Co., Armstrong Cork Co., Atlas Press Co., Black & Decker Mfg. Co., California Redwood Association, Carborundum Co., Cleveland Twist Drill Co., Delta Power Tool Division — Rockwell Manufacturing Co., DeVilbiss Co., Devoe & Raynolds Co., DeWalt Division — American Machine & Foundry Co., Douglas Fir Plywood Association, E. I. duPont de Nemours & Co., Franklin Glue Co., Henry Disston & Sons, National Lumber Manufacturers Association, National Paint, Varnish and Lacquer Association, National Retail Lumber Dealers Association, Nicholson File Co., Northern Hemlock & Hardwood Manufacturers Association, Northern Pine Manufacturers Association, Pittsburgh Plate Glass Co. — Brush Division, S. C. Johnson & Son, Sherwin-Williams Co., South Bend Lathe Works, Southern Pine Association, Stanley Works, U. S. Department of Agriculture, U. S. Forest Service — Forest Products Laboratory, United States Plywood Corp., United States Steel Corp., Western Pine Association, and Yale & Towne Manufacturing Co.

The author is indebted to the following architects and designers for some of the plywood plans: Mary Lund Davis, Pat and Jerry Gropp, and Walter D. Widmeyer.

Table of Contents

CHAPTER 1

Wood and Wood Products

Wood and wood products are the materials chiefly used by the home mechanic, because they are easy to handle and to fasten together with nails, screws, or glue, and they can be made highly ornamental. When properly dried and cured, they are not affected by varying temperatures, as they are poor conductors of heat. If damaged they can be repaired easily.

STRUCTURE AND CLASSIFICATION

The home craftsman should become acquainted with the structural differences of the types of woods used in home construction and repairs. The two general classifications are hardwoods and softwoods.

Wood is made up of cells similar to those of a honeycomb, but wood cells are much smaller, and they vary in size and shape. The relative size and the arrangement of these cells is fairly constant in each species of wood, but varies among the different species. This variation is a reliable means of distinguishing one wood from another.

Just beneath the bark, a layer of wood is added each year on the outside of the layer previously formed. In trees that grow in a temperate climate, the cells formed at the beginning of each year's growth are considerably larger than those formed later in the season. This decided contrast forms a definite boundary to each year's growth of a tree. In a cross section of a tree trunk, these layers of wood are well defined and are known as annual rings.

1

The soft open-celled wood formed in the spring is called the springwood, while the harder and denser wood formed later in the season is known as the summerwood. In some types of wood, such as birch, maple, and gum, the distinction between springwood and summerwood is not clear.

Some species, such as the red oaks, willow, and certain types of pine, usually have wide annual rings, while others, such as the white oaks, sugar maple, and longleaf pine, have narrow rings. While the width of the rings is used to help identify woods, do not place too much emphasis on this factor. The rate of growth, which determines the width of these rings, is also dependent upon the soil, climate, and density of forest in which the tree grew.

Wood can be cut in three distinct planes with respect to the annual rings (Chap. 3). The end of a piece of wood shows a cross section of the annual layers or rings of growth. This is called the end surface, or transverse surface. It shows the size and arrangement of the cells better than any other surface or plane. When wood is cut lengthwise through the center, or pith, of the tree, the exposed surfaces are called radial or quartered surfaces. A longitudinal surface that does not pass through the center is called a tangential surface. Lumber classified as plain-sawed is tangentially cut.

Structure of hardwoods. Pores, technically called vessels, are confined almost entirely to the hardwoods, or woods derived from broad-leaved trees. These pores are hollow tubes made up of large cells with open ends set one above the other. For this reason, hardwoods are also known as porous woods. In conifers, or evergreen trees, the cells are closed at the ends. Conifers therefore are classed as nonporous woods.

In coarse-textured, or open-grained woods, such as oak, ash, or walnut, the pores are plainly visible, but in fine-textured woods, such as beech, maple, and basswood, they are visible only with a fairly good hand lens.

In some types of. hardwoods, the pores are comparatively large at the beginning of each annual ring, but decrease in size more or less abruptly toward the summerwood, thus forming a distinct porous ring in the springwood. These woods are classed as ring-porous woods. Oak, chestnut, ash, and elm are examples of this class.

In other hardwoods, the pores are of practically uniform size throughout the outer portion of the summerwood. These are called diffuse-porous woods, of which birch, gum, poplar, and maple are outstanding examples. The pores in the summerwood of ring-porous woods are arranged in various recognizable ways, described later in the identification of each type of wood.

The pores of some hardwoods, except in the outer sapwood, are filled with a frothlike growth, called a tylosis, formed by ingrowth from neighboring cells. Tyloses are especially abundant in woods of the white-oak group.

Wood fibers constitute most of the denser part of hardwoods. They are very narrow, comparatively long, thick-walled cells, but they cannot be distinguished without a microscope. Though part of the cellular structure of wood, their arrangement can rarely be used for identification purposes. Conifers have no true wood fibers.

Included in the cellular structure of hardwoods are cells known as parenchyma cells. These are comparatively short, usually thin-walled cells. They are too small to be seen individually without a strong microscope, but collectively they can be recognized in the cross section of the wood by the light-colored tissue which they form. In some hardwoods, for example, in some types of elm and maple, the parenchyma cells are so scattered that they are not noticeable. In hickory and in white and green ash, the parenchyma surrounds the pores and projects in tangential lines. In other species of hardwoods, such as black ash, the parenchyma surrounds the pores, causing a halo to appear around them. In yellow poplar, the parenchyma is confined to a narrow layer on the outer portion of each annual ring.

Flecks, or pith flecks, are abnormal groups of these parenchyma cells which appear on the end surface of some woods as small discolored spots, and as darkened streaks on the longitudinal surface. These pith flecks are caused by the larvae of insects that burrow into the young wood under the bark, the passages afterward being filled by the parenchyma cells. Flecks are abundant in some types of birch, red and silver maple, basswood, and a few other species. While they are an added means of identification, their presence or absence should not be relied on too much. However, if a specimen of birch is found to contain numerous pith flecks, it is considered a good indication that it is neither sweet nor yellow birch.

If flecks are found abundantly in maple, the specimen is not sugar maple.

Medullary rays, also known as pith rays or simply as rays, are narrow bands of cells that extend radially inward from the bark at right angles to the grain. In the oaks, some of the rays are comparatively wide and conspicuous, and give the beautiful silver grain to quartered oak. They are also evident in such woods as sycamore, beech, maple, and cherry. In other woods, such as chestnut and cotton gum, these rays are so fine as to be inconspicuous on the radial surface and invisible on the end surface without a lens.

Structure of softwoods (conifers). Softwoods, or conifers, differ in cellular structure from hardwoods in the absence of pores and true wood fibers, in the radial arrangement of the fibrous cells, called tracheids, and in the presence of resin ducts or resin cells.

A large percentage of the wood is made up of tracheids. These are elongated cells that take the place of both the pores and the wood fibers found in hardwoods. In cross section, the tracheids are considerably narrower than most pores, but wider than most wood fibers of hardwoods. In conifers, the tracheids are practically uniform and are arranged in definite radial rows. They are somewhat flattened radially and thick-walled in the outer parts of each annual ring, thus producing a harder and darker band of summerwood. In the harder types of pines and Douglas fir, the summerwood is conspicuous, and because of its density adds greatly to the strength of the wood and to easy identification.

Conifers, especially Douglas fir, pine, and spruce, contain resin ducts. These are more or less continuous passages parallel to the grain of the wood vertically, and within certain medullary rays at right angles to the grain, horizontally.

Vertical resin ducts usually can be seen in some of the pines without a lens, on smoothly cut end surfaces where they appear as dark- or light-colored specks or small pores, which should not be confused with the pores of hardwoods. Smaller than vertical ducts, horizontal resin ducts are not visible without a microscope.

Pitch pockets, resin streaks, and exudations of resin on end surfaces are positive indications of the presence of resin ducts. The absence of such accumulation of resin does not necessarily mean the absence of resin ducts, however. As a rule, resin will not exude from cuts made after the wood has been seasoned. However, warming pieces of spruce or, especially, pine or Douglas fir in an oven usually causes specks of resin to appear on the ends, showing beyond doubt the presence of ducts. This is especially true of pine and Douglas fir. On longitudinal surfaces that have been exposed to the air for some time, resin ducts will appear as brownish lines.

The medullary rays in conifers are very narrow, with the exception of those that contain horizontal resin ducts, which are slightly wider. These wider rays are technically known as fusiform rays, and are found only in the pines, spruces, larches, and Douglas fir. These fusiform rays occasionally help to determine the presence of resin ducts, especially in the spruces in which the vertical resin ducts sometimes are not easily discernible. On the radial surfaces, however, the horizontal resin ducts often may be recognized as brownish lines, especially in the pines.

Sapwood and heartwood. The outer light-colored area on the end surface of a log is known as the sapwood, while the inner dark core is known as the heartwood. All young wood is light-colored, but when the tree becomes older, the inner part is infiltrated with gums, resins, and other materials, the exact nature of which has not been determined. These color the wood to a greater or lesser degree. In some types of woods the heartwood is extremely dark, while in others there is little difference in color between the sapwood and the heartwood. The spruces, the true firs (not the Douglas fir), hemlocks, cedars, and buckeye belong to the latter class. In cottonwood, beech, gum, sycamore, and basswood the heartwood is only slightly darker than the sapwood. The sapwood often is not white, but slightly tinged with the same color found in the heartwood. The bark will sometimes discolor the sapwood by leaching or staining it after the tree has been cut and give it a bluish color. This is especially true in pines and red gums.

Douglas fir sometimes contains zones of light-colored wood inside the heartwood. These zones are known as internal sapwood. They have been found to take preservative treatments just as well as the outer sapwood.

Sapwood width varies with the age and strength of the tree, the distance from the stump, and the particular species. Young and vigorous trees sometimes have wider sapwood than matured trees, although more annual rings are usually present in the sapwood of older trees because of their slower growth in diameter. As the sapwood decreases in width from the stump to the top and often varies in different directions from the center, an annual ring may be sapwood in one part of a tree while it is heartwood in another part.

Identification by color. The color is sometimes useful in identifying woods, but it must not be relied on entirely, since in some species it is variable.

Some woods can be identified at once by their color. For instance, the lustrous red-brown of cherry wood, the dingy reddish brown of red gum, and the bright reddish hue of most Douglas fir are unmistakable.

Color also is more or less an indication of the durability of the wood. It is well known that dark woods like redwood and black walnut are more durable than such light-colored woods as maple, ash, beech, white fir, and spruce. Those cedars that have no very dark heartwood are an exception, and their durability is ascribed to certain natural resins and oils in the wood.

Identification by odor. Many woods give off a distinctive odor when they are wet. Therefore, to determine the odor of wood it should be sawed, and the fresh sawdust held to the nostrils. The odor is more pronounced in the heartwood than in the sapwood. Most of the pines have a distinct resinous odor, while the cedars have an agreeable fragrance. Cypress has a mild rancid odor, while Alpine fir has a rank odor when dry, which distinguishes it from all other firs.

TYPES OF WOOD USED PRINCIPALLY FOR EXTERIORS

Douglas fir. Douglas fir, sometimes called Douglas spruce or red fir, is distinguishable by its annual rings, which are very distinct and vary from narrow to wide, with the summerwood always conspicuous as a denser and darker band. The heartwood of Douglas fir ranges in color from orange-red to red, with the springwood as well as the summerwood being colored. This fir is used principally in home construction for framing and for doors. The finer grades are used for plywood and veneers.

Hard (southern yellow) pine. This wood is known also as long-leaved pine, hard pine, and Georgia pine. It is recognizable by its annual rings, which are very distinct. They are usually narrow, especially several inches from the center, and are very often irregular in width, with the summerwood often occupying half of the annual ring. The heartwood ranges from yellowish to orange-brown. This wood is heavy and hard, straight-grained, and recognizable by a distinct resinous odor. When properly dried, it works easily and does not tend to warp or check or to split in nailing. It holds paint better than most woods and for this reason is ideal for outdoor construction. It is used principally in sidings and for window frames, doorframes, porch stairs and rails, and the like.

Spruces (eastern and Sitka). There are two varieties of eastern spruce—white and red—which resemble each other closely in general structure. For home construction, the red spruce is more generally used. It is somewhat lighter in weight than the white and is straighter-grained with a more even texture. The heartwood of red spruce is nearly white with a slightly reddish tinge, while the white spruce has a light yellow heartwood and a nearly white sapwood. Red spruce has a pearly luster and is exceptionally strong for its weight. Both are used in millwork and for all general building purposes, such as studding, scaffolding, lathing, and concrete forms.

Sitka spruce, grown in the far West, is one of the most important varieties of spruce in the United States. This tree attains a height of 275' to 300' with a diameter of 8', thus producing lumber in much larger sizes than the eastern varieties. The wood is light in weight, with the heartwood ranging from straw color to pink with a thin lighter-colored sapwood. Sitka spruce is straight-grained with the growth rings even and narrow. It is comparatively free from warping and checking and is easily dried. It is generally used for exterior finish, siding, and general construction work.

Cypress, southern. Southern cypress is variously known as red, black, white, and yellow cypress. It is generally classified according to the region where it has grown. For instance, cypress from the deep swamps or the coastal plain regions near tidewater is commercially called tidewater or red cypress. Inland or upland cypress is lighter in color and not quite so durable as the red, and is known as white or yellow cypress. The heartwood of the tidewater cypress varies from slightly reddish to a deeper red, or even almost black. In the inland species, the heartwood is usually slightly reddish or even lighter in color. Cypress is known as one of the most decay-resistant types of lumber. The great durability of its heartwood, probably more than any other property, gives cypress the place of distinction it holds.

Annual rings of cypress are distinct and irregular in width and outline. The summerwood is very noticeable as a dense dark band and in the lighter grades is slightly less conspicuous. The resinous cells are abundant and can be seen with the aid of a hand lens. They are usually arranged in irregular tangential bands, and on a split surface are very distinct, appearing as dark lines running with the grain.

Southern cypress is used extensively for the outside finish of buildings, such as sidings, casings, sashes, doors, cornices, railings, steps, and porches. Because of its great durability, it is a preferred material for tanks, tubs, and outside vats, and especially in the construction of greenhouses, where the wood is subjected to extremes of heat and moisture.

Hemlocks (eastern and western). The eastern hemlock is sometimes called hemlock spruce or spruce pine. The annual rings are narrow to moderately wide, with the springwood soft, of a reddish hue and passing gradually into the narrower, harder, and darker summerwood. The sapwood is occasionally slightly lighter in color, usually not distinct from the heartwood, which is a pale brown with a reddish hue.

The western hemlock is also known as Alaska fir, Alaska pine, and gray fir. It has the same general structure as the eastern variety, but a distinguishing feature is that this wood has abnormal resin passages forming tangential rows in the outer portion of the summerwood. Both woods are moderately light in weight and straight-grained. They are used for general exterior building and construction and are generally accepted as the equal of Douglas fir for this purpose.

Cottonwood. Cottonwood is also known as poplar and whitewood. The pores are discernible with the naked eye, especially in the springwood. They decrease slightly in size toward the outer portion of each annual ring. The annual rings are distinct, but not outstanding, and they are defined by a slight difference in the size of the pores of the summerwood and of the succeeding spring-wood. While pith flecks are occasionally present, they are not conspicuous. The heartwood is grayish white to a light grayish brown, with the sapwood not clearly defined and passing more or less gradually into the heartwood.

While this wood is not so strong in comparison with others, it is strong in proportion to its weight. It is tough and extremely light when well dried, has a close, even texture, is only moderately hard, and generally works and finishes well.

Cottonwood has a wide range of uses and is used for certain purposes in place of more costly woods such as white pine and poplar. It is used principally for partitions, sidings, and sheathings. When properly finished it makes effective door panels, porch railings, and the like. In certain sections of the South and Southwest, it is used extensively for barn framing and for roof boards.

TYPES OF WOOD USED FOR INTERIORS

Sugar pine. Grown principally in California and southern Oregon, sugar pine is one of the species of true white pine that are of outstanding importance in the home-construction industry.

While it has many of the characteristics of northern white pine, sugar pine can be classified among the more durable species of white pine. It is free from any tendency to warp and twist and holds its shape well after being properly dried. It is lighter-colored than the other pines and changes color less on exposure.

Sugar pine is recognizable by its conspicuous resinous ducts and is slightly coarser-textured than the other white pines. It is light in weight, straight-grained and comparatively free from defects, and easily worked. The heartwood is cream-colored and darkens slightly after exposure. Since sugar pine is the largest of the white pines, a great deal of the lumber from it is cut into wide widths of thick stock. It is estimated that over 50% of sugar pine goes into the manufacturing of mill products, such as indoor sashes, blinds, flooring, and so forth.

Idaho white pine. Idaho white pine is sometimes called western white pine. This is another of the three commercial species of genuine white pine found in the United States. As its name indicates, it is grown principally in Idaho. Its cellular structure and other characteristics are similar to the other white pines, but as a rule, it can be distinguished by the color of its knots. Idaho white pine is light in color, light in weight, straight-grained, and durable. It shrinks and swells a little more with changes in moisture content than the other pines, but on the whole, compares very favorably with them.

Idaho white pine is used principally for knotty-pine paneling, for pattern-making, and for general construction purposes. It is also used for made-to-order millwork such as kitchen cabinets, doors, window frames, and both carved and turned work.

Ponderosa or California white pine. Ponderosa is another type of pine used extensively for interior work. It grows throughout the Rocky Mountain section westward to the Pacific and is known by various trade names, such as California white pine, Arizona white pine, Oregon white pine, Oregon pine, western pine, and western white pine.

The ponderosa pine that originates in California and southern Oregon is sold under the trade name of California white pine. These two regions produce approximately 90% of the total cut of this wood. In appearance it closely resembles the northern white pine in many respects, and is put to many of the same uses. The wood is light, extremely straight-grained, and easy to work, with color varying from creamy white to straw. California white pine, because of its low-density cellular structure, is an excellent insulating material. It is recognizable by its pronounced zones of springwood and summerwood, with the heartwood a light reddish brown in color. It is used extensively as a general house-building wood for sheathing, sidings, sashes, doors, millwork, moldings, and finishes.

Redwood. Grown on the Pacific Coast slope, these giants of the forest have produced as much as 300,000 feet of board measure per tree. Redwood is easily recognizable: its sapwood is a very narrow band that is almost white and presents a startling and clearly defined contrast to the distinctive heartwood, which varies in color from cherry to dark mahogany. The annual rings of redwood are moderate and regular in width, and are very distinct, because the summerwood is more pronounced than in other varieties of wood. Besides being unusually durable, this wood is generally straight-grained, comparatively light in weight, and non-resinous.

Because of a minimum of shrinkage when properly seasoned, redwood is classed in use as a "still" wood. It is comparatively clear of knots and other defects. This, coupled with the extremely high percentage of clean lumber and the ease (because of the great diameter of the trees) with which wide clear boards and timbers can be obtained, has led to the extensive use of redwood for beamed ceilings and for paneled and wainscoted walls. It is also used for the better grades of general millwork, such as doors and sashes.

Beech. Lumber cut from beeches in which the heartwood is reddish is usually called redheart beech, and lumber from beeches with white heartwood is known as whiteheart beech. On plain-sawed surfaces, the annual rings of beech are inconspicuous and the pores are not visible, but the medullary rays appear as short dark dashes from $\frac{1}{16}''$ to $\frac{1}{8}''$ in height. On quarter-sawed surfaces, the rays are conspicuous as dark pith flakes of various lengths depending on how nearly radially the lumber has been cut. For a description of plain- and quarter-sawed lumber see Chap. 3 of this section. However, these are not large enough to give this wood a figure or distinctive grain of any value.

Beech is used to a great extent in the manufacture of chairs and exterior parts of furniture which are painted or stained so as to obscure the identity of the wood. It has a tendency to bend easily and is well adapted for curved parts of furniture, such as the backs of chairs. Because of its hardness when properly dried, it is also well suited for rocker runners. Beech is used exclusively by cabinetmakers for drawer sides and runways, frames, and other substantial interior parts of cabinets and furniture. Because of its excellent wearing qualities, beech is also used extensively for finish flooring (Fig. 1).

Oak. While there are over sixty species of oak in the United States, only about fourteen of these are of commercial importance as woods used for interiors. All fourteen belong to two groups generally known as white and red oaks. Various species of oak are known by different common names in different localities. For practical purposes, it is not necessary to be familiar with all of the local names, but it is important to ascertain whether a piece of lumber belongs to the white-oak or to the red-oak group.

The heartwood lumber of the white-oak group is distinguishable by its grayish brown color with an occasional reddish tinge. The heartwood of the red-oak group, as a rule, has a reddish tinge,

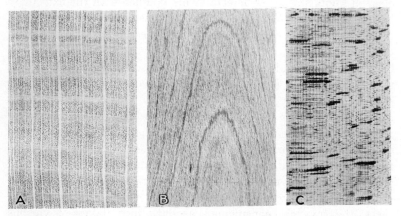

Fig. 1. Beech. A, end surface; B, plain-sawed; C, quarter-sawed.

although sometimes it resembles the white oak in color. The sapwood, which varies from one to several inches in width, is white in both of the groups unless discolored by some external agency. The figure in oak is produced by the annual rings and medullary rays which are very distinct in both the white and the red oaks. Usually, those of the red oaks are wider and also more pronounced, as they contain larger open pores in greater quantity at the beginning of each year's growth.

While individual pores in the denser outer portions of the annual rings of both white and red oaks are too small to be seen without a magnifying glass, their characteristic arrangement in V-shaped groups or lines extending across the annual rings is apparent to the naked eye. On lumber that has been sawed lengthwise, the annual rings in the red oaks are made conspicuous by zones of large pores alternating with zones of denser, less porous wood. These large pores are plainly visible as fine grooves in red oak, while in white oaks the tyloses fill up the grooves more or less.

On plain-sawed surfaces, the ends of the large medullary rays of the oaks can be seen as dark- or sometimes light-colored lines from a fraction of an inch to several inches in height along the grain(Figs. 2 and 3). However, on quarter-sawed surfaces, perfectly radial large rays appear as patches or flakes measuring from a small fraction of an inch to 3″ or 4″ along the grain and the full

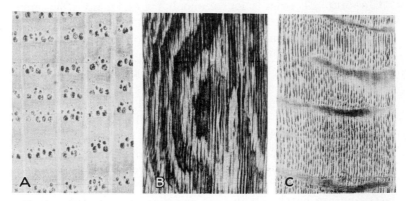

Fig. 2. White oak. A, end surface; B, plain-sawed; C, quarter-sawed.

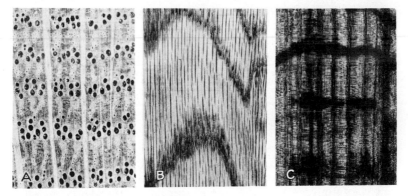

Fig. 3. Red oak. A, end surface; B, plain-sawed; C, quarter-sawed.

width of the board across the grain. The small rays are also visible on quarter-sawed surfaces.

Oak is one of the woods most commonly used in furniture, both in the form of solid lumber and as veneer. Its abundance, hardness, and strength, coupled with its good appearance as well as adaptability to various kinds of finishes, qualify this wood for all grades of interior finish, finish flooring, cabinetwork, and furniture. The white species is preferable for woodwork that is to be given a natural finish, because it is usually free from the reddish tinge common in the other group. For darker pieces and concealed parts, however, little discrimination is made between the two oaks.

Chestnut. Chestnut is not commonly known by any other name. Its heartwood is usually grayish brown and the thin sapwood almost white. Plain-sawed chestnut has a figure much like that of plain-sawed oak, even more strongly outlined by the broad zone of large pores at the beginning of each annual ring. The annual rings are made conspicuous by several rows of large pores at the beginning of each year's growth. However, in the outer, denser portion of each ring, the pores are so small that they cannot be seen individually without the aid of a lens. On plain-sawed and quarter-sawed lumber, the annual rings are clearly defined on longitudinal surfaces, with the larger pores plainly visible as grooves. The medullary rays are not distinct on plain-sawed surfaces and are barely distinct on quarter-sawed surfaces of this lumber (Fig. 4).

Chestnut is sometimes used for flooring, but principally for veneer cores of table and dresser tops, drawer fronts, and other veneer panels in cabinets and medium-priced furniture. Its softness, lightness, ease of drying, and ability to hold glue facilitate manufacturing. It is comparatively free from warpage, and the fact that it shrinks or swells very little, either during manufac-

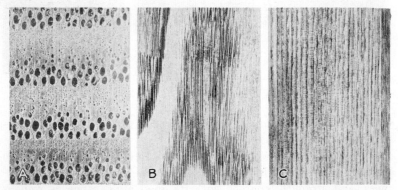

Fig. 4. Chestnut. A, end surface; B, plain-sawed; C, quarter-sawed.

ture or while in use, gives it a stability that is found in few other species of wood used for veneer cores. When chestnut is used with oak veneer, exposed edges of the core need not be covered, since chestnut is similar to oak in appearance.

Elm. Three species of elm are used commercially: American elm, slippery elm, and rock elm. American elm is sometimes known as white or gray elm, slippery elm as red elm, and rock elm as hickory or cork elm.

Annual rings of all species of elm are made distinct by a zone of large pores at the beginning of each year's growth. In the American and rock elms, the zone consists of one row of pores, whereas in slippery elm it consists of several rows, making the last-named species look more porous than the others. These pores are all clearly distinguishable without magnification, except in the rock elm species, in which they are smaller. The smaller pores are arranged in conspicuous wavy tangential lines, but are individually invisible without a lens. This wavy arrangement of the small pores is a distinctive characteristic of the elms (Fig. 5).

The heartwood of the American rock elms is light grayish brown, often tinged with red; that of slippery elm is dark reddish brown or chocolate-brown. The sapwood of all types of elm is white. In slippery elm the sapwood is rarely over ½″ in width. In the other species, it is usually from one to several inches wide.

Plain-sawed elm has a conspicuous growth-ring figure and a characteristic delicate wavy figure within each annual ring (Fig.

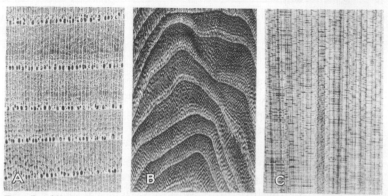

Fig. 5. Slippery elm. A, end surface; B, plain-sawed; C, quarter-sawed.

5). Quarter-sawed, this wood is without a figure of any value. Elm is used extensively for interior trim and finish. Although not considered a cabinet wood of the first rank, it has a pleasing appearance when plain-sawed and properly filled and varnished. It bends well, a property which makes it especially desirable for curved parts of furniture such as chair backs. Elm is used also for an inside finish wood because of its moderate amount of figure and pleasing light and dark shades when finished in a natural color.

Birch. The two species of birch commonly used for interior woodworking are yellow birch and sweet birch. Yellow birch is known also as gray, silver, or swamp birch. Sweet birch is sometimes called cherry, black, or mahogany birch.

On end surfaces, the annual rings of the birches, while not conspicuous, are clearly defined by fine lines and occasionally by a slight difference in the size of the pores at the end of one year's growth and the beginning of the next. While these pores individually are almost entirely invisible without the aid of a lens, they are fairly uniform in size and are evenly distributed. On longitudinal surfaces, while the layers of annual growth are usually distinct, they are not so conspicuous as in oak, chestnut, or similar woods that have definite zones of larger pores.

The heartwood of the birches ranges from light to dark reddish brown, that of the sweet birch being somewhat darker than that of the yellow birch. The sapwood of both, which usually is wide, is practically white.

In quarter-sawed birch, the figure consisting of stripes produced by the annual rings of growth is in itself monotonous, but the wavy grain that is occasionally present produces a pleasing natural effect (Fig. 6).

Plain-sawed birch and rotary-cut birch veneer exhibit a narrow pattern formed by the annual rings. In some logs, the annual rings follow numerous small depressions and elevations which give the lumber an undulating figure that usually is referred to as curly birch. A large proportion of curly birch is used in the form of veneer. Both birches are sufficiently strong and hard, and they hold their shape well. These physical properties of birch make it particularly suitable for furniture and various cabinets and fixtures in the home. Although birch shrinks more than the lighter types of wood, this is not a serious handicap if the lumber has been properly dried.

Birch is used to some extent in natural finish, but often it is stained reddish brown in imitation of mahogany or chocolate-brown in imitation of walnut. It is used extensively for cabinet

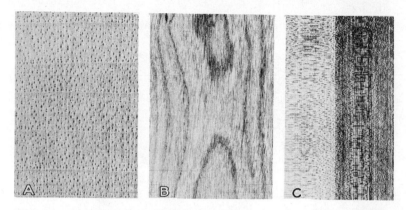

Fig. 6. Yellow birch. A, end surface; B, plain-sawed; C, quarter-sawed.

interiors and in the form of veneers, furniture, moldings, and the like.

Maple. There are four species of maple: sugar maple, red maple, silver maple, and big-leaf maple. Sugar maple is commonly called hard maple to differentiate it from the red and silver species that are generally known as soft maple. Sugar maple also is called rock maple and in one variety is called black maple. Red and silver maple are rarely given any other name but soft maple, although occasionally the red is called swamp, water, or scarlet maple, and the silver is called white, water, or river maple. Big-leaf maple is sometimes called broad-leaved or Oregon maple (Fig. 7).

The annual rings on end surfaces of maple are distinctly defined by thin reddish brown layers. The pores are invisible without a lens. In sugar maple, some of the rays are very small, and in other varieties they are comparatively large and very distinct to the naked eye. In the two soft maples, they are more uniform in size and appear to be more numerous.

On plain-sawed longitudinal surfaces, the thin reddish-brown layers defining the annual rings are clearly visible. The medullary rays appear as exceedingly fine dashes that run parallel with the grain. On quarter-sawed surfaces, the rays, though small (less than $\frac{1}{16}''$ high), are conspicuous as reddish-brown flecks, especially in sugar maple. The pores are not visible on longitudinal surfaces.

The soft maples are susceptible to attack by the larvae of an

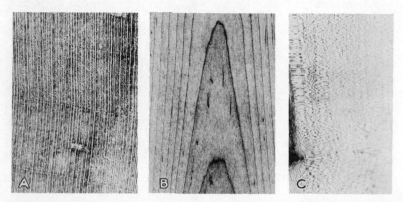

Fig. 7. Red maple. A, end surface; B, plain-sawed; C, quarter-sawed.

insect, whose grub holes produce pith flecks. These are brown streaks running more or less parallel with the grain of the wood. Pith flecks are not always present in wood of the soft maples, and they occur occasionally in sugar maple. Their presence or absence therefore cannot be used as the sole means of distinguishing the maples. But whenever pith flecks are abundant, there is ample reason to believe that the wood is one of the soft maples.

The heartwood of all four maples is light reddish brown, while the wide sapwood is practically white when fresh, but may stain to a pale brown if it has been improperly seasoned. The sapwood of maple often is used separately from the heartwood, in which case it is usually known as white maple. Sugar maple has more luster than either of the two.

Sugar maple is one of the principal American cabinet and furniture woods. When used for exposed parts it is usually given a natural finish. For this reason the wood with a curly or bird's-eye figure is more desirable. With the natural finish, it is used principally for bedroom, porch, and kitchen furniture. Maple is comparatively easy to work, and if properly dried is not subject to shrinkage or warping. It is capable of taking a fine polish, stain, and finish (Fig. 8). In addition to being used for furniture, maple is used also for interior trim, and the hard species of maple is used for fine finished flooring, for stair treads, and for door and panel veneer.

Sycamore. Sycamore is known also as plane tree, buttonwood,

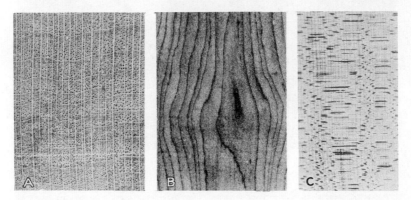

Fig. 8. Sugar maple. A, end surface; B, plain-sawed; C, quarter-sawed.

and buttonball. The sapwood, which usually is narrow, is a pale reddish brown; the heartwood is a deeper reddish brown in color, but is not sharply defined from the sapwood. Under a lens, the pores of a sycamore appear very numerous and fairly evenly distributed, except in the narrow outer portion of the annual rings.

Next to oak, the sycamore has the largest rays of any of our native commercial woods. They appear as numerous distinct lines on cross sections. On longitudinal surfaces, the annual rings are not conspicuous, although the whitish lines limiting the growth of the rings are usually visible. On tangential surfaces, the rays are distinct as crowded dashes up to $\frac{1}{4}''$ in height, but mostly not over $\frac{3}{16}''$, darker than the surrounding surfaces.

On radial surfaces, the rays are very conspicuous on account of their comparatively large size and darker hue. If a sycamore board is perfectly quarter-sawed, many of the rays will extend across the full width of the face. But usually, because the quartered lumber is cut at a slight angle with the rays or because the rays curve slightly in and out, they appear as short flakes (Fig. 9). Sycamore can be kiln-dried easily, but extreme care must be exercised in handling and piling it properly to prevent warpage. Sycamore is used extensively for interior trim and fancy

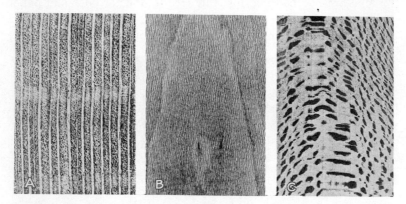

Fig. 9. Sycamore. A, end surface; B, plain-sawed; C, quarter-sawed.

paneling. It is desirable for the construction of doors and built-up panels.

Cherry. Of the several species of cherry, only that known as black cherry is used commercially.

On end surfaces, the annual rings are fairly distinct, being sharply defined by an abrupt difference in the size of the pores in the adjoining portions. While these pores are small and are not visible to the naked eye, nevertheless, because they decrease in size toward the outer portion of each annual ring, the boundaries of the rings are very distinctly marked. The rays in cherry are very clear and numerous.

On plain-sawed surfaces, the annual-growth layers are fairly distinct, but are not conspicuous, with the pores visible as very fine grooves. On quarter-sawed surfaces, the annual layers are poorly defined, with the rays very distinct but small.

The heartwood of cherry ranges from light to dark reddish brown with the narrow sapwood nearly white. Cherry has no striking figure, except in finished pieces cut from burls. Its relative scarcity prevents it from being used extensively in the manufacture of furniture and interior trim, but because of its rich color and its ability to take a high polish, it is sometimes used in combination with other woods and for various mill products, such as panels, doors, and parts of cabinets.

Yellow poplar. Yellow poplar, also known simply as poplar, is called whitewood in New England. This wood is rather light, ranging from soft to medium, fine-textured, easy to work, and finishes smoothly. The color of the heartwood varies from olive-green to yellow or brown and is often streaked with steel-blue. The sapwood is white and in second-growth trees is very thick. The annual rings are defined by a distinct light-colored band. Poplar has a moderate shrinkage and is kiln-dried easily. Despite its light weight, it is a durable wood. It stains easily and uniformly, can be painted evenly and smoothly, and is an excellent base for smooth hard enamel finishes. Because of these qualities, its uses in the home are numerous. It is used extensively for sashes, doors, cabinets, moldings, and all interior mill-work.

Red gum. Red gum is known also as sweet gum, star-leaved gum, hazelwood, and sometimes, especially in European countries, satin walnut. However, the name red gum is applicable commercially only to the heartwood. The sapwood is known in the lumber trade as sap gum and is pinkish white. As its name indicates, the heartwood is of a reddish hue. A great deal of red-gum lumber contains irregular dark streaks due to natural deposits of coloring matter in the wood itself, which closely resemble those found in Circassian walnut. Lumber of this type is identified in the trade as figured red gum; that without such streaks as plain gum. The figure is equally pronounced in both plain-sawed and quarter-sawed lumber (Fig. 10).

The annual rings on both end and longitudinal surfaces of red gum, while present, are not very distinct. The rays show up fairly clearly without magnification and are comparatively numerous.

As the result of intensive research, red gum has been developed into one of the leading furniture woods of the country. In the manufacture of the better grades of furniture and cabinetwork, the heartwood is preferred, but the sapwood also is used extensively for veneered panel cores and sometimes even for exteriors.

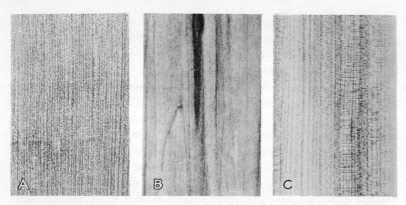

Fig. 10. Red gum. A, end surface; B, plain-sawed; C, quarter-sawed.

Red-gum heartwood not only lends itself easily to various finishes, but often has a beautiful figure of its own and so deserves recognition under its proper name. The sapwood, pale in color and sometimes nearly white, is stained easily in various shades. Improved seasoning methods and the use of veneers on crossbanded panels have practically done away with the former difficulties experienced in handling this type of work. The ease with which it can be worked with both power and hand tools and its adaptability to various finishes are among the chief qualities that have made red gum prominent and extensively used for all types of interior trim and for various articles of furniture.

Walnut. Walnut sometimes is called American walnut or black walnut. The heartwood varies in color and ranges from light to dark chocolate-brown, but present occasionally are irregular streaks that run more or less lengthwise of the wood. The narrow sapwood of walnut, usually pale brown, sometimes is darkened artificially by steaming to make it resemble the heartwood.

Straight-grained quarter-sawed lumber has a figure that consists mainly of stripes formed by the annual layers of growth, or by zones differing slightly in shades of color and occasionally showing a wavy figure. In plain-sawed lumber, the figure consists of stripes, irregular curves, and parabolas outlining the annual layers of growth.

Veneer cut from stumps and crotches of walnut usually shows

an irregular figure of short waves and curly contortions of the fiber, and is known as mottle or butt wood. On the end surfaces, the annual rings of walnut are very distinct and are marked by an abrupt difference in the size of the pores at the boundaries of adjacent rings. However, the decrease in size from the inner to the outer portion of each ring is gradual. Most of the pores contain glistening tyloses. The rays are so fine and inconspicuous that they cannot be seen without the aid of a magnifying lens.

On longitudinal surfaces, the annual rings are clearly marked, but they are not quite so conspicuous as on the end surfaces. The pores are visible as fine grooves or dark lines in both the plain-sawed and the quarter-sawed cuts (Fig. 11).

Walnut has sufficient hardness and strength for general use, but is not hard enough to dull woodworking tools excessively. It has a rich color, luster, and a distinct figure. It is comparatively free from warpage and has excellent gluing qualities. Because of these properties, walnut is used extensively for building both solid and veneered furniture, and for the more expensive types of interior trim, millwork, and general fine cabinetwork.

Mahogany. While true mahogany is rarely given any other name, it is sometimes known by its place of origin, such as Cuban and Honduras mahogany. But if the place of origin is not known, it cannot be determined from the wood itself.

The heartwood of mahogany varies in color from a pale to a deep reddish brown, becoming darker on exposure to light. The narrow sapwood varies from white to light brown.

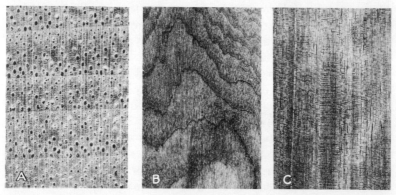

Fig. 11. Black walnut. A, end surface; B, plain-sawed; C, quarter-sawed.

The predominating figure that distinguishes mahogany is due to differences in the reflection of light from adjacent portions of the surface of the wood. Since mahogany nearly always has interlocked grain, quarter-sawed surfaces usually have a ribbon, or what is known as a strip figure. Occasionally, mottle, rain-drop, and other curly figures are present in the quarter-sawed lumber, and these naturally enhance its value. Lumber and veneer cut from crotches in the tree trunk also have a distinctive figure of their own and are more valuable (Fig. 12).

On end surfaces, growth layers varying from ¼₆″ to ½″ or

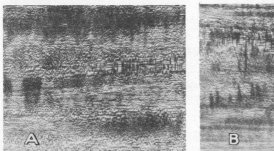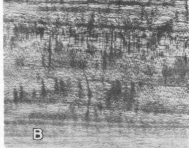

Fig. 12. Stripe and figure in mahogany. A, broken stripe, and B, mottled figure, in quarter-sawed mahogany.

more in width are plainly seen, bounded by narrow light-colored concentric lines. The pores in mahogany are visible to the naked eye. They are fairly uniform in size and evenly distributed. Many contain dark reddish-brown gum. Occasionally, and especially in the heavier grades of mahogany, the pores contain minute white deposits. The rays, though very fine, are also distinctly visible (Fig. 13).

On longitudinal surfaces the light-colored layers that define the annual-growth rings on mahogany are very distinct, forming approximately straight lines on quarter-sawed surfaces and curved lines or ovals on plain-sawed surfaces. These layers usually appear rather dark because of the way in which the light is reflected. The pores are visible as small grooves that are often partly filled with dark gum. The rays of mahogany are very distinct on quarter-sawed surfaces and may appear lighter or darker than the wood fibers, according to how the light strikes them. On plain-sawed surfaces, the rays are often in rows running at right angles to the fibers of the wood, producing very fine ripple marks. The distinctness and the abundance of these marks are an aid in distinguishing true mahogany from most other woods erroneously called mahogany.

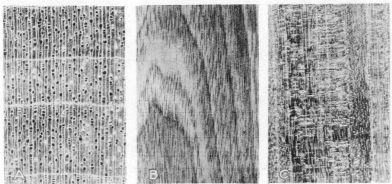

Fig. 13. True mahogany. A, end surface; B, plain-sawed; C, quarter-sawed.

Because of the high cost of true mahogany, it is most often used in the form of veneer. The more expensive types of furniture, cabinetwork, and many really antique pieces are made of solid mahogany. The principal characteristics of this wood, which have made it a prime favorite, are its variety of pleasing figures, negligible shrinkage, stability, and ease in working. A considerable amount of mahogany is also used for the interior finish of fine rooms and for paneling of libraries and executive meeting rooms. Mahogany is also used for high-priced mill products, such as doors and panels.

PLYWOOD AND OTHER CROSSBANDED PRODUCTS

Plywood. Plywood is a term generally used to designate glued wood panels that are made up of layers, or plies, with the grain of one or more layers at an angle, usually 90°, with the grain of the others. The outside plies are called faces or face and back,

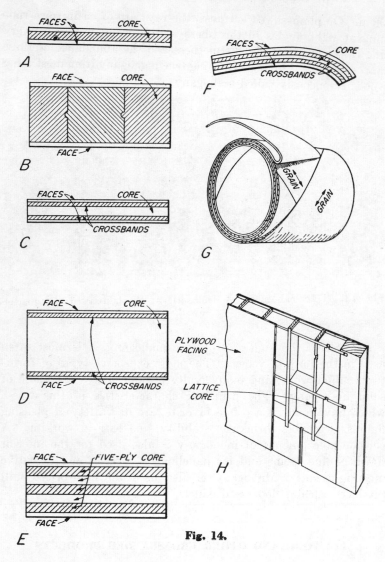

Fig. 14.

Types of plywood and crossbanded construction: *A*, 3-ply (all veneer); *B*, 3-ply (lumber core); *C*, 5-ply (all veneer); *D*, 5-ply (lumber core); *E*, 7-ply (all veneer); *F*, 5-ply bent work (all veneer); *G*, 5-ply, spirally wrapped (all veneer); *H*, section of hollow-core door.

the center ply or plies are called the core, and the plies immediately below the face and back, laid at right angles to them, are called the crossbands (Fig. 14). The essential features of plywood are embodied in other glued constructions with many variations of details. The core may be veneer, lumber, or various combinations of veneer and lumber; the total thickness may be less than $\frac{1}{16}''$ or more than $3''$; the different plies may vary as to number, thickness, and kinds of wood; and the shape of the members may also vary. The crossbands and their arrangement largely govern the properties, particularly the warping characteristics, and the uses of all such constructions.

As compared with solid wood, the chief advantages of plywood are its approach to equalization of strength properties along the length and width of the panel, greater resistance to checking and splitting, and less change in dimensions with changes in moisture content. The greater the number of plies for a given thickness, the more nearly equal are the strength and shrinkage properties along and across the panel and the greater the resistance to splitting.

The cheaper types of plywood are used extensively for sheathing, underflooring, and for concrete forms. The more expensive types of plywood, with mahogany, walnut, and other figured veneers, are used for interior paneling and for such furniture as bookcases, fireplaces, radio cabinets, and partitions, and for toys. Plywood can also be procured with a laminated plastic top. This type is used extensively for children's furniture, table and cabinet tops, and similar articles. Plywood is worked the same as wood; it can be nailed, screwed, and glued.

Veneer. Veneer is a form of plywood with an outer layer very much thinner than the core. The core of veneer plywood is an inexpensive wood, and the outer layers are more expensive hardwoods of attractive grain or figure. Veneer plywood is used for wall panels and to a great extent for furniture panels (Figs. 12 and 15). The sizes are approximately the same as those of ordinary plywood. The cost is considerably higher, depending on the type of wood used on the outside layers.

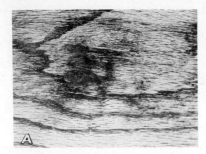 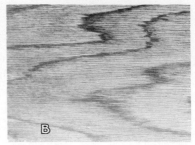

Fig. 15. Oak and oak veneer. Growth-ring figure in A, plain-sawed oak, and B, rotary-cut oak veneer.

ARRANGEMENT OF PLIES

The tendency of crossbanded products to warp as the result of stresses caused by shrinking and swelling is largely eliminated by balanced construction. This construction consists of arranging the plies in pairs about the core, so that for each ply there is an opposite, similar, and parallel ply. Matching the plies involves a consideration of (1) thickness, (2) kind of wood with particular reference to shrinkage and density, (3) moisture content at the time of gluing, and (4) angle or relative direction of the grain.

The use of an odd number of plies permits an arrangement that gives a substantially balanced effect; that is, when 3 plies are glued together with the grain of the outer 2 plies at right angles to the grain of the center ply, the stresses are balanced and the panel tends to remain flat with moisture content changes. With 5, 7, or some other uneven number of plies, the forces may be similarly balanced. If only two plies are glued together with the grain of one at right angles to the grain of the other, each ply tends to distort the other when moisture content changes occur, and cupping usually results. Similar results are likely when any even number of plies are used, unless the 2 center plies are parallel and act essentially as 1 ply.

The use of balanced construction is highly important in thin panels that must remain flat. In thicker members some deviation from balanced construction is possible without serious consequences. *For example*, with lumber cores that are properly crossbanded the face and back plies may be dissimilar without any noticeable effect; whereas if dissimilar face and back plies were used in thin three-ply panels, the warping might be very objectionable. In certain curved members, the natural cupping tendency of an even number of plies may even be used to advantage.

Since the outer or face plies of a crossbanded construction are restrained on only one side, changes in moisture content induce relatively large stresses on the outer glue joints. The magnitude of stresses depends upon such factors as thickness of plies, density and shrinkage of the wood involved, and the amount of change in moisture content. In general, one-eighth inch is about the maximum thickness of face plies that can be held securely in place when dense woods are used and large changes in moisture content occur, and thinner faces are advisable under such conditions of service.

QUALITY OF PLIES

In thin plywood the quality of all the plies affects the shape and permanence of form of the panel. All plies should be straight-grained, smoothly cut, and of sound wood.

In thick, five-ply lumber-core panels the crossbands, in particular, affect the quality and stability of the panel. Imperfections in the crossbands, such as marked differences in the texture of the wood or irregularities in the surface, are easily seen in the panel through thin surface veneers. Cross grain that runs sharply through the crossband veneer from one face to the other causes the panels to cup. Cross grain that runs diagonally across the face of the crossband veneer causes the panel to twist unless the two crossbands are laid with their grain parallel. Lack of observance of this simple precaution accounts for much warping in crossbanded construction.

The best woods for cores of high-grade panels are those of low density and shrinkage, of slight contrast between springwood and summerwood, and of species that are glued easily. Edge-grained cores are better than flat-grained cores because they shrink less in width. In softwoods with pronounced summerwood, moreover, edge-grained cores are better because the hard bands of summer-wood are less likely to show through thin veneer and the panels show fewer irregularities in the surfaces. In most species, a core made entirely of either quarter-sawed or plain-sawed material remains more uniform in thickness with moisture content changes than one in which the two types of material are combined.

Distinct distortion of surfaces has been noted, particularly in softwoods, when the core boards were neither distinctly flat-grained nor edge-grained.

GRADES AND TYPES OF PLYWOOD

Broadly speaking, two classes of plywood are available—*hardwood* and *softwood*. Most softwood plywood is made of Douglas-fir, but western hemlock, white fir, ponderosa pine, redwood and other species are used. Hardwood plywood is made of many species.

Various grades and types are manufactured. "Grade" is determined by the quality of veneer, and "type" by the moisture resistance of the glue joints. The types and grades in general use are listed in commercial standards established by the industry with the assistance of the Department of Commerce. Separate commercial standards cover Douglas-fir plywood, western softwood plywood, ponderosa pine and sugar pine plywood, and hardwood plywood.

Douglas fir plywood. Two types of Douglas fir plywood are listed in Commercial Standard CS45-48—interior and exterior. The *interior type* is expected to retain its form and practically all of its strength when occasionally subjected to a thorough wetting and subsequent normal drying. It is commonly bonded with soybean glue or with an extended resin glue of the phenol type. *Exterior-type* plywood is expected to retain its form and strength when repeatedly wet and dried and otherwise subjected to the elements and to be suitable for permanent exterior use. It is commonly bonded with hot-press, phenol resin glue.

Within each type, several grades are established by the quality of the veneer on the two faces of a panel. In descending order of quality, the veneer is designated as A, B, C, or D. Grade A-A

plywood, *for example*, has Grade A veneer on both faces, and
Grade A-D plywood has Grade A veneer on one face and Grade
D on the other. As a general rule, Grade C is used for the inner
plies of the exterior type and Grade D for the inner plies of the
interior type.

Softwood plywood other than Douglas fir. The requirements
of Commercial Standard CS122-49 for western softwood plywood
resemble those of the commercial standard for Douglas fir. The
same two types—*interior* and *exterior*—are provided for, and the
grade is determined by the quality of veneer used on the two faces
of each panel. The grades of veneer are designated A, B, C, and
D, as with Douglas fir veneer, but one higher grade, A-1, is provided.

Commercial Standard CS157-49 provides for only an interior
type of ponderosa pine and sugar pine plywood. The grades of
veneer are designated in descending order of quality as good,
sound, solid, sheathing, and backs. Provisions are made for
eight grades of plywood, as for example "good 2 sides" and "solid
1 side," depending upon the quality of veneer used on the faces
and backs.

Hardwood plywood. Four types of hardwood plywood—Technical, Type I, Type II, and Type III are described in Commercial
Standard CS35-49. For the most part the difference between
the types is based on the resistance of the glue bond to severe
service conditions, although technical differs from Type I in the
permissible thickness and arrangement of plies. Glue bonds conforming to the requirements of both technical and Type I plywood are high in durability and correspond closely to those required for exterior-type Douglas fir plywood. In general, resistance of the glue bonds of Type II hardwood plywood resembles that of interior-type Douglas fir plywood. Good dry strength
but no water resistance is required of the glue bonds in Type III
hardwood plywood.

The grade of the plywood is determined by the quality of the
veneers used on the faces and backs of the panels. The veneer
is graded 1, 2, 3, and 4 in order of descending quality. The requirements are the same for all hardwood species for Grades 2, 3,
and 4; Grade 1 requirements are described separately for each

species. The plywood grade is designated by combining the designation of the grade of the veneer on the face and back, as Grade 1-2 or Grade 2-3. Veneers of Grade 2 or 3 are generally used for inner plies.

Plywood for special purposes. Most of the plywood produced in the United States conforms in general to the commercial standards. Some plywood, however, is produced to meet specific demands or to conform to specifications that were drawn to secure a product suitable for a special purpose.

Unless very large quantities are involved, procurement of special-purpose plywood is difficult, costly, and often wasteful. For most purposes, plywood conforming to commercial standards is adequate.

CHAPTER 2

Woodworking Hand Tools and How to Use Them

BASIC TOOLS

Before we describe the various hand tools used in woodworking, the following important facts must be noted by the home craftsman. He should purchase tools of good quality only. The difference in cost between an excellent tool and one of inferior manufacture is negligible when it is realized that the performance of a good tool is far superior to that of a cheap tool. Good tools keep their edges longer, are more easily sharpened, and withstand harder usage.

The following basic tools have, from experience, proved to be adequate for most needs:

Hammer, 16 oz.	Nail set, $\frac{1}{16}''$
Screw drivers, 3″ and 5″	Awl
Handsaw	Spokeshave
Bit brace, 8″	Vise
Auger bits, $\frac{1}{4}''$ and $\frac{3}{4}''$	Marking gauge
Gimlet bit, $\frac{3}{8}''$	Zigzag rule, 4'
Screwdriver bit, $\frac{5}{16}''$	Try and miter square, $7\frac{1}{2}''$
Chisels, $\frac{1}{4}''$ and $\frac{3}{4}''$	Combination oilstone
Pair of pliers	

Additional tools to be secured as required are:

Hand ripsaw	Jack plane
Compass saw	Gouge chisels, $\frac{1}{2}''$ and 1″
Coping saw	Hand drill

Expansive drill	Glass-cutter
Monkey wrench	Grinding wheel (hand)
Countersink	Handsaw set
Miter box	Files
Steel tape	Carriage makers' clamps
Caliper rule	Hand screws

WOODWORKING HAMMERS

The essential parts of a *claw* hammer, the most commonly used woodworking hammer, are shown in Fig. 1. Other types illustrated are the *ripping, upholsterer's,* and *tack* hammers. Hammer sizes

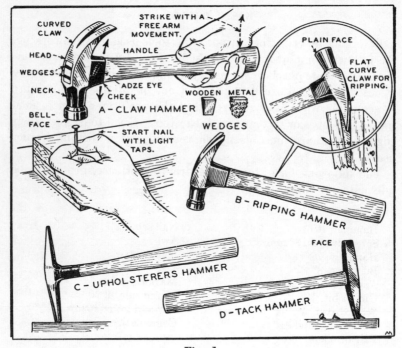

Fig. 1.

are determined by the weight of the head, which ranges from 5 to 28 oz. The heavier hammers are for driving larger nails into soft material or ordinary nails into harder wood. For general use, a 16-oz. hammer is recommended.

Smooth-face hammers are either plain or bell-face. The *bell-face* type is slightly more convex than the *plain*. While the novice cannot drive a nail as straight and as easily with a bell-face hammer, this type is more frequently used because, with a little experience, a nail can be driven flush and sometimes even below the surface of the work without leaving any hammer marks.

Correct method of using a hammer. *Driving nails*—The effectiveness of a hammer is dependent on its weight and the manner in which the blow is struck. To use a hammer correctly, grip it firmly in the right hand, close to the end of handle (Fig. 1). Always strike with a free arm movement. Grasp the nail with the thumb and forefinger of the other hand and place it exactly at the point where it is to be driven. Unless the nail is to be driven at an angle, it should be held perpendicular to the surface of the work. To set the nail, center the face of the hammer on the head of the nail and give it several light taps before removing the fingers. Then drive the nail in as far as desired with a few firm blows, using the center of the hammer face. Nails that do not go in straight or bend shoould be drawn out and thrown away. If, after several attempts, the nail continues to bend or go in crooked, the work should be investigated. If there is a knot or some other obstruction, drill a small hole through the obstruction and then drive the nail through.

Pulling out nails—When nails are pulled out with the claw end of a hammer, the head of the nail should clear the surface of the work sufficiently to permit the claws to grip it. To prevent marring the work and to secure extra and safe leverage, place a small block of wood under the head of the hammer as shown in Fig. 2. Be careful to place the block of wood in the correct position, that is, against the nail, to avoid enlarging the hole from which the nail is pulled.

Clinching nails—For added holding power, nails are sometimes *clinched*. The nails used for clinching must be long enough to penetrate the wood so that at least an inch and a half of the point protrudes from the underside. The protruding point is then bent over in direct line with the grain of the wood and hammered flat. When clinching nails, rest the work on a solid surface and be careful to avoid splitting the wood (Fig. 2).

Toenailing—Driving nails obliquely is called *toenailing*. This type of nailing is employed when the end of one piece of wood is fastened to the side of another, as shown in Fig. 2.

Driving corrugated fasteners—Corrugated fasteners, as shown in Fig. 2, are often called *wiggle nails*. They are used to a large extent in the making of screens and picture frames and for similar purposes. They are procurable with either a plain or saw edge.

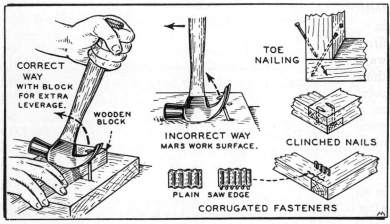

Fig. 2.

The *plain-edged* fastener is used for hard wood; the *saw-edged* type for soft wood. When driving corrugated fasteners, use a medium-weight hammer. Strike evenly distributed light blows. It is important that the lumber being fastened together rest on a solid surface while the work is being done.

Ripping—To rip woodwork apart, insert the claw part of a *ripping* hammer into a crack as near to a nail as possible. Use a quick, jolting movement to loosen each nail. Pull out the nails as previously described. Then rip out the boards or woodwork as required (Fig. 1).

Replacing a broken hammer handle—Machine-made hickory handles in various sizes can be secured at most hardware stores. The portion of the broken handle that remains in the hammer head must be removed. The simplest and most effective method of doing this is to drill through it with a twist drill to remove as much wood as possible. It is then easy to split out several small pieces and thus remove the old wedged-in handle.

The end of a new handle is usually larger than required and must be scraped or pared slightly before it will fit into the head of the hammer. However, do not pare it too much, since it must fit very tightly. After the small fitted end of the handle is inserted into the opening in the head of the hammer, tamp the other end of the handle against a solid surface until the head is in place. To prevent the head of the hammer from flying off, the end of the handle must be expanded, after it is in place in the hammer head, by inserting several wooden or metal wedges (Fig. 1). Wooden wedges can be made of either maple or hickory wood. Metal wedges can be secured at any hardware store and are preferable. Do not insert the wedges until the head is on the handle as far as it can go. When using wooden wedges, make a saw cut about as long as the wedge in the end of the handle before inserting it into the head of the hammer. Saw cuts are not necessary when using metal wedges.

HANDSAWS

The essential parts of a handsaw are shown in Fig. 3.

There are many types and sizes of handsaws. The ripsaw and the crosscut saw are most commonly used.

The *ripsaw* is designed specifically for cutting with the grain (Fig. 3). The teeth of the ripsaw are set alternately, that is, one tooth is bent slightly to the left and the next one to the right for the entire length of the saw to give the proper clearance when cutting through the work. A good ripsaw usually has five and one-half points to every inch, with each tooth acting like a vertical chisel, chipping out a small portion of the wood from the *kerf*, or cut.

Crosscut saws are designed to cut against, or across, the grain of the wood. The teeth of a crosscut saw are ground to a *true taper* for the additional clearance required when cutting across the grain. The front faces of the teeth have an angle of 15°, and the backs have an angle of 45°. The upper halves of the teeth are set alternately to the right and to the left to insure proper clearance. The teeth of a crosscut saw have an action similar to that of a chisel (Fig. 3).

The *backsaw* is useful for all types of cabinetwork. Its fine teeth and stiff back make possible the smooth, accurate cutting

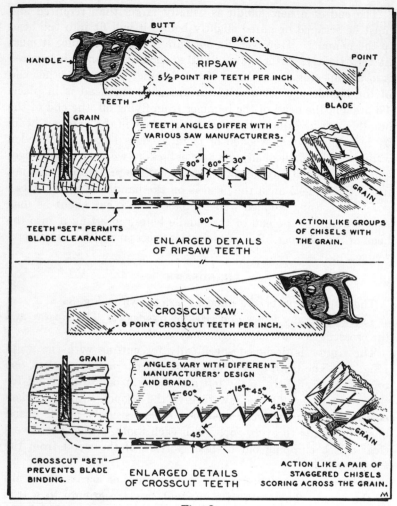

BUTT

BACK

HANDLE

POINT

RIPSAW

5½ POINT RIP TEETH PER INCH

TEETH

BLADE

GRAIN

TEETH ANGLES DIFFER WITH VARIOUS SAW MANUFACTURERS.

90° 60° 30°

90°

GRAIN

TEETH "SET" PERMITS BLADE CLEARANCE.

ENLARGED DETAILS OF RIPSAW TEETH

ACTION LIKE GROUPS OF CHISELS WITH THE GRAIN.

CROSSCUT SAW

8 POINT CROSSCUT TEETH PER INCH.

GRAIN

ANGLES VARY WITH DIFFERENT MANUFACTURERS' DESIGN AND BRAND.

60°   15° 45°

45°

45°

GRAIN

CROSSCUT "SET" PREVENTS BLADE BINDING.

ENLARGED DETAILS OF CROSSCUT TEETH

ACTION LIKE A PAIR OF STAGGERED CHISELS SCORING ACROSS THE GRAIN.

Fig. 3.

necessary for making joints. It is the ideal saw to use for cutting light stock, such as moldings and screen and picture frames. Backsaws are available in 8″, 10″, 12″, 14″, and 16″ lengths, with from 12 to 16 points to the inch. The 12″ length, with 14 points to the inch, is the most popular size (Fig. 4).

There are a great many uses for a *compass saw* in the home

workshop. It may be used for cutting curves and circles and for starting a cut from a hole bored in wood (Fig. 5). It is extremely useful for cutting holes in board and plaster walls and in floor boards to receive gas or water pipes. The compass saw is taper-ground from the tooth edge to a thin back, allowing for clearance. It also tapers to a sharp point and is toothed to the point for easy access to holes and for cutting sharp curves.

An ideal type is an interchangeable compass saw. Different lengths and types of blades are available for it and the handle can be adjusted to any convenient angle. The three blades shown in Fig. 5 can be used for a variety of purposes. The *compass* blade in the center of the illustration is 14″ long, with 8 points to the inch, and can be used for cutting curves and shapes in material up to ⅜″ thick.

Fig. 4. Backsaw.

Fig. 5. Compass saw.

The top blade, known as a *pruning* blade, is 16″ long and, in addition to being used for pruning trees, can also be employed as a general-purpose saw. The other blade in the set is a *keyhole* blade, 10″ long, 10 points to the inch. It can be used for cutting keyholes, sharp curves, and similar small work.

The *keyhole saw* is a special-purpose saw for cutting keyholes and for doing all kinds of cutout pattern, or fretwork, and similar light work. (Fig. 6).

The *coping* saw is designed for cutting curves (Fig. 7). It is

Fig. 6. Keyhole saw.

also used for shaping the ends of molding, for scrollwork, and similar light work on thin wood or plastic. It has very narrow blades, only ⅛″ wide, fitted at each end with a pin that is inserted in a stretcher at each end of the frame. A square nut forced into the handle engages the threaded end of the stretcher. By turning the handle, the blade is tautened. The blade, when stretched tight in the frame, may be turned as required for cutting sharp angles. The frame of a coping saw should be made of good steel. It is usually ⅜″ wide, 3⁄16″ thick, and 4½″ deep from the tooth edge to the inside of the back. The blades of a coping saw should be made of good spring steel ⅛″ wide, 17 points to the inch, and 67⁄16″ in length from pin to pin.

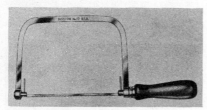

Fig. 7. Coping saw.

Using a handsaw. Each type of saw is designed for a specific purpose and should be used for that purpose only. If you value your tools and the material on which you are working, never use a crosscut saw for work that requires a ripsaw, or vice versa. Ripsaws are specifically designed to cut with the grain of the wood. This is called *ripping.* Crosscut saws are designed for *crosscutting* (sawing against the grain).

To hold a saw properly, grasp the handle firmly with the right hand, with the thumb and index finger touching the sides of the handle (Fig. 8). This grip makes it easy to guide the direction of the saw cut. Always start a saw cut with an upward stroke, using the thumb of the left hand to guide the saw. Never under any circumstances start a saw cut with a downstroke. Draw the saw slowly upward several times at the point where the cut is to be made (Fig. 8). Do this very slowly or your saw will jump; instead of a well-cut piece of lumber you will have a badly cut thumb. When the line of cut has been started properly, proceed to cut on the downstroke.

For ripping, use a ripsaw to permit long, easy strokes. Cutting with just a few inches of blade in the middle of the saw usually makes it difficult to keep the line of cut straight. When ripping lumber, support the work on sawhorses, and start the cut by using the finer teeth at the end of the blade. If the work cannot be supported on sawhorses, place it in a vise. A cutting angle of 60° between the edge of the saw and the face of the work gives best results (Fig. 8).

To begin a crosscut, rest the blade on the waste side of the line of cut, support the side of the blade with the thumb, and draw the saw upward a few times until a slight groove appears (Fig. 8).

When either crosscutting or ripping, it is good practice to cut on the outer, or waste, side of a line; do not attempt to saw directly on the line.

In crosscutting, 45° is the proper angle to maintain between the saw and the face of the work. Extending the forefinger along the side of the handle aids considerably in guiding the blade (Fig. 8). Take long, easy strokes to utilize a maximum of the saw's cutting edge. Always keep saw square with surface of wood (Fig. 9).

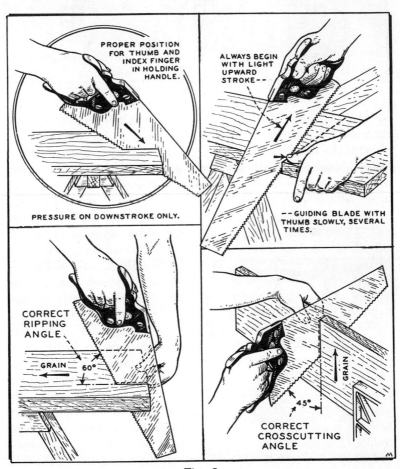

Fig. 8.

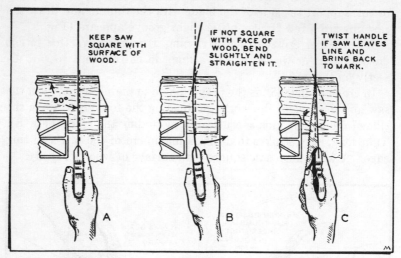

Fig. 9.

When the cut is nearly completed, support the piece to prevent the wood from splintering on the underside. Never twist the piece off with the saw blade or in any other way; cut right through to the end, using light final strokes to avoid splitting.

Using a backsaw. When using a backsaw in a miter box, be sure that the work lines up with the slots in the box. Hold the work against the back of the box (Fig. 10). Start the cut carefully with a backstroke, holding the handle of the saw slightly upward. As the cutting proceeds, level the saw gradually and continue cutting with the blade horizontal. Hold the saw firmly for clean, straight, accurate cutting.

Fig. 10. Using a backsaw in a miter box.

If a miter box is not used, it is advisable to support the work with a bench hook. For long material, two bench hooks are necessary. A bench hook and its use is shown in Figs. 11 and 12.

Using a coping saw. A *coping* saw is used to cut curves and intricate patterns in thin wood or plastic. The correct position for use is shown in Fig. 13. A coping saw is generally used with a saddle to support the work. The *saddle* consists of a board cut

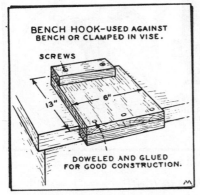

Fig. 11. Bench hook.

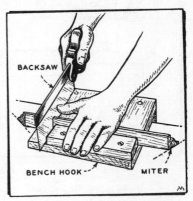

Fig. 12. Using bench hook.

with a V-notch, about 3″ wide and 3½″ deep, attached to a support. Hold the blade so that it moves vertically. Cutting strokes should be as long as possible to avoid overheating the blade. In cutting scrollwork, furniture overlay, and similar articles, the piece marked with the design to be cut out is held on the saddle and shifted so that the saw can cut along the curves as it progresses. To avoid breakage of blades, change the angle of the blade in the frame when making sharp turns.

Setting and sharpening a handsaw. A good saw is a fine tool and will give a lifetime of service if properly handled. The saw teeth will require setting and

Fig. 13. Coping saw.

sharpening from time to time. This may seem to be an involved operation, but if directions are followed carefully, it is not difficult.

A special *saw clamp* (Fig. 14) and several files are all the equipment needed. The following table indicates the file to be used.

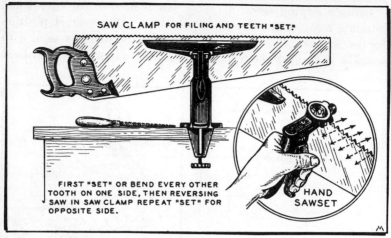

Fig. 14.

Points to the Inch	File to Be Used
4½, 5, 6	7″ slim taper
7, 8	6″ slim taper
9, 10	5″ to 5½″ slim taper
11, 12, 13, 14, 15	4½″ slim taper
16 or more	4½″ or 5″ superfine, No. 2 cut
For jointing teeth	8″ or 10″ mill bastard

Examine the teeth of the saw to see if they are uniform in size and shape and are properly set. A good saw will not need resetting of the teeth every time it is sharpened. If the teeth are touched up occasionally with a file of the proper size, they will cut longer and better and retain sufficient set to enable the saw to clear itself. The proper amount of set is shown in Fig. 15.

Before proceeding to set and sharpen a handsaw, study the shape of the teeth. The teeth of saws for crosscutting and for ripping should be similar to those shown at *A* and *B* in Fig. 15. A saw cannot do a good cutting job unless the teeth are even and properly shaped. If the teeth are found to be uneven, it is necessary to joint and file them, using the following procedure.

Jointing handsaw teeth. *Jointing*, or filing, the teeth to the same shape and height is necessary when they are uneven or incorrectly shaped or when the tooth edges are not straight, or slightly breasted. Unless the teeth are regular in size and shape it is wasted effort to set and file a saw.

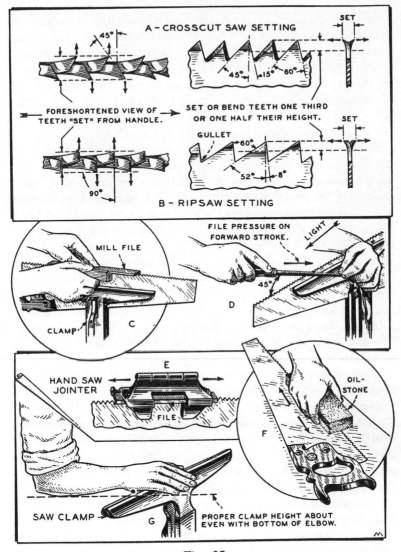

Fig. 15.

To joint a saw, place it in a saw clamp, with the handle of the saw to the right (*C* and *G*, Fig. 15). Lay a mill file, of the proper size, flat lengthwise on the teeth. Pass it lightly back and forth across the tips of all the teeth, for the full length of the blade. If the teeth are very uneven, it is better not to make all of them the same height the first time they are jointed. Joint only the highest teeth first, then shape the teeth that have been jointed. Proceed by jointing the teeth a second time, passing the file along the tops of all the teeth until every tooth is touched by the file. Never allow the file to tip to one side or the other—always file flat. The use of a handsaw jointer is shown at *E*, Fig. 15.

Shaping handsaw teeth. After jointing, proceed with *shaping* the teeth. All the teeth must be filed to the correct shape, with all the gullets of equal depth (Fig. 15). The fronts and backs must have the proper shape and angle. The teeth must be uniform in size, disregarding the bevel, which will be taken care of later. To bring the gullets down to equal depth, place the file well into each gullet and file straight across the saw at right angles to the blade (*D*, Fig. 15). Never hold the file at any other angle during this operation. If the teeth are of unequal size, file in turn the ones with the largest tops until the file reaches the center of the flat top made by jointing; then move the file to the next gullet. File until the rest of the top disappears and the tooth has been brought up to a point. Do not attempt to bevel any of the teeth at this time.

After all the teeth have been properly shaped and are even in height, the next step is setting the teeth.

Setting handsaw teeth. As mentioned previously, the teeth of a good handsaw do not need to be reset every time they require a little sharpening. If it is not necessary to joint and shape the teeth, carefully examine the saw to see if the teeth have the proper amount of *set* (*A* and *B*, Fig. 15). If they have the proper set, the saw is ready for filing; if not, they should be set. Always set the teeth after they have been jointed and shaped but before final filing, to avoid injury to the cutting edges.

The operation of setting saw teeth has a distinct purpose. *A* and *B*, Fig. 15, show end views of saw teeth; the teeth of both crosscut saws and ripsaws are sprung alternately left and right (not more than half the length of each tooth) for the entire length of the tooth edge of the saw. This arrangement enables the saw to cut a kerf, or path, slightly wider than the thickness of the blade itself, giving the necessary clearance and preventing any friction that would cause the saw to bind in the cut. The depth of the set should never exceed half the tooth, whether the saw is fine or coarse. A taper-ground saw requires very little set, because its blade tapers thinner both toward the back and along the back toward the point, thus providing sufficient clearance for easy running.

The simplest method of setting a saw is by the use of a special tool known as a *saw set* (Fig. 16). Fasten the saw in the saw clamp, as shown in Fig. 14. Start at one end of the saw and place the saw set over the first tooth bent away from you. The plunger in the saw set should strike the tooth firmly and squarely. Holding the saw set firmly in place, compress the handle: the tooth will then bend against the saw clamp. Work across the entire length of the saw and set alternate teeth. Reverse the saw in the clamp and set the remaining teeth in the same manner. With the saw still in the clamp, joint the teeth by

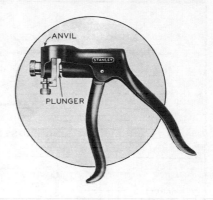

Fig. 16. Saw set.

lightly rubbing a file lengthwise over them until they all have flat tops, which will provide a proper guide for filing.

Extreme care must be taken to see that the set is even and regular. It must be the same width from end to end of the blade and the same width on both sides of the blade, otherwise the saw will run out of line and cuts made with it will not be true. After the saw has been properly set, the next step is to file the teeth.

Filing handsaw teeth. The type of file to use for filing the teeth is determined by the number of tooth points to the inch. For a crosscut saw, measure one inch from the point of any tooth. For a ripsaw having 5½ or fewer points to the inch, the teeth near the point of the blade are finer than the rest; therefore measure the regular-size teeth at the butt of the blade. For the best working position, align the top of the clamp with the elbow. Place the saw in the clamp with its handle at the right. Allow the bottom gullets to protrude ⅛″ above the jaws of the clamp, otherwise the file will chatter or screech.

Filing a crosscut saw. To file a crosscut saw, stand at the first position shown in Fig. 17. Start at the point and pick out the first tooth that is set toward you. Hold the file in the position shown in the illustration. Place the file in the gullet to the left of the tooth, holding it directly across the blade. Swing the file handle left to the correct angle, as shown in Fig. 17. Hold

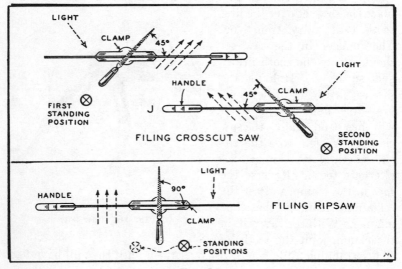

Fig. 17.

the file level and maintain this angle; never allow it to tip either upward or downward. Be certain at all times that the file is set well down into the gullet. Let it find its own bearing against the teeth it touches. For guidance in filing, study and duplicate the shape and bevel of some of the least-used teeth, those near the handle end.

File on the push stroke only: the back of the left tooth and the front of the right tooth are thus filed simultaneously. File the teeth until half of the flat tops previously made on them are cut away; then lift the file from the gullet. Skip the next gullet to the right and place the file in the second gullet toward the handle. Repeat the filing operation as previously described, filing at the same angle as for the first set of two teeth. Proceed by placing the file in every second gullet until the handle end of the saw has been reached.

For the second position, turn the saw around in the clamp with the handle to the left. Take the position shown in Fig. 17 and place the file in the gullet to the right of the first tooth set toward you. This is the first of the gullets skipped when the reverse side of the saw was filed. Now turn the file handle to the desired angle toward the right. Proceed to file until the other half of the flat top made on each tooth as a guide has been cut away and the tooth is sharpened to a point. Continue by placing the file in every second gullet until the handle of the saw is reached.

Be sure that in the final sharpening all the teeth are of the same size and height, otherwise the saw will not cut satisfactorily. When teeth are of uneven sizes, stress is placed on the larger or higher teeth, thus causing the saw to jump or bind in the kerf.

Filing a ripsaw. The procedure for filing ripsaws is similar to that for crosscut saws, with a single exception (Fig. 17). Ripsaws are filed with the file held straight across the saw at a right angle to the blade. Place the file in the gullet so as to give the front of each tooth an angle of **8°** and the back an angle of **52°**. Place the saw in the clamp with the handle toward the right. Place the file in the gullet to the left of the first tooth set toward you. Continue by placing the file in every second gullet and filing straight across. When the handle of the saw is reached, turn the saw around in the clamp. Start at the point again, placing the file in the first gullet that was previously skipped when filing from the other side. Continue to file in every second gullet to the handle end of the saw.

One final precaution: never try to avoid reversing the saw in the clamp or attempt to file all the teeth from the same side of the blade. This procedure is certain to make the saw run to one side.

Angle and bevel of teeth. The angle of the teeth in crosscut saws is of great importance. Imagine that Fig. 18 is a board, across which a deep mark with the point of a knife is to be made. If the knife is held nearly perpendicular, as at *B,* it will pull harder and will not cut so smoothly as when it is inclined forward, as at *A*. It follows, then, that the cutting edge of the crosscut saw should be at an acute angle, as at C, rather than perpendicular, as at D.

The angles of 15° front and 15° back for crosscut saws, and

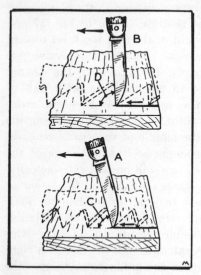

Fig. 18. Shapes and angles of saw teeth.

8° front and 52° back for ripsaws, as set at the factory, prove most satisfactory for general use. When a saw has less angle at the front of the teeth than specified above, it is said to have more *hook* or *pitch*. If too much hook is given to the teeth, the saw often takes hold too keenly, causing it to "hand up" or stick suddenly in the cut, thus kinking the blade. When there is too much set, the teeth may be broken, as the resulting strain is out of proportion to the strength of the blade.

In filing saws for crosscutting, the file is held at an angle; therefore the teeth are given an angle. This angle on the front and back of the teeth is called *bevel*.

How to bevel teeth. The proper amount of bevel to give the teeth is important. If there is too much bevel, the points of the teeth will score so deeply that the wood fibers severed from the stock will not clear and will have to be removed with a file or rasp. In Fig. 19, B shows a tooth (enlarged) of a crosscut saw with the same amount of bevel front and back; suitable for softwoods where rapid work is required.

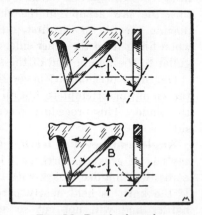

Fig. 19. Bevel of teeth.

A, in Fig. 19, shows a tooth (enlarged) of a saw suitable for medium hardwoods. It has less bevel on the back, which gives a shorter bevel to the point, as at *B*.

These illustrations show that the bevel on the front of the teeth is about the same, but the bevel of the point (looking lengthwise along the blade) is quite different, depending on the difference in the angles of the backs of the teeth. Experience will indicate what bevel is best.

For the beginner, the instructions given under Filing the Teeth should be followed carefully.

Side-dressing saws. After jointing, setting, and filing the saw, side-dress it by laying it on a flat surface and lightly rubbing the sides of the teeth with an oilstone as shown in *F*, Fig. 15.

SCREWDRIVERS

Types of screwdrivers. There are many sizes and several types of screwdrivers. The size is always given by the length of the blade: a 6″ screwdriver has a 6″ blade, and so on. Narrow-tipped blades are designed for small screws, and blades with larger tips for heavier screws. The following types are in general use: common screwdriver, ratchet, spiral ratchet, offset, Phillips.

Common screwdriver—The common screwdriver is available in many sizes, each for a specific size of screw. The various parts of a common screwdriver are shown in Fig. 20.

Ratchet and spiral ratchet screwdrivers—Two variations of the common screwdriver are shown in Fig. 21. They are the ratchet and the spiral ratchet types. Similar in operation to the common screwdriver, the ratchet type drives screws in much faster and works semiautomatically. Blades of various sizes can be secured for both types of ratchet screwdriver, and both types can be set for driving screws in or extracting them. The handle of the ratchet screwdriver turns back and forth in the direction set.

The spiral ratchet screwdriver operates even faster than the ratchet. It can be set for either in or out. To drive the screw, set the blade in the screw slot and push on the handle, steadying the blade with the other hand. The blade makes several turns for each push.

Offset screwdriver—Offset screwdrivers are designed for driving screws located where there is insufficient space to use the conventional type of screwdriver (Fig. 22). The offset screwdriver is made from a piece of either round or octagonal steel with two

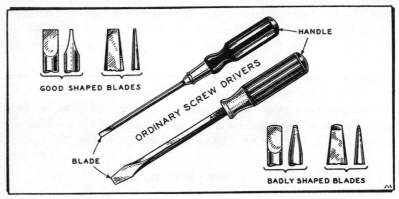

Fig. 20.

blades at right angles to one another and to the shaft at opposite ends. When screws have to be driven in or extracted in inaccessible places, it is sometimes necessary to use both ends of the

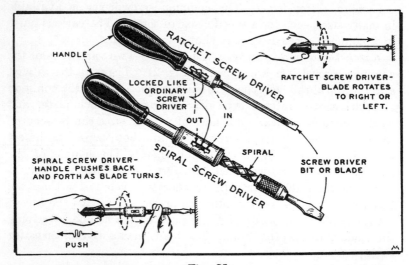

Fig. 21.

offset screwdriver, turning the screw a short distance with one end and then with the other.

Phillips screwdriver—The Phillips screwdriver is used only for driving the Phillips screw (Fig. 22). Phillips screws have a head with two V-slots which cross at the center. The tip of the Phillips screwdriver blade is shaped like a pointed or beveled cross to fit into these slots. To keep the blade in the cross slots of the

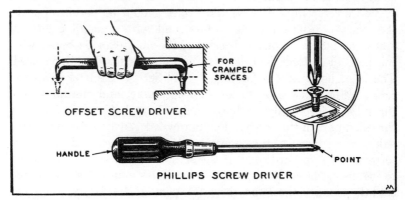

Fig. 22.

screw more downward pressure is used. Phillips screws are used to a great extent in radio sets, on moldings, the trim of automobiles, and furniture and cabinetwork. This type of screwdriver cannot slip out of the slot or otherwise damage expensive finishes.

Correct method of using a screwdriver. Choose the right size of screw and screwdriver, and be sure to use the longest screwdriver that is available and convenient for the particular job. The blade of the screwdriver must fit the screw slots. It must be neither too small nor too large. If it is too small, the blade may break. If it is too large, it may slip out and mar the surface of the wood.

The quickest way to ruin any screwdriver is to use it as a can opener, a putty- or paint-mixer, or as a lever.

The tip of a screwdriver must be square. A round-tipped screwdriver is dangerous: it is apt to slip when driving a screw, causing serious injury.

When driving screws with a common screwdriver, grasp the

handle with the thumb side of the hand toward the blade. Use automatic screwdrivers according to directions given by the manufacturer of each type. Place the screw in the pilot hole, hold it straight with the left hand, set the blade in the slot, and start turning the screwdriver, exerting pressure with the right hand. As soon as the screw has taken hold of the wood, remove the left hand, and continue driving the screw in. Hold the screwdriver steady, with the blade in a direct, straight line with the screw.

Before screws are driven, pilot holes should be bored. Locate the exact positions for the screws, and with a small *brad awl* mark the places. For small screws, the holes can be bored with the awl. For large screws, bits or twist drills should be used. The pilot holes should be slightly smaller in diameter than the screw. For softwoods, such as spruce, pine, and similar types, the pilot holes should be bored only about half as deep as the threaded part of the screw. For hardwoods, such as maple, birch, oak, and mahogany, they must be drilled almost as deep as the screw itself. In hardwood, if the screw is large or if you happen to be using brass screws, the pilot holes must first be bored slightly smaller than the threaded part of the screw, then enlarged at the top with a second drill of the same diameter as the unthreaded portion of the screw.

When two pieces of wood are to be fastened together with screws, two sets of holes must be drilled. The top piece is clamped to the lower piece only by the pressure of the screw head, and for this reason the holes are drilled so that the threaded portion of the screw takes hold of only the under piece of the wood. Locate the positions for the screws and mark each with a brad awl. Bore the pilot hole of smaller diameter than the threaded portion of the screw. This pilot hole must be bored all the way through the upper piece of the wood and for about half the length of the threaded part of the screw into the lower piece. Enlarge the pilot hole in the upper piece of wood to the same diameter as the unthreaded portion of the screw. Countersink the clearance hole in the upper piece of wood. Drive all of the screws firmly into place; then tighten each consecutively.

Where flathead or oval-head screws are used, the upper end of the pilot hole should be bored out or countersunk to match in size the diameter of the heads of the screws that are used. Countersinking is a simple operation, and the tool used is called a *countersink* (Fig. 23), its size depending on the size of the screw. It fits into a brace (Fig. 23).

Driving screws into hardware, hinges, and handles. While steel screws are used generally in woodworking, brass screws also are used to some extent for fastening small hinges and hardware on cabinets and furniture. General directions for the use of brass screws are approximately the same as for steel screws.

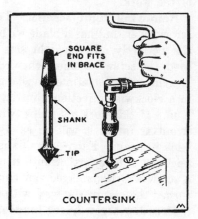

Fig. 23.

Directions for fastening hinges and other types of hardware, where a recess must be made before the fixtures can be mounted, are described in Chap. 3, devoted to hanging doors and similar work.

When the work does not need to be recessed, place the hardware in the required position and mark the screw holes with a brad awl. Bore the pilot holes, following the directions given in the previous paragraphs on the Correct Method of Using a Screwdriver. Where screws are short, only a pilot hole is needed, but long screws require a clearance hole of the same diameter and length as the unthreaded part of the screw.

Use the largest size of screw that will slip easily through the holes in the hardware. If the holes in the hardware are counter-sunk, oval-head or flathead screws to fit the countersink should be used; if they are not countersunk, use round-head screws. Do not tighten the screws until all of them have been driven in.

Concealing screws with plugs. It is sometimes necessary to set screws below the surface of the wood and to conceal them with a plug of the same type of wood. For instance, the planking on boats is usually fastened to the frames in this manner. Wooden plugs of various diameters, made from mahogany, oak, pine, cedar, and cypress, can be bought from dealers in boat supplies for this purpose.

To conceal screws with wooden plugs, bore a hole with the bit and brace to fit the plug, then bore the pilot and clearance holes for the screws, and drive the screws into place. To insure a tight fit, put glue or wood filler in the plug hole and drive in the plug with a hammer. When the glue or filler is set, pare off the top of the plugs with a chisel, and sandpaper it even with the surface of the work.

Removing tight screws. To remove a tight screw, use a screwdriver that has a blade with parallel sides, and fits the screw slot perfectly. If the right size and shape of screwdriver is not used, the screw becomes "chewed," making the job more difficult. A tight screw sometimes can be started by giving it a slight twist in a clockwise direction, that is, the same direction which drives it in. If this does not help, twist the screw both ways, backing it out as far as it will go easily, and then turning it part way back in again. Each time this is repeated, the screw usually will back out a little farther until it is all the way out. In some cases, a screw with a damaged slot can be backed partly out, and then turned the rest of the way with a pair of pliers.

Dressing screwdriver blades. A screwdriver is not a cutting tool and for that reason does not have to be sharpened, but it must be dressed or kept in condition. This is done by occasion-

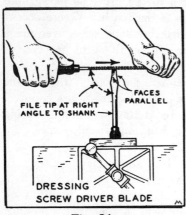

FACES PARALLEL

FILE TIP AT RIGHT ANGLE TO SHANK

DRESSING SCREW DRIVER BLADE

Fig. 24.

ally grinding it on an emery wheel or by filing the blade with a flat file. Correct and incorrect shapes for a screwdriver are shown in Fig. 20.

When dressing a screwdriver with a file, hold the screwdriver in a vise and file the tip absolutely straight across both ends, at right angles to the shank and the sides, with the faces near the tip as parallel as possible to each other (Fig. 24). Never bevel or round the tip of a screwdriver.

When using an emery wheel for dressing a screwdriver, do not hold the blade against the wheel too long, or the friction wheel will heat the steel and draw the temper or soften the blade. When dressing a screwdriver, dip the blade in water at frequent intervals.

PLANES

Planes are used for roughing down the surface of lumber and as finishing tools. They are classified as either *bench* or *block*. The bench plane is always used with the grain of the wood; the block plane for cutting across the grain. Bench planes are made in several types, each of which has outstanding features.

The bench planes in common use are the *smoothing, jack, fore,* and *jointer types* (Fig. 25). The smoothing plane, the shortest of these, is used for finishing or leveling flat surfaces after the rough surface and unevenness has been removed with a jack plane. It is handy to use where only small areas are to be leveled off, as its short length makes it simple to locate and remedy these uneven spots.

The smoothing plane is smaller than a jack plane, but considerably larger than the block plane. It does not cut the end grain of lumber as well as a block plane. It ranges in size from 5½″ to 10″ in length and is made like a jack plane, but has a shorter sole or bottom. A plane-iron cap to coil and break the shavings is attached to the plane iron. The cutting edge on the blade of a smoothing plane must be set rather close to make a fairly fine shaving.

A fore plane is merely a shorter type of jointer plane, and is sometimes preferable because of its light weight. When it is necessary to true up edges of boards preparatory to fitting them closely or jointing them, the jointer plane is used. These four types of planes are shown in Fig. 25.

Roughing or scrub plane. When more than ¼″ of waste is to be removed from a board, a *roughing* or *scrub* plane is used. This plane is available in two sizes, 9½″ and 10½″ long. A roughing or scrub plane is equipped with heavy rounded blades. It is used to clean up rough, dirty timber and to true up large pieces of wood to approximate size, preliminary to doing a finish job with either the smoothing or jack plane.

Circular plane. This special-type plane has a flexible steel bottom which is adjustable to form a curve for planing either

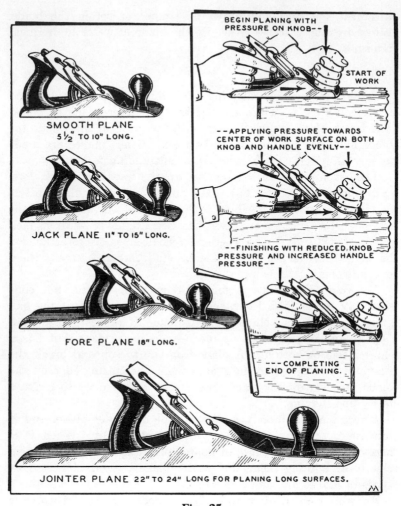

BEGIN PLANING WITH
PRESSURE ON KNOB--

START OF
WORK

SMOOTH PLANE
5½" TO 10" LONG.

--APPLYING PRESSURE TOWARDS
CENTER OF WORK SURFACE ON BOTH
KNOB AND HANDLE EVENLY--

JACK PLANE 11" TO 15" LONG.

--FINISHING WITH REDUCED KNOB
PRESSURE AND INCREASED HANDLE
PRESSURE--

FORE PLANE 18" LONG.

---COMPLETING
END OF PLANING.

JOINTER PLANE 22" TO 24" LONG FOR PLANING LONG SURFACES.

Fig. 25.

concave or convex surfaces down to a minimum radius of **20″**.

Rabbet plane. Rabbet planes are used to cut out *rabbets*, which are rectangular recesses at the ends or edges of a plank to form what is known as a *rabbet joint*. Rabbet joints are described more fully in Chap. 3 (page 125). The sole, or bottom, of this plane is cut away so that the edge of the cutting iron is in line with the side of the plane. When fitted with a special iron called a *spur*, the rabbet plane can be used also for planing across the grain (Fig. 26).

Modelmaker's plane. The *modelmaker's* plane, also called a *violin* plane, is only 3″ to 4″ in length. The sole is curved in both directions and the blade is rounded, conforming to the same

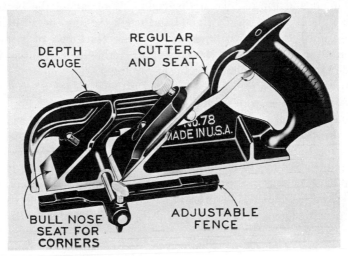

Fig. 26. Parts of a rabbet plane.

curvature. It can be used to remove excess wood from a flat, convex, or concave surface of any radius down to a minimum of 12″. It is used by patternmakers, violin- and other instrument-makers, and professional modelbuilders. It can be bought only on special order.

Spokeshave. While a spokeshave is not strictly a plane, it sometimes is used for the same purpose and in the same manner. It is an excellent tool for shaping curved pieces.

Adjustment of plane irons. A plane is a cutting tool set in a block of metal or wood which serves to act as a guide to regulate the depth of the cut. The plane iron, a chisel-like tool, does the actual cutting. Like all cutting tools, it must have a keen, sharp edge and be adjusted correctly.

Bench planes, that is, the smoothing, fore, jointer, and jack planes, have a plane-iron cap clamped to the cutting blade to stiffen the iron and break and curve the shavings as they come up through the throat of the tool. The position of the cap in relation to the plane iron is adjustable by loosening the clamping screw. In general, the edge of the cap should be about $\frac{1}{16}''$ back of the cutting edge of the iron. To regulate the thickness of shavings, turn the plane upside down, holding the knob in the left hand and the handle in the right. Look along the bottom of the plane, and with the right hand begin turning the adjusting screw until the blade projects about the thickness of a hair. Then turn the adjusting lever left or right to straighten the blade: the blade should never be at an angle.

In block planes, the blade is locked in position by a lever cap or by a cam lever, which differ slightly in planes produced by different companies. Moving the lever-cap screw, or the lever, in one direction locks the plane iron; moving it in the opposite direction unlocks the iron when it is necessary to remove it from the plane. By means of an adjusting screw, the sharpened lower edge of the plane iron can be moved in and out of the mouth of the plane. A block-plane iron is beveled on only one side of the sharpened edge, and it is set in the frame of the plane with the bevel up.

To adjust a block plane, hold it up with the toe, or front, of the plane facing forward, and the bottom level with the eye. To regulate the thickness of shavings, turn the adjusting screw until the sharp edge of the iron projects slightly through the sole. This is called a vertical adjustment. To produce even shavings, a lateral adjustment is made by loosening slightly the lever-cap screw or the lever cam. Sight along the bottom of the plane. Press the upper end of the blade near the adjustment screw either to the right or left to bring the cutting edge of the blade parallel to the bottom of the plane. Never set one corner of the blade farther out of the throat of the plane than the other. Do not set the blade too far out of the throat; it should project just enough for the edge to be visible and to be felt with the fingertips (Figs. 27 and 28).

Correct method of using a plane. Grasp the handle of the plane with the right hand, holding the knob firmly between the thumb and forefinger of the left hand, with the finger joints of the left hand protruding slightly over the edge of the plane. At

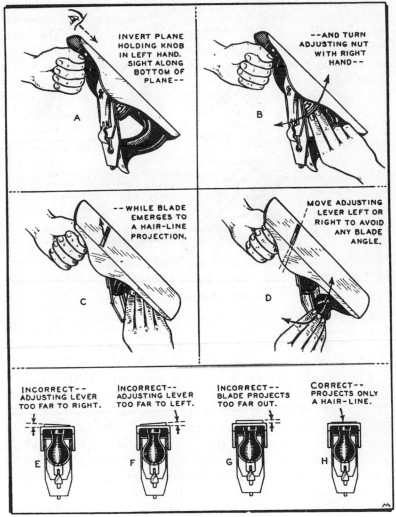

Fig. 27. Adjusting a plane.

the beginning of each stroke, the pressure and driving force is exerted by the left hand. As the stroke progresses, the pressure of the left hand is gradually lessened, and that of the right hand correspondingly increased until the pressure from both of the hands is approximately equal. Continue increasing the pressure

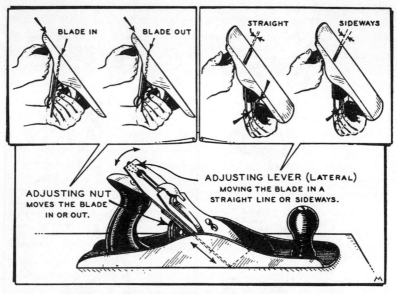

Fig. 28. Adjusting a plane.

from the right hand. At the end of the cut, the right hand will
be exerting the power and driving the plane, while the left hand
will be guiding the tool (Fig. 26).

When planing, always hold the plane level. If the plane is
tilted, it will produce uneven, thick shavings and ruin the trueness
of the work. To avoid dulling the cutter unnecessarily, lift the
plane above the work on all return strokes. When working on
long surfaces, begin at the right-hand side of the board, taking
a few strokes; then step forward and take the same number of
strokes, repeating until the entire surface of the board has been
planed, always *with* the grain. As the work progresses, use a try
square and level to determine the accuracy. For the first cuts
on any wide surface, a jack plane should be used. Its long face
rides over the low spots and dresses down the higher ones. The
cutter on a jack plane is ground in a slightly convex form, which
facilitates the removal of thick shavings, and at the same time
avoids a rectangular shaving that would tend to choke up the
throat of the plane. Thus all parts of the blade coming in contact
with the work cut smooth, even shavings. This important fact is

also true of the cutter on a fore plane, except convexity is slightly less. The convex cutters of both planes will leave a series of slight grooves, but these are easily removed with either a smoothing or a jointer plane.

For cutting against the grain, the block plane is used. Only one hand is employed; grasp the sides of the tool between the thumb and the second and third fingers, with the forefinger resting in the hollow of the finger rest at the front of the tool, and with the lever cap under the palm of the hand. Pressing down and forward at the beginning of each stroke and maintaining an even pressure throughout the forward motion is the secret of properly using a block plane. To avoid splitting, plane the end grain halfway, alternately from each edge. If the plane is pushed all the way across an end grain, the corners and the edge of the work are apt to split off.

Sharpening a plane iron. Sharpening a plane iron involves two operations: *grinding* and *whetting*. As a rule, the cutting edge can be whetted several times before grinding is necessary. A plane iron requires grinding only when its bevel has become short or when the edges have been nicked. Because whetting is done after grinding, the process of grinding is described here first.

While the grinding of a plane iron is similar to grinding a chisel or gouge, two important points must be considered: avoiding burning the cutting edge and maintaining the correct bevel. If a motor-driven grinder is not available, use a small hand-driven grinder equipped with a carborundum wheel of the right type for chisels and plane irons. Either type of grinding wheel must be provided with an adjustable tool rest, which is set to a grinding angle of 25°-30° to produce the desired bevel (Fig. 29).

Grinding a plane iron on a dry emery or carborundum wheel requires considerable care and some experience. Burring can be avoided by grinding

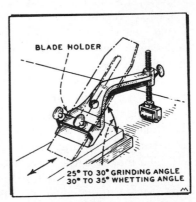

BLADE HOLDER

25° TO 30° GRINDING ANGLE
30° TO 35° WHETTING ANGLE

Fig. 29. Grinding a plane iron.

very lightly and by dripping either kerosene or water onto the wheel to keep it from getting too dry, and by frequently dipping the plane iron in water. If these precautions are not taken the edge will overheat or burn, turning a blue-black color, and will lose its temper. Steel that has lost its temper is softened and can never be resharpened.

The edge of a grinding wheel must always be dressed smooth. If it becomes grooved or out of true, dress it with a carborundum stick especially made for the purpose. Hold the carborundum stick against the revolving wheel until the wheel has been smoothed out.

Preparatory to grinding, the plane iron must be removed from the plane. If it is a double plane-iron type, the iron must be separated from the cap by loosening the screw and sliding it along to the end of the slot, where its head will pass through the hole.

The right bevel or grinding angle for plane irons is 25° to 30°. Maintaining it throughout is a simple matter if the adjustable tool rest is used. Turn the wheel toward the tool, at the same time moving the tool from side to side against the wheel. Exert only a slight pressure against the wheel, as too much will cause overheating, thus spoiling the tool. Grind the plane iron until a fine bevel or wire edge appears.

Whetting a plane iron. A plane iron must be whetted after grinding to remove the burr or wire edge and to produce a clean cutting edge. When a plane iron has become only slightly dull, whetting it without prior grinding will usually restore a keen cutting edge. A common oilstone with a fine surface on one side and a rough surface on the other is used, with a light oil, such as kerosene or kerosene mixed with a light motor oil, to float the particles of steel and prevent them from filling up the pores of the stone. The whetting bevel is usually 30° to 35°, slightly greater than the grinding bevel. The bevel must at all times be kept straight. With a steady motion, move the tool parallel to the stone and with a figure-eight movement make certain that all parts of the cutting edge come in contact with the stone (Fig. 30). To maintain the correct bend, use the toolholder shown in the same illustration. After this bevel is cut, or if the blade has been ground, the back of the blade will have a wire edge. Remove this edge by reversing the plane iron and taking several strokes with the blade flat on the stone (Fig. 30). Then complete the whetting by drawing the edge over a small wooden block or a leather strap. Hold the blade up to the light to determine its sharpness. A sharp edge does not reflect light. A dull edge will show as a fine white line; if this occurs, repeat both operations.

Reassembling a plane iron. Reassemble a newly sharpened plane iron with extreme care to avoid nicking its keen edge. Lay the plane-iron cap across the flat side of the iron with the screw in the slot. Pull it down and away from the cutting edge, and turn the cap parallel to the iron when it is almost at the end of the slot. Hold the cap and iron together and slide the cap forward until its edge is about $\frac{1}{16}''$ back of the cutting edge of the iron. To avoid nicking or dulling the blade, do not move the cap or drag it across the cutting edge. When the cap is in proper position, hold the cap and iron firmly together and tighten the screw that will hold the two parts of the double plane iron together. When not in use, lay the plane down on its side to protect the blade, and set the blade far in so that it cannot be damaged by other tools falling against it (Figs. 31 and 32).

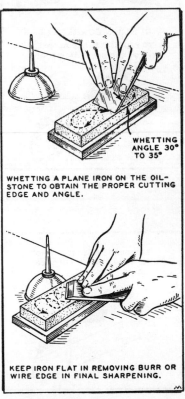

WHETTING
ANGLE 30°
TO 35°

WHETTING A PLANE IRON ON THE OIL-
STONE TO OBTAIN THE PROPER CUTTING
EDGE AND ANGLE.

KEEP IRON FLAT IN REMOVING BURR OR
WIRE EDGE IN FINAL SHARPENING.

Fig. 30. Whetting a plane iron.

CHISELS AND GOUGES

There are many kinds of woodworking chisels and gouges: paring, firmer, framing, packet, sikh, corner, gouge, butt, and mill chisels (Fig. 33). Those most generally used in the home workshop are the framing, butt, and packet types, each of which is available with either a straight or a bevel edge, according to its intended use. All chisels and gouges come in two types known as the tang and the socket (Fig. 34). For general use the socket type is preferable because it is more durable. One end of the steel blade of the socket chisel is formed into a funnel-shaped socket that fits over the tapered end of either a wood or plastic handle. The

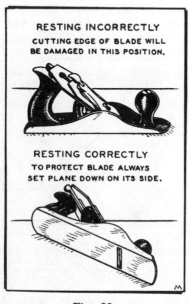

RESTING INCORRECTLY
CUTTING EDGE OF BLADE WILL BE DAMAGED IN THIS POSITION.

RESTING CORRECTLY
TO PROTECT BLADE ALWAYS SET PLANE DOWN ON ITS SIDE.

Fig. 31.

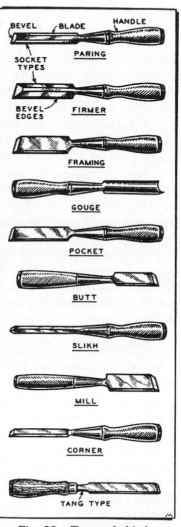

BEVEL   BLADE   HANDLE

SOCKET TYPES   PARING

BEVEL EDGES   FIRMER

FRAMING

GOUGE

POCKET

BUTT

SLIKH

MILL

CORNER

TANG TYPE

Fig. 33. Types of chisels.

SET BLADE IN SO IT CANNOT BE RUINED, WHEN FINISHED USING PLANE.

Fig. 32.

lighter chisels range from ⅛″ to 1″ in width in gradations of ⅛″. The heavier type range from 1″ to 2″ in width in gradations of ¼″.

While each type of chisel is designed for a specific job, a set of nine or ten, which includes four or five of each of the firmer and framing type, is considered sufficient for general work. The firmer chisel is sturdier than the paring chisel, is capable of doing fairly heavy work, and is used for paring and light mortising work. The framing chisel is a heavy-duty tool that cuts deeply, and it will stand considerable hard handling.

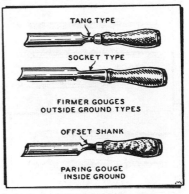

Fig. 34. Types of gouge.

The keen cutting edge of a chisel demands constant care. A chisel never should be used as a can opener, wedge, putty knife, nail remover or screwdriver. When a chisel is not in use, protect its cutting edge from rust with a coat of oil and hang it up to prevent damage.

Gouges are chisels with rounded edges. There are two main classes of gouges: firmer and paring. The firmer gouge is either outside- or inside-ground. The paring gouge is ground on the inside only. Firmer gouges are used for cutting hollows or grooves. Paring gouges are used to cut surfaces or ends in irregular forms, and are used by patternmakers almost exclusively for the shaping of core boxes and patterns. Both types are available with either socket or tang handles, and the sizes range from ⅛″ to 2″ in gradations of ⅛″.

Wood-carving chisels and gouges. Wood-carving chisels and gouges differ considerably from the ordinary types. The sides, instead of being parallel, taper toward the shoulder, and they are beveled. For general wood-carving, gouges are available in eleven different curves, graduating from almost flat to a deep U-curve. They are classified according to their shape (Figs. 35 and 36).

The small, deep U-shaped gouges are called veiners. Fluters are the larger ones that have quick turns. Flats are those that have a slight curve and are almost flat. In addition to these, there are three V-shaped gouges also known as parting tools, further classified as being acute, medium, and obtuse.

Wood-carving chisels are classified as firmers and skew firmers, and are either square or oblique on the ends (Fig. 37). Skew firmers with bent

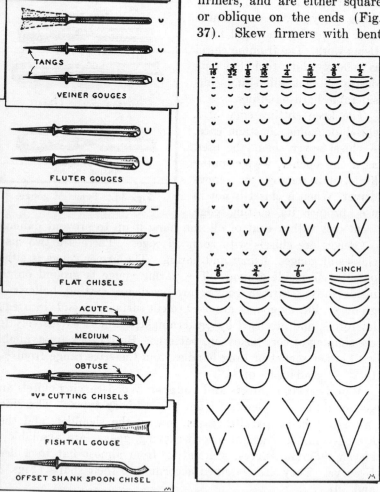

Fig. 35. Wood-carving chisels and gouges.

Fig. 36. Chart of sizes and cutting edges of wood-carving chisels and gouges.

shanks are also available for either right- or left-hand use. Wood-carving chisels are available in eighteen different sizes, from $\frac{1}{32}''$ to $1''$ in $\frac{1}{16}''$ gradations. They are fitted with either straight or bent shanks. The firmers range from $\frac{1}{64}''$ to $1''$ in $\frac{1}{16}''$ gradations. The other wood-carving chisels are available in six sizes from $1''$ to $2''$ in $\frac{1}{4}''$ gradations. All the smaller sizes are available with either spade- or fishtail-shaped blades. These specially shaped blades afford greater clearance back of the cutting edge and are used only when carving intricate designs (Fig. 35).

Using a chisel. To preserve the fine cutting edge of a chisel or a gouge, use another tool, such as a saw, auger, or plane, to remove as much of the waste part of the wood as possible. A chisel should be used only for the finishing cuts.

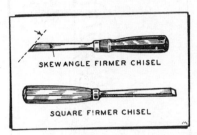

SKEW ANGLE FIRMER CHISEL

SQUARE FIRMER CHISEL

Fig. 37.

Grasp the handle of the chisel firmly with the right hand, which supplies the driving power. Hold the blade with the left hand to control the direction of the cut. Secure the work in a vise, and keep hands away from the cutting edge of tool to avoid injury. Do not start to cut directly on the guideline, but slightly away from it, so that any accidental splitting will occur in the waste portion rather than in the finished work. Shavings made with a chisel should always be thin, especially when making the finishing cut. Always cut with the grain as much as possible, for cutting against the grain splits the fibers of the wood, leaving it rough. Cutting with the grain leaves the wood fairly smooth. Make chiseling cuts either horizontally or vertically. Vertical chiseling cuts are usually made across the grain.

When using a chisel, hold it at a slight angle to the cut instead of straight. This produces a clean shearing cut that is smooth when made with the grain and on end grains (Fig. 38). On cross-grained wood, work from both directions (Fig. 39).

To cut curves on corners or edges, first remove as much waste as possible with the saw. To cut a concave curve, hold the chisel with the bevel on the work, and make the cut by pushing down and then pulling back on the handle (Fig. 40). For a convex cut, hold the chisel with the flat side of the tool on the work and the beveled side up, with the left hand holding the tool and applying the necessary pressure, while the right hand guides it and acts as a brake at the same time. To secure a clean shearing cut, hold the chisel tangent to the curve and move from side to side.

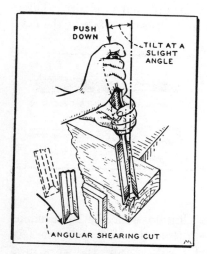

Fig. 38.

When paring on corners and ends, observe the direction of the grain and begin the cut at the edge of the work (*A*, Fig. 41). This prevents the work from splitting. Round corners are pared in the same manner (*B*, Fig. 41). When making a shearing cut, bring the chisel from a straight to a slanting position, sliding it from side to side as you press it down on the work, as shown at *C* and *D*, Fig. 41.

When paring a shoulder of a joint or cleaning out a corner, first hold the chisel vertically, then tipped to get a shearing cut when you draw it toward you, as shown at *A* in Fig. 42. The position of the chisel for flat or horizontal paring is shown at *B*. When making a shearing cut in a recess or other close place, take half the cut, as in *C*. When it is necessary to work across the grain, the position of the tool for vertical paring is shown at *D*.

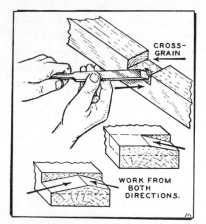

Fig. 39. Cross-grain paring.

Using a gouge. Gouges are used for cutting hollows and grooves, and are handled in the same manner as chisels, with the following exceptions.   Gouge cuts are always started at the edge of a cut and driven toward the center.   When gouging out a large hollow, cut across grain. Gouges with inside bevels are used in the same manner as chisels with the bevel up, those with outside bevels as chisels with the bevel down.

Using a wood-carving gouge or chisel.   Wood-carving chisels and gouges are used in carving designs in low relief.   Sketch or trace an outline of the required design on the wood (*A*, Fig. 43).   Use a small-sized gouge, or what is known as a pattern tool, to go over the entire outline of the design, cutting on the background side of the outline (*B*, Fig. 43).   When doing this, be careful to note the direction of the grain in the raised part of the design.   Observe the curves of the design and cut out the outline with the proper curved chisel or gouge, tapping the tool with a mallet (*C*, Fig. 43).   Use a gouge to cut out the background.   The final step in carving is to model the face of the design by putting in the details with the veiners.   Then

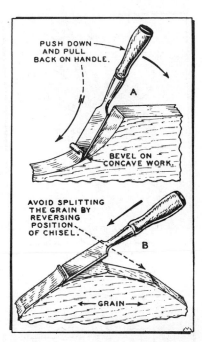

Fig. 40.   Cutting concave and convex curves.

clean out the edges and background of the work and even it off (*D*, Fig. 43).   To have a really effective piece of wood carving, be careful to avoid cutting under the outline of the design, making the edges too sharp, or even giving too smooth a finish to the carved-out background.

Many beautiful designs can be executed by merely outlining with one of the small gouges or veiners.   Work can be improved further by cutting or stamping down the background and by slightly modeling the raised part of the design. The skew chisel is used for chip carving, which is very simple and, when not overdone, very effective (Fig. 44). Trace or draw the design on the work. Make the necessary vertical first cuts with the carving tool to the required depth (*A*, Fig. 44). Then make the second or tapering cut toward the bottom of the first cut. If properly

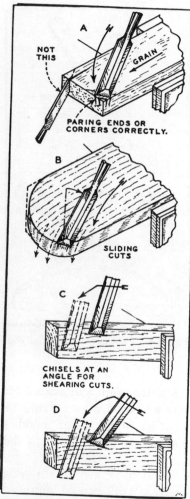

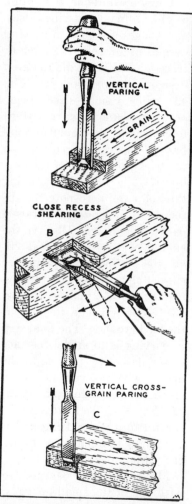

Fig. 41. Paring corners and end sections.

Fig. 42. Cleaning corners and paring shoulders of joints.

SKETCH OR TRACE OUTLINE OF DESIGN ON WOODEN SURFACE.

A

PARTING OR GOUGING OUT BACK-GROUND.

B

LIGHTLY TAPPING CHISEL WITH MALLET.

C

CLEAN-UP EDGES AND BACK-GROUND.

D

Fig. 43. Wood-carving procedures.

cut, the portion to be removed will come out in one chip (*B*, Fig. 44). Another method used for chip carving is shown at *C*, Fig. 44.

Sharpening a chisel or gouge. When the cutting edge of a chisel or gouge becomes dull, whetting will restore its keenness. While the procedure for whetting and grinding a chisel is the same as for a plane iron, the following must be considered. The large bevel of 25° to 30° must be whetted on the coarse side of the oilstone and the small bevel on the fine side. Remove the burr or wire edge on the fine side of the stone. When the cutting edge has become badly nicked or when the tool has lost its original bevel, grinding is necessary. To sharpen a chisel by either whetting or grinding, see the directions for Sharpening a Plane Iron, just a few paragraphs back (Fig. 45).

Whetting and grinding a gouge. Directions for sharpening a gouge are to a large extent the same as for a plane iron or a chisel, with the exception that a gouge is curved and must be sharpened by being turned from side to side as it is pushed forward on the oilstone (*D*, Fig. 46). A slipstone must be used for removing the burr wire edge of a gouge with an outside bevel and for whetting a gouge with an inside bevel (*A, B,* and *C,*

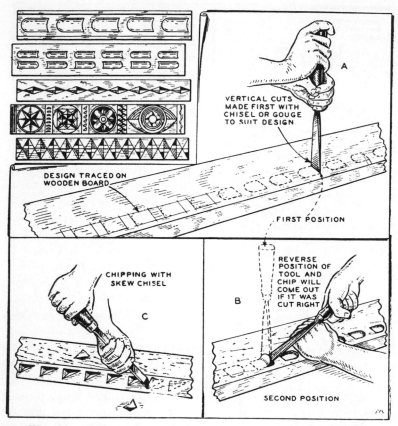

Fig. 44. Chip carving procedures and suggested border designs.

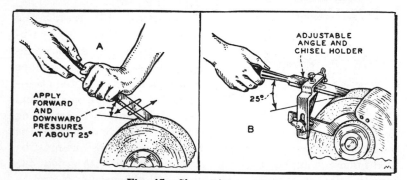

Fig. 45. Sharpening a chisel.

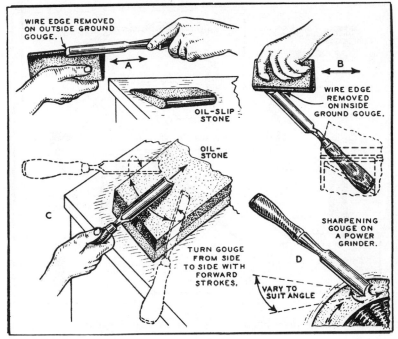

Fig. 46. Whetting and sharpening a gouge.

Fig. 46). When holding the slipstone in the hand, be careful to keep the cutting edge of the gouge true. The wire edge of the gouge with an inside bevel is removed by holding the unbeveled side flat to the stone (Fig. 46).

BRACES AND BITS

The three types of braces are the plain, the ratchet, and the corner brace (Fig. 47). The brace and bit are used for boring holes in wood. The bit bores the holes, while the brace holds the bit in the chuck and turns it. The chuck is adjustable and can hold any type or size of auger bit. A brace can also be utilized as a screwdriver by inserting a screwdriver bit in the chuck.

The most practical type of brace for general use is the one with the ratchet control. This has a ball-bearing handle which

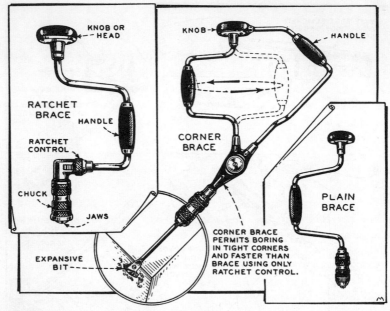

Fig. 47.

makes it easy to turn, and the ratchet can be locked or made to operate in either direction. This brace can be used in places where it is impossible to make a full turn of 360°. In corners or other inaccessible places, the corner brace is used.

Types and sizes of auger bits. Auger bits are available in sizes from ¼″ to 1″ in diameter, graduated by ¹⁄₁₆″. For boring holes smaller than ¼″ in diameter, drills, gimlet bits, and even awls are used. For boring holes larger than 1″, expansive or Forstner bits are used. Sizes of auger bits are indicated by a number stamped on the shank of the bit which gives the diameter

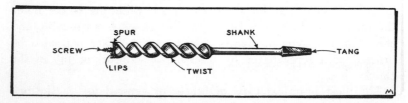

Fig. 48. Parts of the auger bit.

of the hole it will bore, in sixteenths of an inch. A **No. 8** auger bit bores a hole ½″ in diameter and a $\frac{5}{16}$″ auger is marked No. 5, and so on.

An auger bit is essentially a cutting tool. The working parts of the bit are the screw, the spurs or nibs, and the lips (Fig. 48). The spurs or nibs score the circumference of the hole, the lips cut the shavings, and the twist or thread of the bit pulls the shavings out of the hole. The three types of auger bits are the single-twist, double-twist, and straight-core or solid-center.

The single-twist and the straight-core types are more generally used in woodworking. These are fast borers, and they clear themselves of chips more readily and quickly than the double-twist type. They are generally used for hard and gummy woods. While the double-twist type works slower than the single-twist, it makes a more accurate and smoother hole. It is generally used for working with softwoods.

Dowel bits. The dowel bit is a shorter bit, averaging about one half the length of the auger bit. As the name indicates, it is used principally for drilling holes for the insertion of dowels (Fig. 49).

Gimlet bits. Considerably longer than any of the other bits, gimlet bits are from 18″ to 24″ in length (Fig. 49). They are used to bore holes through very thick timbers and planks in

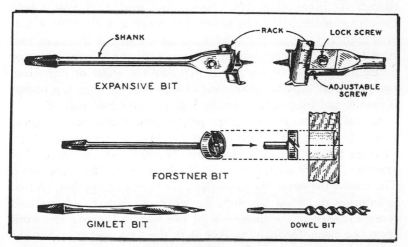

Fig. 49. Types of bits.

heavy construction work. Some gimlet bits have neither screw nor spur.

Forstner bits. The Forstner bit has neither screw, spurs, nor twist (Fig. 49). The lack of a guiding screw makes this bit more difficult to center than the conventional type. Cutting is accomplished by the two lips and a circular steel rim, with the rim centering the bit and scoring the circumference of the hole. These are very accurate bits and are made in sizes up to 2″ in diameter, with the size indicated in sixteenths of an inch on the tang of the tool.

Centering a Forstner bit is a little tricky, but it can be simplified by drawing a circle on the work equal in diameter to the size of the hole that is to be bored. Then start the bit so that the rim cuts into the circumference of the circle. Although more difficult to use than the ordinary type, the Forstner bit has certain advantages. It is used in end wood, where an auger bit does not bore so well, and to bore holes near an end in very thin wood, where the screw on an auger bit would split the stock. A Forstner bit is used to bore holes straight through cross-grained and knotty wood, and to bore a larger hole where a smaller hole has previously been bored. The latter cannot be done with an ordinary auger bit without plugging up the smaller hole.

Using a brace and bit. Insert the bit in the chuck and tighten the brace (Fig. 47). Secure the work in a vise, locate the center of the hole to be bored, and mark it with either a nail or a brad awl. Place the lead screw of the bit on the mark and start boring. To bore a straight hole, check the perpendicular or horizontal position of the bit by sighting the auger or drill from two points 90° apart. Make one of these sights when the boring is begun, and two more after the hole is fairly well started.

Another method of testing the perpendicular or horizontal position of the auger bit is with a small try square. Continue boring, rotating the handle in a clockwise direction, at the same time exerting pressure on the head of the brace with the other hand. The harder the wood, the more pressure has to be applied. Avoid splintering the wood by stopping when the bottom of the lead screw appears on the underside of the work. Remove the work from the vise, reverse it, replace it in the vise, and complete the boring from the reverse side (Fig. 50).

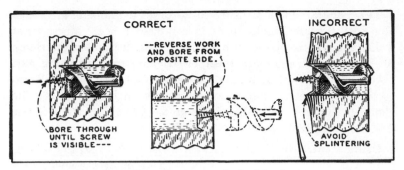

Fig. 50. Correct method of boring.

Boring a hole at an angle is just as simple as boring a perpendicular hole. The only difference is in the sighting. A simple method is to lay out the required angle on a piece of cardboard or thin wood and use this angle in sighting the direction of the auger bit. If the bit is kept parallel to this template, it will bore the hole at the desired angle.

Depth Gauge. A depth gauge is used to bore a hole to a desired depth (Fig. 51). While ready-made gauges are available, a wooden gauge can be made from a small block of wood. Bore a hole in a block, slightly larger in diameter than the bit. The height of the block will vary inversely according to the depth of the hole that is to be bored. The depth gauge is slipped over the bit prior to boring.

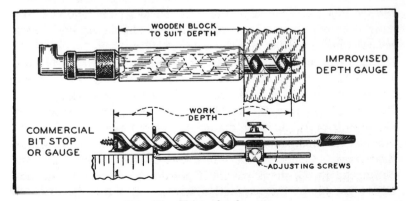

Fig. 51. Using depth gauges.

Twist drills. Twist drills from $\frac{1}{16}''$ to $\frac{3}{4}''$ in diameter are available with tapered shanks to fit in a ratchet brace. Morse twist drills (Fig. 52) are made with a straight shank to fit in the chuck of either a hand, automatic push, electric, or breast drill (Fig. 53). The three-jaw chuck in a hand or electric drill will take drills up to $\frac{1}{4}''$ in diameter. For a larger size, use a breast drill. The chuck on a breast drill takes drills up to $\frac{1}{2}''$ in diameter. Twist drills are available in over fifty sizes.

Using a twist drill. A twist drill must be held steady and be driven at moderate speed in a straight direction. The shank of a twist drill is made of soft steel and will bend if too much pressure is exerted on it. The body of the drill is of tempered steel and if strained or twisted it will snap off. When driven at excessive speed, a twist drill bites rapidly into the wood and the chips do not clear out of the flutes of the drill. The drill then becomes hot, at times hot enough to char the wood and spoil the temper of the drill, ruining its keen cutting edge. When the flutes of a twist drill become jammed with chips, the drill squeaks as it revolves. To clear the chips from the flutes, the drill should be withdrawn several times from the hole during the drilling.

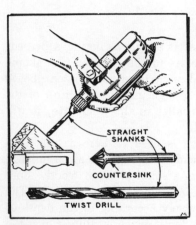

Fig. 52. Morse twist drill and countersink bit.

Expansion or extension bits. *Expansion* or *extension* bits are used to bore holes larger than $1''$ in diameter (Fig. 49). These bits fit into the chuck of a brace. Two sizes are available: one for boring holes from $\frac{1}{2}''$ to $1\frac{1}{2}''$ in diameter, the other for boring holes from $\frac{7}{8}''$ to $3''$ in diameter. They have adjustable cutting blades which can be set to bore holes of any diameter within their range. Loosening the screw that fastens the spur and the cutting lip to the shank makes it possible to move the spur and adjust the bit to the required diameter. Before using, tighten

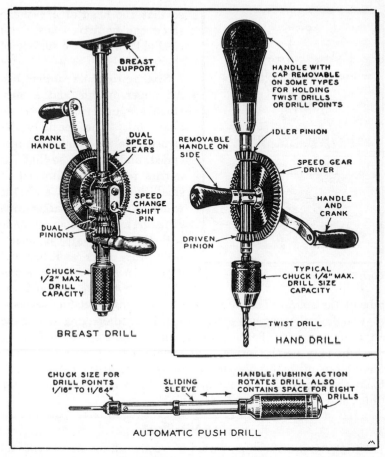

Fig. 53. Types of hand drills.

this screw so that the spur will not slip. The accuracy of the adjustment that has been made should be tested by boring a sample hole through a piece of waste wood. Expansion bits are secured in the chuck of the brace and used in the same manner as other types of bits.

Countersink bits. *Countersink* bits are available in two types: one with a tapered shank fitting into the chuck of a brace, the other with a straight round shank fitting into the chuck of a drill. Countersinks are used to shape the upper portion of a hole

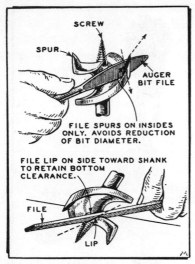

Fig. 54.   Sharpening an auger bit.

so that the head of a flathead screw can be driven flush with or slightly below the surface of the work.

Sharpening an auger bit. An auger-bit file and a slipstone are used to sharpen an auger bit. The specially designed file is small, double-ended, and tapered so that the narrow portion can be used on small-diameter bits and the wider portion on larger bits (Fig. 54). One end is made with the sides "safe" or uncut, while the other end has cut edges. In sharpening an auger bit, file both the lips and the nibs of the spurs. The safe section of an auger-bit file makes it easy to file either the lips or the nibs without damaging any of the adjacent surfaces. To keep the original diameter of the bit, file the nibs only on the inside. To maintain the proper clearance, file the lips of the bit only on the top surface of the cutting edge. Hold the bit in a vise and maintain its original bevel. After filing, use a slipstone.

SCRAPERS

The two types of scrapers used in woodworking are the *cabinet* scraper (Fig. 55)) and the *hand* scraper. The three styles of hand scrapers generally used are shown in Fig. 56. All are available with either bevel or straight edges.

Cabinet scraper. The cabinet scraper is used as a finishing tool. It takes a finer cut than a plane and is used only on flat surfaces to remove marks left by a plane or to prepare the surface for painting or finishing. It produces a smooth cut on cross-grained wood. The beveled blade, which is set in a two-handled metal frame (Fig. 55), can be removed by loosening the adjusting screw and the clamp thumbscrew. Insert the new blade with the beveled side toward the thumbscrew.

Using a cabinet scraper.   Before using a cabinet scraper, place it on a flat wooden surface and adjust the blade so that it is even with the bottom of the scraper by pressing it down lightly against the wood.   Tighten both the clamp screw and the adjusting screw and make a test cut on some waste wood.   Continue to tighten the adjusting screw between test cuts until the blade projects far enough to produce a thin shaving.

The work should be secured in a vise.   Hold the tool in both hands and either push or pull it over the surface of the work. As a rule, it is pushed rather than pulled (Fig. 55).

Hand scrapers.   The two types of one-hand scrapers generally used are the hand scraper, which is rectangular, and the molding

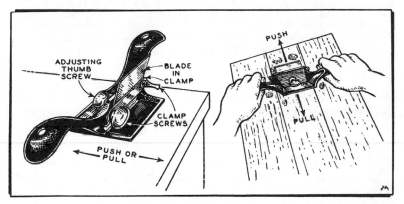

Fig. 55.   Cabinet scraper.

scraper, which is curved (Fig. 56).   They are made of high-tempered steel in various sizes and can be used on both flat and curved surfaces.   They are available with both square and beveled edges.   The square-edge type produces a smoother and flatter surface, but is not so fast as the bevel-edge type, and becomes dull sooner.   Square-edge scrapers are used for furniture, moldings, and cabinetwork.   Bevel-edge scrapers are used for scraping floors and other large areas.

Using a hand scraper.   A hand scraper produces finer shavings than a cabinet scraper.   While it may be either pushed or pulled, better work results when it is pulled.   Hold the blade with the thumb and fingers of both hands; it cuts best when

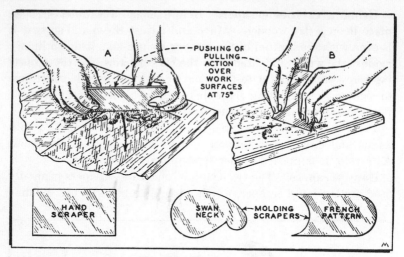

Fig. 56.   Hand scrapers.

slightly curved.   When either pushed or pulled, a hand scraper
must be held at an angle of 75° to the work (*A* and *B*, Fig. 56).

Sharpening a scraper blade.   Directions for sharpening a
scraper blade are similar to those for a plane iron, with a few
exceptions.   The cutting edge can be dressed several times before
it requires grinding and whetting (Fig. 57).   To sharpen a bevel-
edge scraper, place the blade, cutting edge up, in a vise.   With
a smooth mill file held against the side, not the edge of the blade,
remove the old burr.   The worn-down bevel is restored by filing

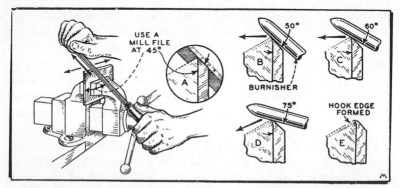

Fig. 57.   Sharpening bevel-edge hand scraper and drawing edge.

or grinding the blade to a 45° angle. Maintaining this angle, whet the bevel on the smooth side of an oilstone. To remove the wire edge, whet the blade face-down on the stone. Lay the blade, bevel side down, on the work, with the edge projecting slightly over the edge of the bench. With the burnisher held perfectly flat against the flat side of the blade, a few firm strokes will be sufficient to draw the edge to the required 50°. Proceed to form the hook edge as shown at *C*, *D* and *E*, Fig. 57.

The procedure for sharpening a square-edge scraper is as follows: Hold file at 90° angle and file edge square (*A*, Fig. 57). Whet edge on oilstone and turn blade on side to remove wire edges. Draw edge with burnisher as shown at *B;* then proceed with steps *C*, *D* and *E*, Fig. 58.

MEASURING AND LAYING-OUT TOOLS

Prior to cutting lumber to any required size or shape, guiding lines must be accurately measured and laid out. The measuring and laying-out tools are *rules, straightedges, squares,* and *gauges.*

Rules. Rules are used for measuring material to exact dimensions. Those most generally used in woodworking are made of wood and are called *zigzag* and *boxwood.* Both the zigzag and

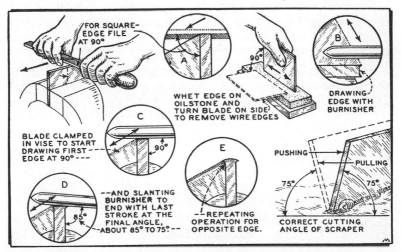

Fig. 58. Methods of sharpening square-edge hand scraper.

boxwood types fold into 6″ lengths. Boxwood is the smaller of the two, can be opened to either 2′ or 3′, and is marked in inches and graduations to ⅛″. The zigzag rule opens to a length of 6′ and is marked in inches and graduations to $\frac{1}{16}$″ (Fig. 59).

Steel tape rules are used to measure the diameter of dowels and drills, the thickness of boards and for inside direct measurements.

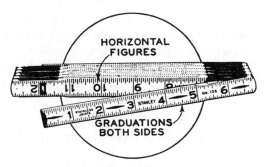

Fig. 59. Zigzag rule.

They are more accurate than other rules for these specific purposes (Fig. 60). They are available in several sizes, ranging from 2′ to 8′ in length, and are graduated in feet, inches, and fractions of inches on both sides.

Where absolute accuracy to $\frac{1}{32}$″ is necessary, the caliper rule shown in Fig. 61 is used for both inside and outside measurements. The boxwood caliper rule is used to measure outside diameters or thicknesses (Fig. 62).

Steel straightedges. Steel straightedges are strips of hardened tempered steel that have been accurately ground. They are available in lengths ranging from 1′ to 6′. Unlike rules, they are not

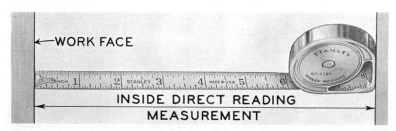

Fig. 60. Steel tape rule.

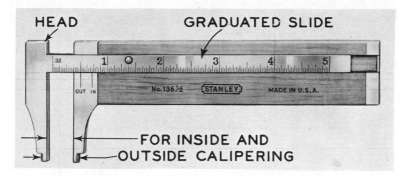

Fig. 61. Inside and outside caliper rule.

graduated in inches or fractions of an inch. They are used as guides for scribing working lines with a knife or pencil when extreme accuracy is required. Straightedges are also used for testing flatness of surfaces.

Squares. The several types of squares used in woodworking are the *carpenter's* or *framing* square, the *try square* with fixed blade, and the adjustable *miter and try square* with sliding blade and spirit level.

Carpenter's or framing squares. The carpenter's or framing square is made of flat steel. It is available in two standard sizes, 24″ by 16″ and 24″ by 18″. The 24″ side is called the body, and the shorter dimension at right angles is called the tongue. Both are marked not only in inches and fractions of an inch, but with several essential tables and scales. They can be used both as rules and as straightedges (Fig. 63).

Try squares. Try squares are constantly used in woodworking for testing the trueness of edges and ends with adjoining edges and with the

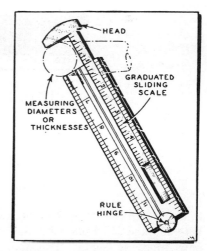

Fig. 62. Boxwood caliper rule.

face of the work after the work has been cut or planed. The common or fixed type is constructed of two parts, a thick wood or iron stock, and a thin steel blade, fixed at 90° to each other;

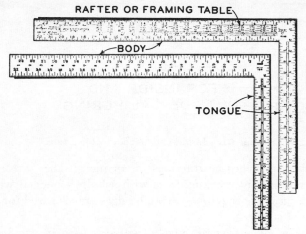

RAFTER OR FRAMING TABLE

BODY

TONGUE

Fig. 63. Carpenter's or framing squares.

the blade is graduated in inches and fractions of an inch. The sizes of the blades vary from 2″ to 12″ (Fig. 64).

The adjustable miter and try square is similar in every respect

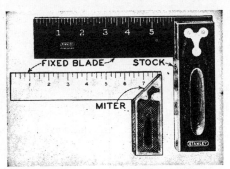

FIXED BLADE   STOCK

MITER

Fig. 64. Try and miter squares with fixed blade.

to the fixed-blade type with the exception that it can be used for both 45° and 90° work (Fig. 65). Its blade can be locked at any point along its length. The stock is fitted with a spirit level.

Using a square. In using a square, a guideline must always be marked across the surface of the work. When it is necessary to cut, plane, or chisel a board square, either a try square or a carpenter's square is used to lay out the work or to mark the necessary guideline. A pencil is quite satisfactory for marking guide-

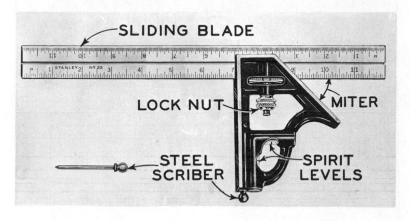

Fig. 65. Adjustable try and miter square.

lines for roughing out woodwork, but where accuracy is necessary, guidelines should preferably be laid out with the blade of a pocket-knife or a bench knife. The tip of the blade should be used to get a clean, accurate line. A guideline must be exactly located and must always be square with the edges of the work. If a board is wide, that is, if it averages wider than the blade of a try square, a carpenter's square must be used. To square a line with a try square, press the stock of the try square firmly against the edge of the board, and mark the guideline along the blade with the point of the pencil or the knife blade (*A*, Fig. 66).

In squaring a line across a board, one edge and one face of the board should be marked with X's so that they can be distinguished as the working edge and face. Then square a line from the working edge across the working face (*B*, Fig. 66). Be certain that the working edge is perfectly flat so that the square does not rock. Always square lines from the working face across both edges. Then, holding the stock of the square up against the

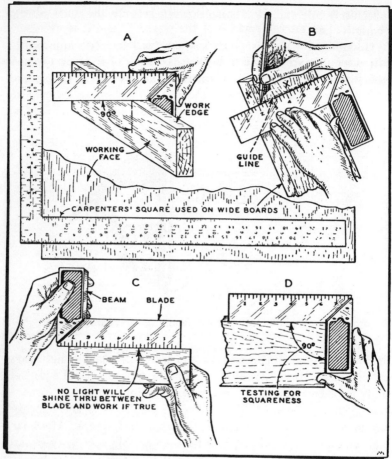

Fig. 66.

working edge, square a line across the face on the side of the board opposite the working edge.

Testing for squareness. To test a board for squareness, place the inside edge of the stock of the square in contact with one surface. Face the light so that it will shine on the work. Slide the square downward and observe where the blade first comes in contact with the surface of the work. If the angle is square and the surface of the work is true, no light will be visible. If the angle does not happen to be square, or if the surface of the work is not absolutely true, light will shine through between the blade and the work (*C* and *D*, Fig. 66).

Gauges. Two types of gauges are used by the woodworker: the *marking* gauge and the *mortise* gauge. The marking gauge is the one more commonly used when absolute accuracy is required. Constructed of either wood or metal, the marking gauge consists of an 8″ bar on which the head of the gauge slides. The head can be secured at any desired point on the bar by means of a thumb-screw (Fig. 67). A sharpened pin or spur affixed near the end of

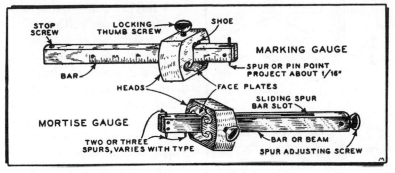

Fig. 67. Two types of woodworking gauges.

the bar scores the gauged line on the work. The bar of the marking gauge is graduated in inches and fractions of an inch.

The mortise gauge is a marking gauge with two spurs instead of one and is used for laying out mortises and tenons. The two spurs, one of which can be set independently, are used to score parallel lines.

Using marking gauges. Set the head of the gauge the required distance from the spur or pin, and secure it in place with the locking screw. Grasp the gauge with the palm and the fingers of the right hand. Press the head firmly against the edge of the work to be marked, and with a motion of the wrist, tip the head forward slightly until the point of the spur just touches the wood. Score the line by pushing the gauge away from you, keeping the head firmly against the edge of the work (Fig. 68). Note that the point of the spur must always be filed sharp and project approximately $\frac{1}{16}$″.

The mortise gauge is used in approximately the same manner as the marking gauge, the only difference being that the two spurs are set the required distance apart by securing the movable one with the thumbscrew in the end of the beam, before the head is adjusted (Fig. 68).

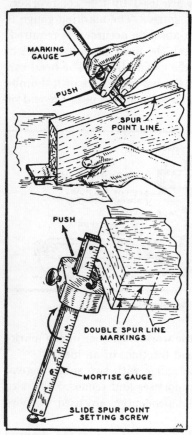

Fig. 68. Marking gauges.

LEVELS

A level is a simple tool that indicates true vertical and true level positions. It may have either an aluminum or a wooden frame in which two or four glass liquid-and-bubble tubes are mounted. Levels made of aluminum are light in weight and do not warp or rust. When there are four tubes, they are mounted in sets of two, each set at right angles to the other.

Using a level. The use of a level on either a flat or a vertical surface is shown in Fig. 69. In either position, when the bubble in one of the tubes is absolutely in the center—that is, between indicated lines on the tube—the work is level or plumb. When the bubble is off center, the work is not level.

CLAMPS

Clamps used in woodworking are the bar clamp, C clamp, hand screws, cabinetmaker's clamp, and cramping clamp. All are used to hold work together under pressure until glue has set firmly. These clamps and their use are shown in Chaps. 3 and 5.

GLASS CUTTER

The procedures for the use of all types and sizes of glass cutters are identical. When cutting glass with this simple tool, a steel ruler or straight edge must be used to guide the tool. Set rule where cut is desired. Exert an even pressure of the wheel of the tool on both the glass and the edge of the ruler or straight edge to score a line at required place on glass. After line has been scored, grip the waste part of the glass in the groove of the cutter and snap gently to break the glass along the scored line.

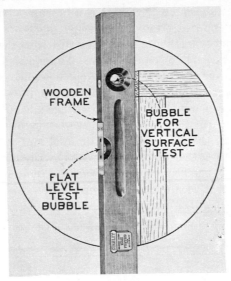

Fig. 69. Vertical plumb test with wood-type level.

TOOL STORAGE AND RUST PREVENTION

Every tool in the workshop should have its proper place. Tools that are most often in use should be kept at hand on a tool rack specially designed for that purpose. Plans and directions for building a tool rack are given in Chap. **18.**

Tools that are not used frequently should be stored in a tool chest or in the individual boxes in which they were originally

packed.   During the damp spring and summer months, each tool
should be coated with a film of oil or grease to prevent rust.   When
tools are to be stored for any length of time, it is good practice,
in addition to coating, to wrap them in paper for protection from
moisture and dust.

The cutting edges of tools must be protected at all times.   In
addition to the tool rack, a well-designed tool chest or a sturdy
workbench in which each tool has its own place is desirable.   Plans
and directions for building a workbench are given in Chap. 18.

Removing rust from tools.   When rust forms on hammers,
chisels, saws, and screwdrivers, it can be easily removed.   While
there are several rust-removing solutions that work fairly well, the
most satisfactory method of removing rust from these tools is with
No. 240 emery paper or emery cloth.   To remove a heavy coating
of rust from surfaces that must be kept true, like the bottom of a
plane, or a surface on which graduations and scales are marked,
place this fine emery cloth on a flat surface and rub the tool on it.

This method of removing rust serves a double purpose, for it
helps to retain the true surface of the tool and also removes any
high or low spots that have been caused by the formation of rust.
After the rust has been removed, rub the tool clean with a dry
cloth and coat it with a film of oil or grease.

CHAPTER 3

Working with Wood

— ⋮ ————————————————————————————————

CLASSIFICATION OF LUMBER

Plain-sawed and quarter-sawed lumber. Lumber is usually
cut longitudinally in two directions: at right angles to the rays, or
tangentially to the growth rings, producing what is known in the
trade as *plain-sawed* or *flat-grain* lumber; or parallel to the rays
across the growth rings, producing *quarter-sawed* or *edge-grained*

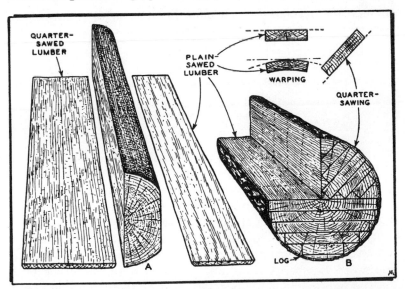

Fig. 1. Quarter-sawed and plain-sawed boards cut from log.

lumber. For hardwoods, plain-sawed and quarter-sawed are the terms in common use.

Plain-sawed lumber is cut with less waste and generally costs less than quarter-sawed. In some types of wood, such as ash, elm, or chestnut, and in all the coniferous species, plain-sawed lumber has a figure or grain superior to that of quarter-sawed (Fig. 1).

Despite its usually higher cost, quarter-sawed lumber has certain advantages that must be considered. It shrinks less in width and is less subject to checking or twisting. Quarter-sawing produces considerable lumber that is cut at more or less of an angle to the rays. In some of the woods, such as oak and mahogany, quarter-sawed lumber has a much more attractive grain, and for that reason is preferable to plain-sawed in spite of its higher cost (Fig. 2).

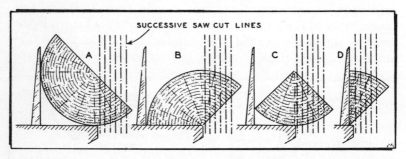

Fig. 2. Common method of quarter-sawing lumber. Dash-and-dot lines represent successive saw cuts.

HARDWOOD LUMBER GRADING

All species of hardwood lumber. Most hardwood boards are not used in their entirety but are cut into smaller pieces to make furniture or some other fabricated product.

The *rules* that are considered standard in grading hardwood lumber in the United States are those adopted by the National Hardwood Lumber Association. In these rules, the grade of a piece of hardwood lumber is determined by the proportion of the piece that can be cut into a certain number of smaller pieces of material clear on one side and not less than a certain size. In other words, the grade classification is based upon the amount of usable lumber in the piece rather than upon the number or size of growth features that characterize softwood yard grades. This usable material, commonly termed "cuttings," must have one face clear and the reverse face sound, which means free from such things as rot, heart center, and shake that materially impair the strength of the cutting. The lowest grade requires only that cuttings be sound.

The highest grade of hardwood lumber is termed "Firsts" and the next grade "Seconds." Firsts and Seconds, or, as they are generally written, "FAS," nearly always are combined in one grade. The third grade is termed "Selects," followed by No. 1 Common, No. 2 Common, Sound Wormy, No. 3A Common, and No. 3B Common

A brief summary of the standard hardwood lumber grades follows. This summary should not be regarded as a complete set of grading rules, as there are numerous details, exceptions, and special rules for certain species that are not included. The complete official rules of the National Hardwood Lumber Association should be followed as the only full description of existing grades. The summary is intended only as a preliminary guide in distinguishing between the general qualities to be expected under the various grades.

STANDARD LENGTHS

Standard lengths are 4, 5, 6, 7, 8, 9, 10, 11, 12, 13, 14, 15, and 16 feet, but not more than 50 per cent of odd lengths will be admitted.

STANDARD THICKNESSES

Standard thicknesses for hardwood lumber are given in Table A.

TABLE A

Standard thicknesses for hardwood lumber

Rough (inches)	Surfaced 1 side (S1S)	Surfaced 2 sides (S2S)	Rough (inches)	Surfaced 1 side (S1S)	Surfaced 2 sides (S2S)
	Inches	*Inches*		*Inches*	*Inches*
3/8	1/4	3/16	2½	2 5/16	2¼
½	3/8	5/16	3	2 13/16	2¾
5/8	½	7/16	3½	3 5/16	3¼
¾	5/8	9/16	4	3 13/16	3¾
1	7/8	13/16	4½	(1)	(1)
1¼	1 1/8	1 1/16	5	(1)	(1)
1½	1 3/8	1 5/16	5½	(1)	(1)
2	1 13/16	1¾	6	(1)	(1)

[1] Finished size not specified in rules. Thickness subject to special contract.

Summary of Standard Grades of the National Hardwood Lumber Association

WOODS INCLUDED[1]

Alder, red
Ash
Aspen
Basswood
Beech
Birch
Boxelder
Buckeye
Butternut
Cedar, red
Cedar, Spanish
Cherry
Chestnut
Cottonwood
Cypress

Elm:
  Rock (or cork)
  Soft
Gum:
  Black
  Red and Sap
  Tupelo
Hackberry
Hardwoods (Philippine)
Hardwoods (Tropical American other than mahogany and Spanish cedar)
Hickory
Locust
Magnolia

Mahogany:
  African
  Cuban and San Dominican
  Philippine
Maple:
  Hard (or sugar)
  Soft
Oak:
  Red
  White
Pecan
Poplar
Sycamore
Walnut
Willow

[1] Species names are those used in grading rules of the association. Two of the woods included, namely, cedar (eastern redcedar) and cypress (bald-cypress), are not hardwoods. Cypress lumber has a different set of grading rules from those used for the hardwoods.

DESCRIPTION OF STANDARD HARDWOOD GRADES

A description of the standard hardwood grades is as follows:

The highest grade, Firsts, calls for pieces that will allow 91⅔ per cent of their surface measure to be cut into clear-face material; that is, not more than 8⅓ per cent of each piece can be wasted in making the required cuttings. In the grade of Seconds 83⅓ per cent of the surface measure of the pieces must yield clear-face cuttings. Boards 6 to 15 feet surface measure will admit of 1 additional cutting to yield 91⅔ per cent of clear face. Both Firsts and Seconds require pieces not less than 6″ wide and 8′ long. In the grade Selects the minimum width is 4″ and the minimum length is 6′. Both Firsts and Seconds and the face side of Selects must, in addition to cutting requirements, meet specified requirements as to knots, holes, and other imperfections. The cutting requirements of Selects are 91⅔ per cent of clear face in pieces with 2 and 3 surface feet. In larger pieces the cutting requirements are the same as for Seconds on tne face side. The reverse side of the cuttings in Selects must be sound or the reverse side of the piece not below No. 1 Common.

The next 2 grades, No. 1 Common and No. 2 Common, call for lumber not less than 3″ wide and 4′ long and require 66⅔ per cent and 50 per cent of clear-face cuttings, respectively. Exceptions in No. 1 Common are pieces with 1′ surface measure and 2′ surface measure, which require 100 per cent of clear face and 75 per cent of clear face, respectively, and in No. 2 Common pieces with 1′ surface measure, which require 66 per cent of clear face. The minimum size of cuttings in these 2 grades is reduced from 4″ by 5′ or 3″ by 7′ in Firsts, Seconds, and Selects to 3″ by 2′. The number of allowable cuttings in grades No. 2 Common and better are limited by the hardwood grading rules according to the surface measure of each piece.

A grade of hardwood lumber called Sound Wormy has the same requirements as No. 1 Common except that wormholes and limited sound knots, and other imperfections are allowed in the cuttings.

The grade of 3A Common admits pieces that will furnish 33⅓ per cent of clear face in cuttings not less than 3″ wide and 2′ long.

This grade will also admit pieces that grade not below No. 2 Common on the good face and have the reverse face of the cutting sound. The lowest grade, No. 3B Common, allows pieces that will cut 25 per cent in sound material not less than 1½″ wide by 2′ long.

HARDWOOD DIMENSION STOCK

Hardwood dimension stock, as used by furniture and cabinet manufacturers is generally graded under the *rules* of the Hardwood Dimension Manufacturers' Association. These rules apply primarily to dimension stock cut from kiln-dried rough lumber and cover three classes of material—kiln dried glued dimension, solid dimension flat stock, and solid dimension squares. Each class may be rough, semifinished, or finished. Solid dimension flat stock has five grades—Clear Two Faces, Clear One Face, Paint, Core, and Sound. Solid dimension squares have three grades—Clear, Select, and Sound.

SOFTWOOD LUMBER GRADING

Softwood lumber, unlike hardwood lumber, is graded under a number of different association rules. Not only are the different kinds of softwoods graded under different rules, but the same softwoods in a number of cases are graded under different association rules.

The agencies promulgated grading rules for commercial use have based their rules on the American lumber standards for softwood lumber. These include California Redwood Association, Southern Cypress Manufacturers' Association, Southern Pine Association, West Coast Lumbermen's Association, Western Pine Association, Northern Hemlock & Hardwood Manufacturers' Association, and Northeastern Lumber Manufacturers' Association.

NOMENCLATURE OF COMMERCIAL SOFTWOODS

The names of lumber adopted by the trade as American lumber standards are not always identical with the names of trees adopted as official by the Forest Service. Table B has therefore been prepared to show the American lumber standards commercial name for lumber corresponding to the Forest Service tree name used in this chapter.

TABLE B

Nomenclature of commercial softwoods

CEDARS AND JUNIPERS

Official Forest Service tree name used in this handbook	Name adopted as standard for lumber under American lumber standards	Other names sometimes used
Alaska-cedar	Alaska cedar	Yellow cedar, Sitka cypress, yellow cypress.
Alligator juniper	Western juniper	Juniper
Atlantic whitecedar	Southern white cedar	White cedar, swamp cedar.
Eastern redcedar	Eastern red cedar	Red cedar, cedar, juniper.
Incense-cedar	Incense cedar	Cedar, white cedar.
Northern whitecedar	Northern white cedar	Arborvitae, cedar, swamp cedar, white cedar.
Port-Orford-cedar	Port Orford cedar	Lawson's cypress, Oregon cedar, white cedar.
Rocky Mountain juniper.	Western juniper	Juniper
Utah juniper	----do----	Juniper, white cedar.
Western juniper	----do----	Juniper, cedar.
Western redcedar	Western red cedar	Red cedar, cedar, western cedar.

CYPRESS

Baldcypress	Red cypress (coast type), yellow cypress (inland type), white cypress (inland type).	Cypress, tidewater red cypress, Gulf coast red cypress, Louisiana red cypress, bald cypress, black cypress.

DOUGLAS-FIR

Douglas-fir	Douglas fir	Red fir, Oregon fir, Douglas spruce, yellow fir, Puget Sound pine.

TABLE B

Nomenclature of commercial softwoods **(continued)**

TRUE FIRS

Official Forest Service tree name used in this handbook	Name adopted as standard for lumber under American lumber standards	Other names sometimes used
Balsam fir_____	Balsam fir_____	Balsam, eastern fir_____
California red fir_____	White fir_____	Red fir_____
Fraser fir_____	Balsam fir_____	Balsam, eastern fir_____
Grand fir_____	White fir_____	Yellow fir_____
Noble fir_____	Noble fir_____	Red fir_____
Pacific silver fir_____	White fir_____	Red fir, fir_____
Subalpine fir_____	____do_____	Balsam_____
White fir_____	____do_____	Colorado white fir_____

HEMLOCKS

Carolina hemlock_____	Eastern hemlock_____	Hemlock, hemlock spruce, spruce pine.
Eastern hemlock_____	____do_____	____do_____
Mountain hemlock_____	Mountain hemlock_____	Weeping spruce, Alpine spruce, hemlock spruce.
Western hemlock_____	West coast hemlock_____	Hemlock, hemlock spruce, Pacific hemlock, Alaska pine.

LARCH

Western larch_____	Western larch_____	Tamarack, larch_____

PINES

Eastern white pine_____	Northern white pine____	White pine, cork pine, soft pine, northern pine, pumpkin pine.
Jack pine_____	Jack pine_____	Scrub pine_____
Loblolly pine_____	Southern yellow pine____	Old-field pine, slash pine, shortleaf pine, Virginia pine, sap pine, yellow pine, North Carolina pine.
Lodgepole pine_____	Lodgepole pine_____	Scrub pine, spruce pine___
Longleaf pine_____	Longleaf yellow pine, southern yellow pine.	Southern pine, yellow pine, hard pine, Georgia pine, pitch pine, heart pine, fat pine.

TABLE B

Nomenclature of commercial softwoods   *(continued)*

Official Forest Service tree name used in this handbook	Name adopted as standard for lumber under American lumber standards	Other names sometimes used
Pitch pine	Southern yellow pine	
Ponderosa pine	Ponderosa pine	Bull pine, Arizona white pine, western soft pine, western pine.
Red pine	Norway pine	Hard pine, northern pine.
Shortleaf pine	Southern yellow pine	Yellow pine, spruce pine, oldfield pine, Arkansas soft pine, North Carolina pine.
Slash pine	Longleaf yellow pine, southern yellow pine.	Swamp pine, pitch pine.
Sugar pine	Sugar pine	Big pine.
Virginia pine	Southern yellow pine	
Western white pine	Idaho white pine	White pine, soft pine.

REDWOOD

Redwood	Redwood	Sequoia, coast redwood.

SPRUCES

Black spruce	Eastern spruce	
Blue spruce	Engelmann spruce	
Engelmann spruce	do	White spruce, silver spruce, balsam, mountain spruce.
Red spruce	Eastern spruce	
Sitka spruce	Sitka spruce	Spruce, tideland spruce, western spruce, yellow spruce, silver spruce.
White spruce	Eastern spruce	

TAMARACK

Tamarack	Tamarack	Larch, hackmatack, red larch, black larch.

YEW

Pacific yew	Pacific yew	Yew, western yew, mountain mahogany.

STANDARD LUMBER PATTERNS

Figure 3 shows six typical patterns of lumber: Flooring, standard match; ceiling, edge beading; drop siding, shiplapped; bevel siding; dressed and matched, center matched; and shiplap.

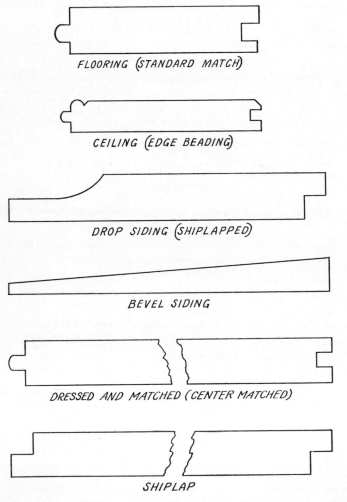

FLOORING (STANDARD MATCH)

CEILING (EDGE BEADING)

DROP SIDING (SHIPLAPPED)

BEVEL SIDING

DRESSED AND MATCHED (CENTER MATCHED)

SHIPLAP

Fig. 3. Six typical patterns of lumber.

With softwood flooring, "standard match" means that the upper lip of the groove is thicker than the lower. The thickness of the lower lip is the same for all standard thicknesses of flooring, and hence the differences between upper and lower lips becomes more pronounced in the heavier thicknesses. Ceiling, which is thinner than 1″, is usually machined with a V. Partition usually has the bead and V, also, but on both sides, and it is thicker than ceiling.

Drop siding is usually made from 1″ lumber and probably is made in more patterns than any other product except molding. Some of these patterns are shiplapped, and others are tongued and grooved. Bevel siding is made by resawing 4/4″ or 5/4″ lumber on an angle. Square-edged lumber in either boards, timbers, or dimensions, of course, forms only rectangles of different dimensions. Boards are frequently dressed and matched (D & M), in which event the tongue-and-groove are in the center, making the pieces center matched. For some uses it is considered preferable to shiplap boards.

LUMBER ITEMS USUALLY CARRIED IN RETAIL YARDS

The small retail yards throughout the United States carry softwoods required for ordinary construction purposes and sometimes small stocks of one or two hardwoods in the grades suitable for finishing or cabinetwork. Any particular hardwood desired, however, may be obtained by special order through the retail lumber yard. Hardwoods are used in building chiefly for interior trim, cabinets, and flooring. In modern practice, trim items are cut to size in standard pattern at millwork plants and are sold in such form by the retail yards. Cabinets are usually made by the millwork plant ready for installation on the job by the carpenter. Hardwood flooring invariably is a planing-mill product and is available to the buyer only in standard patterns.

The assortment of species in general construction items carried by retail yards depends largely upon geographical location. For instance, in the Pacific Northwest local yards will, as a rule, stock Douglas fir, spruce, ponderosa pine, western hemlock, and western red cedar. An Iowa yard may stock eastern hemlock, ponderosa pine, southern yellow pine, and Douglas fir. For some species only certain items of various species may be available; *for example*, southern yellow pine or Douglas fir may be stocked only in the form of dimension, eastern hemlock only in sheathing and 1″ boards, cypress and redwood in finish boards or in siding. A New York market might stock eastern spruce and hemlock, eastern white pine, cypress, ponderosa pine, southern yellow pine, and Douglas fir. In the eastern part of the United States lumber from the Pacific coast is readily available because of low-cost water transportation via the Panama Canal.

Wholesalers do not ordinarily stock lumber. However, some large wholesalers located in extensive lumber-consuming districts have yards stocked with many kinds of lumber, both of hardwood and softwood.

Lumber is sold in a number of standard general-purpose items and also in certain special-purpose items. Retail yards carry all of the general-purpose items, but as a rule only the more important of the special-purpose items. Some of these lumber items come in one group of grades and some in another. There are not many items made in the complete range of grades. Among the typical special-purpose items are stepping, casing and base, silo staves, molding, battens, window and door jambs, and porch columns.

How to order lumber. The standard sizes of hardwoods usually carried in stock by local lumberyards range from ½″ to 6″ in thickness, from 3″ to 12″ in width, and from 2′ to 16′ in length. If small quantities of wood are required, the dealer often has pieces known in the trade as shorts. Shorts are equal in quality to boards of standard sizes, but sometimes can be had at a lower price.

Lumber is available either rough or surfaced. Whenever possible, purchase lumber that has been surfaced on at least two sides, or at least on one side and one edge. But when ordering surfaced lumber, remember that surfacing removes some of the material and thus reduces the dimensions of the board. Therefore, the exact dimensions must be specified, especially thickness and width.

Most lumber is sold by a unit measurement called a board foot. A board foot is the equivalent of an amount of lumber 1″ thick by 12″ wide by 12″ long.

When ordering lumber, list each required size. First list the number of pieces of each size, then the thickness, followed by the width, and finally the length. If you require 20 pieces of lumber of various sizes, the order should be listed as:

$$10 \text{ pieces } 1'' \times 12'' \times 12'$$
$$5 \text{ pieces } 1'' \times 10'' \times 12'$$
$$5 \text{ pieces } 1'' \times 6'' \times 12'$$

The amount of board feet in the above order is calculated as follows:

$$1 \times {}^{12}\!\!/_{12} \times 12 = 12 \text{ board feet per piece}$$
$$10 \text{ pieces total } 120 \text{ board feet}$$
$$1 \times {}^{10}\!\!/_{12} \times 12 = 10 \text{ board feet per piece}$$
$$5 \text{ pieces total } 50 \text{ board feet}$$
$$1 \times {}^{6}\!\!/_{12} \times 12 = 6 \text{ board feet per piece}$$
$$6 \text{ pieces total } 36 \text{ board feet}$$

$$\text{Total required} \ldots \ldots \ldots 206 \text{ board feet}$$

Lumber is always quoted at a specified price per M (thousand) board feet.

Plywood and veneer panels are sold by the square foot. Shingles and laths are sold by the bundle. Moldings are sold by the linear or running foot.

PREPARING PIECES FOR USE

Cutting lumber out in rough. All lumber must be squared, to find any deviation from a right angle, straight line, or plane surface, and trued to the required size before proceeding with the actual work. The tools required for squaring, truing, and preliminary cutting are: a jack or smoothing plane, block plane, straightedge, rule, marking gauge, saw, knife, and pencil.

Cut the lumber out in rough, and wherever possible discard the parts that have large knots, knotholes, bad rips, or similar imperfections. Make an additional allowance of ¼″ to ⅜″ in width and ½″ to 1″ in length for material to be removed during the squaring and the truing-up operations. This allowance from time to time will vary slightly from the given amount.

Preparing a working face. The first step in preparing a working face on rough lumber is to test for straightness. When two diagonally opposite corners of a board are higher than the other two corners, a board is said to be "in wind." It is then necessary to plane with the jack or smoothing plane across the high corners until the board is straight. To find out whether a board is in wind, place a straightedge on each end of the surface across the grain (*A*, Fig. 3). Sight under the straightedges in the direction of the grain of the wood. If the straightedges are par-

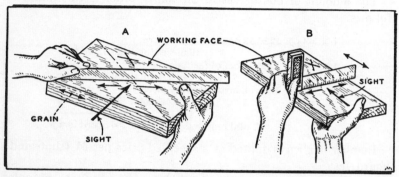

Fig. 3. Testing with straightedge for flatness of lumber.

allel, the surface of the stock is not in wind. If they are not parallel, then the pieces in wind must be trued up.

To test for general straightness lengthwise, sight or use a straightedge along the grain of the board.

To test for straightness across the grain, place the blade of an inverted try square on the surface of the stock, hold the board at eye level, and sight toward the light (*B*, Fig. 3). If there is light between the blade and the stock, the surface is not level.

The next step is planing for smoothness. Use either the smoothing or the jack plane, pressing down firmly on the top of the plane at the beginning of the stroke, and gradually releasing the tension at the end of the stroke. If a board is slightly warped, the working face can be trued up easily by planing across the grain until full-length shavings are obtained.

Preparing a working edge. When the trueness of the face of the lumber has been checked by making the three tests just specified, mark the tested working face with a cross to show that it has been squared and trued (*A*, Fig. 4). This marked face is now the side from which all other tests for squareness and trueness should be made (*A*, Fig. 4).

To prepare a working edge, use either a jack or smoothing plane. Secure the work, which we will now term the stock, in a vise and take several light, even shavings on the edge of the stock (*B*, Fig. 4). Between each of the shavings, test the edge by pressing the handle of the try square against the marked working face and the blade on the edge of the stock. Slide the

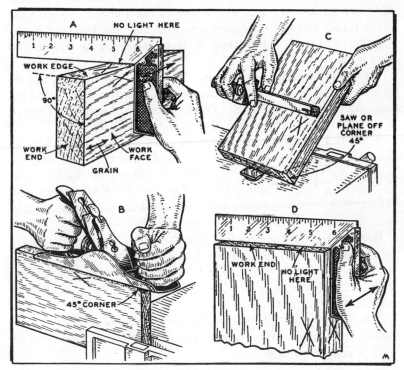

Fig. 4. Preparing, squaring, and testing working surfaces.

blade along the edge of the stock. When no light can be seen between the blade and the edge of the stock, the working edge is square and true. Mark the edge with a cross to show that it is the working edge.

Preparing a working end. To prepare a working end, mark the required width on the working face of the stock with the marking gauge. This is a guideline to show how much of the corner can be cut off by the saw prior to planing the ends. Cut off the corner outside the gauged line with the saw at about a 45° angle to prevent the stock from chipping or splitting while planing against the grain to that corner (*C*, Fig. 4).

Now square a line around the entire piece, holding the handle of the try square first against the working edge and then against the working face (*D*, Fig. 4). Plane to the marked line with the block plane, and test for squareness with both the face and working edge, and mark with a cross to denote the working end (*B* and *D*, Fig. 4).

Squaring to required length. To square the stock to the required length, measure from the working end and mark off the required length of the board. From this mark, proceed as directed for preparing a working end (*B*, *C*, and *D*, Fig. 4).

Squaring to required thickness. Set the marking gauge to the required thickness and mark a line around the edges and the ends of the stock, with the head of the gauge held tight against the working face. Using either a jack or smoothing plane, and taking thin, even shavings, plane the stock down to the marked line, testing frequently for squareness and trueness.

Removing surface defects. Lumber often has surface defects caused by the mill planers or shapers or by the tools used in truing and squaring the lumber. These usually can be removed with a cabinet scraper and sandpaper. The use of a cabinet scraper is shown in Chap. 2.

Where the grain of the wood has been torn slightly, plane lightly with a smoothing plane and scrape the surface smooth with a cabinet scraper.

When the grain has been torn badly, use either a commercial wood filler, or a sawdust-and-glue filler, described later in this chapter.

First remove all loose splinters from the torn section with the point of a brad awl or knife. With the knife blade, fill the torn section with the filler slightly above the surface of the board. Allow approximately 24 hours for it to set and harden and then sand it down to the surface of the board.

Solid or firm knots can be smoothed down to the surface of the lumber with a scraper and sandpaper, but loose knots must be removed and the hole filled.

Lumber that has been handled roughly may have a number of dents, which often can be eliminated by dropping a few drops of water on the dented surface and by picking at the spot with the point of a knife or brad awl. This causes the fibers of the wood to swell and thus fill the dent. After the moisture has dried out, sand down the spot even with the surface of the board.

Small splits sometimes can be removed by the use of a filler. A bad split in the end of a board can be repaired by cutting out a wedge-shaped section of the board where the split occurs, and by gluing in a piece cut exactly to fit the opening.

NAILS, SCREWS, OTHER FASTENERS, AND HARDWARE

Common and finishing nails. Although there are many varieties of nails, the two kinds most generally used are common and finishing nails. Common nails are used for the framework of buildings, and for subfloors and general rough woodworking. They have flat heads and pyramid-shaped points and are available in various sizes and gauges (Fig. 5).

Finishing nails are used to secure trim and all finishing woodwork into place. They have pyramidal points and small heads, called brad-heads. Finishing nails are usually countersunk (Fig. 5).

Sizes of both common and finishing nails are designated by the old English penny system. When and how this system originated is rather vague, but it is still in use. The standard abbreviation for the English penny is *d,* and this abbreviation is used in specifying common or finishing nails.

Special-purpose nails. Special-purpose nails are nails that have been modified to meet special requirements. There are over

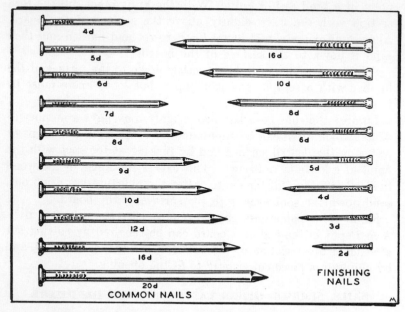

Fig. 5. Two types of nails generally used (⅔ actual size).

a hundred varieties of such nails in use today. They are made for plasterboard, concrete forms, shingles, crates, boats, flooring, and many other specific purposes (Fig. 6). Some special-purpose nails are graded in sizes according to their length in inches, others are designated and graded by the penny system.

Brads and wire nails. Brads are pyramid-pointed brad-headed nails of small diameter. The heads are considerably smaller than the heads of finishing nails. Brads are used in cabinetwork and other types of fine work where it is necessary to countersink nailheads.

Wire nails are flat-headed and pyramid-pointed, and are smaller in diameter than common nails. Wire nails are used in working with light, thin wood which a common nail invariably would split.

COMMON NAILS*

Size in Penny	Length in Inches	Diameter Gauge Number	Diameter of Head in Inches	Approximate Number to a Pound
2 d	1	15	$\frac{11}{64}$	830
3	$1\frac{1}{4}$	14	$\frac{13}{64}$	528
4	$1\frac{1}{2}$	$12\frac{1}{2}$	$\frac{1}{4}$	316
5	$1\frac{3}{4}$	$12\frac{1}{2}$	$\frac{1}{4}$	271
6	2	$11\frac{1}{2}$	$\frac{17}{64}$	168
7	$2\frac{1}{4}$	$11\frac{1}{2}$	$\frac{17}{64}$	150
8	$2\frac{1}{2}$	$10\frac{1}{4}$	$\frac{9}{32}$	106
9	$2\frac{3}{4}$	$10\frac{1}{4}$	$\frac{9}{32}$	96
10	3	9	$\frac{5}{16}$	69
12	$3\frac{1}{4}$	9	$\frac{5}{16}$	63
16	$3\frac{1}{2}$	8	$\frac{11}{32}$	49
20	4	6	$\frac{13}{32}$	31
30	$4\frac{1}{2}$	5	$\frac{7}{16}$	24
40	5	4	$\frac{15}{32}$	18
50	$5\frac{1}{2}$	3	$\frac{1}{2}$	14
60	6	2	$\frac{17}{32}$	11

FINISHING NAILS*

Size in Penny	Length in Inches	Diameter Gauge Number	Diameter of Head Gauge Number	Approximate Number to a Pound
2 d	1	$16\frac{1}{2}$	$13\frac{1}{2}$	1351
3	$1\frac{1}{4}$	$15\frac{1}{2}$	$12\frac{1}{2}$	807
4	$1\frac{1}{2}$	15	12	584
5	$1\frac{3}{4}$	15	12	500
6	2	13	10	309
8	$2\frac{1}{2}$	$12\frac{1}{2}$	$9\frac{1}{2}$	189
10	3	$11\frac{1}{2}$	$8\frac{1}{2}$	121
16	$3\frac{1}{2}$	11	8	90
20	4	10	7	62

* The above tables are reprinted from the *Catalog of U.S.S. American Nails* by courtesy of the American Steel and Wire Company.

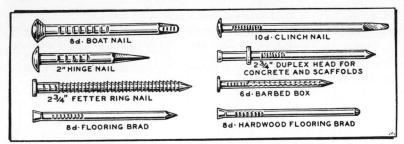

Fig. 6. Special-application nails (⅔ actual size).

Brads and wire nails are available in sizes from $\frac{3}{16}''$ to $3''$ in length. Their diameter is measured by the American Steel and Wire Gauge Standards and ranges from No. 24 to No. 10 gauge.

Wood screws. The two most commonly used wood screws are the flat-head and round-head. Two variations of the round-head screw are the oval-head and fillister-head types (Fig. 7).

Wood screws are sized according to their diameter and length. Diameters range from No. 0, which is .060″, to No. 24, .372″. The length of a flat-head screw is the over-all length; the lengths of both fillister- and round-head screws are taken from the point to the underside of the head of the screw; while that of the oval-head type is computed from the point to the head (Fig. 7).

Corrugated screws. Corrugated fasteners are sometimes called wiggle nails. They are available in various sizes, with either a plain edge or a saw edge, and are used for fastening the miter joints in window screens and frames and in screen doors, and also for tightening loose joints in furniture and woodwork.

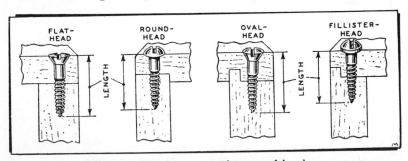

Fig. 7. Wood screws and types of heads.

The one with a saw edge is used for softwoods, the plain edge type for hardwoods. When fastening work with a wiggle nail, it is necessary to rest the work on a solid surface. Drive in the fastener with a medium-weight hammer, using evenly distributed light blows.

Dowels. Dowels are round wooden sticks ranging in size from ⅛″ to 1½″ in diameter and to 3′ in length. They are used for strengthening edge-to-edge joints, for plugging screw holes, and for many other special purposes in woodworking.

Screw fasteners. Screw fasteners are made from either plain or galvanized steel, and are available in various sizes and forms. They are easily installed wherever required and are widely used as hooks (Fig. 8).

Hooks and eyes. Hooks and eyes are available in many shapes and sizes, and are made either of brass or of plain or galvanized steel. They are used as fasteners on screen and cellar doors, on storm windows, and for many other purposes (Fig. 9).

Bolts and nuts. Various types and sizes of bolts and nuts are used on the standard equipment found in modern houses. The carriage bolt and the machine bolt are the two types in general use.

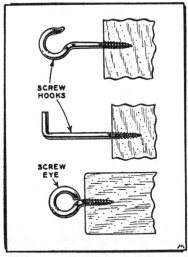

Fig. 8. Typical screw fasteners.

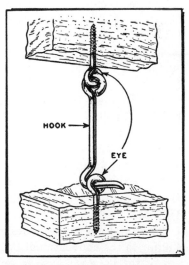

Fig. 9. Hook-and-eye fastener.

The carriage bolt has an oval head and is square for a short distance below the head. This square portion of the shank keeps the bolt from turning when it is screwed into place. The machine bolt has no square section on its shank, but it has a square head which is held with a wrench or pliers while the nut is tightened.

Other types are wing bolts, wing nuts, cap screws, cap nuts, and lock nuts. Wing nuts and bolts are useful as fasteners when a nut has to be taken off at frequent intervals.

Washers. Washers are disks of steel, cast iron, or brass with a hole in the center. They are available in various sizes. A washer is inserted over the end of a bolt before the nut is screwed on to prevent the nut from digging into the wood. Washers give added strength to assembled parts and separate moving parts that are held together by a bolt.

Hinges. The types of hinges most often used are the butt, strap, tee, spring, and rule-joint.

The butt hinge has a removable pin, making it possible to remove a door from its frame without removing the hinges (Figs. 10 and 12). Butt joints are available in iron, brass, bronze, and other ornamental metals, in various sizes and in a wide range of prices.

The strap hinge is used primarily on gates and on cellar and storm doors (Figs. 10 and 13). It has two long triangular-shaped leaves, each tapering from the pin to the end. One of the leaves is screwed to the flat surface of the door, and the other to the surface of the frame, instead of to the edges of both door and frame.

The T-hinge has one rectangular-shaped leaf similar to an ordinary hinge, and the other leaf is triangular-shaped, similar to a strap hinge (Figs. 10 and 13). The T-hinge is used when there is not enough room on the doorframe for a strap hinge. This type is available in sizes ranging from 2″ to 8″.

The spring hinge is a special type fitted with an inner spring. It is used only on screen doors and is available in sizes from 1½″ to 3″ (Fig. 11).

The rule-joint hinge is designed for use on table leaves. It is similar to the conventional type of hinge, with the exception that one of the leaves is approximately twice the length of the other. It is available in sizes ranging from ¾″ to 2″.

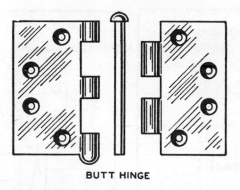

BUTT HINGE

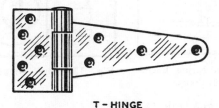

T - HINGE

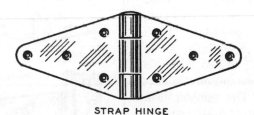

STRAP HINGE

Fig. 10. Hinges.

Locks. There are hundreds of varieties of locks available for use on house doors and on furniture drawers, but there are only two classifications of locks: the mortise and the rim lock. The mortise lock is installed in a slot or mortise in the door or drawer, while the rim lock is secured to the inside surface. Mortise locks are used extensively in better modern construction; rim locks in older houses and those of cheap construction.

Both the mortise and the rim lock may be either a cylinder or tumbler type of lock, and there are a great many styles and

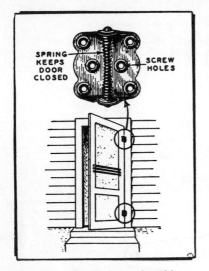

Fig. 11. Fast pin spring hinge used on screen doors.

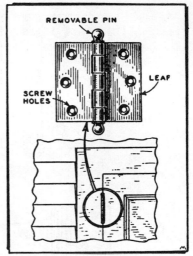

Fig. 12. Butt hinge with loose pin.

varieties of each type (Fig. 14). The cylinder lock is opened with a small, flat, grooved key, notched along one edge. Doors equipped with cylinder locks can be double-locked, and this type is used extensively on outside doors. The tumbler lock is opened and closed with a large key that has a notched blade at the end. Tumbler locks are found in older types of houses, and in modern construction are used on bedroom, bathroom, and other inner doors.

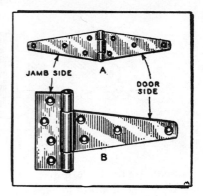

Fig. 13. A, strap hinge; B, T-hinge.

Latches. Latches are used if closet and cupboard doors are to be kept shut but not locked (*A*, Fig. 15). They consist of a beveled bolt that fits into a slot and is held in place by a spring. To open the latch, the bolt is withdrawn by turning a handle to the right.

Another type of latch generally used on screen doors is shown at *B*, Fig. 15.

Hasps. Hasps are generally used on cellar doors, barns, outhouses, and places where other fixtures to prevent entrance are not required. They are available in a variety of sizes, and are usually of galvanized steel (*C*, Fig. 15).

Mending plates. Mending plates are used to strengthen weak joints, to reinforce corners, to mend splits, and for general reinforcement purposes.

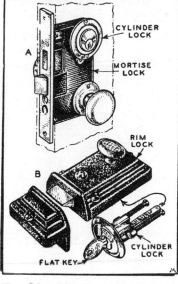

Fig. 14. Mortise and rim locks with pin tumbler cylinders.

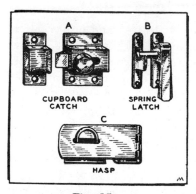

Fig. 15.

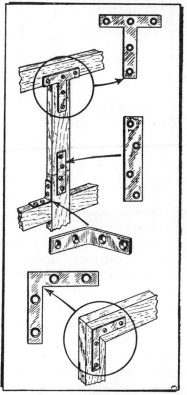

Fig. 16. Types of mending plates and how they are used.

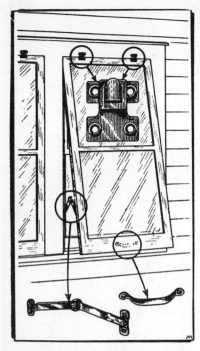

Fig. 17. Types of window and screen hangers and where they are used.

They are made of flat steel in a variety of shapes and sizes, with countersunk holes drilled for the flat-head screws used to secure them (Fig. 16).

Storm window and screen hangers. Storm window and screen hangers are fixtures installed on the top edges of storm windows and screens to enable them to swing outward (Fig. 17). They are usually made of galvanized steel and are available in several sizes. These hangers are demountable, that is, they are designed so that the windows or screens can be lifted off the hangers when swung to a horizontal position. Together with these hangers it is advisable to use a type of hook or bracket to hold storm windows in any desired open position (Fig. 17).

HOW TO MAKE WOODWORKING JOINTS

In woodworking, the making of well-fitted and properly constructed joints is of utmost importance. Although nails, screws, bolts, and other types of fasteners are used extensively in the construction and maintenance of a house, the home craftsman also should be familiar with the common joints used in woodworking and with the proper methods of making them before he attempts to construct, alter, or repair furniture or cabinets.

The common joints in woodworking are the lap, butt, rabbet, dado, mortise-and-tenon, dovetail, miter, and tongue-and-groove joints. All of the joints used are shown in Figs. 18 to 21.

Lap joints. The types of lap joints are the half lap, halved cross lap, end or corner lap, and middle half-lap. They are used

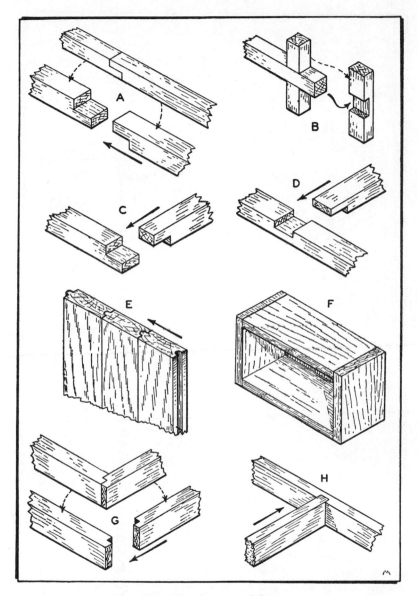

Fig. 18. Common joints.

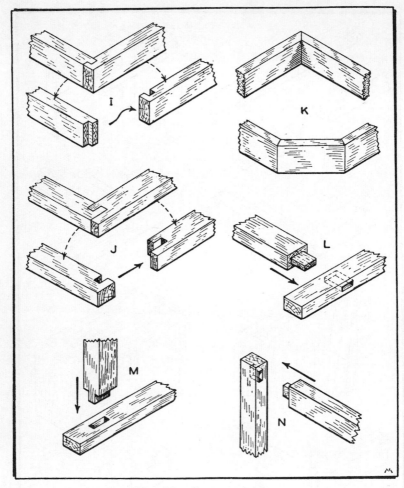

Fig. 19. Common joints.

in the construction of book shelves, stretchers on chairs, easels, kitchen cabinets, and in similar projects (Figs. **22**, **23**, and **24**). The middle half-lap joint is the most commonly used. This joint is laid out by superimposing one piece of the wood upon the other to mark accurately the width of each cut (*A*, Fig. **25**). Then clamp the two pieces together in a vise, and with the try square draw the lines for the width of this cut accurately square across both work edges. Remove the work from the vise, and again using the try square, square the shoulder lines of both the face and the edge of the work (*B*, Fig. 25). Gauge and mark the depth of the required notches with the marking gauge (*C*, Fig. 25).

Again secure the work in the vise, and saw down to the required depth with the backsaw. Be sure to make the saw cuts on the waste part of the stock (*D*, Fig. 25). If the notches are more than ¾″ in width, make several cuts to facilitate the removal of the waste material. Chisel down to the gauge line on each side of the notch. To prevent breaking the grain of the wood and to produce a clean, smooth cut, the chisel should be slanted outward very slightly (*E*, Fig. 25). The final step in the making of the middle lap joint is to finish the cut to a uniform depth (*F*, Fig. 25).

The end half-lap joint is made in the same manner as the middle

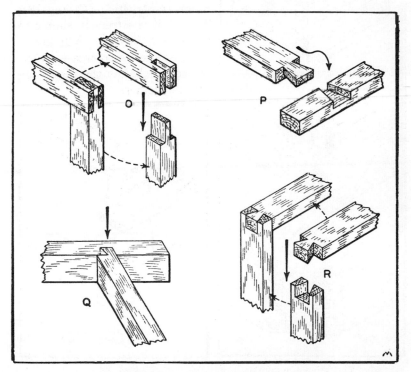

Fig. 20. Common joints.

lap joint, with the exception that only one shoulder is to be cut and the line of the bottom of the joint is gauged across the end of the stock. As the bottom of this joint is accessible from the end of the stock, it can be sawed out and trimmed to the line with the chisel.

The other types of lap joints are merely variations of the two just described, and directions for making them are similar.

Butt joints. The butt joint is the simplest joint and is the only one in which nails or screws must be used. It is used only for rough construction (*F*, Fig. 18). Though it is extremely simple to make, test the edges to be joined for absolute squareness with the try square before the pieces are fitted together.

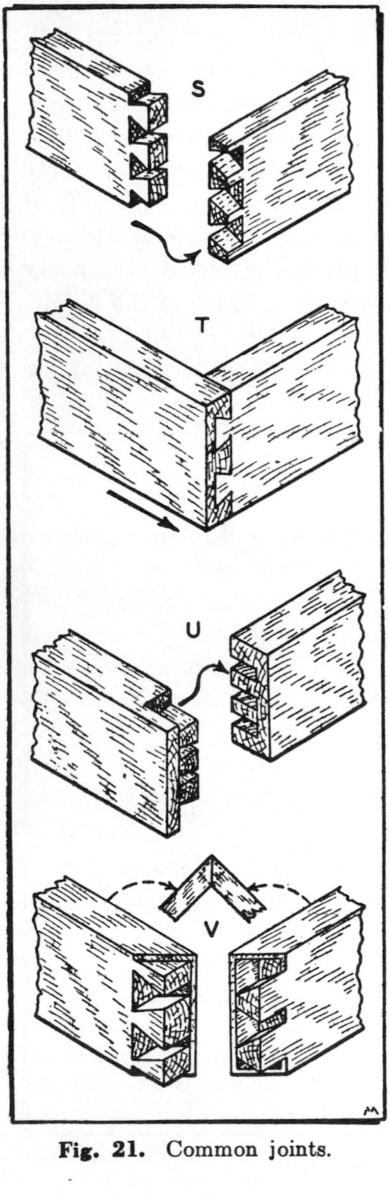

Fig. 21. Common joints.

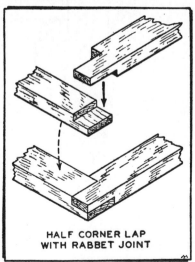

HALF CORNER LAP
WITH RABBET JOINT

Fig. 22.

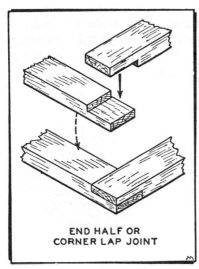

Fig. 23.

END HALF OR
CORNER LAP JOINT

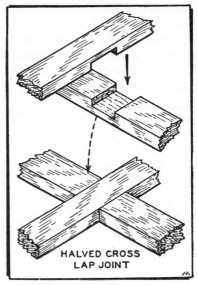

Fig. 24.

HALVED CROSS
LAP JOINT

Rabbet joints. Rabbet joints are formed by recesses, or rabbets, cut out on the edges of the work so that they may be fitted into each other or secured further with a spline fitting into them. Rabbet joints are used in the construction of cabinets, table-tops, and similar projects. The rabbet joints commonly used are the rabbet on end and the rabbet on edge (*A* and *B*, Fig. 26). The shiplap (*C*, Fig. 26) and the rabbet and fillet (*D*, Fig. 26) are two variations of the lap joint.

To make a rabbet on end, lay out the joint by squaring a line for the side or shoulder of the joint across the face of the board and down the edges. This line should be as far from the end of the board as the thickness of the joining piece (*A* and *E*, Fig. 26). Then gauge the required depth of the rabbet, and mark the lines on the two edges and on the end with the marking gauge (*F*, Fig. 26). Cut out the material to be removed with a backsaw (*G* and *H*, Fig. 26).

A handy tool for cutting rabbets is the rabbet plane (Chap. 2). The depth gauge and fence on the rabbet plane regulate the width and depth of the recess to be cut.

The rabbet on edge is cut in the same manner as the rabbet on end, except that the recess is cut on the edge instead of on the end of the board.

Dado joints. Dado joints are grooves cut across the grain of the board, into which a second piece of wood is fitted accurately. They are used in the construction of end tables, cabinets, bookcases, and similar projects. A housed dado joint is one in which

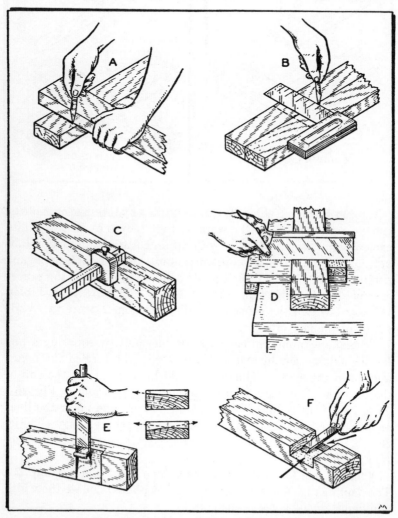

Fig. 25. Making middle half-lap joints.

the entire end of the second piece fits into the dado, or groove (*G*, Fig. 28). In a stopped or gained dado joint, the dado does not extend entirely across the face of the work (*E*, Fig. 27). Other types are the dovetail and shoulder-housed dado (*I*, Fig. 28), (*F*, Fig. 27).

Fig. 26. Rabbet joints and how to make them.

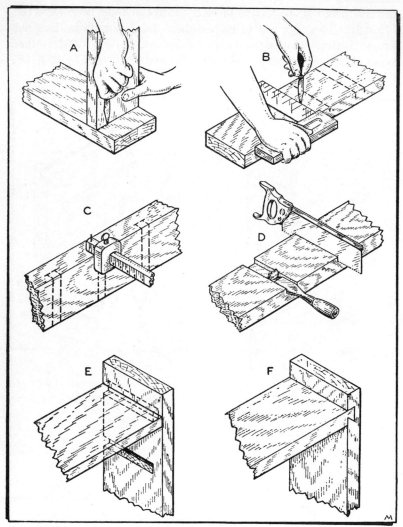

Fig. 27. Dado joints.

To lay out a plain dado, set the board to be housed on end on the face of the board in which the dado is to be cut, and mark the width of the dado accurately on the face of the board (*A*, Fig. 27). Square lines with a try square across the face of the board through the marks and down both edges (*B*, Fig. 27). Then mark

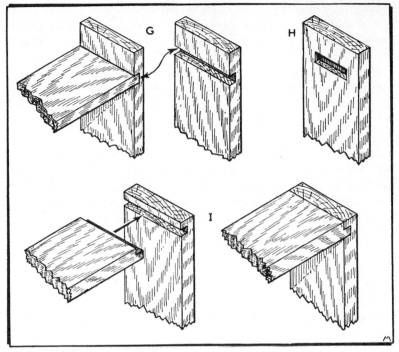

Fig. 28. Dado joints and stopped dado.

the required depth with a gauge, connecting the two marked lines
(*C*, Fig. 27). Using a backsaw, make the necessary cuts; remove
the waste wood with a chisel (*D*, Fig. 27) as previously described
in the paragraphs on Lap Joints.

A stopped dado is laid out in the same manner as a plain dado,
with the exception that it does not extend across the full width of
the board (*E*, Fig. 27). The depth is marked on the work edge
only. To fit the housed piece into a stopped dado, lay out the
shoulder of the housed piece, mark, and cut in one corner to a
length equal to the depth of the dado. When making a stopped
dado, cut a small section of the inner end of the dado with a chisel
to regulate the depth and to assist in sawing the sides. Cut the
sides with a backsaw, and remove the bottom of the cut with a
chisel. Sawing and chiseling should be done alternately, a little
at a time, to avoid cutting the inner part of the joint too deep.

The dovetail (*F*, Fig. 27), housed (*G*, Fig. 28), and grooved types (*H*, Fig. 28) are three other variations of the dado joint.

A combined dado-and-rabbet joint is laid out and made in the same manner as a plain dado, except that a rabbet, or a recess, is cut on the end of the housed piece (*I*, Fig. 28).

Mortise-and-tenon joints. The mortise-and-tenon joint is used extensively by skilled woodworkers. When properly laid out and accurately made, it is strong and dependable. To assure maximum strength and rigidity, it must be fitted very accurately. Mortise-and-tenon joints are used in the construction of desks, tables, chairs, and cabinet furniture that will be subject to hard usage. While there are several kinds of these joints, the directions given here are for the type known as the blind mortise-and-tenon joint. The description and drawings of the procedure in making this joint will help the woodworker to lay out and make any of the other types (Figs. 19 and 20).

The tenon section should be made first. Cut and square both pieces of the work to the desired dimension and plainly mark both faces of each piece for easy identification. From the end of the piece in which the tenon is to be cut, measure back a distance equal to the length of the tenon, then square the shoulder line and mark it around this piece (*A*, Fig. 29).

For general purposes, the tenon in this type of joint should be one-quarter to one-half as thick as the entire board. To lay out the thickness of the tenon correctly, locate the exact center of one edge, accurately measure with a rule one-half the thickness of the tenon each way from the center, and mark these places with the point of a knifeblade or a brad awl (*B*, Fig. 29). Set a marking gauge to these points, and mark both lines across the end and down both edges to the shoulder line previously marked around the board. All gauging must be done from the face side of the work (*C*, Fig. 29).

The width of the tenon also must be laid out very carefully, and the lines gauged through these points across the end and down both sides to the shoulder line (*D*, Fig. 29). With the try square as a guide and using the point of a sharp knife, score the shoulder line repeatedly, to a depth of about $\frac{1}{16}''$ (*E*, Fig. 29).

Fasten the work securely in the vise, and using a very sharp chisel, cut a narrow triangular groove along the outside of the scored line on the waste material (*F*, Fig. 29). Fasten the work

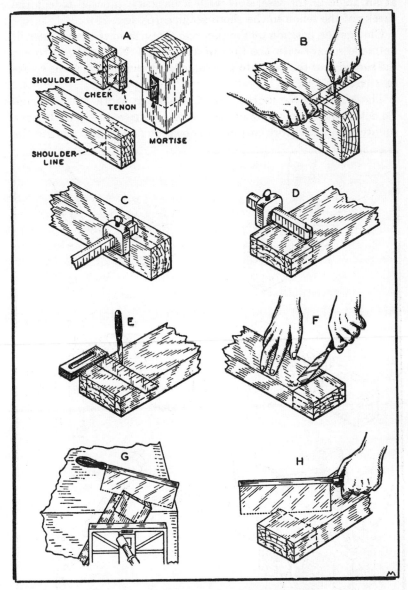

Fig. 29. Making mortise-and-tenon joints.

at an angle in the vise, and with a backsaw proceed to cut the cheeks of the tenon to the shoulder line (*G*, Fig. 29).

Change the position of the piece in the vise so the next cut will be made square with the face of the work. Now proceed to cut the shoulder of the tenon to the required dimension with the backsaw (*H*, Fig. 29).

The length of the mortise must equal the width of the tenon. To determine the position of the mortise, square lines with the try square across the work at points shown at *I*, Fig. 30. Locate the

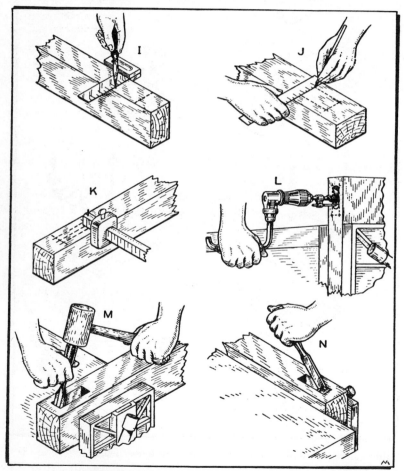

Fig. 30. Making mortise-and-tenon joints.

exact center of the piece, and measure each way from the center exactly one-half the thickness of the tenon to lay out the correct width of the mortise on the other board. Mark these points (J, Fig. 30). Now, carefully check the width of the mortise to make sure that it is equal to the thickness of the tenon. Gauging from the working face, mark through these points, stopping at the end of the mortise. A center line should also be gauged lengthwise of the mortise, as shown at K, Fig. 30.

Secure the work firmly in a vise. Select an auger bit $\frac{1}{16}''$ smaller than the width of the mortise, and adjust the bit gauge to bore holes $\frac{1}{8}''$ deeper than the length of the tenon. Place the spur of the bit on the center line, keeping the bit exactly perpendicular to the face of the work. Begin boring a series of overlapping holes, with the first hole just touching the end of the mortise and the last hole touching the opposite end (L, Fig. 30).

With the work held securely in the vise, as shown at M, Fig. 30, and using a small, sharp chisel, clean out the waste material by cutting out both sides of the mortise as the depth increases. Pare the walls of the mortise to the gauge line, keeping them perpendicular to the face of the work (N, Fig. 30). The final step is to square the ends and remove waste material from the bottom by using a chisel a little narrower than the width of the mortise.

Dovetail joints. Dovetail joints are used by skilled woodworkers in the construction of fine furniture, drawers for tables or desks, and projects where good appearance and strength are desired. A dovetail joint has considerable strength, due to the flare of the projections, called pins, on the ends of the boards, which fit exactly into similarly shaped dovetails. The spaces between the pins and between the dovetails are called sockets, or mortises. The pins are visible on the ends of the work, and the dovetails are visible on the face of the work.

The angle of the dovetail must not be made too acute; this would defeat the purpose of additional strength because an acute angle is weakened by the short grain at the corners of the angle.

The first step in determining the angle of the dovetail is to square a line from the edge of the board, measuring 5'', 6'', 7'', 8'', or 9'' along the board from the edge. Measure 1'' from the line along the edge, and connect the points with a line (Fig. 31). To mark the other angles make a template, that is, a pattern of cardboard or thin wood, of the angle selected (Fig. 32), and use it as a guide.

While the strongest joints are those in which the pins and the dovetails are the same size, for the sake of appearance the dovetails are usually made larger than the pins, though not more than

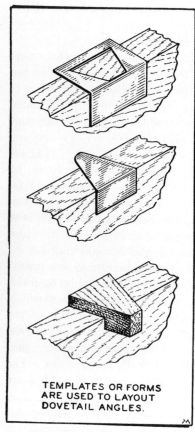

TEMPLATES OR FORMS ARE USED TO LAYOUT DOVETAIL ANGLES.

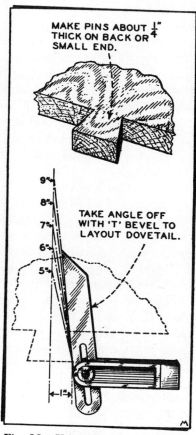

MAKE PINS ABOUT $\frac{1}{4}$" THICK ON BACK OR SMALL END.

TAKE ANGLE OFF WITH 'T' BEVEL TO LAYOUT DOVETAIL.

Fig. 31. Using templates.

Fig. 32. Using bevel for laying out dovetails.

four times the width of the pins. The thickness of the pin and the width of the dovetails will vary in a great many instances, but it is considered good practice to make the pin or its corresponding socket about ¼" on the narrow side.

The three most widely used types of dovetail joints are the half-lap dovetail, the single dovetail, and the multiple dovetail. Dovetail joints are not easy to make, and the beginner is strongly advised to practice on waste material before attempting an actual project.

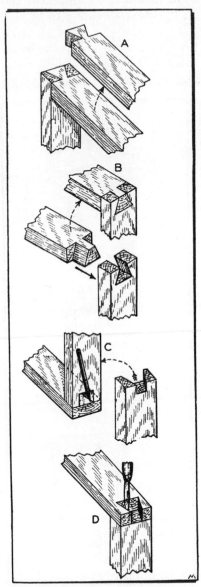

The single dovetail joint shown in *A*, Fig. 33, is the most commonly used.

To make it with two half tongues and a whole dovetail (Fig. 33), first locate the shoulder lines of the joint by measuring the thickness of each piece of wood. Mark the position of the shoulder line and square this line. On one piece, lay out the tongue with a template and cut to required size (*A*, Fig. 33). Saw the sides of this piece with the backsaw (*B*, Fig. 33) and then remove the waste material to the shoulder line with a chisel (*C*, Fig. 33). Hold this piece on the other board to mark the shape of the dovetail (*D*, Fig. 33). Cut out with saw and chisel (*E* and *F*, Fig. 34).

To make the joint with a whole pin fitting into a socket between two half dovetails, square these marks across the end and reproduce the angle on the other side, reversing

Fig. 33. Making a single dovetail with two half-pins.

the procedure outlined for the first type. That is, the sockets between the two half dovetails are first laid out, marked, and cut; then the pin is laid out from the sockets and cut to fit.

A through multiple dovetail joint is merely a series of single dovetails extending along the entire length of the end of the board (Fig. 34). The first step is to mark and square a shoulder line (*A*, Fig. 34). Divide and mark this width into as many divisions

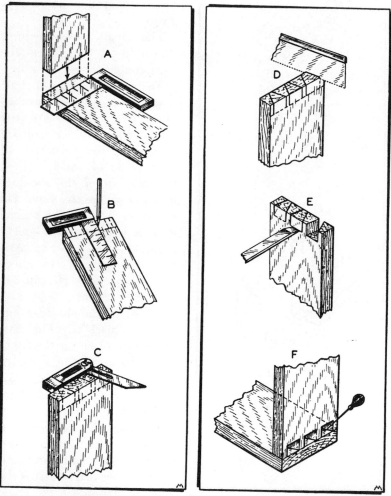

Fig. 34. Making multiple dovetail joints.

as required for dovetails, and measure half the thickness of the pins from each edge and from each side of the divisions (*B*, Fig. 34). Square the divisions to the end, and using a template or bevel, mark the slant on the other side (*C*, Fig. 34). Saw the sides of the pins with the backsaw (*D*, Fig. 34). Finish by chiseling the bottoms of the sockets and cleaning them out with a smaller chisel (*E*, Fig. 34). Now mark the dovetails from the pins with either the point of a knife or a brad awl, and cut out the pins in the manner described for the sockets (*F*, Fig. 34).

Miter joints. Miter joints are used almost exclusively in making picture frames and screens. They are merely butt joints with the angle at the corner halved between the two pieces that are to be joined (Fig. 35). Miter joints are usually cut at an angle of 45°.

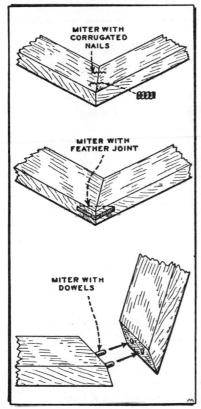
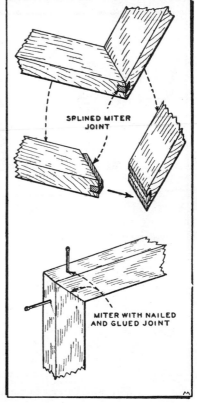

Fig. 35. Miter joints.

While it is a simple matter to mark out an angle of 45°, miter joints are usually sawed in a miter box (Chap. 2).

A miter box is an accurate tool for reproducing an angle of cut, from 30° to 90°, in pieces that are to be fitted together. The material is set in the miter box at the required angle and is cut with the backsaw. When a large number of miter joints are to be nailed or glued together, a special clamp or picture-frame vise is used (Figs. 36 and 37).

Dowels, tongues, or slip feathers are sometimes used instead of nails to strengthen the joint further. When tongued miter joints are made, each of the pieces is grooved, and a wooden tongue of required size is glued into the groove. This strengthens the miter joints, and also prevents the pieces joined in this way from warping.

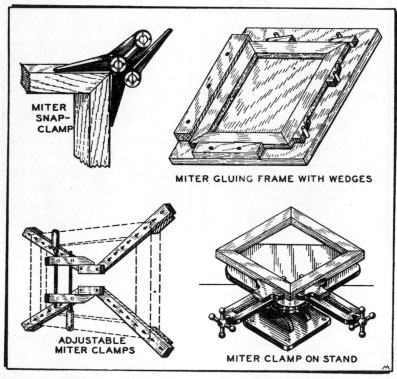

Fig. 36. Various methods of clamping glued miters.

In making a slip-feather miter joint, a groove is cut only part way through with a backsaw. A thin piece or sliver of wood is

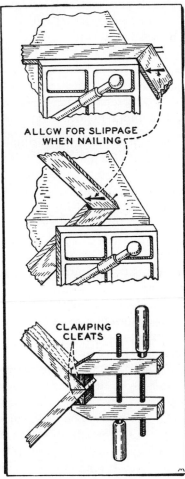

ALLOW FOR SLIPPAGE WHEN NAILING

CLAMPING CLEATS

Fig. 37. Nailing and clamping miters.

glued into the groove, and the protruding excess wood is trimmed flush with the work with a chisel (Fig. 35).

When dowels are used to reinforce a miter joint, the holes for them are drilled at an angle to a depth of from 1″ to 2″. Use a drill slightly larger than the diameter of the dowels. Before insertion of the dowels, file or sand off the square corners. Insert some glue in the holes and coat the dowel with the glue. Fit together and clamp (Fig. 35).

Other methods used for reinforcing miters are shown in Fig. 35.

Tongue-and-groove joints. It is impractical to make tongue-and-groove joints in the home workshop, as finished tongued-and-grooved lumber, when specified, is supplied by the dealer. This type of joint is made by cutting a groove longitudinally with the grain of the wood on one side of a board and a tongue on the other side to fit the groove of an adjoining piece. The tongue-and-groove joint is used principally in flooring.

CHAPTER 4

Working with Plywood

———— : ————————————————

LAYING OUT PLYWOOD FOR CUTTING

The large size panels in which plywood is manufactured simplifies every step of construction. With panels at hand, the only step that has to precede actual construction is laying out the work for cutting. It is worth while to do this with care and to avoid waste and simplify your work. When many pieces are to be cut from one panel, you will find it easiest to sketch the arrangement on a piece of paper before marking the plywood for cutting. Be sure to allow for a saw kerf between adjacent pieces.

Try to work it out so that your first cuts reduce the panel to pieces small enough for easy handling.

One of the most important points to watch in planning your sequence of operations is to cut all mating or matching parts with the same saw setting. Watch the direction of the face grain when cutting. Except where indicated otherwise in the plan, you will usually want this to run the long way of the piece. Mark on the better face of the plywood unless you are going to cut it with a portable power saw; in that case, mark it on the back.

Hand-sawing. When hand-sawing, place plywood with good face up (Fig. 1). Use a saw having 10 to 15 points to the inch. Support the panel firmly so it will not sag. You can reduce splitting out of the underside by putting a piece of scrap lumber under it and sawing it along with the plywood. It also helps to hold the saw at a low angle as shown in illustration. Be sure to use a sharp saw.

Power sawing. Power sawing on a radial or table saw should be done with good face of plywood up. Use a sharp combination

Fig. 1.

Fig. 2.

blade or a fine-tooth one without much set. Let the blade protrude above the plywood just the height of the teeth (Fig. 2).

You will find handling large panels an easier one-man job if you build an extension support with a roller. It can have a base of its own or may be clamped to a saw horse.

Portable power saw. A portable power saw should be used with the good face of the plywood down, as shown in Fig. 3. Tack a strip of scrap lumber to the top of each saw horse and

Fig. 3.

Fig. 4.

you can saw right through it without damaging the horse. Be sure to keep your saw blade sharp.

Planing plywood edges. Planing plywood edges with a plane or jointer will not be necessary if you make your cuts with a sharp saw blade. If you do any planing, work from both ends of the edge toward the center to avoid tearing out plies at the end of the cut (Fig. 4). Use a plane with a sharp blade and take very shallow cuts.

Sanding. Sanding before sealer or prime coat is applied should be confined to edges (Fig. 5). Fir plywood is sanded smooth in manufacture—one of the big timesavers in its use—and further sanding of the surfaces will merely remove soft grain. After sealing, sand in direction of grain only.

PLYWOOD CONSTRUCTION JOINTS

Butt joints. Butt joints, like those shown in Fig. 6, are simplest to make, suitable for ¾" plywood. For thinner panels, use a reinforcing block or nailing strip to make a stronger joint as shown in Fig. 6. In both cases, glue will make the joint many times stronger than if it were made with nails or screws alone.

Fig. 5.   **Fig. 6.**

Fig. 7.   Fig. 8.

Frame construction. Frame construction shown in Fig. 7 makes it possible to reduce weight by using thinner plywood, since it has amazing strength. Glue as recommended in Chapter 5.

Dado joints. Dado joints (Fig. 8) quickly made with a power saw, produce neat shelves. Use a dado blade (shimmed out) to produce these grooves in a single cut.

Fig. 9.   Fig. 10.

Rabbet joints. Rabbet joints like this one shown in Fig. 9 are neat and strong, and easy to make with power tools. You will find this an ideal joint for drawers, buffets, chests, or cupboards.

PLYWOOD FASTENERS

Nails. Nail size is determined primarily by the thickness of the plywood you are using. Used with glue, all nails will produce strong joints. For ¾″ plywood, 6d casing nails or 6d finish nails. For ⅝″, 6d or 8d finish nails. For ½″, 4d or 6d. For ⅜″, 3d or 4d. For ¼″, use ¾″ or 1″ brads, 3d finish nails, or (for backs where there is no objection to heads showing) 1″ blue lath nails. Substitute casing for finish nails wherever you want a heavier nail (Fig. 10).

Pre-drilling is occasionally called for in careful work where nails must be very close to an edge. As shown in Fig. 11, drill bit should be slightly smaller diameter than the nail to be used.

Space the nails about 6″ apart for most work (Fig. 12). Closer spacing is necessary only with thin plywood where there may be slight buckling between nails. Nail and glue work together to produce a strong, durable joint.

Fig. 11.   **Fig. 12.**

Fig. 13.

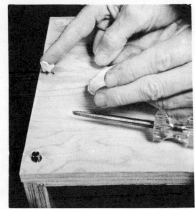

Fig. 14.

Flat-head wood screws. Flat-head wood screws are useful where nails will not provide adequate holding power. Glue should also be used if possible. Sizes shown here are minimums; use longer screws when work permits. This list gives plywood thickness, diameter and length of smallest screws recommended, and size of hole to drill: ¾″ plywood, No. 8, 1½″, ⁵⁄₃₂″ hole; ⅝″ plywood, No. 8, 1¼″, ⁵⁄₃₂″ hole; ½″ plywood, No. 6, 1¼″, ⅛″ hole; ⅜″ plywood, No. 6, 1″, ⅛″ hole; ¼″ plywood, No. 4, ¾″, ⁷⁄₆₄″ hole (Fig. 13).

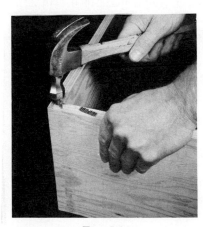

Fig. 15.

Fig. 16.

Screws and nails should be countersunk and the holes filled with wood dough or surfacing putty as shown in Fig. 14. Apply filler so it is slightly higher than the plywood, then sanded level when dry. Lubricate screws with soap if hard to drive. Avoid damage to plywood surface by using Phillips head screws.

Corrugated fasteners. Corrugated fasteners can reinforce miter joints in ¾″ plywood and hold joints together while glue sets as shown in Fig. 15. For some kinds of plywood jobs, sheet-metal screws are valuable. These screws have more holding power than wood screws, but come only in short lengths and do not have flat heads. Bolts and washers are good for fastening sectional units together and for installing legs, hinges or other hardware when great strength is required.

DRAWER CONSTRUCTION

Drawers made with hand tools. This drawer, shown upside down in Fig. 16, is easily made with saw and hammer. Butt joints are glued and nailed. The bottom should be ⅜″ or ½″ fir plywood for rigidity. The drawer front extends down to cover the front edge of the bottom.

Additional strip of wood, glued and nailed to front panel, as shown in Fig. 17, reinforces the bottom of this second type of drawer made with hand tools. Reinforcing permits use of economical ¼″ fir plywood for drawer bottoms.

Drawers made with power tools. Power tools make sturdy drawers easy to build. Figure 18 shows one side (dadoed on outer face for drawer guide) being put into place. Rabbet drawer front (at right) to take sides; dado sides to fit drawer back. All four parts are grooved to take ¼″ plywood bottom.

Two types of guides, both calling for the use of power tools, are shown in Figs. 19 and 20. The drawer side has been plowed before assembly to fit over a strip glued to the side of the cabinet (Fig. 19). Procedure is reversed for the version in Fig. 20. Here the cabinet side has been dadoed before assembly. A matching strip is glued to the side of the drawer. Even heavy drawers slide easily on guides like these if waxed or lubricated with paraffin after finishing.

Fig. 17.   Fig. 18.

Drawer bottom forms guide. Hand tools only are required to make the drawer shown in Fig. 21. The secret is its bottom, made of ⅜″ or ½″ plywood. This bottom extends ⅜″ beyond the sides of the drawer to form a lip. Ease edges and apply paraffin for easy operation. Power tools will permit making a stronger and lighter version of the same drawer. Bottom is ¼″ plywood cut ⅜″ wider than the drawer on each side. See details of construction shown in Fig. 22.

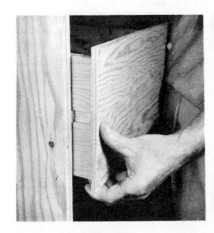

Fig. 19.   Fig. 20.

Extended bottom of drawer described and shown in Fig. 23 fits into slots formed by gluing pieces of ⅜″ plywood to the inner surface of each side of the cabinet. Gap just wide enough to take the lip is left between the pieces. The drawer shown in Fig. 24 slides in slots dadoed into the ¾″ plywood sides of the cabinet. When power tools are used, this is one of the simplest of all methods of drawer-and-guide construction.

Fig. 21.

Fig. 22.

Fig. 23.

Fig. 24.

SHELF HANGING

The neatest and strongest way to hang a shelf is by making a dado joint or using metal shelf supports. A dado shown in Fig. 8 requires power tools and does not permit changing shelf height.

Figure 25 shows inexpensive shelf supports that plug into blind holes ⅝″ deep drilled in the plywood sides of the cabinet. Drill additional holes to permit moving shelves when desired. Another device is the use of slotted metal shelf strips into which shelf supports may be plugged at any height. For a better fit, set shelf strips flush in a dado cut, or cut out shelves around shelf strips.

SLIDING DOORS

Close-fitting plywood sliding doors are made by rabbeting top and bottom edges of each door (Fig. 26). Rabbet back of front door, and front of back door. This will let doors almost touch, leaving little gap for dust and increases the effective depth of the cabinet. For ⅜″ plywood doors rabbeted half their thickness, plow two grooves in top and bottom of cabinet ½″ apart. With all plywood doors. seal all edges and give backs same paint treatment as front to maintain plywood's balanced construction.

Fig. 25.

Fig. 26.

For removable doors, plow bottom grooves $\frac{3}{16}''$ deep, top grooves $\frac{3}{8}''$ deep (Fig. 27). After finishing, (see previous paragraph) insert door by pushing up into excess space in top groove, then dropping into bottom. Plowing can be simplified by the use of a fiber track made for sliding doors of this type.

Only hand tools are required when this version of the sliding-door is used. Front and back strips are stock $\frac{1}{4}''$ quarter-round molding. The strip between is $\frac{1}{4}''$ square, as shown in Fig. 28. Use glue and brads or finish nails to fasten strips securely.

Fig. 27.   Fig. 28.

CABINET BACKS

Standard method of applying backs to cabinets and other storage units calls for rabbeting sides. Cabinet at left in Fig. 29 has rabbet just deep enough to take plywood back. For large units that must fit against walls that may not be perfectly smooth or plumb, the version at right in this illustration is better. This rabbet is made $\frac{1}{2}''$ or even $\frac{3}{4}''$ deep. The lip that remains after back has been inserted may be easily trimmed wherever necessary to get a good fit between plywood unit and house wall.

When hand tools are used, attach strips of $\frac{1}{4}''$ quarter-round molding for the back to rest against (Fig. 30). Glue and nail back to molding.

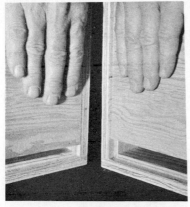

Fig. 29.

Fig. 30.

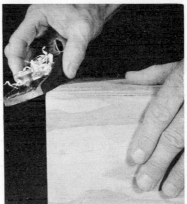

Fig. 31.   **Fig. 32.**

Two methods of applying cabinet backs without rabbets or moldings are shown in Fig. 31. One by nailing the back flush with outside edge. Second by setting the back ½″ to ⅞″ away from edges. The back becomes inconspicuous when cabinet is against the wall.

Bevel cabinet backs that must be applied without a rabbet to make them less conspicuous are made as shown in Fig. 32. Install ⅜″ plywood back flush with the edges of the cabinet, then bevel with light strokes of a block plane.

Nail the cabinet back into rabbet by driving nails at a slight angle as shown in Fig. 33. Use 1″ brads or 4d finish nails. Where back will not be seen, the 1″ blue lath nails shown in illustration may be used.

Two-hand staplers are excellent for nailing cabinet backs (Fig. 34). They drive long staples, setting them below the surface if desired, and greatly speed up the work. They are sometimes available on loan or rental.

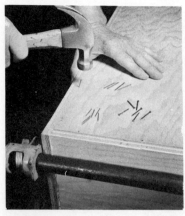

Fig. 33.

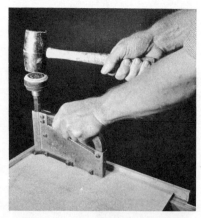

Fig. 34.

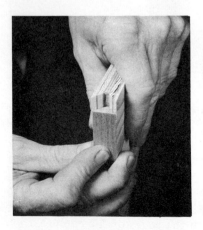

Fig. 35.

Fig. 36.

EDGE TREATMENT

Figures 35, 36, and 37 show three ways to finish plywood edges. You can achieve handsome, solid results by cutting a V groove and inserting a matching wood strip, but this method is comparatively difficult.

Thin strips of real wood edge-banding (Fig. 36) now are available in rolls ranging in various widths. They are coated with

Fig. 37.

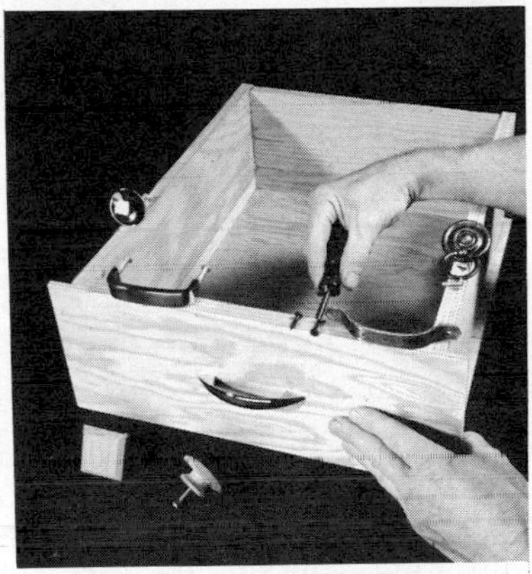

Fig. 38.

Fig. 39.

Fig. 40.

pressure sensitive adhesive. Simply peel off backing paper and apply to plywood edges according to the manufacturer's recommendations. Figure 37 shows one edge already covered with strip of Douglas fir to match plywood.

Laminated plastic surfacing materials may be applied to edges of tables with same contact cement used in applying to table tops. As shown in Fig. 37, apply to edges first, then to counter or table top. A thicker, more massive effect can be secured by nailing a 1″ or 1¼″ strip all around underneath edge.

To fill end grain on plywood edges that are to be painted, several varieties of wood putty are available; either powdered, to be mixed with water, or prepared, ready for use. Plaster spackling also works well. Sand smooth when thoroughly dry and then finish the job.

PULLS, HANDLES, AND CATCHES

Drawer pulls and door handles. Drawer pulls and door handles of the types shown in Fig. 38 are widely available. Use them in metal or wood to style your job. They come in a variety of traditional and ranch styles as well as in many modern designs.

Sliding and rolling doors are most easily equipped with finger cups that you simply force into round holes. For large doors, use the rectangular cups or large round ones that are fastened in with screws. Round pulls at top are suitable where clearance is adequate, or you can make simple rectangular grips from wood (Fig. 39).

The simplest drawer pull of all is a notch cut into the top of the drawer front. It may be rectangular, V shaped, or half-round. You can omit the notch from every other drawer, opening it by means of the notch in the drawer below, as shown in Fig. 40. By sloping drawer fronts, the drawer may be pulled out by grasping the projecting bottom edge.

Catches come in many varieties besides the conventional friction type shown in Fig. 41. The touch type shown in illustration and being installed, permits the door to open at a touch. Magnetic catch has no moving parts to break. Roller catches and the new ones made of polyethelyne are smoother and more durable than the plain steel friction catches.

Fig. 41.

Fig. 42.

Fig. 43.

Fig. 44.

DOOR HARDWARE

Surface hinges. Surface hinges are quickly mounted. They require no mortising, add an ornamental touch, and are available in many styles. A pair of H or H-L hinges will do for most doors; for larger doors or to add rigidity to smaller ones, use a pair of H-L plus one H (Fig. 42), or use three of the H type. Tee or strap hinges help prevent sag in large doors. On tall doors, one or two added hinges between those at top and bottom help to minimize warping.

Overlapping (lipped) doors are neatly hung with semi-concealed hinges (Fig. 43). They are excellent for plywood since screws go into flat grain. These have ½" inset, are made for doors of ¾" plywood rabbeted to leave ¼" lip. Such hinges are made in many styles and finishes, semi-concealed or full-surface.

 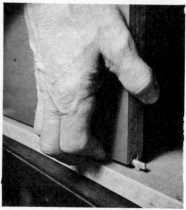

Fig. 45.   Fig. 46.

Concealed pin hinges. Concealed pin hinges give a neat modern appearance to flush doors (Fig. 44). They mount directly onto the cabinet side. Construction is simplified, because no face frame is necessary. Only the pivot is visible from the front when the door is closed. Use a pair of these hinges for small doors, three (called *a pair and one-half*) for larger doors.

Semi-concealed loose-pin hinges. Semi-concealed loose-pin hinges like these offer the same appearance when door is closed as ordinary butt hinges, since only the barrel shows (Fig. 45). They are much better, though, for flush plywood doors because screws go into flat plywood grain. A variation called a chest hinge may be used in the same way.

T guides. Door bottom is kept in line by a simple T guide for each door as shown in Fig. 46. Two strips of ¼" quarter-round molding, with ¼" space between, will form slot if power tools are not available for making the slot.

Metal brackets. Two metal brackets should be fastened to the top of each door with a pair of screws. Nylon wheels with ball bearings roll in a double-lipped track that is fastened to the door frame with screws (Fig. 47). (Single-lipped track is also made for single doors.) Installation is very simple, with no mortising

Fig. 47.   **Fig. 48.**

required.

Rollers. Rolling doors for closets and large storage units may have rollers mounted at either top or bottom (Fig. 48). Top-mount hardware shown in Figs. 46, 47, and 48, usually is smoother in operation, particularly when the door is tall and narrow.

CHAPTER 5

Glues and Gluing Methods

Gluing is done extensively in woodworking, and in the production of various types of wood products. Modern glues, processes, and techniques vary as widely as the products made, and developments have been many in recent years. In general, however, it remains true that the quality of a glued joint depends upon the kind of wood and its preparation for use, the kind and quality of the glue and its preparation for use, the details of the gluing process, the types of joints, and the conditioning of the joints. Depending on the glue used, service conditions also affect the performance of the joint to a greater or lesser extent.

GLUING PROPERTIES OF DIFFERENT WOODS

Table A gives the gluing properties of the woods widely used for glued products. The classifications are based on the average quality of side-grain joints of wood that is approximately average in density for the species, when glued with animal, casein, starch, urea resin, and resorcinol resin glues. A species is considered to be glued satisfactorily when the strength of the joint is approximately equal to the strength of the wood.

Whether it will be easy or difficult to obtain a satisfactory joint depends upon the density of the wood, the structure of the wood, the presence of extractives or infiltrated materials in the wood, and the kind of glue. In general, heavy woods are more difficult to glue than lightweight woods, hardwoods are more difficult to glue than softwoods, and heartwood is more difficult than sapwood. Several species vary considerably in their gluing characteristics with different glues (Table A).

158

TABLE A

Classification of various hardwood and softwood species according to gluing properties

HARDWOODS

Group 1	Group 2
(Glue very easily with different glues under wide range of gluing conditions)	(Glue well with different glues under a moderately wide range of gluing conditions)
Aspen.	Alder, red.
Chestnut, American.	Basswood.
Cottonwood.	Butternut.
Willow, black.	Elm:
Yellow-poplar.	American.
	Rock.
	Hackberry.
	Magnolia.
	Mahogany.
	Sweetgum.

Group 3	Group 4
(Glue satisfactorily under well-controlled gluing conditions)	(Require very close control of gluing conditions, or special treatment to obtain best results)
Ash, white.	Beech, American.
Cherry, black.	Birch, sweet and yellow.
Dogwood.	Hickory.
Maple, soft.	Maple, hard.
Oak:	Osage-orange.
Red.-	Persimmon.
White	
Pecan.	
Sycamore.	
Tupelo:	
Black.	
Water.	
Walnut, black.	

SOFTWOODS

Group 1	Group 2	Group 3
Baldcypress.	Cedar, eastern red-.	Cedar, Alaska-.
Cedar, western red-	Douglas-fir.	
Fir, white.	Hemlock, western.	
Larch, western.	Pine:	
Redwood.	Eastern white.	
Spruce, Sitka.	Southern yellow.	
	Ponderosa.	

GLUES USED FOR VARIOUS JOBS

Animal glues have long been used extensively in woodworking; *starch glues* came into general use, especially for veneering, early in this century; *casein glue* and *vegetable protein glues,* of which *soybean* is the most important, gained commercial importance during and immediately following World War I for gluing lumber and veneer into products that required moderate water resistance. *Synthetic resin glues* were developed more recently but now surpass many of the older glues in importance as woodworking glues. *Phenol resin glues* are widely used to produce plywood for severe service conditions. *Urea resin glues* are used extensively in producing plywood for furniture and interior paneling. *Resorcinol* and *phenol-resorcinol resin glues* are useful for gluing lumber into products that will withstand exposure to the weather. *Polyvinyl resin emulsion glues* are used in assembly joints of furniture.

Broadly, synthetic resin glues are of two types—*thermosetting* and *thermoplastic.* Thermosetting resins, once cured, are not softened by heat. Thermoplastic resins will soften when reheated.

Many brands of glues made from fish, animal, or vegetable derivatives are sold in liquid form, ready for application. Their principal use in woodworking is for small jobs and repair work. They are variable in quality and low in water resistance and durability under damp conditions. The better brands are moderate in dry strength and set fairly quickly. They are applied cold, usually by brush, and are pressed cold. They stain wood only slightly, if at all.

CHOOSING THE RIGHT TYPE OF GLUE

No one glue is ideal for every project. Choose the best type of glue suitable for the job at hand from the following descriptions.

Liquid hide glue. Liquid hide glue has several advantages. It is very strong because it is raw-hide-tough and does not become brittle. This glue is easy to use, light in color, resists heat and mold. It has good filling qualities and gives strength even in poorly fitted joints Liquid hide glue is excellent for furniture work, and wherever a tough, lasting wood-to-wood bond is needed. It is a favorite glue for cabinetwork and general wood gluing. Because it is not waterproof, do not use it for outdoor furniture or for boat building.

Liquid resin glue. Non-staining, clean and white liquid resin glue can be used at any temperature, and is recommended for quick-setting work where good clamping is not possible. It is a fine all-around household glue for mending and furniture making and repair, and is excellent for model work, paper, leather, and small assemblies. Liquid resin glue is not sufficiently moisture-resistant for anything to be exposed to weather, and is not so strong and lasting, as liquid hide glue for fine furniture work.

Resorcinol. Resorcinol is a very strong and waterproof glue. It works better with poor joints than many other glues do. This type of glue should be used for work that may be exposed to soaking: outdoor furniture, boats, and wooden sinks. *Do not* use it for work that must be done at temperatures below 70°. Because of its dark color and mixing, it *should not* be used unless waterproof quality is needed.

Powdered resin. This light-colored almost waterproof powdered resin is very strong, but brittle if the point fits poorly. It should be used for woodworking and general gluing whenever considerable moisture resistance is needed. *Do not* use powdered resin with oily woods or with joints that are not closely fitted and tightly clamped. When using this resin, be sure to mix it for each use.

Powdered casein. Powdered casein is strong, fairly water-resistant, works in cool locations, and fills poor joints well. It can be used for most woodworking jobs and is especially desirable with oily woods, such as teak, lemon, and yew. Powdered casein will stain acid woods such as redwood, and is not moisture re-sistant enough for outdoor furniture. It must be mixed for each use.

Flake animal. Flake animal glue has the same advantages as liquid hide glue, but it must be mixed, heated, kept hot, and used at high temperatures. It is good for quantity woodworking projects that justify the time and trouble of mixing and heating the glue. This glue is not waterproof, and is too much trouble to use for small jobs or most home shop work.

GLUING METHODS

Successful wood gluing ordinarily means a joint that lasts almost forever and is stronger than the wood itself. Liquid hide glue is ideal for furniture building and repair. It has the rawhide toughness that has made hide glue the craftsman's choice for generations. It can be purchased in ready-to-use liquid form, that eliminates tedious preparation and the necessity for speed and critical temperature control.

Select a fine glue and then follow the six simple steps shown in Figs. 1 to 6.

Scrape or sandpaper the old wood until it is bare and clean, making sure that all the old glue is removed (Fig. 1). Most glues work by penetrating the porous wood grain.

Test the fit of the joint before applying the glue (Fig. 2). With the poor fit often unavoidable in repair work, be sure to use a glue with good gap-filling qualities.

A brush is the best applicator, particularly if your glue comes in a wide-mouth can as shown in Fig. 3. Be sure to apply glue to both of the surfaces to be jointed.

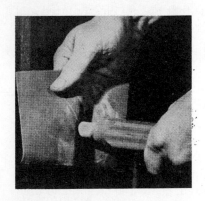
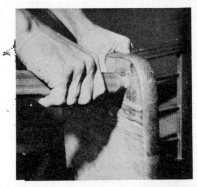

Fig. 1.   Fig. 2.

Fig. 3.   Fig. 4.

You will get a strong joint more quickly if you let the glue become tacky (Fig. 4) before joining the parts.

The joint should be pulled tightly together and held in that position (Fig. 5). (See section on clamps in this chapter.)

Most glues set better and faster in a dry, warm (not hot) room. It is safest not to disturb the joint until the glue is set, following the time given in Table B. An ordinary heat lamp (Fig. 6) will speed up the drying of the joint.

Fig. 5.   Fig. 6.

TABLE B

GLUE TYPE	ROOM TEMPERATURE	HOW TO PREPARE	70° Clamping Time Hardwood	Softwood
Liquid Hide	Sets best above 70°. Can be used in colder room if glue is warmer.	Ready to use.	2 hours	3 hours
White Liquid Resin	Any temperature above 60°. But the warmer the better.	Ready to use.	1 hour	1½ hours
Resorcinol	Must be 70° or warmer. Will set faster at 90°.	Mix 3 parts powder to 4 parts liquid catalyst.	16 hours	16 hours
Powdered Resin	Must be 70° or warmer. Will set faster at 90°.	Mix 2 parts powder with ½ to 1 part water.	16 hours	16 hours
Powdered Casein	Any temperature above freezing. But the warmer the better.	Stir together equal parts by volume glue and water. Wait 10 minutes and stir again.	2 hours	3 hours
Flake or Powdered Animal	Must be 70° or warmer. Keep work warm.	For each ounce glue add 1½ ounces water (softwood) or 2 ounces water (hardwood).	1 hour	1½ hours

HINTS ON APPLYING GLUE

Work at proper temperature. Temperature is important, and you will get better results if the work, the glue, and the room are all 70° or warmer. Flake animal glue should be used hot. Liquid hide glue must be warm to spread it properly (Fig. 7). Resorcinal and powdered-resin glues will not set properly at less than 70°. If you must work at a lower temperature, liquid resin glue, which can be used at any temperature above 60°, should be used.

Size end grain. The end grain of any wood is highly absorbent, and if it is permitted to soak up the moisture of the glue a weak joint may result. This can be avoided by giving the end grain a thin preliminary coat of the glue you are using (Fig. 8), applying it a few minutes ahead of time. When you spread the glue over the rest of the joint, be sure to give the end grain a second coat of the glue.

Fig. 7.

Fig. 8.

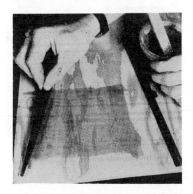

Fig. 9.

Fig. 10.

Use suitable applicator. Old saw blades with fine teeth, such as hacksaw or utility saw blades, make good spreaders for covering a large area. Figure 9 shows a plywood cupboard door panel being prepared for covering with burlap. Discarded windshield wipers are good spreaders too.

Oil can. Chair rungs and similar joints can be reglued even when it is not feasible to pull them apart. Drill a small hole into the joint and inject the glue with an oil can (Fig. 10).

Glue tube. Glue tube is a handy applicator for gluing small objects (Fig. 11). It is useful too for running a line of glue around the edge of an article, or for applying glue to a long strip of molding.

Cover all surfaces evenly. A *roller* of the type sold in camera shops permits putting a thin, uniform coat of glue on a big surface. Large *paint brushes* can also be used. The small brush shown in Fig. 12 is a whisk broom cut off short for stiffness. With this type of brush you can get a thinner coat than with an ordinary soft brush.

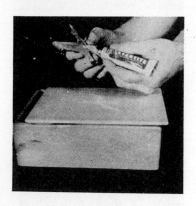

Fig. 11.

Fig. 12.

CLAMPING

Common gluing clamps. Good woodworking depends on good gluing. Good gluing depends on adequate clamping. Therefore, building a clamp collection is an important step toward better work. A good place to begin is with an assortment of C-clamps. They are the least expensive and most versatile of clamps. Next, you will want long clamps for gluing up stock and large frames— two or preferably three of them. Wooden-jaw hand screws do so many jobs that they are like a third hand. As need for them arises you will want to add many special clamps such as press screws, edge-clamp fixtures, miter clamps, spring clamps, surface clamps, and a band clamp.

Hand screw. The hand screw is the woodworker's favorite, because its jaws are wood and it may often be applied directly to the work without danger of marring it. The adjustable type hand screw works on odd shapes like the ironing board shown in Fig. 13.

The right and wrong use of the hand screw are shown in Fig. 14. The clamp at the left is properly adjusted so that its jaws are parallel. The clamp at the right is not properly adjusted. These clamps can be quickly adjusted by gripping both handles and twisting them at the same time.

Fig. 13.

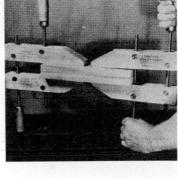

Fig. 14.

Fig. 15.

Fig. 16.

Surface clamp. The surface clamp or the bench clamp can be fastened to any table or bench top. Its special bolt drops below the surface when the clamp is slipped off, leaving the top clear for other work. This kind of clamp is very handy when gluing small objects since it requires only one hand (Fig. 15), leaving the other free to hold the work.

Spring clamps. Many delicate jobs can be done with spring clamps like the one shown in Fig. 16 that no other kind of clamp will do as well. These overgrown clothespins come in assorted sizes, and are handy for light assemblies. Some of these clamps have rubber-covered jaws to protect the work.

Fig. 17.

Fig. 18.

Fig. 19.

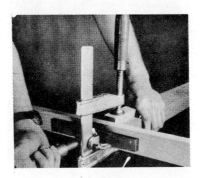

Fig. 20.

C-Clamps. C-clamps will do a wide assortment of jobs and substitute reasonably well for many other types of clamps. Protect the work by inserting small blocks of wood under the jaws of the clamps (Fig. 17).

Deep-throat C-clamps. As shown in Fig. 18, deep-throat C-clamps can do many jobs that ordinary clamps cannot. They can reach to the center of small work and put on the pressure where it is needed most. As with other C-clamps their metal jaws call for scraps of wood to avoid marring the work.

Quick clamp. The quick clamp does the work of a heavy C-clamp. In construction it is actually a short bar clamp. Its special virtue is that it can be adjusted in an instant by sliding the head along the bar (Fig. 19). The screw is needed only for putting on pressure

Edge-clamp fixture. This fixture works with a quick clamp to solve a common and difficult gluing problem. It is used most often to glue strips to the edges of boards, or as shown in Fig. 20 to join work in the shape of a T. The quick clamp grasps the work and the edge clamp puts on the pressure.

Pipe type or long clamps. These clamps can be purchased complete as shown in Fig. 21, or you can buy just the fixtures and put them on ordinary water pipe. With these fittings you can make your own long clamps at a small cost, and have any length you want.

Fig. 21.

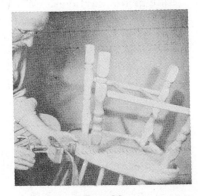

Fig. 22.

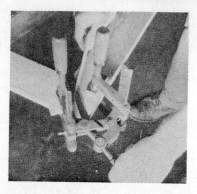

Fig. 23.

Band clamp. The band clamp wraps itself around curved or irregular shapes and squeezes from all directions. The bands are either made of steel or heavy canvas. Steel is best for round objects, and canvas for odd shapes. For general home-shop use with varying shapes, it is best to use canvas (Fig. 22).

Miter clamp. This clamp is a clever extra pair of hands. You can put it on a miter joint or something like the joint in the back of a chair, open the joint by twisting the handles, apply glue, then close the joint tightly (Fig. 23).

TYPES OF GLUED JOINTS

Side-grain surfaces. With most species of wood, straight, plain joints between side-grain surface (Fig. 24, A) can be made substantially as strong as the wood itself in shear parallel to the grain, tension across the grain, and cleavage. The tongued-and-grooved joint (Fig. 24, B) and other shaped joints have the theoretical advantage of larger gluing surfaces than the straight joints, but in practice they do not give higher strength with most woods. Furthermore, the theoretical advantage is often lost, wholly or partly, because the shaped joints are more difficult to machine than straight, plain joints so as to obtain a perfect fit of the parts. Because of poor contact, the effective holding area and strength may actually be less on a shaped joint than on a flat surface. The principal advantage of the tongued-and-grooved and

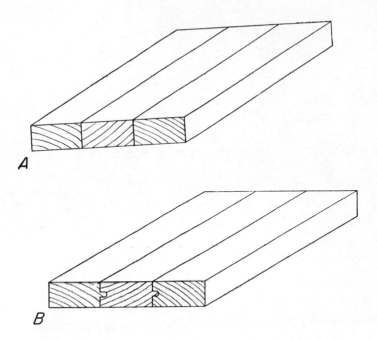

Side-to-side-grain joints: *A*, Plain; *B*, tongued-and-grooved.

Fig. 24.

other shaped joints is that the parts can be more quickly aligned in the clamps or press. A shallow tongue-and-groove is usually as useful in this respect as a deeper cut and is less wasteful of wood.

End-grain surfaces. It is practically impossible to make end-butt joints (Fig. 25, A) sufficiently strong or permanent to meet the requirements of ordinary service. With the most careful gluing possible, not more than about 25 percent of the tensile strength of the wood parallel with the grain can be obtained in butt joints. In order to approximate the tensile strength of various species, a scarf, serrated, or other form of joint that approaches a side-grain surface must be used (Fig. 25). The plain scarf is perhaps the easiest to glue and entails fewer machining difficulties than the many-angle forms.

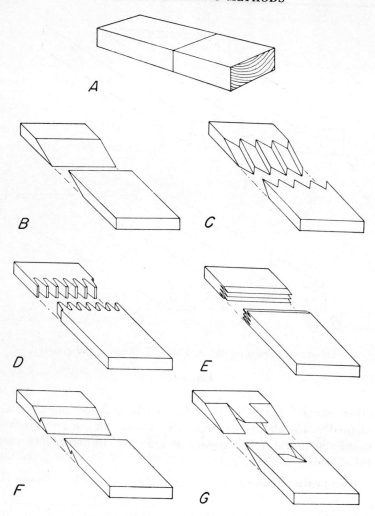

End-to-end-grain joints: *A*, End butt; *B*, plain scarf;
C, serrated scarf; *D*, finger; *E*, Onsrud; *F*, hooked scarf;
G, double-slope scarf.

Fig. 25.

End-to-side-grain surfaces. End-to-side-grain joints (Fig. 26) are also difficult to glue properly and, further, are subjected in service to unusually severe stresses as a result of unequal dimensional changes in the two members of the joint as their moisture content changes. It is therefore necessary to use irregular shapes of joints, dowels, tenons, or other devices to reinforce such a joint in order to bring side grain into contact with side grain or to secure larger gluing surfaces (Fig. 26). All end-to-side-grain joints should be carefully protected from changes in moisture content.

Conditioning glued joints. When boards are glued edge to edge, the wood at the joint absorbs water from the glue and swells. If the glued assembly is surfaced before this excess moisture is dried out or distributed, more wood is removed along the swollen joints than elsewhere. Later, when the joints dry and shrink, permanent depressions are formed that may be very conspicuous in a finished panel.

When pieces of lumber are glued edge to edge or face to face, the glue moisture need not be dried out but simply allowed to distribute itself uniformly throughout the wood. Approximately uniform distribution of glue moisture can usually be obtained by conditioning the stock after gluing for 24 hours at 160° F., 4 days at 120° F., or at least 7 days at room temperature with the relative humidity, in each case, adjusted to prevent significant drying.

In plywood, veneered panels, and other constructions made by gluing together thin layers of wood, it is advisable to condition the panels to average service moisture content. In cold-gluing operations, it is frequently necessary to dry out at least a part of the moisture added in gluing. The drying is most advantageously done under controlled conditions and time schedules.

Drying such glued products to excessively low moisture content materially increases warping, opening of joints, and checking. Following hot-press operations, the panels will often be very dry, and it may be desirable to recondition them under circumstances that will cause them to regain moisture.

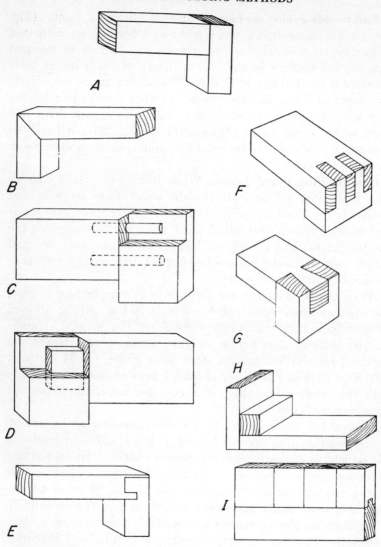

End-to-side-grain joints: *A*, Plain; *B*, miter; *C*, dowel; *D*, mortise
and tenon; *E*, dado tongue and rabbet; *F*, slip or lock corner;
G, dovetail; *H*, blocked; *I*, tongued-and-grooved.

Fig. 26.

HOUSEHOLD GLUING JOBS

A clean-working white glue will add to the ease and pleasure of doing a variety of household jobs. It can be used for joining many kinds of porous materials (wood, paper, felt, canvas, plaster, and leather) to each other.

Leather. Leather and leather substitutes like this fabric-supported plastic material (Fig. 27) are most easily repaired with liquid resin glue Use liquid resin glue or liquid hide glue in covering chests, radios, and other furniture with supported plastics or leather. Where extra flexibility is needed with these materials add 1 part of glycerine to each 20 parts of glue.

Furniture repairs. Small tubes of liquid glue comes in handy for small repairs. Screws holding drawer pulls (Fig. 28) will not work loose if there is good glue in the joints to help them.

Quick-setting. Quick-setting properties make liquid resin glue a good choice for light gluing where clamping is not possible (Fig. 29). The wooden buttons forming the dial of this built-in clock will grip the plywood tightly enough to hold themselves in place after a few seconds when glue is used.

Fig. 27.

Fig. 28.

ADHESIVES FOR SPECIAL JOBS

There are some materials on which wood glues will not do the best possible sticking job, therefore, they call for the use of special adhesives, which in turn, are not suitable for gluing wood to wood.

There are cements available that will grip nonporous surfaces, as well as porous ones. You can use these cements on such objects as tile, glass, mirrors, metal plates, asbestos board, bricks, foil, and plastics. In many cases these cements will give a surprisingly strong bond, but do not expect them to do the kind of job that a good wood glue can do on wood.

Cellulose household cements will do a fair job on *plastics*, but the *solvent cement* recommended for the particular plastic will do better. For problem materials like china, glass, and pottery, a *catalyst-type cement* is best. Figure 30 shows how this cement (it has to be mixed just before using) can make one of the most difficult of all mends—repairing a broken handle.

Fig. 29.

Fig. 31.

Linoleum. Linoleum glued to plywood makes a fine desk top (Fig. 31); using liquid hide glue. For a sink top, use waterproof linoleum paste. Hide and resin glues may also be used with materials of the Formica type if adequately clamped for 24 hours.

Otherwise, use one of the new nonclamping adhesives now available at your dealer, and put on pressure with a rolling pin.

Hardboards. Like most sheet materials, hardboards may be glued like wood. Use liquid hide glue and clamp the joint firmly. Figure 32 shows a second sheet of plywood being used as a clamping aid in veneering hardboard to Douglas fir plywood.

Doors. Cupboard or wardrobe doors can be covered with brightly colored burlap (Fig. 33). Use a liquid hide glue or resin glue. Be sure to spread in a thin even coat of the adhesive.

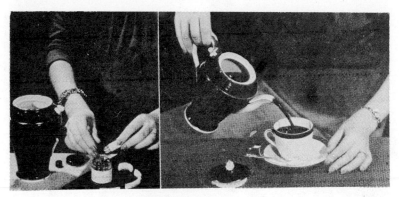

Fig. 30.

Fig. 32.

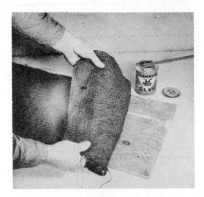

Fig. 33.

GLUES FOR BONDING WOOD TO METAL

Glues capable of producing bonds of high strength and durability between wood and metal are comparatively new in woodworking. Many of them are combinations of a thermosetting resin, often of the phenolic type, and a thermoplastic resin or elastomer, such as a polyvinyl resin or synthetic rubber. The vehicle may be water, alcohol, ethyl acetate, or some other solvent.

Some of these wood-metal adhesives are spread on one or both of the surfaces to be bonded, the solvent is evaporated, and the bonding operation is completed under heat and pressure. With other wood-metal adhesives, the bonding is done in two steps, usually with two different adhesives. In the first step, one adhesive is spread as a primer on the metal and cured at elevated temperatures. In the second step, the primed metal is bonded to the wood with a room-temperature-setting resin adhesive of the woodworking type. The metal surface must be thoroughly cleaned and generally more care is required in removing solvents before bonding than is required in wood-wood bonds.

Adhesives formulated with casein and rubber latex, both natural and synthetic, have been used for several years to bond wood to metal. These formulations have the advantage of curing at room temperature, and the bonds are satisfactory where highest strength and durability are not essential.

CHAPTER 6

Hand Power Tools

PORTABLE ELECTRIC SAWS

Portable electric saws are available in various sizes, ranging from 6½" for the amateur builder, up to 9¼" for the more advanced or professional worker.

Motor. These saws are equipped with a "Universal" type motor and will operate either on D.C. or A.C. current at 25, 40, 50, or 60 cycles, of the specified voltage. Standard voltages are 115 or 220, with 125 or 240 volts available.

Inspect carbon brushes in the motor at regular intervals, and if worn away replace immediately to prevent damage to the motor armature. The manufacturer's service department will be glad to instruct you in brush inspection and furnish the correct brushes.

Current. Be sure to specify the voltage when purchasing a portable electric saw. *Always* check the voltage specifications on the nameplate of your equipment with the voltage of your supply line.

Cable. Three-conductor cable is used on all saws. The third wire is for "grounding." Do not permit the cable to lie in grease or oil which ruins the rubber. Wipe it off occasionally and avoid rough handling. When not in use coil it loosely without sharp bends or kinks and keep it off the floor. Extension cables are described in this chapter.

Grounding. Every electric tool *should be* grounded while in use to protect the operator against shock. Proper grounding is a good habit to develop under all circumstances, but is especially important where dampness is present. The unit is equipped with approved 3-conductor cord and 3-blade grounding type attachment plug cap to be used with the proper grounding type receptacle, in accordance with the National Electrical Code. The green colored conductor in the cord is the grounding wire which is connected to the metal frame of the unit inside the housing and to the longest blade of the attachment plug cap. *Never* connect the green wire to a "live" terminal.

If your unit has a *plug* that looks like the one shown in Fig. 1, A, it will fit directly into the latest type of 3-wire grounding receptacles. The unit is then grounded automatically each time it is plugged in. A special grounding adaptor (Fig. 1, B) is supplied to permit using 2-wire receptacles until the correct receptacle is properly installed. The green grounding wire extending from the side of the adaptor must be connected to a permanent ground, such as a properly grounded outlet box, conduit or water pipe before plugging in the tool.

If the unit has a *plug* like the one shown in Fig. 1, C, no adaptor is furnished and it should be used in the proper standard matching 3-wire grounding receptacle. The unit is then grounded automatically each time it is plugged in.

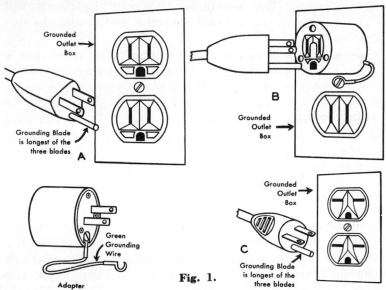

Grounded Outlet Box

Grounding Blade is longest of the three blades   A

B

Grounded Outlet Box

Green Grounding Wire

Adapter

Fig. 1.

Grounded Outlet Box

C

Grounding Blade is longest of the three blades

OPERATION

Connect the grounding-wire first, as described previously in this chapter, and then plug into power supply. Before pressing trigger switch to start motor, rest front of saw "shoe ' or base on the work and line up blade with cutting line. Be sure that blade teeth are not yet in contact with work and that lower blade guard is free. Pull trigger and guide saw through its cut with firm pressure, but without forcing. Undue force actually slows down the cutting and produces a rougher cut.

Keep blades sharp. Dull or incorrectly set teeth may cause the saw to swerve or stall under pressure. If the saw stalls *do not* release trigger switch, but *back* the saw until the blade momentum is regained. Then either shut off motor or start to cut again. This procedure will greatly increase the life of your saw switch.

To make a *pocket cut*, first set the saw shoe at the desired cutting depth. Then rest the toe or heel of shoe against the work (heel, when using 6½″ saw). Carefully draw back the lower blade guard by lifting the provided lever *before starting the motor*. Next, lower the saw until the blade teeth lightly contact the cutting line. This will allow you to release the lower blade guard as contact with the work will keep it in position to open freely as the cut is started. *Now*, start the motor and gradually lower the saw until its shoe rests flat on the work. Advance along the cutting line as in normal sawing. For starting each new cut, proceed as above for your own protection. *Do not* tie back the lower blade guard.

Caution! To insure against accidents *always* disconnect the cable plug before making adjustments or inspection. *Always* disconnect the saw cable when not in active use.

ADJUSTMENTS

Cutting depth adjustments. In cutting any material with steel blades the most efficient depth adjustment is one that permits the tooth depth only of the blade to project below the material (except when using carbide tipped blades, when just ½ of the tooth tip should project below the material). This keeps blade friction at a minimum, removes sawdust from the cut and results in cooler, faster sawing (Fig. 2).

For 6½", 7¼", 8" saws. Correct cutting depth is obtained by adjusting the quick clamping lever on the side at the rear of the saw. Adjustment of the clamping lever on the 6½", 7¼" and 8" saws is made by loosening the set screw, removing and indexing the lever to its proper clamping location, replacing it and tightening the set screw.

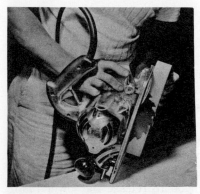

Fig. 2.

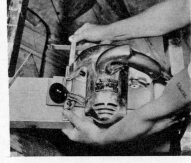

Fig. 3.

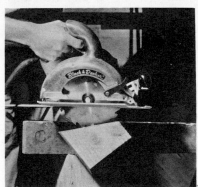

Fig. 4.

Fig. 5.

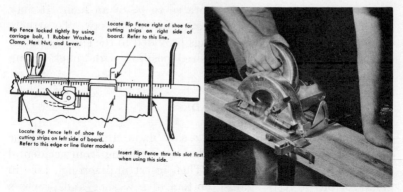

Rip Fence locked tightly by using carriage bolt, 1 Rubber Washer, Clamp, Hex Nut, and Lever.

Locate Rip Fence right of shoe for cutting strips on right side of board. Refer to this line.

Locate Rip Fence left of shoe for cutting strips on left side of board. Refer to this edge or line (later models)

Insert Rip Fence thru shoe slot first when using this side.

Fig. 6.   **Fig. 7.**

For 8¼″, 9¼″ saws. Correct cutting depth for these saws is obtained by adjusting either or both of the built-in front and rear cutting depth adjustments. By using both adjustments, the handle remains in the most comfortable cutting position. *Always* be sure to retighten wing nuts securely after making adjustments.

Bevel Angle Adjustments. The 6½″, 7¼″, 8″, 8¼″ and 9¼″ saws have an adjustable shoe which permits bevel cutting at any angle between 45° and 90°. The quadrant on the front of these saws is calibrated for accurate adjustment. Loosen the wing nut and tilt the shoe to angle desired. Retighten wing nut securely. See Figs. 3 and 4.

ACCESSORIES

Protractor. This is a surprisingly simple and practical device that is calibrated in degrees and can be set to cut any angle by moving the holding arm to correct degree. Use the bevel adjustment on the saw in conjunction with the protractor for compound mitres. To operate, the saw shoe (either side) is lined up with the protractor's straightedge and is advanced along this edge (Fig. 5).

A protractor is also useful for laying out any carpentry work involving angles.

Rip fence. The rip fence saves time in rip sawing (Fig. 6), eliminating the need to scribe guide lines. It greatly improves ripping accuracy. Fence is calibrated to ⅛ of an inch. It may be used on either right or left hand side of the saw. To attach, slide fence through proper openings provided in the shoe as shown in Fig. 7. Clamp firmly at desired position with quick acting lever.

BLADES

Changing blades. To change a saw blade, first disconnect the cable plug to prevent injury or damage resulting from accidental pressure on the trigger switch. Then insert nail through hole in blade so that it rests against bottom of saw shoe and prevents blade from turning. With a wrench, turn holding screw counterclockwise to loosen and remove screw and washer. Retract lower guard and lift off blade. Remove inner clamp washer and clean both faces of each clamp washer, blade, and blade screw threads —this prevents uneven seating of the blade. Replace inner clamp washer, new blade—trade-mark side out (with teeth pointing toward front of saw), outer clamp washer, and blade holding screw and tighten holding screw clockwise with wrench until secure.

Combination blades. This is the latest type, precision engineered, fast-cutting blade for general service ripping and crosscutting (Fig. 8, A). Each blade carries the correct number of teeth to cut chips rather than scrape sawdust. Blade teeth receive less wear and stay sharp longer, and give definitely smoother cuts. Cutting efficiency has been increased by using redesigned sturdier teeth, reduces any tendency of the blade to "flutter" or vibrate.

Extensive tests have shown that a greater number of teeth reduces cutting efficiency, because of an increased scraping action. On the other hand, a lesser number increases the toothload to a point where the cutting edges rapidly become dull and burnt.

Crosscut blades. Crosscut blades were designed specifically for fast, smooth crosscutting (Fig. 8, B). They make a smoother cut than the combination blades.

Planer blades. This blade makes very smooth cuts, both rip and crosscut (Fig. 8, C). It is ideal for interior wood working, and is hollow-ground to produce the finest possible saw-cut finish.

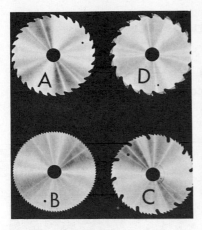

Fig. 8.

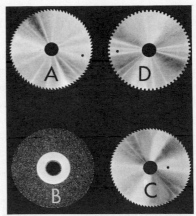

Fig. 9.

Carbide-tipped blades. The carbide-tipped blade is the keenest and most durable blade yet developed for cutting building materials (Fig. 8, D). This blade stays sharp thirty times longer than normal steel blade when cutting lumber. The carbide tips are brazed into a special alloy steel blade. It has been established that the diamond-like hardness of these tips will retain their edges up to 50 times longer than steel.

Flooring blades. Flooring blades should be used on jobs where occasional nails may be encountered (Fig. 9, A). They are especially useful in cutting through flooring, sawing reclaimed lumber and in opening boxes and crates.

Abrasive discs. These blades are all of the top-quality resinoid-bonded, abrasive cut-off type (Fig. 9, B). They are used for cutting and slotting in ceramics, slate, marble, tile, transite, etc. Also for cutting thin gauge, non-ferrous metals.

Non-ferrous metal-cutting blades. These blades have teeth shaped and set for cutting soft, non-ferrous metals, including lead (Fig. 9, C).

Friction blades. Friction blades are ideal for cutting corrugated galvanized sheets. They cut faster, with less dirt, than abrasive discs. Blade is taper-ground for clearance (Fig. 9, D).

COMBINATION ELECTRIC SCREW-DRILL

A completely new combination tool, the electric screw-drill, is an efficient tool for craftsmen, builders, and hobbyists. It is equipped with a positive-clutch electric screw-driving mechanism. The screw-drill has a locking collar that permits operator to quickly convert to direct drive for general-purpose drilling. The unit is amply powered by a "Universal" motor for 115 volts, A.C. or D.C., and includes a 3-jaw geared chuck and key, and screw-driving bit and finder assembly.

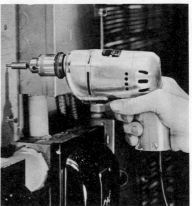

Fig. 10.   Fig. 11.

Used as a drill, the unit is capable of drilling holes up to ⅜" diameter in steel. It can also be used to drive hole saws, masonry bits and wood augers (Fig. 10).

In its screw-driving position, the screw-drill drives wood screws up to #10 x 1½" size, or self-tapping metal screws up to size #12 (Fig. 11).

OPERATION

Chuck. When operating, first, always bottom the bit in the chuck. This permits the chuck jaws to grip the shank fully and prevents cocking the jaws. Second, use *all three holes* in the chuck body to tighten as much as possible. Only one hole is needed to release the bit. Third, use *only* a chuck key to tighten or loosen the chuck jaws. If you lose the chuck key, obtain a new one at once.

To obtain maximum life from the jaw assembly, lock your chuck firmly with the key to prevent drill slippage, and when the chuck is not in use, leave it with the jaws open.

Removing the chuck. To remove the chuck, place the chuck key in the chuck and strike key a sharp blow using a hammer or other object in the same direction that tool normally runs. This will loosen the chuck so that it can be easily unscrewed by hand. *Disconnect* tool before making any changes or adjustments.

Switch. Grasp the tool firmly before pressing trigger switch "ON". The tool will remain "ON" as long as pressure is maintained on the trigger. Releasing trigger automatically turns the motor "OFF".

To lock the switch "ON" pull trigger and hold it "ON"; press in locking button and hold it in; then release trigger. Motor will now stay "ON" until trigger is again squeezed and released— the trigger will snap out and the motor will turn "OFF". Practice this a few times.

Drilling. To adjust the unit for drilling, viewing the unit from the chuck end, rotate the adjustment collar counterclockwise until the word "drill" is at the top of the unit. If the collar stops before reaching this point, turn the chuck slightly; the adjustment collar can then be rotated to the proper position (Fig. 12).

For screw-driving rotate the adjustment collar in a clockwise direction until the word "screw" is at the top of the unit. This will disengage the clutch teeth which will automatically be engaged when pressure is applied in driving screws.

The two Allen set screws located in the front part of the gear case are properly adjusted by the factory and should not be readjusted unless the adjusting collar is loose.

Mark exact center of hole with a center punch or nail to guide the drill bit. Clamp or anchor the work securely to insure accuracy and prevent damage or injury. Thin metal should be backed up with a wooden block to prevent bending or distortion

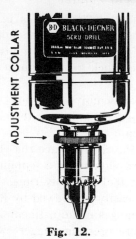

ADJUSTMENT COLLAR →

Fig. 12.　　　　　　　　**Fig. 13.**

of the work. Keep bits sharp and use a lubricant when drilling ferrous metals other than cast iron. Relieve pressure on the tool when bit is about to break through to avoid "stalling" the motor. Be sure that the chuck jaws are tightened securely and do not constantly overload the tool. In general, high speed and light feed are recommended.

When drilling wood, particularly deep holes, partially remove the bit from the hole several times while in motion. This will clear the chips, speed up drilling and prevent overheating (Fig. 13).

In drilling brick, cement, cinder block or similar materials, use carbide tipped masonry drill bits. Ordinary steel bits would be dulled rapidly in this type of work.

Driving screws. Adjust the collar to the screw driving position, then insert the correct screw driving bit into the chuck. (See Fig. 11). Make sure that the chuck jaw rests squarely on the "flats" of the bit. Tighten chuck jaws securely so that there is no chance of slippage. Turn on the unit and the chuck and bit will idle until the bit is engaged in the screw head and pressure is applied. The unit should be grasped firmly with both hands and a steady forward pressure applied—the screw will be driven down tight. At this point the clutch comes into operation and will ratchet or slip until the unit is removed from the screw.

It is suggested that you practice by driving a few screws into a scrap piece of lumber until you get the "feel" of this procedure (Fig. 11).

MAINTENANCE

Brushes. Inspect carbon brushes frequently and replace them when badly worn. Cartridge-type brush holders are used to make this operation easy for you. Merely remove the end cover on the switch handle by taking out screws which hold cover in place. Then remove brush caps with a screwdriver and take out the brush and spring assemblies. Springs should have enough tension to hold the brush firmly against the commutator. Be sure to replace badly worn brush assemblies.

Always keep brushes clean and sliding freely in their guides. After several brush replacements, the commutator should be inspected for excess wear. If a groove has been cut by the brushes, the tool should be sent to the manufacturer for repair.

Cable. The cable is the "life line" of your tool, therefore keep it clean by wiping it off occasionally. Be sure to keep it out of oils and greases which ruin the rubber. Coil it neatly when not in use and avoid dragging it across sharp surfaces or using it as a handle to lift the tool.

When using the tool at a considerable distance from power source, an extension cable of adequate size must be used to prevent loss of power. Use the table below for 115 volt current.

Extension Cable Length in Feet	*Gauge of Cable Wire Required*
25, 50, 75, 100, 200	18, 18, 18, 18, 16

Lubrication. The gears should be re-lubricated regularly in from sixty days to six months, depending on use. Remove gear housing, flush out all old grease with kerosene and, with gears in place, refill the housing only half full. The commutator and armature bearing may be lubricated by one or two drops of oil on the armature shaft through the hole provided in the handle cover.

ELECTRIC HAND FINISHING SANDER

This new dustless finishing sander for use in the home and shop has been designed for simple, quick attachment to any vacuum cleaner, and the unit gives the cleanest sanding jobs possible. Dust is instantly removed from the work surface to provide more healthful working conditions and keeps the abrasive paper sharp for more efficient sanding.

It operates on an orbital-action principle, powered by a special sander motor to deliver 4300 orbits per minute, producing a satin-smooth finish upon any surface. Speed and power of the unit permit sanding *with, against,* or *across* the grain of wood surfaces without danger of swirl marks or scratches. Light, compact, and easy to handle, this sander permits even a novice to get professional results effortlessly, on all sanding or refinishing jobs (Fig. 14).

Fig. 14.

Abrasive Paper. "Electro coated," aluminum oxide abrasive paper is the best to use with your finishing sander; 150 or 4/0 fine grit, open grain paper will give you the smoothest finish; and 60 or 1/2/0 coarse grit, open grain will give you the greatest material removal consistent with the proper wood finishing practice.

Do not use ordinary sand paper as its coating qualities are inferior. However, in certain metal sanding applications, emory cloth of various grits will prove to be more durable.

Attaching abrasive paper. The dustless finishing sander is supplied with a dust collecting skirt, snap-in hose connector, hose and coupling. To attach the abrasive paper to this unit the dust collecting skirt should be removed. Two studs on either side of the skirt clamp around the bottom of the sander housing. With thumb pressure on both sides of skirt and two index fingers on inner edge of skirt, pull out and up. This will release studs and allow skirt to be removed (Fig. 15, A). The sandpaper tightening sprockets are now completely exposed.

After selecting the correct grade of grit apply the abrasive paper between the sprocket and the platen and tighten the sprocket by using the T-shaped key provided, or a screwdriver. (Key may be attached to cable, using the slot provided in the key.) This sprocket should be tightened until the abrasive paper is about ¼″ underneath the sprocket (Fig. 15, B).

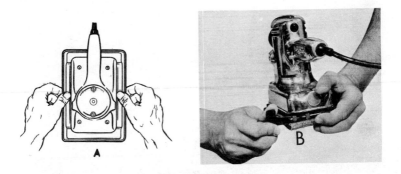

Fig. 15.

Fasten the other edge of the abrasive paper in the same manner.

You will find this new type clamping mechanism holds the abrasive paper taut. If it should become loose during operation, tighten the sprockets immediately. This will preserve the life of your abrasive paper.

ASSEMBLY

The finishing sander, after the abrasive paper has been mounted in place, can be converted to a dustless unit by assembling the dustless equipment as follows:

Remove round plug (Fig 16, A) in the rear of the finishing sander by prying under the edge with a screwdriver or knife. Snap on the dust collecting skirts so that the two studs (Fig. 16, I) fit firmly over the lower edge of the sander housing. Insert the metal coupling (Fig. 16, B) with the detent pin inserted in the rear end of the sander. It may be necessary to manually depress the detent pin. Now attach the hose to the coupling using the smaller hose end (Fig 16, C). To the other end of the hose attach a vacuum cleaner (any type). In connecting the hose to the vacuum cleaner use either the adapter supplied, or hose end itself (which may be attached over or into the inlet). See Fig. 16, depending upon the type of vacuum cleaner connection.

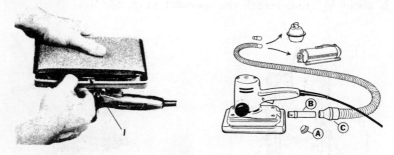

Fig. 16.

OPERATION

Before using the finishing sander, examine the trigger switch. Squeezing this trigger turns the tool "ON"; releasing it turns the tool "OFF". However, on most sanding applications it is more convenient to lock the switch "ON", with the locking pin, which projects from the side of the switch handle, just above the trigger. To do this, first squeeze the trigger and hold it "ON", and press in the locking pin. Then release the trigger. The switch will remain "ON". To turn the motor "OFF", merely pull the trigger and release it. The black molded knob may be screwed into any of three positions to suit the operator. The knob can be threaded into either side or in front of the motor housing.

After turning on the vacuum cleaner, which is attached to your finishing sander, grasp both control handles of the sander firmly, and use the tool freely without forced effort or unnecessary downward pressure. Excessive pressure will slow cutting action and reduce abrasive life. The weight of the tool itself, in most cases, will prove to be sufficient (Fig. 17).

It is not necessary to sand only with the grain of the wood. Move the sander in any direction over the work area to effect rapid and convenient coverage. Sand only long enough to obtain a smooth surface, as the cutting action of the tool is rapid and too much material may be removed with prolonged sanding (Fig. 18).

Fig. 17.   **Fig. 18.**

For best results sand progressively with coarse paper first; then, medium; then, fine paper. To obtain what might be called a "superfinish", wet the surface with a sponge or rag and let it dry. The grain of the wood will rise slightly and the surface feel rough. Now, re-sand with 150 or 4/0 grit paper for extra-smooth results.

Of course, the more effective your vacuum cleaner, the more dust removal; therefore, the bag of the vacuum cleaner should be emptied periodically to assure maximum suction.

Note: To remove metal coupling (Fig. 16), rotate coupling so that arrow is on top and then remove.

MAINTENANCE

Motors. This finishing sander is equipped with a "Universal" motor which can be used, at the voltage specified on the nameplate, with either alternating current at 25, 40, 50 or 60 cycles, or with direct current. Voltage should not vary more than 5 per cent, over or under the voltage shown on the nameplate, or serious overheating and loss of power can result. All motors are tested by the manufacturer, and if the tool fails to operate, proceed as follows: (1) Check supply line for blown fuses; (2) see that plug and receptacle are making good contact; and (3) inspect carbon brushes and replace them if they are worn away.

Brushes. Inspect carbon brushes frequently and replace when badly worn. Cartridge-type brush holders are used to make this operation easy. After disconnecting tool, merely remove both brush caps with a screwdriver and take out the brush and spring assemblies. Springs should have enough tension to hold the brush firmly against the commutator. Be sure to replace badly worn brush assemblies.

Be sure to keep brushes clean and sliding freely in their guides. After several brush replacements, the commutator should be inspected for excess wear. If a groove has been cut by the brushes, the tool should be sent to the manufacturer for repair.

Cable. Be sure to keep the cable clean by wiping it off occasionally as it is the "life line" of your tool. Keep it out of oils and greases which ruin the rubber. Coil it neatly when not in use and avoid dragging it across sharp surfaces or using it as a handle to lift the tool.

When using the tool at a considerable distance from power source, an extension cable of adequate size must be used to prevent loss of power. Use the table below for 115 volt current.

Extension Cable Length in Feet	*Gauge of Cable Wire Required*
25, 50, 75, 100, 200	18, 18, 17, 14, 12

Lubrication. The gears should be re-lubricated regularly from sixty days to six months, depending on use. Remove gear housing, flush out all old grease with kerosene and, with gears in place, refill the housing only half full. The commutator and armature bearing may be lubricated by one or two drops of oil on the armature shaft through the hole provided in the top of the tool.

ELECTRIC HAND POWER PLANE

This hand power plane is designed for a comfortable operating balance. Handles and thumb-rest are so placed as to provide an accurate planing "feel" and afford the correct "inward and downward" pressure for each planing operation.

Motors. The power plane shown in Fig. 19 is equipped with a "Universal" motor which can be used, at the voltage specified on the nameplate, with either alternating current at 25, 40, 50 or 60 cycles, or with direct current. Voltage should not vary more than 10 per cent, over or under, the voltage shown on the nameplate or serious overheating and loss of power can result. All motors are tested by the manufacturer, and if the tool fails to operate take the following action: (1) Check your supply line for blown fuses; (2) see that the plug and receptacle are making good contact; and (3) inspect carbon brushes and replace them if they are worn away.

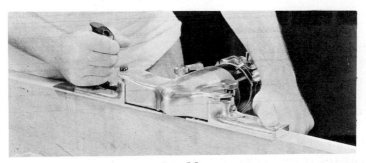

Fig. 19.

Brushes. Inspect carbon brushes frequently and replace them when badly worn. Cartridge-type brush holders are used to make this operation easy for you. Merely remove both brush caps with a screwdriver and take out the brush and spring assemblies. Springs should have enough tension to hold the brush firmly against the commutator. Be sure to replace badly worn brush assemblies.

Keep brushes clean and sliding freely in their guides. After several brush replacements, the commutator should be inspected for excess wear. If a groove has been cut by the brushes, the tool should be sent to the manufacturer for repair.

Cable. When using a power plane at a considerable distance from power source, an extension cable of adequate size must be used to prevent loss of power. Use the table below for 115 volt current.

Extension Cable Length in Feet   *Gauge of Cable Wire Required*
25, 50, 75, 100, 200   18, 16, 16, 12, 10

Grounding. As previously described.

Adjustments. Place a straightedge or scale along the rear shoe of the plane and with a screwdriver, turn adjusting screw (Fig. 20), until the highest cutting edge of the cutter touches the scale of straightedge. This adjustment must be accurate, or poor results would be obtained and, when once adjusted properly, the adjustment should not be changed unless the cutter is replaced or resharpened.

To adjust the depth of cut, place a straightedge or a piece of wood along the rear shoe of the plane and turn the knurled knob (Fig. 21) for the depth of cut desired. This is determined by the space between the front shoe and the straightedge or piece of wood (Fig. 21). The depth of cut is adjustable from zero to $\frac{3}{32}''$. A depth of cut of $\frac{1}{32}''$ is recommended.

The adjustments referred to above are necessary each time a cutter is replaced or sharpened.

To adjust the vertical guide at right angles to the shoe of the plane, slightly loosen wing nuts (Fig. 22, A) and using a square, move the vertical guide so that it is at 90° to the shoe.

The vertical guide is adjustable outward to a 120° obtuse angle and inward to a 45° angle for bevel planing. To adjust the vertical guide for bevel planing, loosen wing nuts (Fig. 22, A) and adjust it to the degree of bevel required. The quadrants at the wing nuts are graduated, however, for very accurate work, a protractor or similar device should be used when adjusting the vertical guide,

Fig. 20.

Fig. 21.

Fig. 22.

after which wing nuts (Fig. 22, A) should be tightened securely.

Lock screws (Fig. 22, B) are used to apply tension on both the front and rear shoes of the plane. These screws are properly tensioned at the factory, but after a long period of use it may be necessary to slightly tighten them with a screwdriver.

OPERATION

When using the power plane, grasp both handles firmly and place the thumb of the left hand on the recess of the top of the shoe (Fig. 19). Place the plane on the board using downward pressure with the left hand until the cutter engages, after which downward pressure is applied by both hands, and the vertical guide should be engaged against the side of the board using side pressure. At the completion of the cut, pressure is relieved from the left hand and exerted to the right hand at the rear of the tool, and the forward feed should be reduced so as to minimize chipping at the end of the cut.

The forward movement of the plane in operation depends upon the type of wood being planed. Softwood such as pine planes very rapidly; however, when planing hardwood and particularly plywood, the forward feed of the plane should be slowed down so that the cutter will cut freely.

If the plane is moved forward too slowly the cutter will have a tendency to burn certain kinds of lumber, and if moved too fast, the speed of the motor would be reduced, causing it to be overloaded and result in premature wear on the cutter. The fact that wood has different densities and occasional knots will be encountered, it is impossible to predetermine the forward movement of the plane. The user will soon learn by the sound of the motor when the forward movement of the plane is correct.

It is suggested that a piece of scrap lumber be used to familiarize the user with the tool. There are instances where the wood being planed would have high spots, and these spots should be removed before making a complete cut the length of the board. This is best done by drawing an accurate line on the side of the board, so that the high spots can be easily located.

To get the most out of your plane keep it clean, blow dust and chips from it when necessary, and always keep both the vertical guide and shoes free of resin or any other foreign matter so that smooth surfaces will always be applied to the board being planed. For the best results keep the cutter sharp at all times. When not in use, store the plane in a dry place. A thin coat of oil or paste wax will retard rust.

Safety procedures. Always disconnect the plane from the power supply when making any adjustments. Be sure to disconnect the plane from the power supply when not in use. Handle sharp cutters carefully to avoid injury.

Lubrication. The power plane is completely lubricated at the factory. All ball bearings are of the closed-type and lubricant lasts the life of the bearings.

ELECTRIC HEAVY DUTY HAND ROUTER

The hand operated router shown in Fig. 23 is the latest development in electric woodworking tools. It is efficiently designed for speed and accuracy in performing the finest joinery, and most beautiful cabinet work such as beading, grooving, routing, fluting, cove-cutting, dovetailing, dadoing, rabbeting, making joints, and similar operations. Its use enables the home woodworker to rapidly accomplish inlay work, decorative edges, and many types of bas-relief carving and wood-finishing. (See Parts shown in Fig. 23)

This router is powered by a special router motor, and operates on a direct-drive principle, no gears are necessary, and the motor speeds up to 21,000 r.p.m. Feeding properly into the work it leaves an extremely smooth finish that requires little or no sanding.

GENERAL OPERATING PROCEDURES

The router consists of two major parts—the *motor* and the *base* (Fig. 24). The motor housing is designed in such a way that it forms a firm support for the router in an inverted position. This extra convenience feature leaves both of the operator's hands free to insert or remove bits and cutters. The base is equipped with a smooth surface sub-base, held in place by three countersunk screws. This sub-base protects the working surface from mars or scratches while doing fine cabinet work. It may be

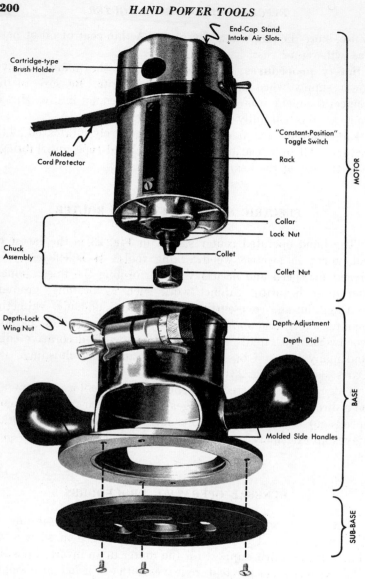

Cartridge-type
Brush Holder

Molded
Cord Protector

Chuck
Assembly

End-Cap Stand.
Intake Air Slots.

"Constant-Position"
Toggle Switch

Rack

Collar

Lock Nut

Collet

Collet Nut

Depth-Lock
Wing Nut

Depth-Adjustment

Depth Dial

Molded Side Handles

MOTOR

BASE

SUB-BASE

Fig. 23.

easily removed to facilitate use of large bits and cutters, or to add depth-of-cut when a longer bit or arbor is not available.

ASSEMBLY

Figure 25 shows the assembled motor and base. To *assemble*, loosen the wing nut (A) on the base, and insert the motor into the base until the rack and pinion (B) which regulates the depth-of-cut, engages. Tighten wing nut and set router up in inverted position. The unit is now ready for inserting a bit or an arbor to hold cutters.

Fig. 24.   Fig. 25.

MAINTENANCE AND CARE

Motor and current. The router is powered by a "Universal" router motor. It operates at nameplate voltage on alternating current (25 to 60 cycles), or on direct current. Voltage variation of more than ten per cent will cause loss of power and overheating. Be sure to check the voltage specifications on the nameplate of your equipment with the voltage of your supply line. Inspect the carbon brushes in the motor at regular intervals, and if worn away replace them immediately to prevent damage to the motor armature as instructed by the manufacturer.

Cable. Every router is equipped with a *three-conductor cable.* The third wire is for "grounding." (See Grounding in section on Portable Electric Saws, Chap. 6.) *Do not* permit cable to lie in grease or oil which ruins the rubber. Wipe it off occasionally and avoid rough handling. When not in use coil the cable loosely without sharp bends or kinks, and keep it off the floor.

If an extension cable is necessary to reach a power outlet, be sure that the cable is made of a wire size large enough to carry current to the router without too great a drop in voltage. A long extension cable of inadequate size will cause a voltage drop, loss of power and damage to the motor through overheating. When using an extension make sure that it is a 3-conductor cable. Connect the third wire of the cable on the tool to the third wire of the extension. Then ground the other end of the extension with the third wire, as described under Grounding. If more than one extension cable is used, connect the various third wires, grounding the one nearest the electrical receptacle.

Use the following table for 115 volt current.

Extension Cable Length In Feet	*Gauge of Cable Wire Required*
25, 50, 75, 100, 200	18, 16, 14, 12, 10

OPERATION SAFETY

Make sure that the tool is *properly grounded* before operating. To operate, grasp the tool firmly, not gingerly in your hand. *Do not* turn the power "ON" until you are in working position. Then place the tool in working position and press the toggle switch.

Always pull the plug before you change bits or cutters.

Every tool is thoroughly tested before leaving the factory and should be in perfect operating condition when it reaches the user. If, at any time, your unit fails to operate, it will save you time and expense to check the following possible causes of failure:

1. Is your supply line dead? Check for blown fuses.
2. Are the receptacle and plug making good contact? Check for bent prongs and loose wires.
3. Are both brushes touching commutator? Check for good

brush contact. Carbon brushes should be inspected at regular intervals and if worn away should be replaced immediately to avoid motor damage.

4. Check voltage specifications on the nameplate with the voltage of your supply line. See Motor and Current previously described in this chapter.

Lubrication. All *routers* are completely lubricated at the factory and are ready for use. All *ball bearings* are of the closed type and are grease sealed with sufficient lubricant packed in them to last the life of the bearing.

ATTACHING BITS AND CUTTERS

Figure 26 illustrates how a straight bit is inserted into the collet-type chuck. The shank of the bit or cutter arbor should be inserted to a depth of at least ½″. *Make sure electric current is disconnected when performing this operation.*

Fig. 26.   **Fig. 27.**

After the bit is inserted, the two open-end wrenches are employed to tighten the chuck, as shown in Fig. 27. One of the two wrenches is fitted to the upper, or collet nut, and the other is attached to the collar at the bottom. Hold the lower wrench stationary and turn the upper wrench from right to left to tighten bit or arbor in chuck securely. Reverse the procedure to loosen and to remove the bit when necessary.

Located between the collet nut and the collar is a *lock nut,* which neither wrench will fit, and which is tightened before the unit leaves the factory. This lock nut needs no further attention from the operator.

REGULATING CUTTING DEPTH

Place the router on flat surface, on its base, loosen wing nut (A), and turn knurled knob (C) until the bit very lightly touches the surface on which it is resting (Fig. 28). Tighten the wing nut and set router up on end.

With router inverted, the built-in micrometer-type depth adjustment (D) is set on the zero calibration. Each graduation on the depth dial represents $\frac{1}{64}$ of an inch. To set bit to desired cutting depth, loosen wing nut, turn outer knob (C), reading depth on dial (D); then tighten the wing nut. The graduated scale provides direct depth-reading in 64ths of an inch, without measuring, up to 1 inch.

OPERATING THE ROUTER

There are a number of fixtures and attachments used to control and guide the router—the straight and circular guide, slot and circle cutting attachment, template guides, dovetail joint fixture, and the hinge mortising template. These, as well as other fixtures such as a home-made T-square are illustrated and described in this chapter.

In using the router, the base should be held firmly and flat on the surface, and the tool should be moved from left to right in straight cutting at a rate sufficient to maintain a high motor speed. In irregular or circular cutting move the router counter-clockwise. Feeding the router too slowly may cause the bit or cutter to burn the wood, whereas excessive speed in feeding will cause undue wear on the bits and cutters and at the same time result in an inferior cut.

Various wood densities make it impossible to set down just how fast this feeding should be done. After short practice in using the router, you will soon acquire the *feel* of the tool for the correct feeding speed.

In some instances, such as extremely hard wood, it is necessary to make several passes at varying depths until the desired depth-of-cut is obtained.

Bits and cutters should be kept sharp at all times.

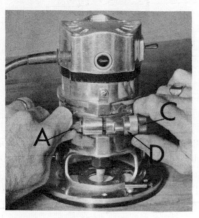

Fig. 28.

Free-hand routing. Although the router is more widely used with some form of guiding device for greater cutting accuracy, there are many applications to which it is put *free-hand*, that is, routing that is guided only by the operator's skill. Raised letter work. A variation of this is routing the letters themselves out of a flat surface. Surface stock removal may be accomplished free-hand, carefully following a pencilled layout: Skilled wood carvers often use a router to gouge out background and prepare work for final carving. The results and beauty of work that can be done in this fashion are limited only by the artistic ability and skill of the operator.

T-square guide. A simple device for guiding the router when making straight cuts on flat surfaces is the home-made T-square (Fig. 29). This T-square can be easily made out of scrap lumber, but make sure its edges are perfectly smooth and straight. It is

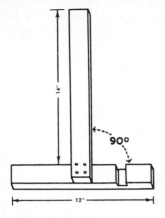

Fig. 29.   **Fig. 30.**

placed on the surface being routed and held in position by means
of a clamp, as shown in Fig. 30. The base of the router is guided
firmly along the edge of the T-square to make a straight cut.
Measurements shown in the illustration are ideal for most applications with the router. They may, however, be altered to suit
your specific needs. Other home-made guiding devices are discussed later in this chapter.

STRAIGHT AND CIRCULAR GUIDE

The straight and circular guide (Fig. 31) is the most popular
device used with the router. It enables the operator to make
straight, curved, or angular cuts with ease and accuracy.

Attaching and adjusting. Figure 32 shows how the straight
and circular guide is attached with four screws through the metal
brackets, and firmly tightened to the router base. The two wing
nuts (A) are loosened and the guide is adjusted along the length
of the round metal rods and positioned in relation to the bit or
cutter where the cut is to be made, after which wing nuts (A)
are tightened.

The guide has a built-in vernier-type adjustment device that
is used to adjust the guide accurately. In making fine adjustments, tighten the wing nut (B), loosen two wing nuts (A), and

turn the knurled knob (C) to either right or left until the guide is accurately positioned, then tighten wing nuts (A) securely. Figure 33 shows operating position.

There are times when the length of the guide is insufficient to give the router ample support. When such is the case, a piece of wood may be attached to the front end of the guide using two wood screws and a piece of smooth lumber about 8″ or 10″ long and 2″ to 3″ wide (Fig. 34). Two holes are provided in the straight edge for this purpose.

Fig. 31.

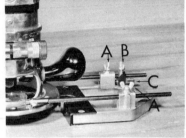

Fig. 32.

Fig. 33.

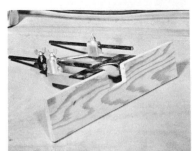

Fig. 34.

Straight cuts. When routing along the edge of straight pieces, the straight edge (Fig. 31) is attached to the guide and held against the straight edge of the work as the router is fed along cutting line as shown in Fig. 33.

Curved and angular cuts. Routing is accurately accomplished along curved or angular edges by removing the straight edge, (AA), from the straight and circular guide. This leaves two points of contact to guide the router along irregularly shaped edges. Figure 35 illustrates this operating position, using the router to put a decorative edge around circular table top.

Fig. 35.

Fig. 36.

Fig. 37.

Fig. 38.

Inside cuts. When cutting inside edges such as rabbeting for screens, the straight and circular guide is attached in the reverse position as illustrated in Fig. 36.

Measuring feature. For added accuracy, the straight and circular guide features a slotted recess along the bottom which permits the insertion of a rule or scale for use in adjusting the edge of the guide in relation to the cutting edge of the bit. Figure 37 shows how this measurement is made, assuring precision results on any routing project.

SLOT AND CIRCLE CUTTING ATTACHMENT

The slot and circle cutting attachment is used with the router for cutting evenly spaced slots and grooves, discs, circular holes and concentric designs. In circle cutting, or slot cutting, the attachment can be adjusted for diameters or lengths from 1″ to 22″ (Fig. 38).

Figure 39 shows the router in operating position when cutting a medium sized circle. Move the router always in a counterclockwise direction. Figure 40 illustrates the completed operation. *Note* that a ¼″ hole was first drilled in the center of the circle to hold the attachment guide pin. A straight bit of sufficient depth to pass through the wood was used—with a scrap piece of lumber being placed underneath the work to prevent cutting into the workbench.

Fig. 39.   **Fig. 40.**

Interesting circular designs can be made using this attachment such as the one shown in Fig. 41. *Note* that two different bits were used to obtain an artistic result. *Note* how a circular opening can be improved by routing an attractive molding as shown in Fig. 42.

With the circle cutting pin removed and a guide bar assembled in its place, this attachment serves as a guide for cutting slots and grooves. In the example shown in Fig. 43, the first slot was made by using the end of the lumber as a guide, and the second slot was cut in the same manner as illustrated. This operation can be repeated, or the distance between slots varied by adjusting the two wing nuts on the attachment.

IT IS EASY TO MAKE CUTS AND JOINTS

MAKING DADO CUTS

Dado cuts, frequently used in the construction of shelving, bookcases, furniture, etc., can readily be made with a router and the correct-size straight bit.

Figure 44 illustrates three types of dado cuts commonly used —the *through dado* (A), the *half-blind dado* (B), and the *blind dado* (C).

When making a *through dado*, it is well to use a piece of scrap lumber on each edge of the board so as to prevent chipout. A *half-blind dado* is accomplished by stopping the machine before it reaches the entire width of the board. *Blind dado* cuts are made by first positioning the router at a given point, then lowering it into the lumber slowly and feeding it forward the required distance.

When making dado cuts, select a bit, if possible, that will be the diameter of the thickness of the board that is to be used in the groove. A strip of wood should be clamped to the board receiving the dado cut to serve as a guide on which the base of the router is supported.

Guiding the router on dado cuts is best accomplished with the straight and circular guide, as previously discussed. The T-square may also be used as shown in Fig. 30.

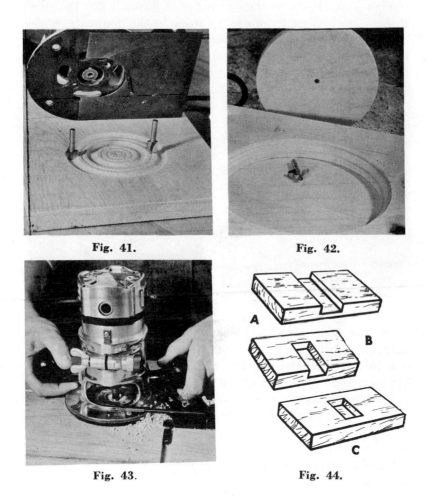

Fig. 41.   Fig. 42.

Fig. 43.   Fig. 44.

THE DOVETAIL DADO

One of the strongest joints possible in fine cabinet work is the *dovetail dado*. It prevents twisting or warping, and is unsurpassed where tightness of finished joint is an important factor, such as in making doors and frameworks of various types. The router, fitted with a dovetail bit is capable of turning out dovetail dadoes with speed and accuracy.

Figure 45 illustrates the routing of a dovetail groove. *Note* that an improvised fixture is clamped to the work for use in controlling the movement of the router. The groove shown is a *half-blind* groove, since it will not extend completely across the board.

Fig. 45.   **Fig. 46.**

After the groove is cut, the same bit is used to rout out the male section. *Note* in Fig. 46 that the piece being routed is held in a fixture, with the straight and circular guide being used, first along one edge, and then along the other edge of the fixture to control the router. When one side is finished, the router is reversed and the opposite side is cut.

The width of the dovetail dado need not be confined to the size of the bit, since several adjacent cuts may be made to provide any desired width-of-joint. This also applies when cutting the male section.

MAKING RABBET CUTS

Rabbet cuts are used for making rabbeted drawer fronts, cabinet doors, and many other types of joints. Figure 47 shows how this operation is performed, using a rabbeting bit.

In Fig. 48, a straight bit is used, which should be placed in the chuck and adjusted to the required depth of cut. The router may be controlled by means of the straight and circular guide, which is adjusted to the desired width of the rabbet cut. It is best to select a bit that is larger in diameter than the width of the finished cut so that a less critical adjustment is necessary in the guide. A simple home-made fixture (Fig. 49) can be used to hold small pieces in routing position as shown in Fig. 48.

When making rabbet cuts, it is usually better to make them across the end grain of the lumber first, and then along the grain. This procedure tends to eliminate chipping at the edges.

Fig. 47.

Fig. 48.

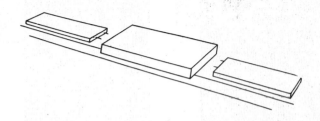
Fig. 49.

TONGUE-AND-GROOVE JOINTS

Tongue-and-groove joints enable two or more boards to be firmly and uniformly joined together to provide a large, flat surface, such as a table or dresser top. They are frequently used in fine cabinet work and interior designing. For maximum accuracy and strength, boards being joined by the tongue-and-groove method should first be made smooth and true.

All grooves are cut first. On the edge of one board, the location and the width of the groove should be outlined with a sharp pencil or knife. The router is fitted with a straight bit, slightly smaller in diameter than the groove, and adjusted to the zero depth setting. The straight and circular guide is attached to the router and adjusted, so that one edge of the bit is positioned against one side of the drawn outline. The built-in vernier adjustment on the guide provides maximum accuracy in making this adjustment. The bit is next adjusted to the desired cutting depth and the cut is made, guiding the router against one side of the board (Fig. 50). The second cut is made by guiding the router on the opposite side of the board. This method assures the groove to be in the exact center of the board. Without changing any adjustments on the router, proceed to cut all grooves in all boards that are to receive them.

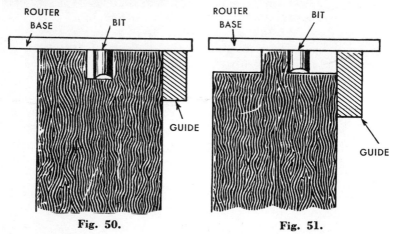

ROUTER BASE   BIT   ROUTER BASE   BIT

GUIDE

GUIDE

Fig. 50.   **Fig. 51.**

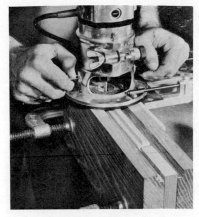 

Fig. 52.   **Fig. 53.**

When cutting the tongues, the depth adjustment should be about $\frac{1}{64}''$ more shallow than the groove, to allow space for glue. The straight and circular guide is adjusted and each side of the board is routed until a tongue of the correct width is made (Fig. 51). Without changing any adjustments, proceed to cut all pieces that are to have tongues.

When routing tongue-and-groove joints on short pieces of lumber, it is advisable to use a fixture for holding the pieces while they are being machined (Figs. 52 and 53).

MORTISE-AND-TENON JOINTS

Mortise-and-tenon joints are frequently used in the construction of furniture, doors, windows, screens, and in many other projects needing firm, strong joints.

Cutting the mortise. To make a joint of this type, first outline on the piece of wood that is to be mortised, the length and width of the mortise. This can be done with a sharp pencil or a knife. When the mortise is to be in the exact center of the board, it is best to use a straight bit, smaller in diameter than the width of the mortise (Fig. 54).

Place the piece to be mortised in a fixture that is suitable to hold it securely. Place the straight bit in the router chuck to at least a $\frac{1}{2}''$ depth, and adjust the bit to zero setting. Attach straight and circular guide to the router and adjust it to ride along the edge of the fixture at a distance to place the edge of the bit exactly on one side of marked rectangle where the cut is to be made.

Loosen wing nut and turn knurled knob on the router until the bit is adjusted to the necessary depth of cut. In hard lumber it may be necessary to make several passes with the router to obtain the necessary depth of mortise.

Fig. 54.

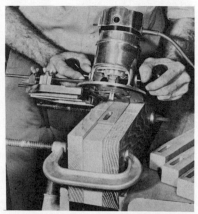

Fig. 55.

Fig. 56.

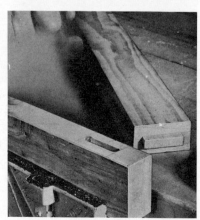

Fig. 57.

Tighten all adjustments securely, start router and lower the revolving bit slowly into the wood that is to receive the mortise, until the base of the router rests flat on top of the fixture. The router is then moved forward to cut the desired length of the mortise.

After this first cut is completed, the router guide is placed against the opposite side of the fixture and the second cut is made to provide the correct width of the mortise. It will be in the exact center of the board. Without disturbing the adjustments on the router, proceed to cut all pieces that are to be mortised.

Fig. 58.

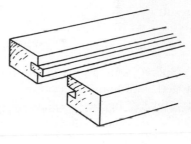

Fig. 59.

There are times when a mortise is to be located to one side of the center of the board, such as in making table legs (Fig. 55). To do this, select a bit of the proper size, adjust it to the proper depth and proceed to cut the mortise as described, guiding the router along only one side of the fixture.

When a large number of mortises are to be made, an improvised stop can be attached to the fixture so as to limit the movement of the router in its lengthwise motion, thereby making all mortises the same length.

Cutting the tenon. The board to receive the tenon is held in the fixture (Fig. 56). A straight bit is placed in the router and the depth of cut adjusted about $\frac{1}{64}''$ less than the depth of the mortise. This provides space for glue when the object is being assembled. The straight and circular guide is attached to the base of the router and adjusted, so that when it is passed along both sides of the fixture, a tenon of the proper width is made. The vernier adjustment on the guide is very helpful in making this adjustment. After the length of the tenon has been cut, it is then cut to width. This is done by guiding the router along the end of the fixture. After one side is cut, the piece is reversed and the other side is cut. Do not change the router adjustments until all tenons have been made.

Note that all mortises will have round ends and the tenons will have square ends as shown in Figs. 57 and 58. The mortise can be made square with a chisel, or the tenon can be made round to fit the mortise with a file. In either case, a satisfactory joint will result.

SPLINE JOINTS

Spline joints are used in joining two or more pieces of lumber together to build up a large surface (Fig. 59). Generally speaking, in ¾″ lumber a spline of ¼″ thickness and a depth of ¼″ to ⅜″ is usually sufficient. The edges of the boards that are to be joined together should be made smooth and true.

The edge of the groove to be cut is outlined on the board with a sharp pencil or knife. A straight bit, smaller in diameter than the width of the groove, should be placed in the router, and then the router should be adjusted to the zero setting. Place the straight and circular guide on the router, and adjust it so that one edge of the bit is along one edge of the drawn outline. Use the vernier adjustment for making these measurements.

The depth of cut is then adjusted, and the cut is made along one side of the board after which the router is used on the opposite side of the board. The result will be a perfect groove in the exact center of the board. When short pieces of lumber are to be joined, it is best to hold the wood in a fixture (Fig. 60). Without changing any of the router adjustments, proceed to cut all grooves.

Plywood is frequently used in making the splines. The same kind of wood being joined can also be used. If it is, the grain in the spline should run in opposite directions to the boards being joined together. Blind spline joints are made where the edge of the glued up pieces is to be uniform in appearance. This is done by starting the groove a short distance in from the end of the board and the cut is stopped a short distance in from the other end of the board. Figure 61 shows how a blind spline joint should be made to join together a heavy frame.

Fig. 60.

Fig. 61.

DOVETAIL JOINTS

Due to their strength and neat appearance, dovetail joints are frequently used in the construction of drawers and boxes. To make them by hand, using a chisel and mallet, requires considerable skill and patience. The dovetail kit shown in Fig. 62 permits this type of joinery to be accomplished with speed and accuracy.

Two sizes of finger templates are available for use with the dovetail fixture (Fig. 63). One is for use with lumber $7/16''$ to $1''$ thick, and the other with lumber from $5/16''$ to $5/8''$ thick. The edges of the two boards that are to be joined are cut at the same time, insuring a perfect fit.

Figure 64 illustrates how the lumber is held in the fixture, and Fig. 65 shows how the cut is made. Figs. 66 and 67 show the

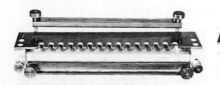

Fig. 62.   Fig. 63.

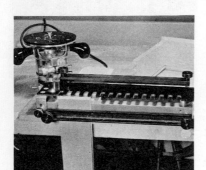

Fig. 64.   Fig. 65.

cuts completed, and Fig. 68 illustrates how the drawer pieces are grooved to accommodate the drawer bottom.

The router can also be used to enhance the appearance of drawer fronts as shown in Fig. 69.

TEMPLATES

The best method of duplicating shapes, especially those of intricate design, is by *template routing*. This consists of transferring the desired design to a pattern, or template, and cutting it out. This template is clamped to the material being routed and the router, fitted with a bit and a template guide is directed along its pattern for perfect duplication. Once the template is cut, it may be reused again and again for production-line uniformity.

Figure 70 shows several types of template guides available for use with the router. These serve to guide and restrict the movement of the router within the desired area being cut. Figure 71 represents the template guide and bit in cutting position. *Note* that the pattern, or template, should be made slightly larger than the opening wanted, to compensate for the size of the template guide used.

Fig. 66.

Fig. 67.

Fig. 68.

Fig. 69.

Fig. 70.

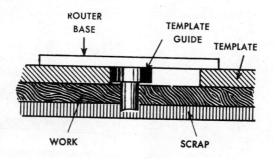

Fig. 71.

Fig. 72.   Fig. 73.

Routing the template. The design is usually first drawn on paper and then transferred to the template material, which may be hardwood, plywood, or composition board (Fig. 72). This design may be cut out with a jig or band saw or the router may be used as follows:

Remove sub-base from the router to provide maximum visibility. Place the drawn template on a piece of smooth scrap material and clamp both to the workbench. Fit the router with a straight bit and adjust the cutting depth to about $\frac{1}{16}''$ deeper than the thickness of the template material. The design is then routed out freehand, with careful guiding, and keeping the bit slightly away from the drawn line. After all first cuts are made, go over them again and slowly rout to the drawn line.

After the template is cut, all edges should be made smooth with a file or sandpaper, for any irregularities in the template will be automatically transferred to the finished piece.

TEMPLATE ROUTING

The template is used as follows:

Tack the template to the piece that is to be routed using small brads and locating them in section that will be scrapped. Place a piece of scrap lumber under the work to protect the bench top, as shown in Fig. 73. With the sub-base and template guide attached to the router, a straight bit is placed in the chuck and adjusted to the desired depth of cut. This depth adjustment will depend on the hardness and the thickness of the wood being routed. Usually several passes of the router at varying depths are necessary to produce a smoother surface than a single heavy cut. Turn the current on and lower the revolving bit into the wood until the base of the router is flat on the template. With the template guide in contact with the template, the router is then guided within the design until the area is completely cut as shown in Fig. 74.

After each section is cut out, turn off the current and allow the bit to stop revolving before moving to the next opening. Continue until all openings have been cut.

Should a bas-relief effect be desired instead of a through cut, the same procedure is followed except that the depth of cut is adjusted so as not to pass completely through the material being routed.

Fig. 74.   Fig. 75.

INLAY WORK

Because of the accuracy and smooth, high-quality cuts possible with the router, it is an excellent tool for inserting inlays. Inlay strips, which greatly enhance the beauty of finished woodwork, and add to its value, can be conveniently purchased in a wide variety of shapes and designs.

In applying an inlay strip around a table top proceed as follows:

1. Draw an outline completely around the entire surface to indicate the exact position of the finished inlay.

2. Fit router with a straight bit of the exact same width as that of the inlay and adjust cutting depth to slightly less than the thickness of the inlay. (The set inlay will protrude slightly above the surface for sanding to a perfectly smooth, flush finish.)

3. With the straight and circular guide attached to the router and set at the correct, outlined position of the inlay, the table top is routed around the entire inlay area, as shown in Fig. 75. When finished, the corners will be round—cut them square with

a thin blade chisel or knife.

4. Place inlay in the routed groove, fit correctly, and miter at each corner.

5. Place glue in the groove, insert fitted inlay, and clamp, using a strip of paper and a long board for protection and uniform pressure along inlay.

6. After the glue sets, remove clamps and thoroughly and carefully sand surface.

7. Follow the same procedure for inlaying in each of the tapered legs. Fit legs and clamp as shown in Fig. 76, while this work is being done.

8. Locate center design (Fig. 77) in the exact center of the table top, and outline by tracing around the inlay piece with a sharp, thin knife blade. Care must be taken not to cut any deeper than the thickness of the inlay, itself.

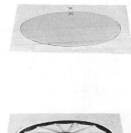

Fig. 76.   **Fig. 77.**

9. Fit the router with a straight bit and, with the sub-base removed, adjust depth of cut to slightly less than the thickness of the inlay.

10. With the correct depth established, rout out center section free-hand, carefully restricting cut to about $\frac{1}{32}''$ from knife-cut outline. (This $\frac{1}{32}''$ is hand-trimmed with knife blade.)

11. Apply glue to the recess, insert inlay, and clamp securely. Most inlays are protected on one side by pressure-sensitive paper. *Be sure* to insert this type of inlay with the paper side up.

12. When glue has set, remove all clamps and sand entire surface to a smooth, even finish.

The care and patience required in accomplishing fine inlay work by hand can only be imagined by one who has not actually tried it. However, with the electric router this same type of work becomes only one of many jobs accomplished with the speed and accuracy of the professional craftsman.

MAKING YOUR OWN MOLDING

Many types of novel and decorative wood molding can be easily accomplished with the router, using either bits or cutters. Such molding cuts can be made directly along the edge of the work, such as table and desk tops, bookcase shelves, etc.; or they can be made separately and fastened wherever desired.

Figure 78 illustrates two types of molding made with the router, using the pilot part of the bit to guide the tool along the edge of the work. After the molding is shaped with the router, a saw is used to cut the molding from the lumber, as illustrated.

Moldings of this type are extremely useful in baseboard work, picture-framing, panelling, etc. By using various combinations of bits and cutters, the unique designs possible are limitless.

Figure 79 shows a molded edge being applied directly to the edge of a table top, using a bit with a pilot end to guide the tool.

Fig. 78.   **Fig. 79.**

The straight and circular guide as shown in Fig. 31 may also be used when the cut desired must be made with a straight bit.

MAKING TAPERED LEGS

Tapered legs, such as are often used in making tables and chairs, can easily be made, using the router and a simple fixture (Fig. 80). The size of the fixture will depend upon the size and length of the leg

Tapering fixture. To make this tapering fixture, proceed as follows:

Secure a board of sufficient size for the base (A). The two upright pieces, (B) and (C) are made from the same stock and shaped as shown in the illustration. They should be about ½″ higher than the thickness of the leg that is to be tapered. Fasten pieces (B) and (C) to base (A), spaced so that the square leg can be placed between them (Fig. 81). A tapered wedge (D) should be made to fit between boards (B) and (C) (Fig. 80). This is used to elevate one end of the leg being tapered.

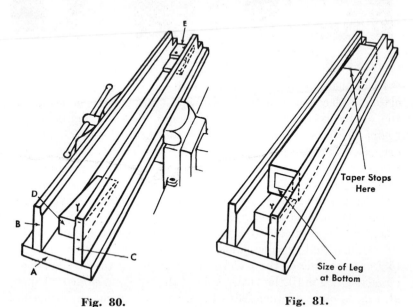

Fig. 80.   **Fig. 81.**

Tapered leg. Most tapered legs are made square a certain distance down from the top in order to accommodate an apron. Therefore, draw a line across the leg where the taper is to stop. Determine the size that the leg should be at the bottom and draw the outline as shown in Fig. 81. It is only necessary to do this with one leg as, after all adjustments are made, all legs will be alike. The fixture should be held in a vise or fastened by clamps to the work bench.

Fig. 82.

Fig. 83.

Place the straight leg in the fixture against the stop (E) and clamp in place. The router, fitted with a straight bit, is rested on top of the fixture (Fig. 82) and, using both the wedge and the router depth-adjustment, bit is set to cut to the depth of the drawn outline on the leg bottom. Be sure that the adjustment for depth of cut is such that the cut will stop where the line has been drawn on the leg to accommodate the apron. When all adjustments are accurately made, a nail is partially driven into wedge (D) to hold it securely.

The router is guided along the outer edge of the fixture, using the straight and circular guide and the cuts are made, using the tool on each side of the fixture and readjusting the straight and circular guide until the entire side of the leg is machined. Taper all legs on one side, then, with the same setting, cut the adjacent sides. A small wedge is used at the tapered end to prevent end-play while leg is being machined (Fig. 83).

Without changing the cutting-depth on the router, cut the remaining two sides of the leg. To set this cutting depth, remove nail holding wedge (D) and move wedge inward until bit meets the drawn outline of the leg bottom. Insert small wedges (Fig. 84)to prevent end-play while routing. Figure 85 illustrates final cut being made.

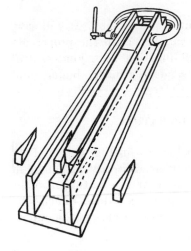

Fig. 84.

Fig. 85.

Legs for fine furniture are often made from hardwood, in which case it may be necessary, depending upon the taper, to make several passes at different depths of cut until the desired depth is obtained. The speed with which the router operates is such that the tapered legs will require only a minimum amount of sanding.

CHAPTER 7

Radial-Arm Machine

$\vdots$

The radial-arm machine is a complete workshop. It will saw, dado, and shape with complete accuracy. With the proper attachments added, the machine will function as a jointer, drill press, router, lathe, saber saw, sander, grinder, buffer, and polisher.

PRINCIPLE OF OPERATION

The radial-arm type of power tool shown in Fig. 1 is in effect a mechanical arm that features the easy dexterity of a human arm. Flexibility with this tool means that the cutting member can be placed in any position throughout all three dimensions (length, width, and depth). This is possible because of the unique

Fig. 1.

Fig. 2.

design allowing full maneuverability through a complete circle in any of the three directions.

The three-dimension flexibility is possible with the motorized mechanical arm, shown in Fig. 2. The radial arm (A) rotates 360° for right- or left-miter cuts. Release clamp (B) and lift latch (C), then easily swing the arm to any angle. The eye-level calibrated miter scale (D), shows the angle required. The "built-in" stops at 0° and 45° automatically locate these common angles. Never shift the lumber for miters, as the radial-arm machine puts the saw at the exact angle, and you pull across for perfect cuts. An accurate measuring scale, on the right side of the arm, gives you instant measuring for ripping.

Figure 3 shows the shoulder action of the mechanical arm. As the arm is raised or lowered, it measures for you. Each full turn of the elevating handle (A) lifts or lowers the arm (B) $\frac{1}{8}''$. One-half turn gives you $\frac{1}{16}''$. This is a precision depth control.

The elbow action of the mechanical arm is illustrated in Fig. 4. The yoke, which holds the motor, is beneath the arm and rides freely on it. Release the yoke clamp (B) and lift the locating pin (C), then swing the yoke right or left. It automatically stops at all four 90° positions, giving quick, positive adjustment for rip and crosscuts. The clamp (D) locks the saw in the desired rip position.

Fig. 3.

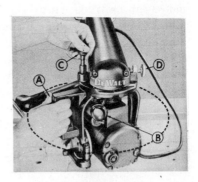

Fig. 4.

Figure 5 shows the wrist movement of the mechanical arm. Pull out the clamp (*A*) and locating pin (*B*). Tilt the motor (*C*) for the angle desired on the bevel scale (*D*). Then, relock *A*. The motor unit automatically locates the popular 0°, 45°, and 90° bevel positions. Your compound angles and bevel cuts are measured for you with unequaled accuracy, and there is no limit to the bevel cuts.

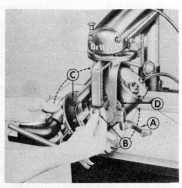

Fig. 5.   Fig. 6.

The flexible operation of this machine is based on the following three simple radial adjustments; the arm can be swung horizontally through 360° around its column; the yoke can be revolved horizontally through 360° under its roller carriage; and the motor can be tilted within the yoke to any angle desired. These adjustments enable you to place the cutting tool easily in any position.

Radial-arm machine sizes. Radial-arm machines are available in a range of sizes from ¾ to 10 h.p., the smallest being the most popular one for home workshop use. This size machine cuts 2½″ deep with a 9″ blade, crosscuts 15″ wide on 1″ stock, and rips to the center of 48″ wide panels.

This machine is equipped with a *direct-drive motor*. There are no belts, pulleys, gears, or other devices to maintain. The cutting tool is mounted directly on the motor spindle, an operation done above the worktable so that there are no table inserts to be concerned with. The motor operates at 3,450 r.p.m. and is available in either 115-volt single-phase 60-cycle alternating current or 220-, 440-, or 550-volt three-phase 60-cycle alternating current models.

The direct-drive motor has grease-sealed-for-life bearings at each end of the motor shaft so that you never have to oil it. Motors of this type are protected against overloading by a manual-reset thermostat that kicks out when the motor is overheated and loaded. To reset the motor, allow a few minutes, then "push in" the red button on the motor.

Safety features. One of the outstanding virtues of the radial-arm machine is its safety features. A *safety guard*, as shown in Figs. 15 and 16, is used to cover the cutting tool so as to provide maximum safety to the operator. It is adjustable and is provided with a kickback device for use in ripping operations, as well as with an adjustable dust spout that directs the flow of sawdust wherever desired. This guard is used for sawing, dadoing, shaping, and other operations, providing safety factors hitherto not possible with ordinary table saws.

Another important factor is an *ignition-type motor-starting key* (Fig. 6). Only this key will start the motor, and it fits a tumbler-type mechanism that is recessed in the side of the arm. This key is especially important in the home where there are children and, of course, prevents unauthorized use by others.

The fact that the *blade* is mounted above the worktable, instead of below it, is possibly the major safety feature of this machine. Since you can always see what you are doing, you can very quickly do accurate cutting, because you can easily follow the layout marks on the top of the material, and the mechanical arm guarantees a true cut regardless of the angle. For most operations the hand guides the saw blade through the work; this lessens the chance of having the blade clip you. It, of course, eliminates overcutting and spoiling of the material.

Regardless of the operation, all setups are made above the worktable to simplify all jobs. The calibrated miter, rip, and bevel scales, as well as all control handles are above the worktable, clear of the work and easy to reach.

Floor space required. The radial-arm machine is fundamentally a one-wall shop, and the over-all floor space required is approximately 3 square feet. It can be set up even in the smallest basement, utility room, garage, or attic. For example, in the attic, the radial-arm machine can be placed back under the eaves, using space that would otherwise be wasted. Unlike a table saw, the radial arm does not require accessibility from all sides.

When locating the radial-arm machine, space should be allowed for handling material of the maximum lengths required. About 10′ on either side will allow for most ripping and handling of long boards. Two feet of the operating area is all that is required at the front of the machine. Table extensions are preferable to support long work, and should be solid or made of wood on metal rollers to help in conveying stock past the blade. Be sure to provide an ample light source, natural or artificial, to enable easy reading of angle and dimension dials and controls. A typical small workshop layout is shown in Fig. 7.

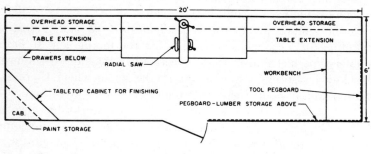

Fig. 7.

The ¾ h.p. machine which takes a 9″ saw blade is practically portable. It may be mounted on saw horses (temporary installation), steel legs, or on a steel cabinet (Fig. 8), or built into a workbench (Fig. 1).

Connecting the machine to the power supply. To obtain the maximum efficiency from your radial-arm motor, the wire from the source of power to the machine should not be less than size 14 (B and S gauge). Be sure that the electric line is fused with a 15-ampere fuse. If an ordinary type of fuse blows during the initial fraction of a second when the machine is turned on, do not put in a new one of higher rating. Replace it with a fuse of the same rating, but of the "slow-blow" or delay type. It contains a special fusible link that withstands a momentary overload without giving way.

Before plugging the cord into the wall or floor outlet, look at the name plate on your machine to see if it is marked 120 volts, because this is the voltage in common use today in homes. If you purchased a radial-arm machine for use on a 240-volt line, be sure the name plate is marked 240 volts. In case the motor runs hot or short of power, call your local power company to check your voltage.

The radial-arm machine, as any other power tool, should *always* be grounded while in use. This precaution will protect the operator against possible electric shock should a short circuit or ground develop while the machine is being connected to the power outlet or during operation. The radial-arm machine offers new and assured grounding protection for your safety. In accordance with a ruling of the National Electric Code, it is equipped with a three-wire cord, one wire being a ground wire. For your complete safety while operating this saw, remember that the three-conductor attachment plug requires a three-prong grounded outlet (5260 series). Just insert the three-prong plug and the machine is instantly grounded (Fig. 9).

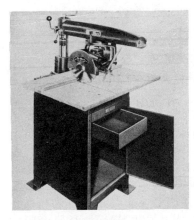

Fig. 8.

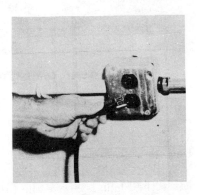

Fig. 9.

To permit use of this tool with a two-prong receptacle, an adapter is available. Match the wider prong of the adapter with the wider hole of the outlet. If you find that the adapter will not fit, file the wider prong to size. When using the adapter, the extending green wire should be connected to the outlet-plate retaining screw (Fig. 10), provided that the outlet itself is grounded, or to any other known permanent ground, such as a water or an electric-conduct pipe.

Caution! If an extension cord is used, be sure it is a three-wire cord and large enough (12 gauge) to prevent excessive voltage loss.

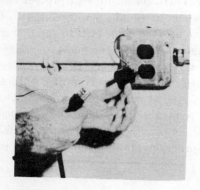

Fig. 10.

Fig. 11.

BASIC OPERATION OF THE SAW

Actually there are only six basic saw cuts in woodworking; *crosscut, bevel crosscut, miter, bevel miter, rip, and bevel rip* (Fig. 11). All other cuts, no matter how intricate, are combinations of these basic cuts.

With a radial-arm saw, the basic cuts are easy and safe. Because the blade is above the table top, you always work on the top side of the material, with your layout marks in clear view. The saw also adjusts to the lumber for all cuts.

CONTROLS

The versatility of the radial-arm saw is due, in part, to its controls. All the controls for depth of cut, miter angles, beveling, etc., are within sight and are easy to reach (Figs. 12, 13 and 14).

Saw-blade kerfs. On the top surface of the table top (*M*, Fig. 13), you will find several saw-blade kerfs ⅟₁₆″ deep which the saw blade (*H*, Fig. 12) will follow or ride in when making most popular cuts. They are a straight crosscut, right 45°, straight 45° bevel, a concave cut in the center of the table for ripping, and a quarter-round circle in the front of the table for the saw blade to follow when swiveling 90° to the in-rip position. The cuts are also made in the guide fence (*N*, Fig. 13).

Elevating handle. The elevating handle (*D*, Fig. 12) raises or lowers the arm, motor, and yoke. Each complete turn of the

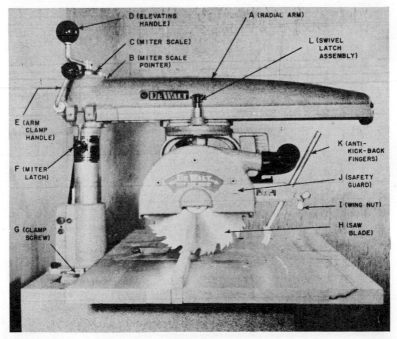

Fig. 12.

crank handle raises or lowers the machine ⅛″. To raise the machine, follow the rotation arrow on top of the column. To lower the machine, turn the elevating handle in reverse of the rotation arrow.

Safety guard. The safety guard (*J*, Fig. 12) is adjustable for cutting any thickness of material up to the capacity·of the blade. To make the guard adjustments necessary for ripping, loosen the wing nut (*P*, Fig. 13) which holds the guard to the motor, and rotate the guard down to ⅛″ above the material that is to be ripped (Fig. 15). Retighten the wing nut. Then on the opposite side of the guard, release the thumbscrew (*I*, Fig. 12) which holds the anti-kickback fingers (*K*, Fig. 12), and lower them to ⅛″ below the top of the material being ripped (Fig. 16). Then retighten the thumbscrew. Adjust the dust spout (*O*, Fig. 13) until it is turned toward the back of the machine so as to carry the dust away from you.

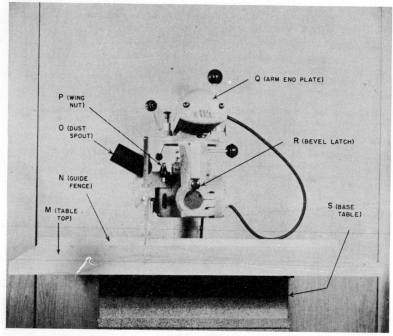

Fig. 13.

Column. The radial arm (A, Fig. 12) revolves a full 360° on the column (EE, Fig. 14). This movement permits you to set the saw for any angle cut desired.

Arm clamp handle. To make this movement, release the arm clamp handle (E, Fig. 12) by pulling it forward and lift the miter latch (F, Fig. 12) from the slot in the column. Swing the arm left or right to the angle desired by following the miter scale (C, Fig. 12) on top of the column, then lock the arm clamp handle.

Miter latch. For quick, positive location for straight cutoff or left and right 45°, seat the miter latch into the proper slot on the column and lock the arm clamp handle.

Yoke and motor. The yoke (X, Fig. 14) and motor (T, Fig. 14) revolve a full 360° on the roller carriage of the radial arm. This movement permits location of the saw in a positive locking position for (1) crosscutting, blade parallel with the arm; (2) in-ripping, swivel yoke and motor left 90° from the crosscut

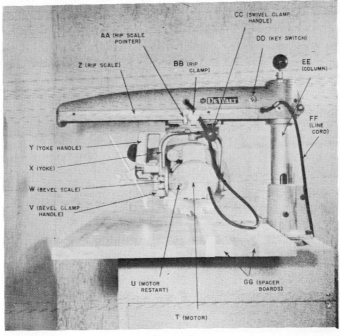

Fig. 14.

Fig. 15.   **Fig. 16.**

position; and (3) out-ripping, swivel yoke and motor right 90° from the crosscut position. To make these movements, release the clamp handle (*CC*, Fig. 14) by pulling it forward and pulling up on the swivel latch (*L*, Fig. 12). Swivel the yoke to one of the above positions. The swivel latch accurately locates the position. Then tighten the clamp handle by pushing it back.

Rip-lock clamp. The rip-lock clamp (*BB*, Fig. 14) locks the roller carriage to the radial arm for all operations where the material is moved to the cutting tool. When setting the saw for ripping, move the pointer (*AA*, Fig. 14) to the desired width of the rip, by following the ripping scale (*Z*, Fig. 14). Then turn the knurled head of the rip-lock clamp clockwise until tight on the radial arm so that the roller carriage cannot move. The saw may then be set for either in- or out-ripping. Most rip cuts can be made from the in-rip position, whereas wide panel ripping is done in the out-rip position.

The motor mounted in the yoke will tilt to any angle or bevel position desired. To make the bevel adjustment, first elevate the column about twenty turns of the crank to provide clearance above the table. Then grip the safety guard (*J*, Fig. 12) with the left hand and release the bevel clamp handle (*V*, Fig. 14) by pulling it forward. After pulling out the bevel latch (*R*, Fig. 13), move the motor to the desired angle by following the calibrated bevel scale (*W*, Fig. 14). Then lock the bevel-clamp handle by pushing it back. For quick positive location at 0°, 45°, and 90°, the bevel latch will drop into these positions automatically.

TYPES OF BLADES

Combination blade. Power saws usually come equipped with a combination blade which will crosscut, miter, and rip equally well. This blade is adaptable to most home workshop needs to do general-purpose work. The combination blade is divided into segments and provides crosscut teeth and one raker tooth in each segment, with a deep gullet between. This arrangement of the teeth permits the blade to cut freely and smoothly both with and across the grain.

In the *flat-ground blade* (two cutting teeth and one raker), the teeth must be set as shown in *A*, Fig. 17.

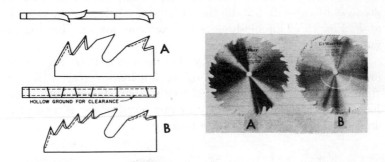

Fig. 17.

Hollow-ground blade. This blade generally has four cutting teeth and one raker, and the teeth have no set (*B*, Fig. 17). The blade is beveled, or hollow-ground, so that it is several gauges thinner near the hub than at the rim. Sometimes called a planer or miter blade, it is generally used by cabinetmakers when cutting stock to finish dimensions, as it cuts very smoothly both with and across the grain.

Carbide-tipped blade. The eight-tooth carbide-tipped saw blade (*A*, Fig. 18) rips and crosscuts like a combination blade, but it remains sharp for long periods of continued operation and outlasts ordinary blades many times over. It is ideal for cutting hardboard, plywood, asbestos board, and other similar materials.

Carbide blades do not, however, produce so smooth a cut in the softer woods as the combination blade.

Ripping blade. The ripping blade (*B*, Fig. 18) is designed to do just one job—cutting with the grain of the wood. The blade will tend to tear the wood on crosscuts, but cuts fast and clean on rip cuts. Since ripping usually puts a heavy load on the motor, this blade is recommended for general ripping jobs.

Cutoff wheels and special blades. Cutoff wheels are flexible abrasive discs which mount on the saw arbor like a blade. The aluminum oxide wheel (*C*, Fig. 18) is used for cutting steel and similar metals, while the silicon carbide wheel (*D*, Fig. 18) works best for ceramics, porcelain, glass, plastics, etc. A special blade (*E*, Fig. 18) is available for cutting non-ferrous metal such as aluminum, copper, etc. It cuts solid, extruded, or tube with the greatest of ease A fine-toothed plywood cutting blade is shown at *F*, Fig. 18. This blade does an excellent job on plywood and gummy, resinous woods.

"Safety" blade. The "safety" blade, shown at *G*, Fig. 18, has only eight teeth, but it is a combination blade, crosscutting and ripping equally well, and it produces a fairly smooth cut. It performs with maximum efficiency at minimum power consumption, and it reduces kickback to a minimum.

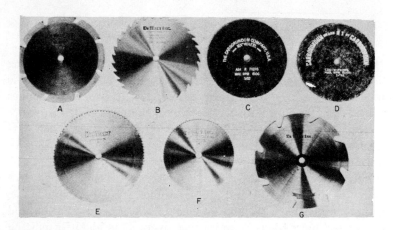

Fig. 18.

MOUNTING A SAW BLADE

When mounting a saw blade, remove the arbor nut and arbor collars. Elevate the radial arm until the blade will slide on the shaft and clear the table top. Then place the ⅜″ arbor collar on the arbor so that the recessed side of the collar will be against the saw blade. Place the saw blade on the arbor. The teeth of the saw blade must point in the direction of rotation when the saw blade is in the proper operating position. (Generally blades are marked "This side out," which means that the side marked should be on the same side as the arbor nut.) Then place the ¼″ arbor collar, recessed side against the saw blade, on the arbor. Now place a wrench on the flat of the arbor shaft to hold it, and tighten the arbor nut with the arbor-nut wrench (Fig. 19). The arbor nut has a left-hand thread, which means that the nut must be turned and tightened counterclockwise.

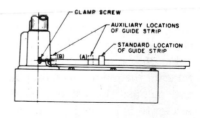

CLAMP SCREW
AUXILIARY LOCATIONS OF GUIDE STRIP
STANDARD LOCATION OF GUIDE STRIP
(B) (A)

Fig. 19.   **Fig. 20.**

Mount the safety guard over the saw blade and adjust it, on the motor stud, to the desired position for the cuts you are going to make and tighten the wing nut.

ALIGNING OPERATIONS

Every radial-arm machine is thoroughly tested, inspected, and accurately aligned before leaving the factory of the manufacturer. Rough handling during transportation may throw the machine out of alignment. Eventually adjustment and realignment are necessary in any machine to maintain accuracy—regardless of the care with which the machine is manufactured.

Checking the guide fence for accuracy. For accurate work, the guide fence must be straight. This wood guide strip is inspected with a master straightedge at the factory before shipment and should arrive in perfect condition. If the machine has been exposed to the weather, it is possible that the wood table-top parts may be warped so that the guide fence is no longer straight.

It can be made straight by planing and sanding and can be checked with a straightedge or square before proceeding with other adjustments. Be sure that the clamp screws at the rear of the table are tightened. The main table board must be flat. If a straightedge shows this to be warped, it should be planed if necessary when you level the worktable top.

The guide fence, as shown in Fig. 20, is located in the most frequently used position on the worktable. This will take care of the normal cutting jobs. If you want maximum crosscut on 1″ material or wider bevel-meter capacity, loosen the clamp screws at the rear of the table top and relocate the guide fence behind the 2″ spacer board, location *A*. Be sure to tighten the clamp screws after this is done.

For maximum width in ripping, loosen the clamp screws and relocate the guide fence by placing it at the rear of the table top and against the column base, location *B*. Tighten the clamp screws to hold the guide fence rigidly in position.

If the guide fence should become cut with many kerfs (and it does over a period of time), it can be replaced with a new one. Use a straight piece of pine or similar softwood the same size as the present fence. Plane, sand smooth, and check it with a straightedge or try square for straightness before putting it in place. For several operations, such as *shaping, sanding,* or *jointing,* special guide fences will be required, but these are very easy to make.

Aligning the work top to the arm travel. The table top must align with the arm travel in every horizontal (parallel) position. The table top is mounted on adjustable steel cleats with adjustable jack nuts. To realign the top, *see* Figs. 21 and 22.

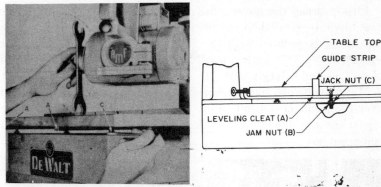

Fig. 21.   **Fig. 22.**

Insert a steel bar about ½″ x ½″ x 12″) or a wrench between the saw-arbor collars in place of the saw blade.

Bring the motor to the forward position on the arm, swing the bar, and adjust the table top until the tip of the bar when oscillated barely scrapes the table top. Repeat at the back section of the table board, to the right and left, without changing the elevation.

Adjust the table top for the height in various positions until it is perfectly level. Loosen the jam nuts (*B*) under the table channel frame (toy flange), and then you can raise or lower the jack nuts (*C*) as required. Be sure to retighten the jam nuts under the table flange after making the adjustments to hold the table board level.

Squaring the saw blade with the table top. The saw blade can be maintained square with the table top (Fig. 23).

Make sure that the table top is level at all points. Remove the safety guard.

Place a steel square (*C*) against the flat of the saw blade. The square should be placed in the saw gullets and not against the saw teeth. Make sure that the bevel latch is properly seated and the bevel clamp handle is locked.

Remove the etched dial plate (*A*) from the motor yoke by taking out the Phillip's-head screws. You can now get at the two adjusting socket screws (*G*).

Release the two socket screws (*G*) approximately two turns with a socket wrench.

Firmly grasp the motor with both hands and tilt it until the saw blade is parallel to the upright steel square (*C*). After the saw blade is squared with the table top, be sure to tighten the socket screws (*G*) with a socket wrench (*B*). Replace the dial plate (*A*) and safety guard.

Many craftsmen nail a "wear" table of plywood or hardboard over the permanent front table, as shown in Fig. 24. This table top takes the saw cuts, and keeps the permanent table from being cut up.

Fig. 23.

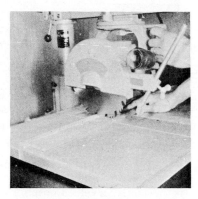

Fig. 24.

A. Nameplate
B. Allen Setscrew Wrench
C. Steel Square
D. Bevel Clamp Handle
E. Bevel Latch Assembly
G. Socket Screws
H. Dial Plate

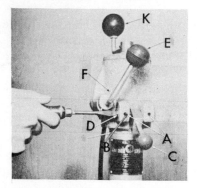

Fig. 25.

A. Allen Setscrew
B. Allen Setscrew Wrench
C. Miter Latch
D. Miter Latch Adjusting Screws
E. Arm Clamp Handle
F. Arm Clamp Handle Stop
K. Elevating Action Handle

Fig. 26.

G. Base Pinch Bolt
H. Hex Jam Nuts
I. Setscrew
J. Allen Setscrew Wrench
L. Column Key Gib

Squaring the crosscut travel with the guide fence. Place a wide board on the table top against the guide fence, and make a cut across with the saw. Check the material for accuracy with a steel square. If the saw blade does not cut square, this means that the arm is out of alignment with the guide fence. To adjust this condition see Fig. 25.

Loosen both the arm clamp handle (*E*) and the miter latch (*C*).

The adjusting screws (*D*) are locked in position by setscrews (*A*). Loosen the screws (*A*) with a ¼″ Allen wrench.

Lay the steel square against the guide fence. Move the saw forward along the steel square to determine which way the arm must be moved.

If the blade moves toward the steel square as you come forward, loosen the adjusting screw (*D*) in the rear (left) with a screwdriver and tighten the adjusting screw (*D*) in the front (right) to bring the arm parallel to the steel square. The arm will be parallel when the saw travels evenly with the steel square for its entire length. If the saw blade moves away from the steel square as you come forward, make the opposite adjustments. Loosen the adjusting screw (*D*) in the front (right) with the screwdriver and tighten the adjusting screw (*D*) in the rear (left). When the saw travel is parallel to the square, lock the adjusting screws (*D*) in the front and rear by tightening both Allen setscrews (*A*) with a setscrew wrench (*B*). Engage the miter latch (*C*) and the arm clamp handle (*E*).

Adjusting the base; gripping, tension, and alignment. If at any time there is some motion at the end of the arm after the arm clamp handle is tightened, this indicates that there is play between the column and base or the gib needs tightening. *See* Figs. 25, 26 and 27.

Loosen the base pinch bolt (*G*), all hex jam nuts (*H*), and all setscrews (*I*).

Rotate the elevating crank handle (*K*) to raise or lower the column. Tighten the base pinch bolt (*G*) so that the column still raises or lowers freely and without play.

The adjusting gib (*L*) must be secured against the column key (*2D*) to prevent side motion in the arm. Tighten the top setscrews (*I*) with a ⁵⁄₁₆″ Allen wrench (*J*) until there is no play (side motion) in the column. Then lock all the hex jam nuts (*H*) securely with an open-end wrench.

Adjusting the arm clamp handle. The arm clamp handle rigidly holds the arm in position for straight or miter cuts. When tightened in position, the arm clamp handle should be upright as shown in Fig. 28. If the arm clamp handle becomes worn so that it goes beyond the vertical position, relocate it.

Remove the clamp-handle stop (*A*) and lift the miter latch (*B*) upward against the side of the arm.

Unwind the arm clamp handle (*C*) by turning it clockwise (to the right). Make about three or four complete turns of this handle.

Push back the arm clamp bolt (*D*) from its hex socket so that the hex head can be turned.

Turn the hex clamp screw (*D*) about one-sixth turn counterclockwise to tighten the arm clamp handle.

Put the hex-screw head (*D*) back in the hex socket, retighten the arm clamp handle (*C*) in the upright position, and insert the arm-clamp-handle stop (*A*).

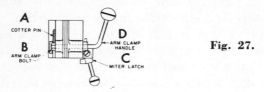

Fig. 27.

Adjusting the roller head bearing to the arm track. The roller carriage is mounted on four ball bearings, two of which are on eccentric shafts whose movement is controlled by $\frac{5}{16}''$ Allen socket screws. To adjust the ball bearings, *see* Fig. 29.

Remove the arm end plate from the arm and bring the saw carriage forward. Swivel the motor into the rip position to get the adjustments.

Loosen the setscrews (*A*) with a $\frac{1}{4}''$ Allen wrench in the front and the rear of the saw carriage since they lock the eccentric shaft (*F*).

Loosen the hex jam nuts (*B*) in the front and rear of the saw carriage so that the eccentric shaft (*F*) can be turned in its socket.

Insert a $\frac{5}{16}''$ Allen wrench (C) in the eccentric shaft (F) and turn this shaft until the ball bearing it controls just touches the arm track. Do not tighten this bearing too much. Repeat on the ball bearing (D) in the rear of the saw carriage. The ball bearing (D) in the front and the rear of the saw carriage should now roll smoothly inside the arm. Tighten the hex jam nuts (B) and lock the setscrews (A) on both ends of the saw carriage.

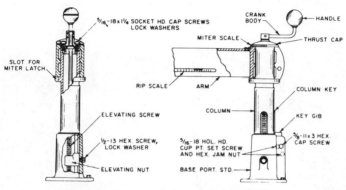

Fig. 28. Details of the Arm Clamp Handle

Adjusting the crosscut travel parallel to the arm. To make sure the saw blade is cutting exactly parallel to the arm tracks, place a board approximately 6″ wide on the table against the guide fence. Make a cut through the board, and stop just as the board is cut off with the back of the blade still in the board. If there is a slight ridge on the material where the blade is stopped, this will indicate the need of adjustment. Another method of checking is, when making the crosscut, to watch the back of the blade where the teeth come up through the board. If the blade is kicking up the wood fibers on the top surface of the board, this will indicate that the blade is not traveling parallel with the arm tracks. To adjust the crosscut travel, *see* Fig. 30.

If the saw blade is "heeling" on the left side of the cut, loosen the setscrew (C) and tighten the screw (A), using a $\frac{5}{16}''$ Allen wrench (F).

If the saw blade is "heeling" on the right side of the cut, loosen the setscrew (A) and tighten the setscrew (C) with a $\frac{5}{16}''$ Allen wrench (F).

After the above two adjustments are made, the heeling may reappear when you place the saw blade in the bevel cutting position, in which case:

Loosen the setscrews (*A* and *C*), each about one-sixth turn, and tighten the setscrew (*B*) if the heeling is on the material on the bottom side of the saw cut.

Loosen the setscrew (*B*) about one-sixth turn and tighten the setscrews (*A* and *C*) evenly if the heeling appears on the upper side of the cut.

Fig. 29.

A. Allen Setscrew	D. Ball Bearing
B. Hex Jam Nut	(on eccentric shaft)
C. Allen Socket	E. Ball Bearing
Wrench	(on permanent studs)
	F. Eccentric Shaft
	G. Wrench

Fig. 30.

A. Allen Setscrew	D. Rear Trunnion Stud
(saw side)	Bushing
B. Allen Setscrew	E. Rear Trunnion Stud
(bottom yoke trunnion)	F. Allen Setscrew
C. Allen Setscrew	Wrench
(opposite saw side)	G. Saw Arbor Collar
	H. Saw Arbor Nut

Adjusting the bevel clamp handle. The purpose of the bevel clamp handle is to hold the motor rigidly in its yoke at any angle even though the bevel latch may be disengaged from the locating holes in the dial plate. The bevel latch locates 90° crosscut, 45° bevel crosscut, and 0° vertical positions only.

To adjust the bevel clamp handle, see Fig. 31.

Loosen the bevel clamp handle (*A*) and the hex jam nut (*F*).

Turn the cap screw (*E*) clockwise (to the right) until the bevel clamp handle rigidly clamps the motor in its yoke.

Be sure to tighten the hex jam nut (*F*) after the adjustment is made.

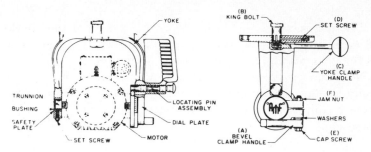

Fig. 31.

Adjusting the yoke clamp handle. There should be no play between the roller carriage and the motor-yoke assembly. The yoke clamp handle in conjunction with the king bolt securely clamp the saw carriage to the yoke. To adjust the yoke clamp handle, *see C*, Fig. 32.

Fig. 32.

A. Screwdriver   C. Yoke Clamp Handle
B. King Bolt   D. Dog Point Setscrew

Remove the saw carriage and the motor yoke completely from the arm.

A dog-point setscrew (*D*) is located in the milled slot on the side of the king bolt (*B*). Its purpose is to keep the king bolt from turning when the yoke clamp handle is loosened or tightened. Remove the setscrew from the slot in the king bolt with a screwdriver (*A*).

Turn the king bolt (*B*) about one-sixth of a turn in a clockwise direction so that the dog setscrew may be located in the next slot in the king bolt. Tighten the dog setscrew in position to hold the king bolt.

This dog setscrew should be drawn up tight and then backed off slightly so that the king bolt can slide freely up and down as the yoke clamp handle is loosened or tightened.

Now that every moving part is in proper alignment, you are ready to start operating the machine. You should, however, observe certain basic rules for maximum safety and efficiency in operation.

BASIC SAW CUTS

The radial-arm saw is a pull-through cutoff type of saw and cuts in a straight line or at any angle. In the crosscutting action, the saw is moved in the same direction as its rotation (*A*, Fig. 33). Ripping must never be done in the same direction as the saw rotation (*B*, Fig. 33). For accurate and smooth cutting, a sharp blade must be used.

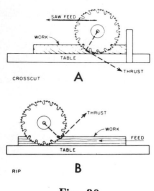

Fig. 33.

Fig. 34.

CROSSCUTTING

When straight crosscutting, the radial arm must be at right angles with the guide fence—indicated as 0° on the miter scale. Locate the miter latch in the column slot at the 0° position, and then securely lock the arm with the arm clamp handle. Now the saw blade should follow the saw kerf in the table top. Use the elevating handle to drop the saw blade until the teeth are approximately $\frac{1}{16}''$ below the top surface of the table in the saw kerf. This clearance is needed to cut through the board. Then return the saw all the way back against the column.

Place the material on the worktable against the guide fence. Adjust the guard parallel to the bottom of the motor, adjust the kickback fingers down to $\frac{1}{8}''$ above the material you will cut off. Turn on the power and give the motor sufficient time to attain top speed. Then pull the saw blade from behind the guide fence in one steady motion completely through the cut (Fig. 34). Never allow it to "walk" too rapidly through the work. Return the saw to the rear of the guide fence before removing the material from the table. Practice to get the "feel" of the cutting action—let the saw blade cut—do not force it.

To cut a board thicker than the capacity of the machine, set the blade just a little over half the thickness of the material. Pull the blade through in the same manner as for straight crosscutting, and then turn it over and complete the cut on the other side.

Right- or left-hand feed. Your first cut will pose the question of whether to use right-hand (Fig. 35), or left-hand feed (Fig. 36). You may have a tendency to use left-hand feed because it puts the holding (right) hand on the side away from the saw. However, right-hand feed generally is more practical and more comfortable, and you will quickly adopt this system.

Fig. 35.

Fig. 36.

Crosscutting wide boards and panels. To cut a board wider than the capacity of the machine, cut to the limit, then turn it over and complete the cut. Large pieces of plywood can be cut with ease by using the method shown in Fig. 37.

Fig. 37.   **Fig. 38.**

Horizontal crosscutting. This crosscut operation (Fig. 38) is used for cutting across the end of any size of stock. To locate the saw in the horizontal position, raise the radial arm by turning the elevating handle until the blade is approximately 3″ above the table top. With the saw in the crosscut position, pull it to the front end of the arm. Holding the top of the safety guard in your left hand, release the bevel clamp handle by pulling it forward and pull out the bevel latch. Swing the motor and saw into the 90° horizontal position and lock the bevel clamp handle by pushing it back. (The bevel latch automatically locks itself in position.) The blade will now be parallel to the table top, and the motor will be in a vertical position. Then adjust the dust elbow on the guard, parallel to the table top. Push the motor and saw and guard back to the column.

Place the material to be cut against the guide fence and lower the saw blade to the point where the cut is to be made. The depth of the cut will be determined by the location of the material in respect to the saw blade.

Turn on the motor, and with the saw behind the guide fence, pull it through the material in the same manner as when crosscutting. If you wish to form a groove, push the saw back against the column and raise or lower the arm a full turn. Bring the saw forward again and then return it to the column. Repeat this procedure until the desired width of the groove is obtained.

BEVEL CROSSCUTTING

Bevel crosscutting, shown in Fig. 39, is similar to straight crosscutting, but the saw is tilted to the desired bevel angle. With the motor and saw back against the column, elevate the machine so that the blade will clear the table top when swiveling the motor in the yoke. Pull the motor and saw to the front end of the arm. To bevel your motor and saw, place your left hand on top of the safety guard to hold the motor from dropping and release the bevel clamp lock by pulling it forward. Pull out on the bevel locating pin and move the motor to the degree desired by following the bevel scale and pointer. Then lock the bevel clamp by pushing it back. Turn the elevating handle down until the saw-blade teeth touch the bottom of the concave kerf in the center of the table top. Push the motor and saw back to the column. If a common 45° bevel is desired, simply let the locating pin fit the 45° slot. Then lock the bevel clamp.

Place the material on the table top against the guide fence. Adjust the guard and keep back your fingers, the same as in crosscutting. You can make your bevel cutoff on the left side—

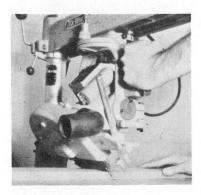

Fig. 39.

Fig. 40.

hold the material with your left hand and pull the motor and saw with your right hand by using the grip handle on the yoke. If cutting on the right side, reverse the hand holds.

MITERING

Mitering is the same as crosscutting except that the radial arm is revolved on a horizontal plane to the angle of the miter.

Right-hand miter. Make sure the motor and saw are back of the guide fence against the column. With your left hand, release the arm clamp handle and lift the swivel latch. With your right hand on the radial arm, swing it to the right to the angle desired by following the miter scales. Then lock the arm clamp handle. The popular 45° miter cut is set quickly with the miter latch seated in the 45° quickset slot in column. Simply lock the arm clamp handle. Now place the material flat on the table top and tight against the guide fence. Adjust the guard parallel to the bottom of the motor; adjust the kickback fingers down to ⅛" above the material you will cut off. Hold the material with your left hand, and pull the saw through the material with your right hand (Fig. 40). Return the saw to its original position at the rear of the guide fence before removing the material from the table top.

Left-hand miter. Move the radial arm to the left to the desired angle in the manner described for a right-hand miter. To get the full capacity on a left-hand miter, move the guide fence to the rear of the table-top spacer boards.

BEVEL MITERING

A bevel miter (sometimes called a compound or double miter) is a combination of a miter and a bevel (Fig. 41). First set the motor and saw to the angle desired by following the bevel scales and then lock the bevel latch and clamp handle. Then release the arm latch and clamp handle and swing the radial arm into the desired miter position, following the same routine as for miter cuts. To make the cut, follow the normal operating routine described under crosscut beveling.

RIPPING

Straight ripping. Straight ripping is done by having the saw blade parallel with the guide fence and feeding the material into the saw blade. You can rip from either the left or right side of the machine. The feeding of the material to the saw depends on the rotation of the saw blade. When ripping from the right side of the table (in-rip), the motor and saw must be swiveled to the left 90° from the crosscut position. If ripping from the left side of the machine (out-rip), swivel the motor and saw to the right 90° from the crosscut position.

In-ripping. To set your saw to the in-rip position, pull the motor and saw to the front end of the radial arm. Release the yoke-swivel clamp handle by pulling it forward and lift up the location pin. Swivel the yoke clockwise 90° from the crosscut position. (The swivel location pin will snap into position automatically.) Now tighten the swivel clamp handle.

 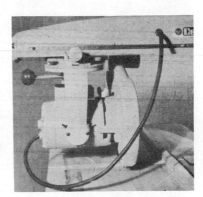

Fig. 41.   **Fig. 42.**

The rip scale or rule on the right side of the arm is set with the guide fence in its standard position, which is between the stationary top and the spacer boards. With the saw blade against the guide fence, the pointer on the roller head should read zero on the *top* side of the ruler marked "in-rip" (Fig. 42). This rule and pointer can be off as much as $\frac{1}{16}$" because of difference in the types of saw blades. Some saw blades have set teeth, while others may be hollow ground with no set in the teeth. To adjust the rule, release the two Phillip's-head screws and adjust the scale to the proper setting. Now set your saw to the desired width of the rip by following the pointer and rule. Then tighten the rip-lock clamp screw to hold the saw in position.

With the saw set to in-rip position, you must feed the material into the saw from the right side of the machine. With your left hand approximately 6″ back of the safety guard, hold the material down and back against the guide strip. Now with your right hand, move the material into the saw by standing on the right front side of the machine and let the material slide through your left hand (Fig. 43). When your right hand meets your left hand, continue the balance of the rip by using a pusher board.

Fig. 43.

Fig. 44.

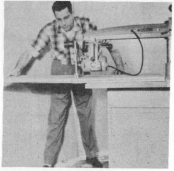

Fig. 45.

Fig. 46.

Hold the pusher board back against the guide fence and against the end of the board you are ripping and continue on through until the board you are ripping clears the saw blade on the opposite side by 2″ (Fig. 44). Now pull the pusher board straight back.

Out-ripping. When ripping wide materials such as panel boards, you should swivel the saw 90° counterclockwise from the crosscut position to out-rip position. With the saw set to out-rip position, follow the lower edge of the rip rule on the radial arm. This rule can be used to a capacity of 17½″ with the guide fence in its standard position. If ripping wider material, it is necessary to move the guide fence to the rear of the table boards. When the saw is set for out-ripping, the material must be fed into the saw from the left side of the machine (Fig. 45).

Resawing. If extremely thick wood or hardwood is being ripped into thinner boards, it is often necessary to cut part way through the board, invert the board, and complete the cut. This operation is generally called "resawing."

When resawing, the saw should be placed in the in-rip position. The blade should be set just a little over half the width of the board when the board is *less* in width than twice the capacity of the saw. To illustrate this, let us assume that it is necessary to resaw a board 4″ wide by ¾″ thick into two boards 4 by ⅜″. Making an allowance of ⅛″ for the kerf or the wastage material by the blade, and taking into consideration that the capacity of the particular saw blade is 2½″, about 1½″ is left for the second cut (Fig. 46). However, when the width of the board to be resawed is greater than twice the capacity of the machine, make the cuts as deep as possible from each edge. Then finish the ripping by hand. When resawing 4″ stock and larger, use a guide fence approximately 3½″ high.

An important point to bear in mind always when resawing is to keep the same surface of the board against the guide fence for both cuts. Always reverse the board end for end, never side for side. Be sure to follow all the safety rules for straight ripping when resawing.

Horizontal ripping. This operation is similar to horizontal crosscutting except that the cut is made on the side of the stock rather than on the end. To place the saw blade in the horizontal rip position, first set the saw in the in-rip location and then turn it to 90° as indicated on the bevel scale described in horizontal crosscutting.

Place the material to be cut against the guide fence, either standard or auxiliary depending on the thickness, and locate the height and depth of the cut. The rip clamp is tightened and the material is pushed past the blade in the same manner as in straight ripping. If a groove is desired, the arm may be raised or lowered a full turn at a time and the operation repeated until the proper width is obtained.

BEVEL RIPPING

Bevel ripping is simply ripping with the saw motor tilted for angle cuts (Fig. 47). With the saw swiveled to the rip position (either in- or out-rip), elevate the column by rotating the handle and then release the bevel clamp handle and latch. Turn the motor within the yoke to the desired angle. If the popular 45° position is wanted the bevel latch will quickly locate it. If any other angle is desired, set it and securely clamp the motor in place with the bevel clamp handle. Adjust the guard on the in-feed end so that it is within ⅛" of the material, but do not adjust the anti-kickback device. Use a pusher board as previously described to prevent kickback of the material. Push the material through as previously described.

Fig. 47.

Fig. 48.

SPECIAL CUTTING OPERATIONS OF THE SAW

By combining the six basic cuts, previously discussed, you are able to perform such special operations as tapering, chamfering, kerfing, cove cutting, or making saw-cut moldings. While this work may seem more complicated, it is easy and safe to do on a radial-arm saw.

KERFING

It is often necessary to bend wood. When the problem of curved surfaces arises, you have a choice of three methods; (1) bending the wood by steaming it (this calls for special equipment), (2) building the curve up by sawing thick segments of the circle on a saber saw (which means that a great deal of expensive wood would be wasted), or (3) cutting a series of saw kerfs to within ⅛" of the outside surface to make the material more flexible for bending. The latter is the most practical method (Fig. 48).

The distance between these saw kerfs determines the flexibility of the stock and the radius to which it can be bent. In order to form a more rigid curve, the saw kerfs should be as close together as possible. To determine the proper spacing, the first step is to decide on the radius of the curve or circle to be formed. After the radius has been determined, measure this same distance (the radius) from the end of the stock as shown in Fig. 49, and make a saw kerf at this point. The kerf can be made in the crosscut position, with the blade lowered to ⅛" of the bottom of the stock.

Now clamp the stock to the table top with a C clamp. Raise the end of the stock until the saw kerf is closed, as shown at *A*. The distance the stock is raised to close the kerf determines the distance between saw kerfs in order to form the curve.

Since most bending operations require many saw kerfs, mark this distance with a pencil on the guide fence. The first kerf is made in the standard crosscut position, with the end of the work butted against the mark. The remaining cuts are located by placing each new kerf over the guide-fence mark and making the new cut.

When the kerfing is complete, the stock is slowly bent until it matches the required curve (Fig. 50). Wetting the wood with warm water will help the bending process, while a tie strip tacked in place will hold the shape until the part is attached to the assembly. Even compound curves may be formed in this manner by kerfing both sides of the work. When kerfing is exposed, veneers may be glued in place to hide the cuts.

When bending wood for exterior work, the kerfs should be coated with glue before the bend is made. After making the bend, wood plastic and putty may be used to fill the crevices. When finished properly, only a close examination will show the method used to make the bend.

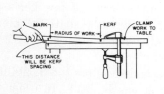

Fig. 49.

Fig. 50.

SAWCUT MOLDINGS

Several attractive moldings can be made with cuts similar to those used for kerfing. The zigzag shape shown in Fig. 51 is commonly called a dentil molding, although this term has a broad application and can include many different shapes.

A spacer mark on the guide fence, as for kerf bending, should be used. The distance from the mark of the blade determines the spacing of the saw cuts. The saw is set in the crosscut position, and the blade is lowered to the depth desired. Repeat cuts are made by alternately turning the work face up and face down, as shown in Fig. 52. The molding is then made by ripping narrow

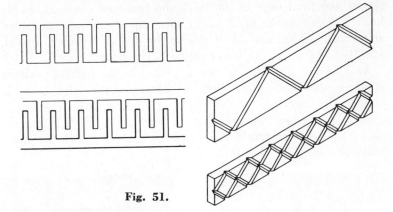

Fig. 51.

strips from the work, as shown in Fig. 53. A ripping operation on work as narrow and delicate as this demands care and accuracy. Use a pusher strip to push the molding past the blade.

Molding should be cut with a hollow-ground or planer blade to assure clean cutting. After the dentil molding is cut, it can be used as an overlay, or the molding can be applied to a heavier backing piece of contrasting color.

TAPER RIPPING

Taper ripping is the process of cutting material to a taper or narrower at one end than at the other. First, make a full-sized drawing or pattern of the taper. Transfer this pattern to a piece of plywood or waste lumber and cut to make the necessary template or jig.

To use the jig, place the flat side against the fence and place the material to be tapered in the stop at the end of the jig. With the saw in the rip position, push the jig past the blade as if it were a normal ripping operation (Fig. 54). Continue the ripping operation on all four sides in the same manner.

Tapering with a radial-arm machine can be done without the use of a specialized jig. This also includes taper ripping long stock which cannot be handled in the jig. Simply by clamping a piece of narrow stock to the lower edge of the material to be ripped, the front edge of the table top becomes a second "guide fence" for this operation. You can taper rip at any predetermined angle with this method. Just decide the degree of taper desired, and then clamp on the lower guide board accordingly.

As shown in Fig. 55, the saw is placed in the out-rip position (that is, swiveled to the right rather than the left) for this tapered-rip operation. This allows the blade to be positioned directly above the front edge of the worktable. Thus, the completed rip cut corresponds exactly to the angle at which the guide board is clamped to the stock.

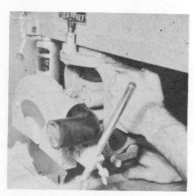

Fig. 52.

Fig. 53.

Fig. 54.

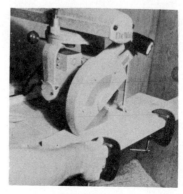

Fig. 55.

Regardless of the method used, a planer blade is the saw to use for taper ripping since it cuts more smoothly.

CHAMFER CUTTING

Chamfer cutting (Fig. 56) is simply making bevel cuts along the top edges of stock. Set the saw in the rip-bevel position at an angle of 20° to 45°. Position the blade so that it overhangs the stock by the desired width of the cut and lock it in place with the rip clamp. Push the stock along the guide fence and through the

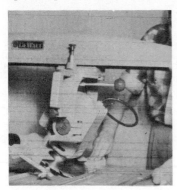

Fig. 56.

Fig. 57.

Fig. 58.

Fig. 59.

blade path. Then reverse the material and cut along the other top edge in the same manner.

Cross-chamfer is achieved by placing the blade in the crosscut-bevel position at the desired angle. Position the blade so that it overhangs the stock by the desired width (as for rip-chamfer). Then pull the motor and saw through in the prescribed crosscut method.

The octagon shape required for spindle lathe work can be cut in the same manner as described for chamfer cutting.

GROOVING

Grooving (Fig. 57) is the same as the horizontal saw cuts previously described. Place the saw in the crosscut or rip position, depending on the type of groove desired, and turn it to the 90° bevel position. Locate the position of the blade (height and depth), place the material against the fence and past the blade, or pull the saw through the material. If the blade strikes the guide fence, the stock should be placed on an auxiliary table. Then raise or lower the blade a full turn at a time and repeat the operation until you obtain the proper groove width.

CONTOUR CUTTING

One of the most novel techniques in radial-arm saw operation is the *contour feed* for cutting coves. On the standard circular saw this is a fairly difficult task, but on the radial-arm saw it is simple. Place the material flat on the table top against the guide fence. Set the saw at a bevel 45° position and swivel the motor 45° to the left. Locate the motor so that the lowest point of the blade is on the center line of the material and tighten the rip clamp. Back the material off from the saw and lower the blade so that it is 1/8″ below the top surface of the stock. Turn on the machine and push the material past the saw blade as when ripping (Fig. 58). Continue this procedure, lowering the blade one full turn (1/8″) at a time, until the desired depth of the cut is obtained. The final cut should be a light one for a smooth finish.

The saw cut can be made in different angle positions for different effects. For instance, you may set the bevel at 45° and the motor swivel at 30°, or the bevel at 30° and the motor swivel at 45°. Experiment with scrap wood until you get the effect you desire.

A half-circle effect, suitable for modern picture frames, is cut by establishing the depth of cut at the edge of the material and pushing the material past the blade in the same manner as just described. (Fig. 59).

Fig. 60.

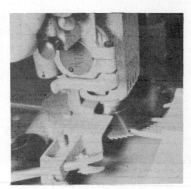
Fig. 62.

SAUCER CUTTING

This cut makes intricate decorative patterns easily. Place the stock flush with the edge of table front and clamp it to the table top. Locate the saw arm so that the lowest portion of the blade is on the center line of the stock, and tighten the rip clamp. Lower the blade until it touches the material, swing the motor to the 90° bevel position, and then lower the motor by turning the elevating handle one full turn. With your left hand on the anti-kickback rod, pull out the bevel latch with your right hand. Then swing the motor in an arc past the stock (Fig. 60). Lower the saw blade one full turn of the elevating handle and continue the cutting process until the desired depth is reached.

LAP-JOINT CUTTING

There are several types of lapped or halved joints (Fig. 61). To make the *end lap*, place the motor in the vertical position (the horizontal crosscut sawing position) and install the auxiliary table in place of the standard guide fence. Both pieces of stock that are to form the joint can be cut at once—laid side by side on the auxiliary table. Make the first cut with the blade passing through the center of the stock, following the technique described for horizontal crosscutting. Then elevate the blade ⅛″ (the width of the blade) by turning the elevating handle one full turn with each successive cut until all excess stock has been removed (Fig. 62).

The other types of lap joints shown in Fig. 61 are combinations of end lap joints and dado cuts.

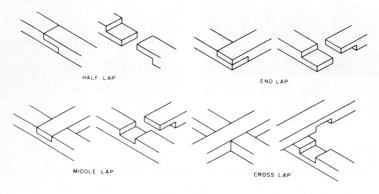

HALF LAP   END LAP

MIDDLE LAP   CROSS LAP

Fig. 61.

LOCK-JOINT

The *lock-joint*, when properly made and reinforced with glue or dowels, can be one of the strongest joints available. It is accomplished with the machine positioned exactly as when making the lap joint. Instead of removing half the stock, however, each alternate ⅛″ is left standing (Fig. 63). Use a standard ⅛″ thick blade to make this joint and judge your cuts by remembering that each complete turn of the elevating handle represents exactly ⅛″. The opposite ends are cut opposite so that the two pieces will mesh together.

TENON AND MORTISE CUTTING

The *tenon* is made in the same manner as the lap joint except that the stock left standing is in the middle rather than on one side of the material (Fig. 64). The full tenon, when combined with a tight-fitting mortise and properly glued or doweled, gives a very strong joint which is widely used in all phases of cabinet-making and general woodworking.

The *mortise* is the other half of the joint into which the tenon fits. Making the mortise consists simply of cutting a groove to the same width as a previously made tenon (Fig. 65).

Fig. 63.

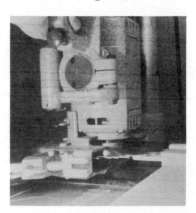

Fig. 64.

BEVEL-SPLINE JOINT

The *bevel-spline joint* (Fig. 66) is made by bevel crosscutting the ends of the stock with the motor locked in the 45° bevel position. To make the slot for the spline, reverse the stock on the table and, with the motor still in the bevel position (but elevated to the proper height, approximately ⅜″, so that the blade will not completely cut through), pull the saw across the previously made bevel crosscut, leaving the shallow slot (Fig. 67). Make the spline itself from any ⅛″ rippings you may have. Simply cut to the size desired to fit the spline joint.

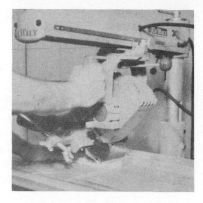

Fig. 65.   **Fig. 66.**

DADO-HEAD OPERATIONS

Dado-heads. The first accessory you most likely will choose for your radial-arm machine is a dado head. It contains a series of saw blades (Fig. 68) that can cut grooves, rabbets, mortises, tenons, dadoes, etc., in thicknesses from ⅛″ to $1\frac{3}{16}$″ in a single pass. In other words, the dado head cuts down the time consumed in making most wood joints.

There are basically two types of dado heads; the *flat ground* and the *hollow ground*. While the latter is more expensive, it produces a much smoother cut and should be used in high-quality work. Either type consists of two outside saws, each about ⅛″ thick, whose teeth are not given any set, and inside saws, or "chippers" as they are called—one ¼″, two ⅛″ (some heads include two additional ⅛″ chippers instead of the ¼″ one), and one $\frac{1}{16}$″ thick (thickness at the hub). The cutting portions of the inside cutters or chippers are widened to overlap the adjacent cutter or saw. When assembling a cutter head, arrange the two outside cutters so that the larger raker teeth on one are opposite the small cutting teeth on the other. This produces a smoother cutting and easier running head. Be sure also that the swaged

teeth of the inside cutters are placed in the gullets of the outside
cutters, not against the teeth, so that the head cuts clean and
chips have clearance to come out. And stagger the inside cutters

Fig. 67.

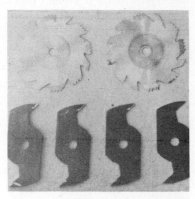

Fig. 68.

so that their teeth do not come together (*A*, Fig. 69). *For example*,
if three cutters are used, they should be set 120° apart.

MOUNTING THE DADO HEAD

The dado head is installed on the motor shaft in the same
manner as the regular saw cutting blade. In other words, for
dado cuts up to ½", place the ⅜" arbor collar on the shaft first,
with its recessed side against the saw; the dado-head assembly
next; then the ¼" arbor collar, with its recessed side against the
dado head; and finally tighten the arbor nut with two wrenches
(Fig. 70). For cuts over ½", omit the ¼" arbor collar. If using
the full dado head, first put on the ¼" arbor collar, the $1\frac{3}{16}$"
dado, and then the arbor nut. Mount the safety guard over the
dado head, adjust for the cut on the motor stud, and tighten the
wing nut.

In a dado head there is quite a mass of metal revolving at a
fairly high speed in the flywheel manner, and if it is not running
true it will set up a noticeable vibration. This can be avoided, of
course, by staggering the teeth properly and tightening the dado
to the full extent.

Never use the chipper blades without the two outside saws. *For example,* to cut a dado ½″ wide, use the two outside saws, each ⅛″ in width, plus a single ¼″ or two ⅛″ chippers. Actually any width dado head can be used (the size being limited only by the length of the motor arbor). However, most dado-head sets have enough blades to make cuts only up to 1¾₆″ wide.

When the width of the finished cut is to be more than 1¾₆″, set up the dado head to a little more than half the required width of the cut and make two successive cuts. Each cut must overlap a bit at the center. If the width of the dado is to be more than

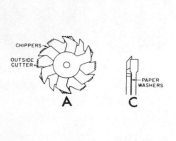

Fig. 69.   **Fig. 70.**

twice the capacity of the cutter head, set it for a little over one-third of the width and make three overlapping cuts. Figure 69 at C shows how the outside saw and the inside chipper overlap, and how a paper washer can be used as needed to control the exact width of the groove. These washers, 3″ to 4″ in diameter, can be cut from paper and are placed between blades and chippers. If you desire to increase the width slightly, cardboard (up to ¹⁄₁₆″ thick) can be substituted for the paper.

The design of the cutting teeth of the dado head permits cutting with the grain, across the grain, or at an angle.

OPERATING THE DADO HEAD

The dado head is operated in the same manner as the saw. The settings for the various cuts are the same.

Plain dado. A plain or cross dado is a groove cut across the grain. It can be done in the way described for crosscutting. With the motor in the crosscut position, elevate or lower the radial arm until the depth of the groove is obtained. Then pull the motor past the stock, which has been placed tight against the guide fence (Fig. 71).

Angle dado. This cut has many uses in cabinetmaking, construction work, and general woodworking. Among other applications, the angle-dado cut is used to recess treads in stepladders, in joining the sill to the upright members of a window frame, and

| Fig. 71. | Fig. 72. |

to recess the narrow strips in shutters, louvers, etc. This cut is made in the same manner as the cross dado, except that the radial arm is moved to the right or left to the desired degree of angle as indicated on the miter scale.

Parallel dadoes. These are a series of dado cuts exactly parallel to one another. With the radial-arm machine, these cuts are easy to make because the material remains stationary, the cutting head doing the moving. As a result, any two cuts made with the radial arm in the same position (whether crosscut or any degree of miter) are always exactly parallel to one another. Mark your guide fence and make successive cuts the exact distance apart.

Parallel dado cuts at right and left miter can be done as shown in Fig. 72.

Blind dado. A blind dado is cut only partly across the board. With the stock against the guide fence, mark off where you wish the dado to stop. Then place a stop clamp on the machine. With the dado head in the crosscut position and the arm set at the proper height, pull the yoke forward until it hits the stop, and then back off the motor. If a square cut at the blind end of the dado is desired it can be made with a wood chisel.

Ploughing. The ploughing operation with a dado head corresponds to the rip cut with a saw blade and is done in the same way. Set the radial arm at 0° (crosscut position); swivel the yoke 90° from crosscut position; move the carriage out on the arm to the desired width and lock; raise or lower the column to the desired depth for the groove. (Remember that each turn of the elevating handle represents exactly ⅛".) For a ¼" groove, lower the column two turns from a position where the blades just touch the top surface of the stock. Adjust the safety guard so that the infeed part clears the stock, lock the wing nut, and then lower the anti-kickback fingers ⅛" below the surface of the board. Push the material against the guide fence past the blade from right to left in the same manner as when ripping (Fig. 73).

Fig. 73.   **Fig. 74.**

Rabbeting. Grooving a notch from the side and top of the lumber is simple and effective with the radial-arm machine. Elevate the arm until you have sufficient space beneath the motor to allow the cutting member to swing to a vertical setting. Then release the bevel clamp and the bevel latch to put the dado head in the vertical position (same as the horizontal sawing position).

To set the width of the rabbet, use the rip scale located on the radial arm. Then lower the arm to the desired depth for the groove and pass the material past the cutters from the right side of the table (Fig. 74).

To lay out a rabbet joint, hold one edge of the second member over the end or side of the first and mark the width of the rabbet.

 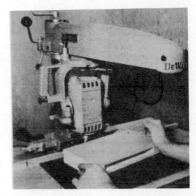

Fig. 75.   Fig. 76.

Then draw a line down the sides or end and measure one-half to two-thirds the thickness of the first member as the depth of the rabbet. If the cutter "burns" the stock, it indicates a minor misalignment. Simply release the arm, and swing it approximately 5° to the right-hand interposition. This will relieve the drag and will result in a clean cut.

The bevel rabbet is made in a manner similar to the straight rabbet except that the motor is placed at some angle less than 90° (vertical position), depending upon the degree of the bevel desired (Fig. 75). This cut is widely used throughout construction, cabinetmaking, and general-millwork operations.

Grooving. Although the term "groove" is used to denote many types of dado cuts, it is properly applied to the dado operation made on the side as opposed to the top or end surface of stock. The operation is exactly the same as for rabbeting except that the arm is lowered so that the cutting head is below the top surface of the lumber.

Blind mortising or *blind grooving* is similar to grooving except that the cut is not carried completely through the ends of the stock. In many cases, where the ends of the lumber will be exposed, it is desirable not to show the side groove. In such cases, the stock is "heeled" or pivoted into the cutting head some inches back from the end (Fig. 76).

Mortising and tenoning. For both operations, the motor is placed in the vertical position (as for horizontal crosscutting). A spacing collar is inserted into the dado head at the proper place so that the stock forming the tenon is left standing. On the auxiliary table, place the material against the fence and mark the stock for the tongue or groove depth desired. The dado head should be located at the proper height, and the motor can be brought to the tenon (Fig. 77).

Mortising is actually a reverse cut of the one used for tenons. Making the mortise consists simply of cutting a groove to the same width as a previously made single tenon. Be sure the length of the tenon and mortise is the same.

Fig. 77.　　　　　　　　　　　Fig. 78.

Cutting lap joints. The lap joint is found in simple furniture legs, tables, frames, and chairs, as well as in many other pieces. The basic one is the *cross-lap* or *middle-half-lap* joint. Adaptations of this are the edge-lap, and half-lap joints. The cross-lap joint is one in which two pieces cross, with the surfaces flush. They may cross at 90° or any other necessary angle. On modern furniture legs, *for example*, they frequently cross at 45°.

The *edge-lap* joint is identical except that the members cross on edge. The *middle-* or *tee-lap* joint is made with one member exactly like the cross-lap joint and the second member cut as a rabbet. The *end-lap* joint, which is used in frame construction, is made by laying out and cutting both pieces as rabbets. The *half-lap* joint is cut in the same way except that the pieces are joined end to end.

The *end-lap* and *half-lap* joints are actually two tenons with the stock removed from *only* one side.

Cross-lap and *edge-lap* joints are cut similar to a cross dado, except that the lap joints are usually wider. Make the layout and cut in the same manner described for cross dadoes (Fig. 78).

In the *middle-lap* joint, one member is cut like a tenon and the second like a dado. Follow the instructions for making each of these two kinds of cuts (Fig. 79).

Radius cutting. This is a dado operation used to produce a concave cut along the face of a piece of lumber. It is accomplished by elevating the column (the radial arm and yoke remain

Fig. 79.   **Fig. 80.**

in the normal crosscut position) and dropping the motor to the 45° bevel position. The motor is moved in or out on the radial arm to the correct position in relation to the stock to be cut and is locked in place. The lumber is then pushed under the cutting head as when ripping or ploughing (Fig. 80). The first cut should be about ⅛″ and the dado head should be lowered one full turn at a time until the desired concave is obtained. This operation is similar to contour cutting with a saw blade, as previously described.

Tongue-and-groove. By cutting a tongue-and-groove, you can make your own flooring, wood panels, etc. The tongue-and-groove is really a combination of tenon and grooving, previously described. With the saw in the horizontal rip position, cut the tongue by using the dado inserts with collars to the exact dimension needed (Fig. 81). Push the stock past the blade to complete the tongue. Cut all the tongues on the panels required first; then turn the stock over and cut the groove (Fig. 82). The groove must match the tongue for a good fit.

Tongue-and-groove cuts can also be made with a molding head on the shaper, as described in the next section of this chapter.

Fig. 81.

Fig. 82.

Fig. 83.

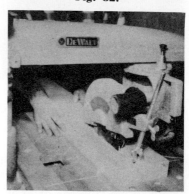

Fig. 84.

Cutting and dadoing. It is possible, by combining a saw blade and the dado head, to get both a cutoff and dadoing operation at the same time. Install the saw blade first on the arbor, followed by the dado head. Then, with the saw in the crosscut position, pull the yoke through the material (Fig. 83). Result—cut-off and dado in the same action. Use a 9″ saw blade and an 8″ diameter dado head, as a rule, for deep cuts.

It is also possible to rip and plough at the same time. Mount the saw blade and dado head on the arbor and put the motor in the rip position. Lower the column to the desired depth and push the stock past the blade and dado head (Fig. 84). Result— both cuts in a single operation.

SHAPER-JOINTER OPERATION

The *shaper attachments* for a radial-arm machine are used for straight and irregular shaping, matched shaping, tongue-and-groove, planing, sizing, and jointing, chamfer cutting, and making drop-hinged leaf joints. It is easy to perform these operations and to turn out the work quickly and accurately. The tilting-arbor shaper of the radial-arm machine offers many advantages over the conventional shaper. For instance, standard makes of shapers are maneuverable in only two directions—the cutting head can be raised and lowered, the guide fence can be moved forward and back. But unlike the radial-arm shaper, there is no provision for tilting the arbor or cutter head. This flexibility adds approximately 50 per cent more shapes to each cutter. Also, you can shape in the center of wide stock, which is impossible with the limited spindle capacity of the ordinary shapers.

Be sure the table is level. It is a good idea to use a ¼″ hardboard top clamped or nailed over the wood table top to minimize friction and to allow the stock to be cut with ease.

SHAPER ACCESSORIES

Nearly all common moldings can be cut on the radial-arm machine with a special cutterhead. Molding heads with a ⅝″ bore come in two- and three-knife styles, either one of which will produce smooth, clean work.

There are also two types of cutters available for shaper work. One is the loose type mounted on a safety head (*A*, Fig. 85) (two styles are illustrated), and the other is the solid cutter (*B*, Fig. 85). The latter is milled from a solid bar of hardened and properly tempered tool steel, ground to the required shape. The loose-type knives are held in the head by means of fillister-head socket screws. Since the spindle moves clockwise and is not reversible, all cutters must point in the same direction.

There are many cutting-knife shapes available. You can start your collection of knives with a few basic types, then add new ones as you need them. There are combination blades that permit different cuts, depending on which part of the contour you

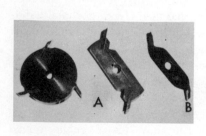

Fig. 85.

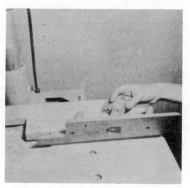

Fig. 87.

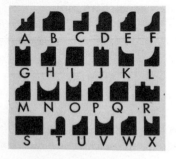

Fig. 86.

A. Miter Lock Joint	M. Cove and Bead
B. Drop-Leaf Table	N. Nosing Cutter
C. Cupboard Door Lip	O. Nosing Cutter
D. Fluting Cutter	P. Bead and Cove
E. Bead and Cove	Q. Surfacing Knives
F. O. G. Molding	R. Tongue and Groove
G. Nosing Cutter	S. Straight Jointer
H. Quarter Round	T. Fluting Cutter
I. Panel Raising	U. Quarter Round
J. Glue Joint	V. Nosing Cutter
K. Cupboard Door Lip	W. Cone and Bead
L. Quarter Round	X. Cupboard Door Lip (7° rake)

use. With these, you can shape table edges, make your own moldings, and do many other decorative jobs.

Standard cutters are each designed to do a specific job and usually require use of the full contour of the blade. These can cut shaped edges for glue joints, door lips, tongue-and-groove joints, drop-leaf tables, and quarter-round molding. Figure 86 illustrates profiles of some of the common types of cutters or knives.

The head is mounted on the arbor of the saw in the same way as a saw blade or dado cutter. To mount the molding head, remove the safety guard, arbor nut, cutting device, and arbor collars from the motor shaft. For the solid type of cutter, replace the $\frac{1}{4}''$ arbor collar (recessed portion on the outside), the cutter, and the arbor nut. The safety guard is used when the molding head is in the horizontal and chamfering positions.

To mount the solid-cutter type, place the arbor collars ($\frac{3}{8}''$ and $\frac{1}{4}''$ thick collars first), the molding head, and the arbor nut. The safety guard is used with the molding head in the horizontal and chamfering position. With this type, be sure that the knives are in place and tighten securely.

Right after use, clean the knives of gum and sawdust and coat them with oil to prevent rust. Store them so that the cutting edges will be protected from nicks. The head itself should also be cleaned, especially the slots in which the knives sit. Never leave knives locked in the molding head.

Shaper-jointer fence. A shaper-jointer fence is available for the radial-arm machine and should be used for straight shaping. This fence replaces the standard guide fence (metal portion on the right side) and fits directly into the standard guide slot. As shown in Fig. 87 the infeed side of the fence is adjustable for any capacity up to a full $\frac{1}{2}''$, while the outfeed side remains in a fixed position. This, of course, is of prime importance in the jointing operation when a portion of the surface of the lumber is being removed. Because the infeed side of the fence can be recessed by the exact amount of stock being removed by the jointer, there is always full support of the lumber both before and after contact with the cutting knives. The result is a smooth, clean surface, free from "ripples" and "dimples."

Since the fence is designed for insertion in the guide slot of the radial-arm machine, either the infeed or outfeed side can be independently moved closer to the center of the table or farther out toward the ends. This flexibility of positioning allows the user to place the center ends of the fence right up to within ⅛″ of the cutting diameter of the shaping or jointing head, no matter what that diameter may be.

For certain types of straight shaping, a high fence is desirable because the material being shaped should never be higher than the fence. Figure 88 shows the construction of an easily made jig to replace the standard guide fence and rear table boards. The jig is clamped into place by tightening the thumbscrews at the rear of the table in the usual manner. Note that a square hole has been cut into the horizontal board to allow the motor shaft and arbor nut to project down through the surface of the table.

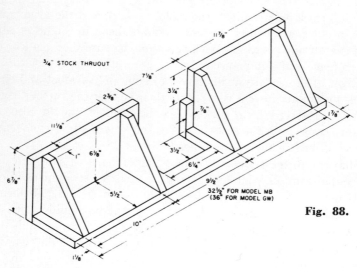

Fig. 88.

Figure 89 shows the action of the molding head extending through the high guide fence and completing the decorative shape on the face of the stock.

Shaper guard. As shown in Fig. 90, the shaper guard totally encloses the cutting knives and the motor spindle. After the shaper guard is fitted into the slotted portion of the motor end bell (Fig. 91), the hole in the guard flange is placed over the stud on the motor in exactly the same manner as when installing the saw guard. To allow the circular wall to be raised to a height permitting the user to check the precision of the cut, two thumbscrews, located on either side of the center wing nut, permit the protecting portion of the guard to be freely raised and lowered on the small circular columns. When raised on the columns, and locked in position by retightening the thumbscrews, the guard permits full access to the cutting knives. Thus you can look and reach beneath the guard (with the motor "off") to position the knives accurately for the desired depth of cut. The easiest way to do this is to place the lumber against the knives. After all adjustments have been made, the guard can be lowered right down to the top surface of the lumber and the shaping operation can begin.

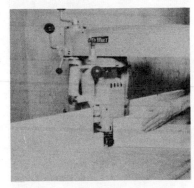

Fig. 89.

Fig. 90.

Shaper ring. To allow the shaping head to follow irregular curves, the standard guide fence must be removed from the table top. Then, to maintain the stock in proper relation to the cutting knives, a circular guide ring of the same diameter as the cutting circle of the head must be provided. Although you can buy a steel shaper ring for this purpose, you may find it more convenient and less expensive to make a variety of these rings for your own use.

Figure 92 shows the simple construction of the shaping ring. To determine the diameter, measure the shortest distance between the cutting surfaces of the opposing shaper knives. This will ensure that the stock will enter the knives to an exact and uniform dimension. The inner circle of wood is removed from the ring to allow the motor shaft to project below the surface. The shaper ring is then nailed to a small piece of 1″ scrap lumber which replaces the standard guide when the machine is to be used for this operation (Fig. 93).

SHAPER OPERATIONS

Shaper operations may be divided into four main classifications, according to the methods used in holding or guiding the material against the cutters:

Fig. 91.

Fig. 92.

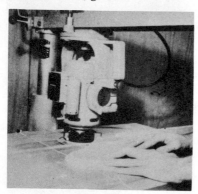

Fig. 93.

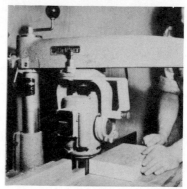

Fig. 94.

Holding the stock against the guide fences. This method is used for cutting stock with straight edges or faces.

Holding and guiding stock against the shaper ring. This method is used principally for cutting stock with curved edges or faces and irregular shapes.

Cutting stock by following patterns. This method is used in production work when many pieces of the same shape have to be made.

Holding stock on special jigs. This method is generally used for stock that cannot readily be held except on special jigs.

General shaper operations are similar to those described in Chapter 13.

JOINTING

Edge jointing. For edge jointing (or face jointing up to two inches) place the four-wing jointer on the arbor shaft and install the jointer fence. To install the jointer, remove everything from the arbor shaft. Then slide on the jointer and tighten the special adaptor nut which comes with the jointer blade. Use the wrenches to tighten. Now place the motor in the vertical position and locate it on the radial arm so that the lead portions of the jointer blades line up with the rear or outfeed fence. Lower the motor to the desired cut by means of the elevating handle.

The 2″ straightedge jointing or surfacing shaper knives can also be used in the same way as the four-wing jointer.

The front or infeed fence must be about $\frac{1}{32}$″ back of the cutter head for light cuts and $\frac{1}{8}$″ back for rough cuts. Turn the handle in back of the infeed fence to bring it in or out. *Always* use the shaper guard whenever possible.

Place the material flat on the table and tight against the infeed fence. Then feed the material past the jointer blade, keeping it against the infeed fence (Fig. 94). When about one-half to two-thirds of the board has passed the cutter head, move your left hand to the board over the outfeed fence. As most of the board passes over the cutter, move your right hand to the board over the outfeed fence to finish the cut. Feed the material slowly past the blade and take two thin cuts rather than one big one.

Face jointing. In face jointing, *always* use a push stick to push the board through. Push the material past the cutter in the same manner as for edge jointing. Always cut with the grain when jointing.

Sizing and jointing. Sizing and jointing in the same operation require an easily made jig (Fig. 95) which has the guide fence located at the front of the table rather than at the rear. The exact width of the finished stock is determined by measuring the distance between the front guide and the cutters. Lock the carriage at the desired position on the arm. Feed the stock into the cutters from the right side of the table (Fig. 96). The result is perfect width and perfect edge with only one cut. To joint the flat surfaces, remove the jig and place the stock against the guide fence. Lower the jointer blade until it hits the top surface and keep lowering it until it takes off the desired amount. Push it past the blade in the rip manner and keep passing it over the surface until the surface is smooth and even.

General jointer operations are similar to those described in Chapter 13.

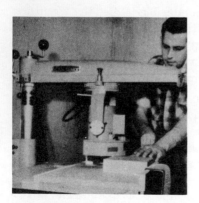

Fig. 95.   Fig. 96.

Rotary surfacer. This attachment, actually a rotary jointer, will quickly and efficiently cut warped boards down to uniform thickness and convert them into usable stock ready for sanding or finishing.

To install the rotary surfacer, remove all items from the motor shaft. Then screw on the rotary surfacer directly to the motor shaft (Fig. 97). Drop the motor to the vertical position (the surfacer will be in a horizontal position), locate the motor on the arm where the surfacing is to be done, lock the rip clamp, and lower the column until the surfacer knives project slightly below the top surface of the material.

Place the stock flat on the table against the fence and feed the work into the rotary planer from right to left, following the grain.

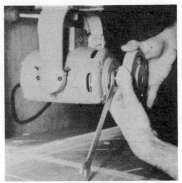 

Fig. 97.   **Fig. 98.**

BORING AND DRILLING

The flexibility of the radial-arm machine brings you unlimited boring capacity. Equipped with the boring bit attachments, it overcomes certain limitations of the conventional drill press. *For example,* you are not restricted in the length or width of material you can bore because of the size of the throat opening or the length of the downstroke of the press. The boring action of the radial-arm machine is horizontal rather than vertical. Thus material several feet in length can be end-bored with perfect precision and accuracy. And the depth of the hole to be bored is limited only by the length of the bit itself, not by the stroke of press.

MOUNTING THE BORING BIT

To mount the boring bit, remove the safety guard, the arbor nut, the cutting device, and the arbor collars from the motor shaft. Replace the two arbor collars (the ⅜″ thick collar first) and then screw on and tighten the special motor-shaft adapter (Fig. 98). The desired size of bit can now be placed in the adapter, and the adapter setscrew should be tightened.

Wood-boring bits for the radial-arm machine are available in the following sizes: ¼, 5⁄16, ⅜, ½, ⅝, ¾, ⅞, and 1″. Since a left-hand feed and point are required with this machine, conventional bits *cannot* be used.

WOOD-BORING OPERATIONS

For various boring operations, a *simple jig* (Fig. 99) is needed to raise the material above the surface of the table top and to provide a higher guide fence. Place a wedge between the jig and column to add support when boring (Fig. 100).

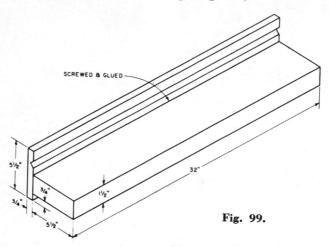

SCREWED & GLUED

5½″

32″

¾″

3⁄4″

1½″

5½″

Fig. 99.

Laying out the work. Accurate layout is a basic requirement of hole boring. The simplest method of marking the location of a hole is to draw lines which intersect at the center of the hole. For such work, a combination square is ideal, since it can be used to draw lines parallel with the edge of the work and as an edge-marking gauge. Dividers are handy when it is necessary to transfer a measurement from one piece to another or to mark off a line in a number of equal spaces. If a pencil is used for marking, select a hard one (3H or harder) and keep it sharp so that the lines will be well defined.

General boring and drilling operations are similar to those described in Chapter 12.

Fig. 100.

Fig. 101.

OPERATION OF THE SABER OR BAND SAW

No tool adds so much to the versatility of the radial-arm machine as a saber or band saw. It will cut all types of intricate scrollwork and irregular curves—either square or beveled—in wood, plastic, or light metal. It can also be used for power filing, sanding, and similar operations.

The *saber saw* shown in Fig 101 will cut material up to 2″ in thickness. The table top of the radial-arm machine allows you to do intricate scrollwork on large panels with full support of the stock, for there is more than 27″ of clearance between the blade and the column.

The *saber-saw unit* mounts directly on the radial-arm motor brackets and takes just about one minute to install (Fig. 102). The Scotch-yoke mechanism encased in the unit converts the rotating motion of the shaft into the reciprocating motion necessary to drive the saber saw. Oil-impregnated bearings eliminate lubrication worries.

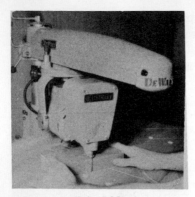

Fig. 102.

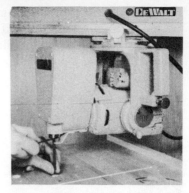

Fig. 104.

MOUNTING PROCEDURES

The installation of the saber saw is a simple operation. Before you make the setup for the first time, you must bore a small hole (about ½" in diameter) through the wood table top to allow the saber-saw blade to project down through the table. This hole can be placed anywhere on the wood top so long as it does not come directly above any of the channel braces in the steel table frame. From experience, a location about three inches to the inside of the second hold-down screw (counting from the rear) is ideal. This position allows maximum use of the table-top working surface.

To mount the saber-saw unit, follow these six steps.

Remove the safety guard and the circular-saw blade (or other cutting tool) from the motor.

Place the pulley, provided with the unit, on the motor shaft (groove toward the motor), then replace and tighten the arbor nut. Check to be sure that the belt is on the pulley in the saber-saw unit. If not, remove the back of the unit by removing the four Phillip's-head screws, slide the belt on the pulley, and replace the back.

Hold the saber saw in your right hand and slightly tilt the bottom in toward the motor. Place the belt in the groove on the motor pulley.

Hook the bottom lip of the saber saw into the groove in the

lower front end of the motor bell (Fig. 103). Then slide the top bracket of the unit into place in the safety-guard stud atop the motor. Replace and tighten the wing nut on the guard stud.

Align the saber-saw blade with the hole in the wood table top by swinging the radial arm to the left and swiveling the motor yoke to the right. Then lock all controls—arm clamp, yoke clamp, and rip lock.

Lower the radial arm by means of the elevating handle until the saber-saw guide barely touches the top surface of the material to be cut.

When saber sawing, the guide fence, in most operations, should be removed from its normal position and placed at the extreme rear of the table.

SABER-SAW BLADES

To operate the saber saw with maximum efficiency, become familiar with the various blades available. For most uses, four blades will do the job. The following table lists various materials and suggests the size of saber-saw blades for cutting them.

Material	Thickness, in Inches	Blade Size, Teeth Per Inch
Softwood	Up to ½	15 or 20
Softwood	Over ½	7 or 10
Hardwood	Up to ½	15 or 20
Hardwood	Over ½	10 or 15
Nonferrous metal	Up to ⅛	20
Nonferrous metal	Over ⅛	15 or 20
Plastic, ivory, bone, etc.		10, 15, or 20

Always use the blade with the coarsest teeth that will cut the material cleanly, and that will cut the sharpest curve in any pattern you are working on. As you progress with your saber sawing, your experience with various materials and blades will help you in choosing a blade for the particular operation on hand.

Mounting the blade. To mount a saber-saw blade, turn the machine on and off until you stop the chuck at the bottom of its stroke. Loosen the Allen-head setscrew on the side of the chuck with a wrench and insert the blade approximately ⅜″ into the chuck against the insert, with the teeth pointing downward (Fig. 104). Then tighten the chuck setscrews and you are ready to start cutting.

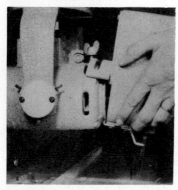

Fig. 103.

OPERATING THE SABER SAW

Since the prime purpose of the *saber saw* is to cut curves and patterns, lay out and plan your work before cutting. Except for simple designs that can be sketched directly on the material, it is necessary to make a full-size pattern of work and transfer it to the stock being cut. Be sure you have a clean outline to follow.

For average work, *always* stand directly in front of the blade with both hands resting comfortably on the table. Guide the work with both hands, applying forward pressure with the thumbs (Fig. 105). Make sure the guide finger on the unit always rests lightly on the work.

Where the work is of such length that it will strike the column before the cut is completed, cutting from the side or using an extension table is necessary.

Side cutting requires the motor to be swiveled until the blade of the saber unit is parallel with the guide fence.

General saber or band sawing procedures are similar to those described in Chapter 10.

THE LATHE

The 12″ lathe shown in Fig. 106 is designed as a radial-arm-saw accessory. It is complete and ready to use, taking its driving power from the saw's motor. The lathe also can be operated as a separate unit with any motor ⅓ h.p. or larger.

LATHE PARTS

Wood lathes are designated according to the maximum diameter of the work that can be swung over the bed. A lathe capable of swinging a 12″ diameter disc of wood is called a 12″ lathe. The lathe shown in Fig. 106 will take work 37″ long between centers.

The principal parts of a lathe are the *headstock, tailstock,* and *tool rest.*

Fig. 105.

Fig. 106.

Headstock. The headstock contains the driving mechanism, the step pulley for changing speeds, and the spindle. The spindle of the headstock lines up exactly with the tailstock spindle. The two main attachments are the spur center, which fits the headstock spindle and is commonly known as the "live center," and the cup center, which fits the tailstock spindle and is known as the "dead center." The work is mounted between these two centers, the spurs of the live center serving as the driving member. The faceplate is fastened to the headstock spindle in certain types of turnings in place of the spurs.

Tailstock. The tailstock assembly can be clamped to the bed at any position. A hand wheel can be turned to move the tailstock spindle in or out 3¼″. This spindle is hollow, with a No. 2 Morse taper. The cup center fits into this end.

Tool rest. The tool rest and holder clamp to the bed and can be adjusted to various diameters of work.

SETTING UP THE LATHE

It is a very simple operation to convert the radial-arm machine into a *wood-turning lathe* by proceeding as follows:

Remove the safety guard and the cutting tool from the motor shaft.

Swivel the motor to the out-rip position and swing the radial arm to the left 90° and lock securely.

Set the lathe on the table top of the radial-arm machine with the base of the lathe tight against the fence. The headstock should be at the left.

Set hold-down clamps with the long part of the L's beneath the machine's table top and the short part resting against the bottom of the lathe base. Locate the two carriage bolts in the holes on the base of the lathe, push them through the clamps, and place the wing nuts on the bolts. Then draw the nuts tight against the bottom of the clamps.

Place the belt pulley on the motor shaft, hub side out, and tighten the setscrew in the hub. Place the arbor nut on the shaft and tighten.

Position the motor directly behind the headstock and align the headstock pulley with the one on the motor shaft. This may require raising or lowering the motor by means of the elevating handle. When aligned, tighten the rip clamp and carriage arm and attach the drive belt.

General lathe turning operations are similar to those described in Chapter 9.

DISC, BELT, AND DRUM-SANDER ATTACHMENTS

With the versatile radial arm, you have a choice of three major types of power sanders—*disc, belt,* and *drum.* Each type has its advantages and uses. But unlike ordinary sanders, the attachments allow you to take full advantage of maneuverability and flexibility of the radial-arm machine. Attached directly to the motor arbor, they can be tilted, swiveled, or elevated, and absolute accuracy is always possible.

ABRASIVES

For power sanding there are four types of abrasive materials to choose from—*flint, garnet, aluminum oxide,* and *silicon carbide.*

Flint. Flint is the oldest of modern abrasives. It is cheap but has little efficiency as compared to other abrasives. Flint paper is good for removing old paint and for other jobs requiring quantity rather than quality.

Garnet. Garnet, a rubylike gemstone, is the hardest of natural abrasives. It is used in most home workshops as the basic paper for finishing wood.

Aluminum oxide. Aluminum oxide is a synthetic abrasive made from bauxite, coke, and iron filings in an electric furnace. Aluminum oxide paper is fast becoming the most widely used all-around paper. It is gray-brown in color.

Silicon carbide. Silicon carbide is another synthetic abrasive made of coke and sand, and is the hardest of all abrasives manufactured today. But it is very brittle and can be used only for glass, ceramics, gemstones, and plastics. Silicon carbide paper appears dark gray to black.

Grit size. This is determined by the number of grains which, end to end, equal 1″. To simplify this situation, many manufacturers label their papers as *fine, medium, coarse,* etc.

Backing. Paper-backed abrasives are generally used for hand sanding. Of the six weights of paper available, the only one suitable for machine sanding is the heaviest weight, *Type E.*

This is satisfactory for disc, spindle, or drum sanders.

There are two weights of cloth backings available to the home craftsman. The heaviest *(Type X)* is drill or twill, a linen or cotton fabric with a diagonal weave.

Type of coating. There are two types of coating—*closed* and *open*. Closed-coat papers have tightly packed abrasive grains that cover the entire surface. The grains on open-coat papers cover 50 to 70 per cent of the surface, leaving open spaces between the grains.

Closed-coat papers are durable and fast cutting, but have the disadvantage of clogging under certain conditions. *Open-coated* abrasives are not so durable, but they are useful for finishing certain surfaces such as soft or gummy woods, paint and other finishes, and soft metals and plastics where the abrasive dust tends to clog the disc or belt.

Forms of abrasives. Abrasive-coated materials can be obtained in *sheets, rolls, discs, drums,* and *belts.*

MOUNTING THE DISC SANDER

Remove the safety guard, saw blade, arbor nut, and two arbor collars from the arbor shaft. Replace the two arbor collars (⅜″ one first and recessed sides together), then place the disc plate on the shaft. Place a wrench on the flat of the arbor shaft to hold it, and tighten the disc plate by turning it counterclockwise (Fig. 107).

The abrasive disc must be cemented or glued to the plate. Any good glue may be used. Spread glue on the metal plate, then set the abrasive disc against it. When glue is used, a wood disc of ¾″ stock the same diameter as the plate will have to be placed over the abrasive so that clamps may be applied. The clamps should remain in place until the glue has set.

OPERATING THE DISC SANDER

The *abrasive* used on the disc sander will depend upon the work.

Sanding. Sanding on the disc sander is usually done freehand, the work being held flat on the auxiliary table and projected into the sanding disc. A smooth, light feed should be practiced. Avoid heavy pressure. The best results on curved work can be obtained by going over the work two or three times with light cuts. Sanding should be done on the "down" side of the disc (Fig. 108). Although it is permissible to sand small pieces on the "up" side, and while it is necessary to use both sides of the disc when sanding end grain on wide work, the surface produced will not be quite so smooth as that sanded only on the side of the disc going down. But with the versatile tilting-arbor disc sander, it is possible to sand large areas with only the down-side portion of the disc.

Fig. 107.   **Fig. 108.**

Surface sanding. To position the machine for general-surface sanding, elevate the radial arm until the motor with disc attached can be tilted to the vertical position. Then move the motor out on the arm until the disc is directly above the path the material will follow along the guide fence, and lock it in position with the rip clamp. Place the stock to be sanded on the table and lower the arm until the disc fits snugly against the top surface of the board. Push the board from right to left along the fence (Fig. 109).

For extra-fine sanding, raise the motor from the 90° bevel position 1° or 2° (indicated as **89** or **88** on the bevel scale). In this position, the sanding will be done on the down-side portion of the disc.

Straightedge sanding. Swing the radial arm 60° to the left and place the motor so that the front of the disc sander is parallel to and along the guide fence (Fig. 110). This is achieved by adjusting the swivel-clamp handle and the swivel-latch assembly. Lock the motor in position with the rip clamp. Lower the radial arm until the disc is within $\frac{1}{16}''$ of the top of the fence.

Butt sanding. Place the motor in the crosscut position and set the auxiliary-table jig in place of the guide fence. With the material tight against the fence of the auxiliary table and making contact with the disc, pull the motor past the material in the same manner as when crosscutting.

Fig. 109.   Fig. 110.

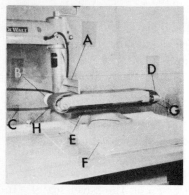

Fig. 112.

A. Work Guide	E. Sanding Belt
B. Pulley	F. Mounting Board
C. Motor Belt	G. Idling Drum
D. Tension Adjuster	H. Driving Drum

Bevel sanding. With the arm in the crosscut position, place the motor at the desired angle of bevel and locate the auxiliary table in place of the guide fence. Position the stock on the jig so that it contacts the sander and pull the disc across the beveled end of the board (Fig. 111). Swinging the motor 1° to 3° to the left will produce a finer job.

Miter sanding. With the motor in the crosscut position, locate the arm at the desired miter angle and replace the guide fence with the auxiliary table. Position the material on the table so that it contacts the abrasive and pulls the motor across the miter end of the board. If finer sanding is required, swivel the motor 1° to 3° to the left.

Rounding corners. Most sanding of corners can be done freehand, sweeping the corner of the work across the face of the sanding disc two or three times until the desired round is obtained. The motor is placed in the crosscut setup and locked into position by the rip lock.

MOUNTING THE BELT SANDER

Before attaching the belt sander to the radial-arm motor, a mounting board must be made. This board is made of ¾″ plywood and the lower projection on it fits into the slot normally occupied by the guide fence. When the spacer-board clamp screws are brought up tight, your 4″ sander will be in place.

Remove the safety guard, arbor nut, saw blade (or other tool), and arbor collars from the motor shaft. Place the pulley on the motor shaft (hub toward the motor) and tighten the setscrew. Replace and tighten the arbor nut.

Now swing the radial arm left until you read approximately 60° on the miter scale. Swivel your motor and extend it out on the radial arm until it is parallel and in line with the pulley on the belt sander. Slip the belt on both pulleys and readjust the motor by extending it farther on the arm or swinging the radial arm right or left a few degrees until the belt is tight. Lock the motor in place by means of the rip clamp. Turn on the machine to check the alignment of the pulleys and the tension on the belt. The belt sander is used mainly for flat work, though with-the-grain edges can be sanded square, beveled, or chamfered.

BELT-SANDER ADJUSTMENTS

The belt sander is provided with two drums over which the abrasive belt travels. The powered drum, the one on which the power pulley is placed, is covered with a rubber sleeve to give traction to the belt. The other drum, which is the idler, is provided with an adjusting device as shown in Fig. 112, which produces the belt tension and keeps the belt tracking. This device consists of four knurled nuts, two at each end of the idler drum.

When placing a belt on the sander, loosen the two inside nuts, releasing all tension, and slip the belt over the pulleys. (Be sure the arrow on the inside of the belt points toward the guide fence.) Tighten both adjustments back to the original position so that there will be sufficient tension for the belt to move when the power pulley is turned over by hand.

Turn the power pulley over several times to determine if the belt is tracking properly. If the belt shifts to the right when doing this, slightly loosen the right outside nut and tighten the right inside nut. This throws the belt to the left. If this does not solve the problem, slightly loosen the left side inside nut and tighten the left outside nut. This will help to throw the belt to the left. Alternate until proper tracking of the belt has been secured. But remember to *loosen lightly* as adjustments are sensitive.

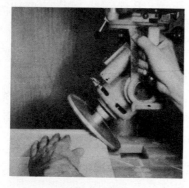

Fig. 111.

Fig. 113.

If the belt is tracking to the left, reverse the procedure given in the previous paragraph. Do not start the machine until you are certain that the belt is tracking on the center of the pulleys.

When the machine is started, it may be necessary to adjust the tension on the belt. To increase the tension, loosen the outside knurled nuts about a quarter turn and tighten the inside nuts until the assembly is forced against the outside nuts. Sometimes it may be necessary to adjust the tension on one side or the other to prevent the belt from shifting to the right or left.

To decrease tension, reverse the instructions given in the preceding paragraph. Too much tension will act as a resistance to your motor and will shorten the life of the abrasive belt.

Occasionally apply a few drops of oil on each end of the drive shaft to lubricate the self-lubricating bronze bearings. Every 4 to 6 months, remove the abrasive belt and screw in the center of the idler pulley. Place a few drops of SAE 30 or 40 oil in the hole. Replace the screw and belt.

OPERATING THE BELT SANDER

Work on a belt sander is generally done freehand, that is, the material to be surfaced is simply placed on the table. Use a light but firm pressure to keep the piece in the proper position. Avoid excessive pressure, since it will scratch the surface being sanded.

MOUNTING THE DRUM SANDER

Small sanding drums come in a range of sizes from 1″ to 3″ in diameter. The most popular is the 3″ size (Fig. 113).

Both the drums and abrasive sleeves are inexpensive and very efficient for edge-sanding curved work.

To mount the 2″ drum, remove the safety guard, saw blade (or other cutting tool), arbor nut, and arbor collars from the arbor shaft. Replace the two arbor collars (⅜″ one first and recessed sides together); then place the drum on the shaft. Place a wrench on the flat of the arbor shaft to hold it, and tighten the drum by hand, turning it counterclockwise. The 3″ drum sander may be used in either the horizontal or vertical position, depending on the operation.

Directions for replacing sleeves are shown in Fig. 114. Cut a 9″ x 11″ sheet of garnet sandpaper of the proper grit into three 3″ x 11″ strips by tearing it against a metal straightedge or hacksaw blade. (Never cut the sandpaper with scissors or a knife, as this will damage the cutting edge of the tool.) Bend the ends of the sleeves by the use of a board as shown at B, Fig. 114. The board must be measured accurately and cut square. Then wrap the sleeve around the drum approximately ¼″ down on it and slip the ends in the slot. Now slip the sleeve on down over the drum. A little talcum powder on the soft-rubber drum will make the sleeve slip on more easily. Squeeze hard to get the slack out of the sleeve and push the ends down into the slot. Then insert the tube that comes with the drum and turn it with a key. The oval tube should fit snugly. Do not force it. If it is too tight, put it in a vise and squeeze the edge; if too loose, squeeze the flat side of the tube.

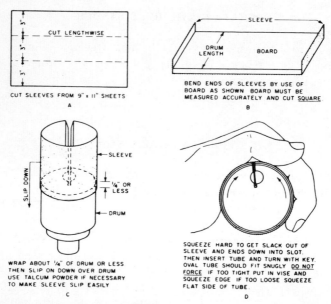

Fig. 114.

To mount the 1″ drum, remove all items from the arbor shaft and replace the two arbor collars (⅜″ one first and the recessed sides together). For this drum operation, use the same adapter as the one used for boring and place it on the shaft. Place a wrench on the flat of the arbor shaft to hold it and tighten the adapter by turning it counterclockwise. The sanding drum is held in place with an Allen-head setscrew in the arbor. The 1″ drum sander can be used in a horizontal position only. One-inch sleeves can be purchased ready made.

VERTICAL OPERATION ON THE DRUM SANDER

When using the 3″ drum sander in the vertical position, locate it over the shaper cutter hole in the table top. The back edge of the guide fence should be notched out for straightedge sanding (Fig. 115). The jointer fence can also be used and be positioned with a 1/64″ offset between the infeed and outfeed edges (Fig. 116).

With the radial arm raised to its fullest extent, place the drum in the shaper hole and, with the motor in the vertical position, bring the arbor shaft over the drum shaft. Lift the drum and mount it as previously described. Tighten the rip clamp on the arm. With the sander in this position, the lower edge of the drum will be a little below the surface of the auxiliary table so that the entire edge of the stock being finished will come in contact with the abrasive.

When using a drum sander, the material being finished should be kept constantly in motion to prevent overheating and scorching the wood. Wire-brushing the sleeve occasionally will prolong its useful life. Ordinarily, this is most effective if done while the machine is running.

Curved sanding. When sanding curved work, move the work past the drum from right to left.

Straight sanding. Although nearly all drum sanding is done freehand, straight work usually requires a guide fence or the use of the jointer fence. With the motor at the rear, bring the sander forward into the shaper slot on the table. Locate the sander so that its leading edge is in a straight line with the out-feed side of the fence and tighten the rip clamp on the radial arm. Place the material against the infeed side of the fence, start the motor, and push the stock past the drum sander.

In sanding straight work, the work must be kept moving at a uniform rate past the drum. If the work is stopped at any point while in contact with the rotating drum, it may be scored or burned. Uneven feed can produce scoring at intervals along the length of the stock. On long stock it will be necessary to shift the hands alternately. Here the trick is to maintain uniform pressure and rate of feed with one hand while the other is being shifted. In some cases an overhand movement gives satisfactory results.

Fig. 115.

Fig. 116.

HORIZONTAL OPERATION OF THE DRUM SANDER

In the horizontal position, the drum sander will do an effective job of surfacing narrow work when used as shown in Fig. 117. For this operation, use either the auxiliary or stationary table. With the motor raised to its full extent, set the motor shaft in a horizontal position. Place the material tight against the fence, and lower the radial arm until the abrasive hits the start of the stock. Withdraw the stock, turn on the motor, and feed the work against the rotation of the drum. If more smoothness is desired, keep lowering the arm a quarter turn at a time.

Wider boards may be handled in the same manner except that several passes will have to be taken with the sander at the same height. *Always remember* in any surface sanding operation do not attempt too deep a bite in one pass; two or more passes will result in a better job.

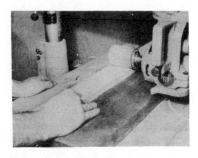

Fig. 117.

Sanding rabbets and similar cuts. Sanding the inside corners of rabbets and similar cuts can be easily executed with the drum sander as follows:

The rabbeted stock is set against the auxiliary-table guide fence, and the drum is set to fit in the corner. Then feed the work forward past the drum to make the cut. For operations like this, the sleeve should be mounted so that it projects about $\frac{1}{32}''$ beyond the bottom of the drum, allowing the inside corner to be finished cleanly.

CHAPTER **8**

Bench or Circular Saws

A good bench saw, sometimes called a circular saw because of the shape of its blade, is an extremely useful and versatile tool. It can be used for fast and accurate cutting, ripping and resawing lumber, beveling stock to any desired angle, and making all types of tapered cuts. Accessories for making dado, rabbet, and tenon joints and for buffing, polishing, and sanding are available.

Design features. In selecting a bench saw, certain fundamental features of design and construction must be taken into consideration. The essential parts of a medium-priced, well-designed bench saw are shown in Fig. 1.

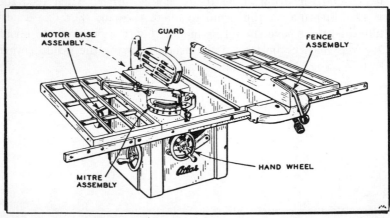

Fig. 1. Typical bench saw and its parts.

306

A bench saw must have a rigid frame mounted on a firm foundation to insure accurate work. It must be equipped with a well-machined, perfectly flat, cast-iron table reinforced with strengthening ribs on the underside. The table must be wide enough to allow the use of the miter gauge from either side of the saw blade. Where larger working surfaces are required, rigid grille-type extensions that can be attached to the table are available (Fig. 2). Avoid the type of bench saw that has large openings in the table around the saw blade, with no provision made for insertion or removal of inserts. This type is extremely dan-

Fig. 2. New grille extensions give large working surface. Grilles are designed for maximum rigidity.

gerous to operate, and in addition will always tend to chip off the bottom of the material being sawed. Be sure that metal inserts are flush with the table surface and easily removable.

In some bench saws, saw blade and arbor are fixed and the table can be raised and lowered. Others have fixed tables with the saw blade and arbor rising and falling. All good bench saws must have an adjustable table or arbor that regulates the steps of the cut. All adjustment controls should be readily accessible. All necessary adjustments must be simple and should be accomplished with a minimum of exertion and effort (Figs. 1, 3, 4, 5, and 6). All good bench saws are equipped with gauges that show the extent of movement made possible by any such adjustments. The better type of bench saw, and this type is especially recommended, in addition to an adjustable table or arbor also has provisions for tilting either the table or the saw. In machines of this type, the tilting should be mechanical and preferably either worm- or screw-controlled (Fig. 3); the latter is positive and is easy to operate. There should also be a gauge to indicate the angle to which the table or the saw is tilted. The indicating scale used in connection with this gauge should be adjustable. Be sure that the manufacturer of the saw has made provision for the adjustment of the alignment of the saw itself with the table, as any unusual strain or accidental bump is apt to put the saw out of alignment. On a well-designed bench saw the arbor should not be threaded for a distance of at least ⅛″

Fig. 3. Wheel at side tilts blade from 0° to 45°. Angle of tilt is shown on a scale. Upper lever locks the tilt mechanism.

from the collar, so as to allow the saw to ride on the arbor and not on the thread.

All efficient bench saws provide for oiling of the bearings, whether they be sleeve or ball bearings. Most of the ball-bearing types are of course dust-sealed, but they will need to be oiled or greased at some future time, and it is inconvenient to have to take an entire machine apart in order to do this. If your bench saw is equipped with oil or grease cups, injection of a little oil from time to time will do no harm.

A circular saw should be provided with a guard that can be adjusted to the various thicknesses of stock, remaining in position over the saw blade even in the tilted position.

When installing power-driven equipment, give serious consideration to the type of motor used. The motor for a bench saw must be of sufficient horsepower to cut wood as thick as the capacity of the saw permits. The saw blade must be at its greatest height at all times when sawing completely through any thickness of wood; in this position less power is required than when the saw is adjusted to just a little higher than the thickness of the wood. To be on the safe side, never use a motor of less than ⅓ h.p. If the saw has a 7″ or 8″ blade and the material that will be used is up to 2″ in thickness, best all-round results will be secured with a ½-h.p. motor. A line shaft providing power for several tools is sometimes used in place of individual motors for each tool. With allowance for power loss in the hanger bearings, plus the number of tools that will be operated at any one time, a considerably more powerful motor will be necessary. However, the ideal home workshop setup has an individual motor for each tool.

The motor in a well-designed bench saw is usually attached to a hinged motor base. The switch box should be mounted on the front of the table for efficiency (Fig. 4).

Checking and adjusting. A standard ½-h.p. motor will pull at one and one-half times its rated power, which means that at capacity load with an 8″ saw this motor will be drawing close to 10 amperes. If the motor is plugged into a circuit that is already overloaded, the line naturally will not supply enough current. As a result the voltage will drop and the motor will overheat struggling to carry the load. Thus perfect motors are frequently condemned for not pulling properly, when the defect really is in the house wiring. It is advisable to have a separate line, made up of at least 10-gauge wire brought in direct from the meter, for the home workshop. If there is a loss of power or motor failure persists, check the line with a voltmeter, checking first with no load and then with a load. Without the load the reading should be approximately that shown on the motor; with a full load the line voltage should not fall more than 5 per cent.

Fig. 4. Box-type switch mounted in handy position at front of table.

Manufacturers of all bench saws provide special instructions for setting them up. Be careful to read these instructions and set up your saw accordingly. Most of the well-constructed machines have been properly aligned before leaving the factory. However, rough handling and unpreventable shocks are likely to change the alignment.

Make the following tests. To check the alignment of the blade with the groove in which the miter gauge is guided, attach a piece of scrap lumber 1¾″ by 1¾″ by 10″ to the miter gauge. Set the miter gauge at 90°. Now, raise the saw to its greatest cutting capacity, using the adjustment control provided for that purpose (Fig. 5). Start the blade running. Move the miter gauge away from you toward the saw in the left-hand groove until the saw cuts halfway through the under edge of the piece of scrap lumber. Now, back the miter gauge away and lift it from the table. Place the miter gauge on the rear end of the saw table and move it toward you until the saw cuts the other end halfway through the underside of the wood. Check both cuts; if they meet exactly the saw is aligned properly. Repeat this same test in the right-hand groove on the table. If the two grooves are equidistant

Fig. 5. Handwheel on front of saw regulates blade height, small knob locks blade when height is set.

from the saw, then you are ready to proceed to the next checking operation. If they are not, make the necessary adjustment of the saw arbor before going ahead with the next test.

Set the miter gauge at exactly 90°. Secure a piece of wood about 8″ wide, hold this tightly against the gauge, and cut one end off. Check the squareness of this cut with an accurate try square. If it is not perfect adjust the miter gauge and make other cuts until the cut is absolutely square. Then file or readjust the indicating point to the correct 90° mark.

Check the alignment of the ripping fence or guide with the

saw (Figs. 6 and 7). Since the saw is correctly aligned with the slots in the table, it is necessary to align the ripping guide with this slot.

If the table is of the tilting type, tilt it to an angle of 90° with the saw blade, then at 45°, and adjust the screws provided for this purpose. The table can then be quickly tilted to either of

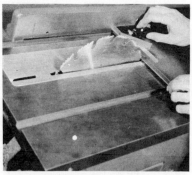 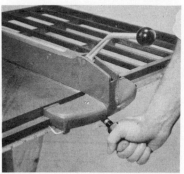

Fig. 6. Checking alignment of miter gauge groove with new blade. The rip fence must first be accurately aligned with the table groove. The fence then makes a convenient surface on which to rest the try square in checking blade alignment.

Fig. 7. Knob permits final accurate adjustment of rip fence. Fence is locked into position with knobbed lever.

these often-used angles, without additional waste of time and labor.

Before attempting to operate the saw make certain that the guard mechanism is properly adjusted and that the guard clears the saw blade. If the saw is equipped with a splitter, check it to be sure that it is directly in line with the saw blade. After all of these preliminary tests, alignments, and adjustments the bench saw is ready for use.

Types of blades. Bench saws are usually equipped with a combination saw, used for ripping, crosscutting, and mitering (Fig. 8). Other types are called planer, fast-cut, and grooving saws.

Planer saws are hollow-ground instead of having the teeth "set." This type of saw requires more power for operation than the combination saw, but makes a smoother cut. However, its use does not by any means entirely eliminate the necessity of planing or jointing the board for final finished edges.

Grooving saws form the two outside parts of a groover or dado

Fig. 8. Saw blades used on the bench saw; left to right: ripping blade, crosscut blade, combination blade, dado blades, dado chippers.

head. The inside members of this type of saw, called "chippers," have two tooth types of different thicknesses, which are used in conjunction with the grooving saws to make different widths of cuts. They cannot be used by themselves. For all general purposes a good ripsaw, a crosscut saw, and a combination saw, together with a dado head that can be built up to ⅞″, will be adequate (Fig. 9).

Mounting the saw. Before mounting or replacing a new blade on the bench saw clean off any sawdust that may have accumulated on the arbor and the collar. Remove the retaining collar nut. Slide the saw on easily, so as not to damage any of the threads. The teeth of the saw nearest to the operator should point down. Replace the retaining collar nut and screw it up tight so that the saw will not work loose. Before starting the motor rotate the blade by hand, to make sure that the saw clears the groove in the table.

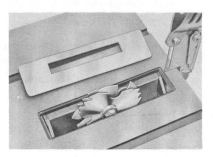

Fig. 9. Dado head in position between the two grooving saws on the bench saw.

Molding cutters and fences. The molding cutter is a bench-saw accessory useful for cutting a large variety of forms or moldings on the edges and ends of boards. It should be perfectly balanced and of solid construction, and the knives should be accurately machined. The knife-holding device must lock the knives firmly in place without their having to be specially adjusted or set. The type of molding cutter shown in Fig. 10 is designed to hold three knives in an automatic-alignment head that saves considerable time and trouble. The knives are made of the best type of high-speed steel, properly hardened and accurately ground to shape. They are available in a number of shapes (Fig. 11).

Fig. 10. Molding cutter.

A molding-cutter fence or gauge is necessary to guide the work while it is being shaped. It is arched in the center to give proper clearance to the head of the cutter when the knives project above the table to the highest point. This type of fence can be set and locked in any required position. It is particularly suitable for the production of several combined shapes (Fig. 11). All of the moldings in this illustration were made with cutters *A, B, C, D, E,* and *F* shown in Fig. 11.

Ripping with the bench saw. Ripping wide boards into narrower pieces is one of the simplest of bench-saw operations, and is one most often used. It relieves the mechanic of one of the most tiresome tasks—that of hand-ripping wide boards. To rip on the bench saw, set the ripping guide by measurement of the distance from the saw blade to the guide, or by setting the ripping guide to the graduated bar on the table. Check the graduated bar frequently, for accuracy in its relation to the saw itself.

The height of the saw above the table is important. To prevent sawdust jamming up the saw, always set it high enough to have several full teeth projecting above the material at the point above the arbor. Unless the teeth project through the wood, the sawdust will not be able to get out and will bind and overheat the saw blade. In ripping without a saw guard on the machine, it will be noted that the higher the saw is adjusted, the more sawdust it will throw up and the more accurately must the ripping guide be aligned with the saw blade.

After making all adjustments place the edge of the board against the guide, start the saw, and proceed to rip the stock.

When the distance between the saw blade and the ripping guide is less than three inches, a pusher stick must always be used. A pusher stick should be specially made for this purpose, preferably of a piece of hardwood, and kept in a handy spot near the saw.

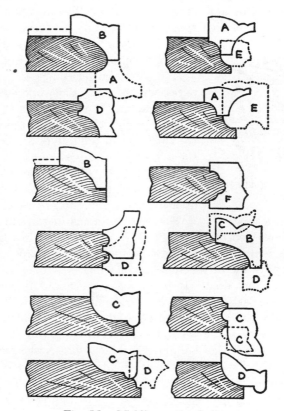

Fig. 11. Molding cutter knives.

To push narrow pieces through without a pusher stick may result in serious injury to the hand.

When ripping warped boards, place the concave side on the table and the convex side up (Fig. 12).

After ripping examine the surface of the cut on both pieces. If one of them appears considerably rougher and shows deeper grooves than the other, it may be because the ripping saw has not been properly aligned or the wood has warped as it passed the blade. The remedy to the former is obvious—realign the saw blade—while the remedy to the latter is to install a splitter. On the better types of bench saws a splitter is incorporated into the saw guard.

Resawing. Another form of ripping is resawing or cutting a board into thinner boards. For resawing, the blade should be set just a little over half the width of the board when the

Fig. 12. Ripping a board with blade tilted. When sawing warped stock be sure convex side is up.

board is less in width than twice the capacity of the saw (Fig. 13). To illustrate this, let us assume that it is necessary to resaw a board 4″ wide by ¾″ thick into two boards 4″ by ⁵⁄₁₆″. Making an allowance of ⅛″ for the kerf or the wastage of material by the blade, and taking into consideration that the capacity of the particular saw is 2¾″, set the blade to 2¾″. This leaves 1⅞″ for the second cut, which should be sufficient to prevent squeezing and binding of the

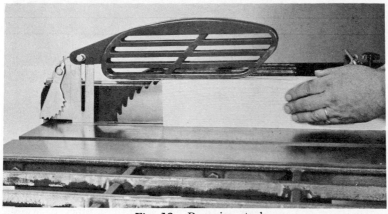

Fig. 13. Resawing stock.

blade. However, when the width of the board to be resawed is greater than twice the capacity of the machine, make the cuts as deep as possible from each edge. Then finish the ripping either by hand or on the band saw. An important point to bear in mind always when resawing is to keep the same surface of the board against the guide for both cuts, then reverse the board end for end, and never side for side. Thus stock twice as wide as the maximum depth of the cut can be resawed. On saw blades of larger capacity, stock can be resawed in one operation. When ripping narrow stock always use a push stick (Fig. 14).

Crosscutting. When crosscutting with a bench saw, particu-

Fig. 14. Always use a push stick when ripping or cutting narrow pieces.

larly where the cut is other than a perfect right angle, accuracy depends on several factors, not the least of which is the operator himself. The miter gauge on most bench saws does not exceed 7″ in length. For this reason extreme care must be exercised in order to hold a board several feet long against such a short length always at the correct angle. One of the first things to do upon acquisition of a bench saw is to attach a straight piece of wood to the miter gauge as a guide for such work. If possible use a piece of laminated plywood, to prevent any warping. This should be at least 17″ by ¾″ by 2″. Near the lower edge, to the left and to the right of the gauge, run a wood screw through to project about $\frac{1}{16}$″ and then file the end of the screw to a point. The edge of a board pressed against this point will not slip, and the small indentations that these points will make on the lumber that is being crosscut are not objectionable. The miter gauge must be set and checked to cut a right angle accurately. It will then automatically cut any other angle to which it may be set. The indicated point on the gauge should be filed to offset any slight inaccuracy.

When a board is held against the miter gauge for either crosscutting or mitering, pressure of the left hand must be directly across the board from the pivot of the gauge and not near one end of the face strip. If the board to be cut off is wider than the distance from the front of the saw to the front of the table, reverse the miter gauge in its slot. Never hold a wide board against the gauge and let one edge of it come down on the saw, or a couple of badly pinched fingers might be the result (Fig. 15). If the board is too wide to be included in the capacity of the miter gauge of your saw, use the ripping guide.

Miter gauges are usually furnished with metal rods that regulate the length of the pieces that are being cut off (Fig. 16). When a miter gauge is used in a left-hand table groove no part

Fig. 15. Crosscutting.

of these rods should extend past the miter gauge from the right. When the miter gauge is used in the right-hand table groove the position must be reversed.

Cutting miters. Mitering, or cutting a board across the grain at an angle to its edge, is another form of crosscutting, and is performed in exactly the same manner. To form a four-sided frame, set the miter gauge at 45°, the most generally used angle. For a six-sided frame the angle is 30°, and for an eight-sided one, 22½°.

Dadoing and rabbeting. While dadoing and rabbeting can be done on a bench saw, this tool is never intended to produce finished dados and rabbets. Therefore only concealed ones should

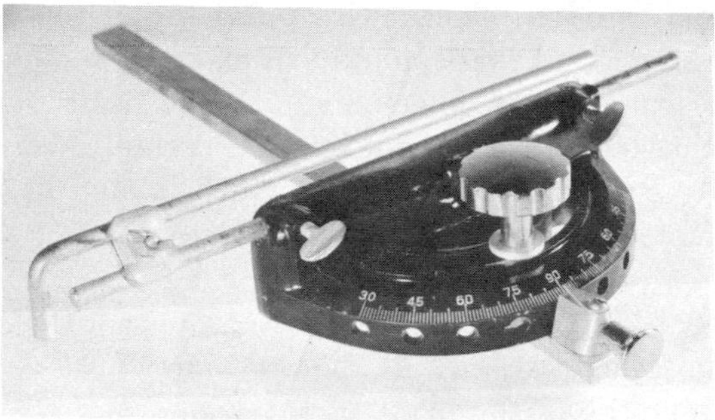

Fig. 16. Miter gauge, provided with stop rods for duplicate work, is used in crosscutting. Graduated 60° left and right and indexed every 15°.

be cut on a bench saw; finished dadoing and rabbeting is to be done on a jointer or shaper. Special accessories for this work are called dado heads and groovers.

Dado heads generally include two outside saws, each about ⅛″ thick, whose teeth are not given any set. While they do not make a finished cut, it is reasonably smooth with very few tool markings on the sides. The inside chippers in dado heads consist of one ¼″, two ⅛″, and one ¹⁄₁₆″ (thickness at the hub). The actual cutting portions of these inside cutters or chippers are widened to overlap the adjacent cutter or saw. When assembling one of these cutter heads, place the swaged or widened portion of the inside chipper or cutter so that it fits into the gullet of the adjacent cutter or saw. The chipper teeth should be staggered around the circumference of the outer saws, to distribute the cutting effort more evenly and produce a smoother cut (Fig. 17).

In setting up a dado head on a bench saw be sure to clean off all sawdust and dirt that has lodged on the saw arbor. In a dado head there is quite a mass of metal revolving at a fairly high speed, and if it is not running true it will set up a terrific vibration. Put on the outside dado or groove saw first, then as

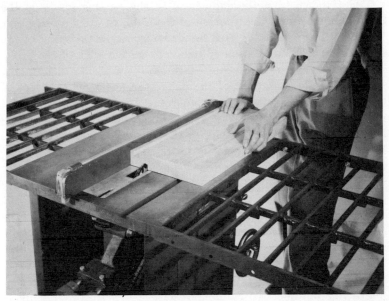

Fig. 17. Cutting a dado. Chippers are used in conjunction with two groover saw blades—never alone.

many chippers as are necessary, then finally the outside saw to make the desired width of cut. Never use the chipper blades without the two outside saws. Dado heads are generally furnished by the manufacturer to make a cut that is variable from $\frac{1}{8}''$ to $\frac{1}{4}''$ and then by sixteenths up to its full capacity of $\frac{13}{16}''$, by combinations of the outside saws and the chippers. For example, to cut a dado $\frac{7}{16}''$ wide, use the two outside saws, each $\frac{1}{8}''$ in width, plus a single $16''$ chipper in order to make the $\frac{7}{16}''$ cut.

When the total width of the finished cut is over $\frac{13}{16}''$, set up the dado head to a little more than half the required width of the cut and make two successive cuts. Each cut must overlap at the center to make up the required width. If the total width of the dado is more than twice the capacity of the cutter head, set it for a little over one-third of the width and make three overlapping cuts. The design of the cutting teeth of the dado head permits cutting with the grain, across the grain, or at an angle to the grain.

The distance from the dado head to the ripping guide on the bench saw regulates the location of the dado or groove being cut. When the miter gauge is used for dadoing across the grain of the material, mark the location of the dado on the edge of the piece, and locate the groove by that marking.

When one or both ends of the dado stop short of the edges of the material it is called blind-dadoing. This can be done accurately by clamping "stops" to the ripping guide in order to regulate the beginning and the end of the cut. The end of the piece being cut should never come into contact with the ripping guide itself during the operation. Use the guide merely as a means for holding the "stops" in place. Where the grooves being cut are of such a length that the stops are beyond the capacity of the ripping guide, temporarily attach a longer piece of wood to the guide, and mount the "stops" on the longer strip.

Rabbeting is merely cutting a groove along the edge of a board. The procedure is essentially the same as for dadoing and requires the same setups.

Cutting tenons. To cut tenons with a bench saw, first make the shoulder cut. Raise the saw blade to project a distance above the table equal to the depth of the shoulder of the tenon. Tighten the adjusting screw to hold the saw firmly at the required height. Then set the miter-gauge as for a square cut, and the stop rods to the required length of the tenons. Cut the shoulders on all the pieces of work requiring this one depth of cut before changing the setting for any other pieces.

The cheek cuts of the tenon are made by clamping or screwing a wide board to the rip fence. Set the rip fence so that the cuts outside the line indicating the cheek cut are nearest the face side of the work. This is necessary in order that the faces of the finished parts will be as flush as possible when they are finally assembled. Make the first cheek cut with the setup shown in Fig. 18. After completing all the pieces required, move the ripping fence and set it for the second cheek cut. For this, hold the face side of the work against the fence as shown in the same illustration.

Taper cutting. Taper cutting is the process of cutting material to a taper, or narrower at one end than at the other (Fig. 19). To cut or rip a board to the desired taper on a bench saw, first

Fig. 18. Cutting a tenon on the bandsaw.

Fig. 19. Adjustable jig is shown cutting a taper on a slender table leg.

make a full-sized drawing or pattern of the taper. Transfer this pattern to a piece of plywood or waste lumber, and cut to make the necessary template or jig. Place the board to be cut against this jig, with the straight edge of the jig against the rip fence of the saw. Then push both the jig and board past the saw blade in the same manner as for straight ripping or cutting (Fig. 12). A right- and a left-hand jig must be made when material has to be tapered on four sides.

Cutting off duplicate work.
In cutting off duplicate work

Fig. 20. Cutting off duplicate work. Note use of stop block instead of stop rods.

stop blocks can be used instead of stop rods as shown in Fig. 20.

Sanding and other operations. The bench saw can be used for cutting composition materials, brake linings, tile, and thin-gauge metals, and for all types of sanding and buffing. Special types of abrasive wheels are available for all of these procedures with center holes the same diameter as the spindle of the bench saw (Fig. 21). Cutting and sanding disks come in various degrees of coarseness, ranging from coarse, which is used for fast cutting or sanding, to fine, for finishing cuts and sanding.

Fig. 21. Sanding disk on bench saw.

Safety rules. It is imperative to stop the bench saw before making any necessary adjustments. While the machine is running never tilt either the table or the saw, adjust the guard, or align the work or the splitters. Adjusting a machine while it is running may result in serious injury to you. Take all necessary precautions to prevent loose ties, sleeves, or other pieces of clothing from coming into contact with any moving parts of the machine.

CHAPTER **9**

The Wood-Turning Lathe

⋮

A wood-turning lathe is a necessary tool for every motorized home workshop. It is used for making turnings, shaping cylindrical parts of woodworking projects, drilling holes, and a great variety of work of this character. The parts of a standard wood-turning lathe are shown in Fig. 1.

While there are a great many kinds of lathes available, it is important that the one purchased be made by a reputable manufacturer who will guarantee his product.

The "swing" or size of a lathe is the maximum diameter of material that can be turned on it. To determine the swing of any particular lathe, measure the height of the centers over the lathe bed and multiply the result by two. If the height of the centers is five inches, then the swing of that particular lathe will

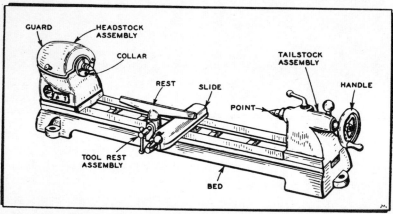

Fig. 1. Typical woodworking lathe and its parts.

324

be ten inches. For general woodworking purposes secure a lathe that is at least 36″ long between centers, with a swing of 9″ or 10″.

The lathe bed should be constructed of heavy steel. Those constructed of either rods or sections of pipe set up vibrations which make accurate wood-turning an impossibility.

The headstock is one of the most important parts of the lathe, as the power for turning the work is applied at this point. A typical well-designed four-speed lathe headstock is shown in Fig. 2. This type of headstock has the necessary strength at the points supporting the spindle. It is solidly cast to eliminate any danger of its working loose. The choice of speeds on this type of lathe makes it an ideal tool for all general wood-turning. Slow speeds are for turning work of large diameter or for roughing-out. The high speeds are used for finishing, sanding, polishing, drilling, routing, or grinding.

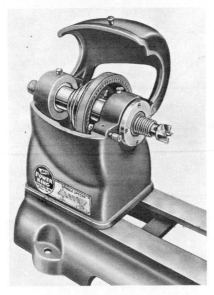

The headstock spindle should be made from a solid bar of hard steel, accurately ground and polished, so that it will have a perfect surface for the precision ball bearings on which it spins. It should be large enough to withstand strains placed upon it in turning large pieces of work.

Fig. 2. Lathe headstock with belt guard raised to show spindle bearings assembly and four-step spindle pulley.

Another important point to consider in the choice of a lathe is the construction of the headstock bearings and the provisions made for lubricating them.

On four-speed lathes the drive pulleys must be accurately made and well-balanced. Pulleys for the V-type belt are especially recommended; this type of belt will not slip.

The tailstock is used to support the other end of the work that is being turned between the centers (Fig. 3). The tailstock, like the headstock, must be of sturdy construction to prevent vibration. It must be accurately machined and fit properly between the rails of the lathe bed (Fig. 4), so that, no matter in what position the tailstock is secured, perfect alignment between the lathe centers is kept. One movement of the lock lever should release the tailstock for repositioning or tightening onto the bed. This eliminates the use of wrenches.

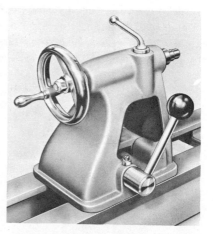

The dead center which fits on the end of the tailstock spindle should be either cone- or cup-shaped with a replaceable pin at its center. The cup-shaped type is preferable for centering the work and keeping it true.

The tool rest must be designed and constructed so that the hand guiding the tool used for turning can be moved easily along the side of the

Fig. 3. View of tailstock showing lever-controlled bedlock built into some of the newer lathes.

tool rest in a parallel line with the work being turned. The base that supports the tool rest must be rigid, and long enough to give proper clearance for the tool rest when turning work of large diameter. To clamp it tightly to the lathe bed the tool rest should have a strong clamping device (Fig. 5).

To do efficient work, the lathe must have a motor of ample power. A good, standard motor of at least 1/4 h.p. will furnish all the power necessary.

All manufacturers furnish detailed instructions for installing and setting up their lathes. These instructions should be closely followed.

Necessary lathe tools and accessories. The following lathe tools and accessories are necessary for wood-turning (Fig. 6):

Gouges, ½" and ¾"   Spear-point tool, ½"
Skews, 1" and ½"   Round-nose chisel, ½"
Parting tool, ⅛"

In addition to the above, the following measuring tools should be secured:

Ordinary rule, 12"   Outside caliper, 6"
Inside caliper, 6"   Pair of 8" dividers

Fig. 4. Lathe bed and tailstock from rear.

All wood-turning tools are divided into three groups: roughing-off tools, smoothing and cleaning-up tools, and scraping tools. All of the cutting tools listed above fall into one or more of these three groups.

Setting up the lathe. Whenever possible the lathe should be mounted on the left-hand side of the workbench. It should be placed so that the headstock end extends slightly beyond the end of the bench. The motor should be mounted below the lathe. A convenient height to set up the lathe (for a person of average height) is with the center of the headstock about 42″ to 45″ from the floor.

Adjustment of turning speeds for various operations.   The

Fig. 5.   Lathe tool rest.

ideal wood-turning lathe has four speeds: 700, 1350, 2200, and 4000 r.p.m.   As far as speeds are concerned, considerable latitude is permitted in wood-turning.   In other words, where a speed of

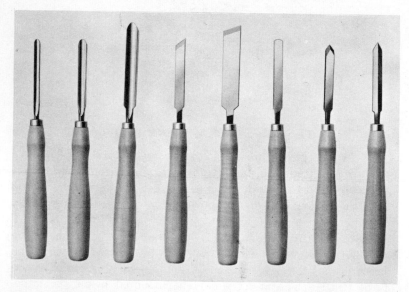

Fig. 6.   Adequate set of wood-turning chisels.   Left to right, 3 gouges, 2 skews, one round-nose, one spear-point, and one parting chisel.

1350 is specified, any speed ranging from 1100 to 1600 can be used with safety.

The turning speed of the lathe is largely governed by the size of the stock being turned. When turning small diameter stock, use a faster speed than when turning larger diameters.

As a concrete example of the various speeds that are used, let us take a piece of stock approximately 3″ square. The first operation will be to rough-off the corners of the stock. For this job use a speed from 600 to 1200 r.p.m. The lower speed is used for hardwoods, and the faster speed is usually used for any of the softer types of wood. After knocking off the corners of the stock by this preliminary operation, use the second speed of the lathe (from 1200 to 1800 r.p.m) for roughing the material down to preliminary size. For the final finishing cuts turn the work at 2000 to 3000 r.p.m. This same speed can be used for sanding a turning. However, for turning material more than 3″ in diameter an entirely different range of speeds is required. The table of speeds for stock of varying diameters is as follows:

TURNING SPEEDS

	Roughing Off	General Cutting	Finishing
3″ dia. stock	500–1,200	1,200–1,800	2,000–3,000 r.p.m.
4″ dia. stock	600–1,000	1,000–1,500	1,800–2,400 r.p.m.
5″ dia. stock	600– 800	800–1,000	1,000–1,800 r.p.m.
Over 5″ stock	200– 500	200– 500	400– 500 r.p.m.

OPERATION OF THE LATHE

Locating center points. Unless the center points on the ends of the stock that is to be turned are not properly located, a considerable amount of vibration will result, and it will be impossible to make an accurate turning. To locate the exact center point on the end of square stock, draw diagonal lines across the end (Fig. 7). On round material determine the center point quickly by the use of a pair of dividers or calipers. Then make two diagonal saw cuts across the end that is to be at the headstock of the lathe. With a soft-faced mallet drive the spur of the headstock faceplate into the saw-cut at the center point

(Fig. 8). Never under any circumstances drive the piece of wood against the headstock of a lathe by hammering on the far end. This will ruin the bearings on the lathe, and in time will knock the headstock out of correct alignment. To keep the lathe in good working condition never do any hammering on the lathe itself.

Methods used in wood-turning. Two methods are used in wood-turning—the scraping method and the cutting method. The scraping method is slower, but is far simpler to master without an instructor, and has the added advantage of being more accurate than the cutting method. Where speed of operation is not important the scraping method of wood-turning is recommended, especially for the beginner. If you have become skillful in this phase of craftsmanship and desire to speed up the work, then by all means attempt the cutting method. In the basic operations that are described in this chapter, the scraping· method will be discussed first.

Mounting the stock. Replace the spur center on the headstock and tighten the

Fig. 7. Locating center of stock by drawing diagonal lines.

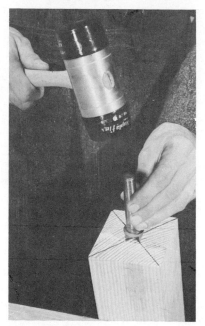

Fig. 8. Driving spur into center with prongs of spur entering saw cuts. Note plastic hammer.

setscrews. Press the work to be turned against the spurs, so that they enter the groove in the end of the material.

Move the tailstock of the lathe so that the point of the dead center of the tailstock is approximately ½″ from the end of the material. Tighten and secure the tailstock firmly to the lathe bed. Proceed by turning the handwheel of the tailstock so that when the head center enters the material it will be set in so firmly that the work cannot be turned by hand. Turn the hand-wheel in the opposite direction to loosen it just enough so that the work can now be turned by hand. Tighten the dead-center clamp at the top of the tailstock to hold the spindle firmly in position.

Adjusting the tool rest. The proper adjustment of the tool rest is the last preliminary operation before starting the actual turning. The tool rest must always be adjusted so that its top is from ⅛″ to ¼″ above the centers (Fig. 9). The top of the tool rest must never be set below the centers or below the center of the piece that is being turned. The top edge of the tool rest must always be parallel to the stock, and about ⅛″ away from the farthest projecting edge of the stock. Revolve the stock by hand to ascertain that it has the proper amount of clearance. Be sure that all clamps are tight and all necessary adjustments made before turning on the power. Take a position in front of the lathe with the left side turned a little nearer to the lathe than the right. When working on a lathe avoid wearing loose apparel that may be caught by the moving parts of the lathe.

Shaping square stock to a cylinder. The first step in the process of shaping a rectangular piece of material to cylindrical form on a lathe is called roughing. This process consists of cutting off the square corners of the material until the piece is approximately cylindrical.

Use a large gouge for making the roughing cuts. The stock must be properly centered and mounted, and the tool rest adjusted. Assuming that the stock is not over 3″ square, the lathe should be run at a comparatively slow speed and the V-belt should be placed on the second largest pulley.

Hold the gouge in the left hand with the hand against the tool rest and the fingers around the tool. Hold the extreme end of the handle with the right hand and drop the wrist slightly, to permit the side of the left hand to act as a sliding guide along the tool rest (Figs. 10 and 11). The cutting end of the gouge must be held above the material with the handle held lower (Fig. 12). To make the necessary shirring cut, roll the gouge just a trifle toward the right (Fig. 12).

Lift the handle slowly as the work revolves and force the cutting edge of the tool into the wood. For proper disposal of the flying chips, hold the tool at an angle to the axis of the work (Fig. 12). Make the first cut several inches from the dead center. Never start a cut at the end of the stock; the cutting tool is apt to catch and be forcibly thrown from your hand. When rounding off the material do not take long cuts; large chips or slivers of wood are apt to fly off, causing injury to you and to the material. Start the second cut several inches to the left of the first and continue in the direction of the first cut until both meet. When combined, these cuts are called the primary roughing cut. When making this primary roughing cut do not attempt to shape the material to a perfect cylindrical form of the required dimension. During roughing, check dimensions of

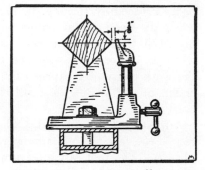

Fig. 9. Proper tool rest adjustment.

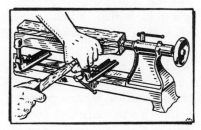

Fig. 10. Correct position to start cut.

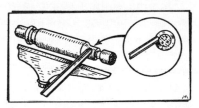

Fig. 11. Where and how gouge is held.

the cylinder with the calipers. Continue to move the gouge back and forth from right to left on the tool rest until the entire piece of stock is cylindrical in form and approximately ⅛" larger than the largest diameter of the turning. Then stop the lathe.

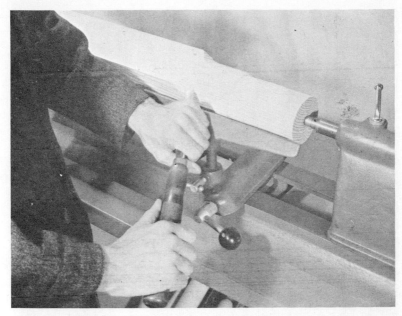

Fig. 12. Shaping square stock to cylindrical form, using a gouge chisel.

The parting tool is used to make the next series of cuts, called sizing cuts. Move the belt to the next smaller pulley to obtain a faster speed.

Readjust the position of the tool rest to $\frac{1}{8}''$ from the cylinder, and tighten in place. For purposes of elementary instruction let us assume that the material is to be turned to a perfect cylinder. Set the calipers to a diameter $\frac{1}{16}''$ greater than that required for the finished work. This allowance has to be made for the finishing cuts and final sanding.

Hold the calipers in the left hand and the parting tool in the right (Fig. 13). Start the lathe running. Using the parting tool, cut a narrow groove in the work several inches from dead center. Take light, thin shavings and do not exert too much pressure on the tool. As the work proceeds check with the calipers the depth of cuts made. Stop cutting when the leg of the calipers passes over the cut without any pressure. Repeat the operation at intervals of about one inch for the entire length of the work. These grooves are called parting or sizing cuts.

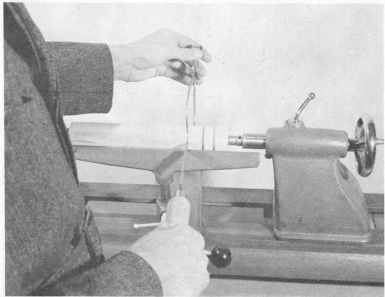

Fig. 13. Sizing stock with parting tool and calipers set ⅟₁₆″ larger than finished diameter. When proper size is reached, calipers will slip over work.

Cutting and smoothing the cylinder to the required dimension is the next and final step. This is called the finishing cut. When making this cut on the lathe by the scraping method, use a square-nose turning chisel or an ordinary woodworking firmer chisel with a long blade. A short-bladed chisel cannot be held properly on the tool rest. Hold the chisel with the beveled side of the blade down and flat against the top of the tool rest. (Fig. 14). Use a scraping action and run the tool along the entire length of the material until the cylinder has been smoothed down to the required dimension. Test for squareness with a straightedge laid lengthwise against the work. If it is not perfectly straight give the work another light scraping with the same tool.

A large skew chisel is the tool used for smoothing cylinders by the more difficult but faster cutting or paring method (Fig. 15). It must be laid on the tool rest with its cutting edge above the work and at an angle of approximately 60° to the surface of the work. Draw the chisel back slowly toward you, and raise it until it begins to cut at a point approximately ¼″ above its heel (Fig.

16). Hold it in the position shown in Fig. 17 when cutting **toward** the right end of the material, and change to the position shown in Fig. 18 when cutting toward the left. Start the cut several inches from the right end of the work and work toward the right by sliding the left hand and the tool along the tool rest. Turn the chisel in the opposite direction and cut the remaining portion to the left

Fig. 14. Finish-turning a cylinder with the chisel used as a scraping tool.

end of the work. The use of the skew chisel in cutting cylinders smooth is more difficult than the scraping method. A close study of the illustrations and directions plus continued practice on scrap

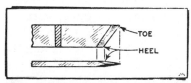

Fig. 15. Parts of a skew chisel.

material are necessary before using the cutting or paring method.

Making sizing cuts. When the material has been turned to a perfect cylindrical form of the required dimension, it is ready for turning or forming to any desired shape or combination of shapes that constitute a finished turning.

Make a full-size dimensioned drawing of the projected turning. Then indicate the points where the sizing cuts are to be made and

Fig. 16. Finish-turning a cylinder with the skew chisel.

mark them on the drawing (Fig. 19). With a pair of dividers transfer these points from the drawing and mark them on the cylinder. Mount the cylinder in the lathe between the two centers. Place the point of a pencil on each of the marks made by the dividers and revolve the cylinder by hand to mark the entire circumference. Set a pair of outside calipers for a diameter $\frac{1}{16}''$ larger than required, as shown in the full-size drawing or pattern at the point where the first sizing cut is to be made.

The parting tool is used to make the sizing cuts. Place its narrow edge on the tool rest with the point above the line of the centers. Set the point on one of the pencil marks on the turning, start the lathe, raise the handle of the parting tool, and push the point into the material. Check the accuracy of the sizing cut by holding the previously set outside calipers in the groove that has been cut. Continue cutting until the calipers slip easily over the work. Set the calipers for each of the subsequent sizing cuts and proceed in the same manner. Sectional views of completed sizing cuts are shown in Fig. 20. Wood turnings usually consist of several types of cuts, called taper, concave, convex, and bead cuts.

Making the taper cuts. The round-nose chisel or the gouge is used to make taper cuts by the scraping method. Always cut from the larger to the smaller end of the taper. With the chisel, cut down to within about ⅛″ of the entire depths of the sizing cuts previously made with the sizing or parting tool, using the same procedure as outlined for forming the stock to cylindrical form. Finish with the square-nose chisel. As cutting proceeds, check the work with the calipers set from the full-size drawing.

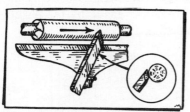

Fig. 17. Using skew chisel in cutting toward the right.

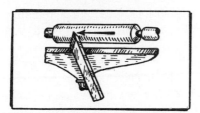

Fig. 18. Position of chisel for left-side cutting.

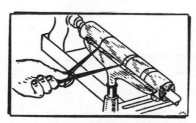

Fig. 19. Cylinder marked with dividers.

The skew chisel is used to make taper cuts by the more difficult cutting method. Place the chisel on the tool rest at an angle of about 60° to the surface of the material and slightly above it. After starting the lathe, draw the chisel back just a trifle, until the heel starts the cut, then draw it a little farther down and back to the original position. Repeat these movements until the actual cutting is being done by the heel of the tool. The entire taper cut can be made with the heel. Avoid the danger of making deeper cuts than required and eventually ruining the turning. The rule of starting the cut from the larger and proceeding to the smaller end of the taper applies also to the cutting method. You should not attempt the cutting method until you have acquired considerable skill in the use of the lathe and lathe cutting tools.

Making concave cuts. The round-nose chisel is used to make concave cuts by the scraping method. After making the parting or sizing cuts and checking dimensions with the calipers, place the round-nose chisel flat on the tool rest with the bevel side down. Hold the tool slightly above the center of the work at right angles to its axis (Fig. 21). Start the lathe and begin the cutting at the top. Complete the concave cut by light cuts with the chisel, working down on each side of the cut previously made by the parting

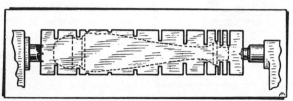

Fig. 20.   How sizing cuts are made in series turning.

chisel, to within $\frac{1}{16}''$ of the required depth (Fig. 21). The remaining material can be removed by light smoothing cuts with the chisel or by sanding.

A gouge is used for making concave cuts by the more difficult cutting method. Hold the tool in a horizontal position with the hollow part up (Fig. 22 and *B*, Fig. 23). Start the cut at the top. Roll and push the tool forward simultaneously to the right and down toward the bottom of the cut, as shown at *A*, Fig. 23, and in Fig. 24. Note the exact position of the gouge, its necessary rolling motion and the angle of the tool to the work (Figs. 25 and 26). Always start the cut from the high point in the design and work to the lowest point. Then reverse the position of the tool and start the cut at the top of the other left side. The bottom of each side must then be cut alternately, and the cutting tool repeatedly shifted from right to left until the required shape of the concave cut has been produced.

Bead cutting. The diamond-point or the parting chisel is used for bead or convex cutting by the scraper method. Mark the cylinder for the beads as for the other cuts previously described. With either tool make the cut to the desired depth. Hold the diamond-point chisel at a slight angle to the work to round out the corners of the bead (Fig. 27). The parting tool can be used instead of the diamond-point chisel when the beads on the turning are not close together. Round out the right-hand corner of each bead first, then reverse the tool to round out the left corner. Repeat the operation for each bead.

The skew chisel is used for making beads or convex curves by the cutting or paring method. Mark the cylinder where the cuts are to be made. Make the cuts to the required depth with the toe of the skew chisel, as shown at *A*, Fig. 28. Then place the skew chisel flat on the tool rest and at right angles to the axis of the turning, as shown at *B*, Fig. 28. Start cutting at the top of the cylinder, with the heel of the chisel (Fig. 29). Turn the tool gradually and draw it toward you simultaneously as the bottom of the curve is reached, as shown in *C* and *D*, Fig. 28. Then reverse the chisel to cut the other side of the bead.

Faceplate turning. When the work to be turned cannot be held between the live and the dead center on the lathe, a faceplate is used. There are several methods of fastening the work onto the faceplate. The choice of the one to be used is largely dependent upon the shape and size of the turning. "Center screw work" is used for forms that do not require any deep cutting in the center, such as knobs or rosettes, and for other small ornamental turnings. For center screw work a hole is usually provided in the center of the faceplate through which a screw is inserted (Fig. 30).

Where work of a larger nature is to be done, or where the

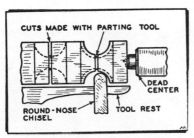

Fig. 21. Scraping method in making concave cuts.

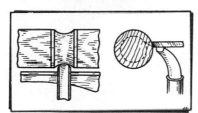

Fig. 22. Cutting method in making concave cuts.

Fig. 23. Right-hand concave cutting direction.

Fig. 24. Concave cutting position.

turning is to be deep, such as a salad bowl, platter, or other large and ornamental piece, a large faceplate is used. This has several holes through which screws are inserted, from the back, into the material that is to be turned (Figs. 31 and 32).

Fig. 25. Gouge position at start of "rolling" cut when making concave cuts by the cutting or paring method.

Before attaching it onto either type of faceplate remove all surplus wood from the material by drawing a circle on it a trifle larger in diameter than desired for the finished work. Cut this circle out with a scroll or band saw. Center the work accurately when screwing it to the faceplate. If the material being used is hardwood, drill small holes in it to start the screws. Use short, heavy flat-headed screws that will enter the work not more than $3/8''$ to $1/2''$. Make certain that the work is securely fastened to the faceplate and that the ends of the screws will not come in contact with the cutting tool when the work is being turned (Fig. 31).

When the shape of the finished work is such that contact with the screws cannot be avoided, the work must be backed up with a disk of the same size. Bore and countersink the holes for the

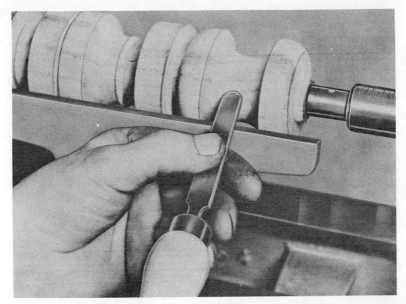

Fig. 26. Proper position of gouge at the end of "rolling" cut when making concave cuts by the cutting or paring method.

screws at points where they will not come in contact with the tool. Screw this extra disk on work and attach the faceplate to this extra disk, or backing piece as it is called (Fig. 32).

Place the faceplate on the end of the lathe spindle and tighten the setscrews.

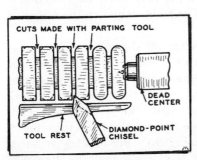

Fig. 27. Diamond-point tool for rounding beads.

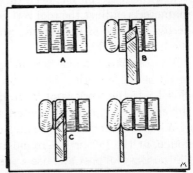

Fig. 28. Method of cutting beads with a skew.

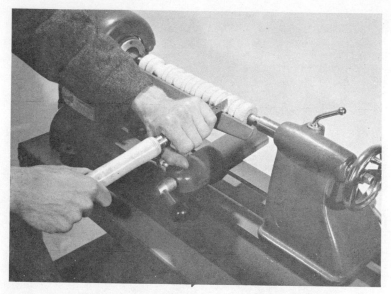

Fig. 29. Forming a bead with the skew chisel.

Next place the tool rest so that its top edge is about ⅛″ above the center of the revolving turning. Use a large chisel to turn the outside of the work roughly to within ⅛″ of the required diameter.

The various speeds used for faceplate work are dependent on the diameter of the stock, and are essentially the same as for cylindrical turnings. Consult the table of speeds given in this chapter. When the material has been turned to approximately the finished diameter, readjust the tool rest to a position where its T-section is across the face of the turning and at right angles to the center of the lathe bed (Fig. 33).

Use the large gouge first in spacing off the turning if the material is not smooth. Then true up the surface with the flat-nose chisel. If the work is of large diameter, use the straight edge of the chisel; on smaller diameters the side of the chisel can be used.

When making concave cuts, use either the large or the small gouge, or the ¼″ or ½″ round-nose flat chisel. Hold it perfectly flat on the tool post and use a scraping cut. For making rounded-off or beaded members use either the skew-point, the diamond-point, or the flat-nose chisel and employ the same type of cuts.

Sandpapering and finishing turnings. To sandpaper turnings in the lathe, Nos. 0, 000, 0000, and 00000 are usually used. Cut strips of sandpaper about 1″ wide. These must be held in both hands with the right hand above, and the left below the turning. To avoid cutting grooves keep the sandpaper in motion while the work is turning in the lathe. Fold the sandpaper and use the edge of the fold to get into the bottom of a V-shaped cut.

Fig. 30. Use of center-screw faceplate for turning.

After sanding the turning smooth, finish and polish it in the lathe. Dilute commercial shellac with an equal quantity of wood alcohol. Make a pad of cheesecloth about 2″ square. Dip this into the diluted shellac and then put several drops of a good grade of machine oil on the pad. Hold the pad lightly on the revolving turning, keeping it in contact with all parts of the work and in motion all of the time. The heat generated by friction will harden and glaze the shellac so that it becomes necessary from time to time to redip the pad. Each time the pad is dipped into the shellac additional oil must also be dropped on the pad.

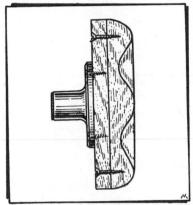

Fig. 31. Faceplate with backing piece.

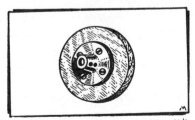

Fig. 32. Faceplate attached to disk for turning.

Another method of finishing turnings is with beeswax, carnauba, or ordinary paraffin wax. Hold the wax in lump form against the turning as it revolves. The heat generated by friction will melt a portion of the wax and deposit a coating on the turning. After the entire turning has been coated, hold a wad made of soft tissue paper against the turning to give it a good polish. If a higher polish is desired, repeat the entire operation.

Maintenance. All manufacturers of lathes issue specific lubri-

Fig. 33. Faceplate turning.

cation directions. To keep the lathe in good working condition these directions must be followed.

Keep the cutting edges of all lathe tools sharp and free from nicks. The procedure for sharpening the chisels and gouges used for wood-turning are the same as those for grinding and whetting woodworking chisels (Chap. 2).

CHAPTER 10

The Band Saw

———— : ————

The band saw is generally used for cutting outside outlines of work. Contrary to general belief it is not limited to the cutting of thin stock. It can cut either a single thick piece or a combination of pieces, provided the thickness of the stock is less than the clearance between the top guide and the table. It can always be used to advantage to cut single- or multiple-curved parts where cuts are started from the edge of the material. A distinct advantage favoring the use of the band saw is that the saw blade in its cutting action carries all of the sawdust downward, thus leaving the marked guiding lines on the work visible at all times. The important parts of a band saw are: the frame, wheels, bearings, guides, and guards (Fig. 1).

The frame must be sturdy, well-designed, and rigid so as to furnish the required strength without any danger of springing or setting up excessive vibrations.

When choosing a band saw, inspect the rims of both saw wheels and make sure they are covered with rubber. This rubber covering protects the teeth of the blade and furnishes proper adhesion between the narrow blade, which is rotating at high speed, and the rim of the wheel. The upper wheel of a well-designed band saw should be adjustable vertically and tiltable either forward or backward. All good band saws are provided with a blade-tensioning device. This device should be located in a convenient position on the upper wheel.

The wheels revolve at a high speed; therefore all of the bearings in the machine must be of excellent quality and made of bronze. Bearings of inferior quality will wear out quickly, resulting in wobbly wheels, inaccurate work, and, frequently, broken blades.

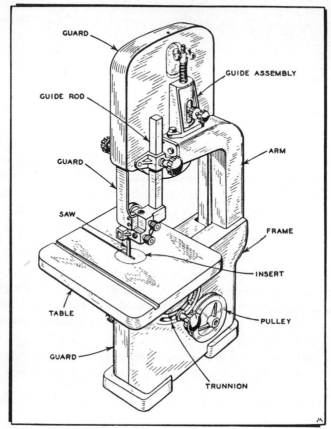

Fig. 1. Typical band saw and its parts.

The bearings must be accessible and fitted with oil cups that will provide sufficient oil to permit running for considerable time without re-oiling.

The drive shaft must be perfectly aligned parallel with the table, or the saw will not run squarely with the table.

Be sure that the table is made of a solid well-ribbed casting that has been machined perfectly smooth and true. The table insert should be made of soft aluminum and must be removable so that it can be replaced quickly and economically whenever necessary. The table must be adjustable and tiltable. An ideal type of table is provided with an accurate scale permitting fast and accurate setting at any desired angle without the use of a protractor. A convenient lockscrew should be provided to lock the table wherever it is set (Fig. 2).

Two blade guides above the table and two below should be pro-

Fig. 2. Underside of bandsaw table showing double trunnions, graduated for angle of table tilt. Ribbing of table casting insures permanent accuracy of table surface.

vided to steady and support the blade and direct it for accurate cutting. They should be made of bronze and must be adjustable (Fig. 3.)

The greatest danger in the operation of a band saw occurs when the blade is forced off the wheel, or when it snaps or breaks while the machine is in operation. All well-designed band saws are provided with proper guards covering the blade at all points except the cutting point, and with an additional guard to protect the mechanic from the moving belt (Fig. 4).

Installation. These instructions for installing, adjusting, and operating a band saw will apply to all of the better band saws available. However, various manufacturers have placed some of the controls in slightly different positions from those described. These altered positions may affect to some extent the adjustment of any particular machine. Before proceeding with any adjustments, be sure to check the manufacturer's printed instructions.

Mount the saw on a sturdy, level bench that is high enough so that the top of the saw table will be slightly lower than your elbows. Before bolting it to the bench, be sure that the base of the band saw rests solidly and squarely on all feet. If a level shows it to be not perfectly square, insert shims, which can be made of thin pieces of metal or hardwood, between the base of the tool and the benchtop.

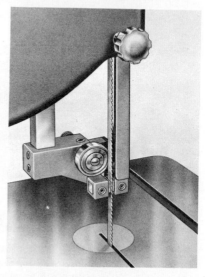

The band saw will require a ⅓ or ½ h.p., 1725 r.p.m. capacitor or repulsion-induction motor. A 2½″ diameter motor pulley (usual size furnished) will deliver a spindle speed of 640 r.p.m. and a cutting speed of 2050 f.p.m., which is just about correct for all types of smooth cutting. The motor can be mounted either behind or below the saw in whatever position is convenient.

Fig. 3. Two bronze blade guides above the table and two below, and a ball-bearing thrust wheel above and below, support and direct the blade for accuracy.

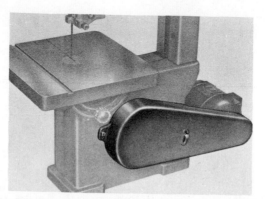

Fig. 4. Safety guard protects operator from moving belt.

You may sometimes experience a slight electric shock when touching the saw. It is possible that this is caused by a static electrical charge set up by the friction of the moving parts and is not necessarily an indication of faulty motor windings or grounds. To correct this condition, ground the saw frame to a water or radiator pipe.

Controls. On most band saws the knob or wheel on the rear controls the blade tension. The double set of knobs controls the tilt of the upper wheel. The outside knob tilts the wheel to track the blade properly and the inside knob locks the tilt setting.

The sliding bar controls the vertical position of the saw guide bracket. When operating the saw place the guide just above the work. To adjust this guide, loosen the lock knob, place guide in proper position, and retighten (Fig. 5).

The table tilt is usually controlled by either a knob or a control wheel under the table. The table can be tilted and locked securely at any angle between 0° and 45°, with the angle shown on a graduated scale.

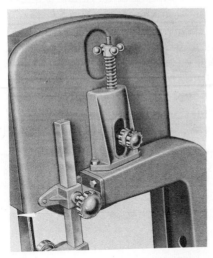

The knobs on the saw guide brackets, two above the table and two below, control the thrust wheel and the blade guide blocks. Be sure always to release the setscrews before making any adjustments to the thrust wheel or guide blocks.

Blades used. For all straight and general circular cutting a ⅞″ blade should be used. This size will cut a circle 2½″ in diameter. A ¼″

Fig. 5. Controls for tension, blade support, and upper saw wheel tilt are located at rear of saw.

blade will cut a 2″ circle and a 3⁄16″ blade will cut a 1½″ circle. When selecting a blade for any specific job use the widest blade with the coarsest teeth that will cut the sharpest contours of the pattern.

Mounting the blade. To mount a saw blade remove the upper and lower wheel guards. Turn the wheel tension control or knob until the tension is released. Remove the setscrew in the table slot. Pass the blade through the table slot, into the left blade guard, then under the lower wheel between the upper and lower blade guides, and finally over the top wheel. Turn the wheel tension control or knob until a slight tension is felt on the blade. Replace the setscrew in the saw table. The next operation consists in tracking. Rotate the upper wheel by hand in a clockwise direction as viewed from front of saw. If the blade runs off the wheel make the following adjustments: Move both the upper and lower thrust wheels and blade guide blocks away from the blade. Turn the lower wheel by hand and adjust the upper one with the tilt knob or control until the blade runs or tracks in the center of both wheels. Tighten the tilt lock knob firmly and securely.

Checking blade tension. Correct blade tension can be acquired only by experience. Do not put too much tension on the blade. Wide blades can stand more tension than narrow ones. A good general rule is to keep the blade at a tension that is just tight enough to produce a low tone when it is struck (Fig. 6).

Adjusting blade guide blocks and thrust wheels. Two pairs of guide blocks, one above and one below the saw table, align the blade and prevent its twisting. To accommodate the different sizes of blades loosen the setscrews and position the blocks so that they just clear the sides of the blade. Check clearance with a piece of paper. To make sure that the blade passes freely between the blocks rotate the upper wheel by hand. After correct setting is obtained tighten the setscrews securely. Proceed by loosening the upper and lower guide-block slide setscrews and position them so that the front edges of the blocks are even with the bottom of the blade teeth. Retighten the screws.

To adjust the thrust wheels, loosen the setscrews that lock them. Set the thrust wheels into position so that they just touch the saw blade. Retighten the setscrews.

Operating the band saw. Before starting the saw, always lower the blade guide until it is just above the work. Check the blade for proper tension. Be sure that it is mounted properly and the teeth point down on the downward stroke. Examine stock carefully before sawing to make sure that it is free of nails. Feed the work evenly and slowly to avoid twisting the blade or crowding it beyond its cutting capacity.

Never force the material with too hard a pressure against the

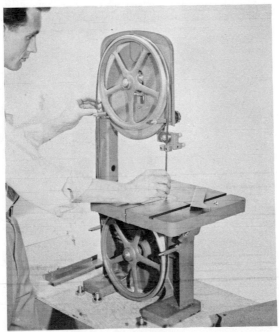

Fig. 6. Correct tension is important in mounting blade.

teeth of the blade. A light contact is sufficient. Move the stock easily and steadily and just fast enough to give.

When the pattern curves, turn the stock so that the blade will follow the line without any danger of twisting. If the pattern has a number of sharp curves, make a series of straight saw cuts in the waste stock opposite each curve before starting. This facilitates removal of waste material and prevents binding.

When it is impossible to continue a cut to the end, cut through the waste stock to the edge of the work and start a new cut at another point. If this is not possible and it is necessary to back out of a cut, draw the work very slowly away from the saw blade. Be sure that the blade follows the saw cut that you are backing out of. Failure to do this carefully may force the blade off the wheels.

Straight sawing. To cut a straight line with a band saw, rest your left hand on the table and use it as a guide while grasping the material and feeding it to the saw with your right hand (Fig. 7).

Cutting curves. In cutting curves either hand can be used as

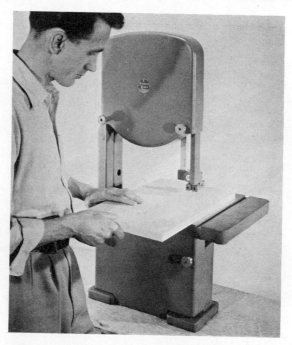

Fig. 7. Making a straight cut with the band saw.

a guide. Cutting curves is quite simple once the knack of properly guiding the saw around them is acquired (Fig. 8). To cut a curve with a sharp, clean edge, exert just a slight pressure of the stock against the side of the blade on the inside of the curve. A ragged instead of a smooth edge will result if you attempt to cut curves freehand, that is, allow the blade to cut without guiding the material. It is important to use a blade of correct width. When cutting small circles use a ⅛″ blade. For larger circles (over 2″ in diameter) a ⅜″ blade must be used. Never attempt to force a wide blade around small curves or circles, and do not use a narrow blade to cut large curves or circles.

Cutting circles. A simple method of cutting circles and true parts of circles is to swing the stock on a pivot (Fig. 9). Cut the board a little wider than the radius of the circle to be cut and clamp it to the saw table. Drive a small nail or brad into this board and file off its head so that it projects about ⅛″ above the

Fig. 8. Cutting curves.

board. This projection will act as the pivot, and should be located at a distance from the blade equal to the radius of the circle to be cut, and on a direct line with the cutting edge of the blade (*C* and *D*, Fig. 9). The radius of the required circle is indicated at *R* in the same illustration. Take care to locate the pivot properly. Then place the center of the stock over the pivot, with one edge against the blade. Be sure that the point of the pivot enters the stock. It is then a simple matter to turn the stock against the blade until a complete circle of the required radius has been cut. If a bevel edge is desired, tilt the table and make the cut in exactly the same manner as for a square edge.

Cutting combination curves. Combination curves, which are cuts combining two or more curves, are cut in series. A typical combination curve is shown in Fig. 10. The first cut is shown at *B*, the second and third cuts are shown at *C*, the fourth and final cut (the fifth cut in this particular case) is shown at *D*.

Cutting circular rails. The method used for making a circular rail out of a narrow piece of stock is shown in Fig. 11. It leaves very little waste and is used principally when cutting top rails out of costly wood or veneer. The dotted line at *A* shows where the first cut is made. After making the cut, glue both pieces together as shown at *B* (the glue joint is indicated by the solid line). The dotted lines at *B* show where the cuts should be made to complete the rail (*C*, Fig. 11).

Multiple cutting. Cutting several pieces of the same pattern or outline at the same time not only saves considerable time but ensures that all of them will be exactly alike. The number of pieces that can be cut simultaneously depends on the thickness of the material and the capacity of the band saw. Multiple sawing can be done very easily if all of the pieces are securely held together with nails at points that will be cut away, that is, in the waste portion of the material, so that the finished work will

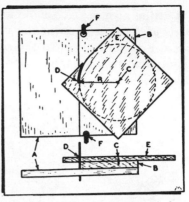

Fig. 9. Jig for bandsawing circles. A, saw table; B, board; C, pivot; D, blade; E, stock; F, clamps.

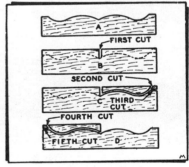

Fig. 10. Steps for cutting combination curves.

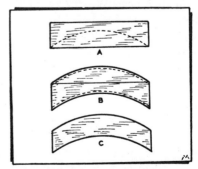

Fig. 11. Making a circular rail.

not be marked. Mark the outline on the top piece and proceed to cut the connected pieces as if they were one solid piece. Make sure that none of the nails come in contact with the teeth of the saw (Fig. 12).

Fig. 12. Multiple cutting. Pieces are nailed together through waste part of stock.

Maintenance and lubrication. Clean sawdust from table trunnions frequently. Make sure that motor and spindle pulleys stay aligned, and keep setscrews tight to prevent scoring of motor shaft and spindle. When saw is not in use, release blade tension. To prevent rust, keep saw table covered with film of oil when not in use. If machine is used frequently, oil bearings or fill oil cups every month with SAE 10 machine oil. Oil the following points at regular intervals of one month (if used infrequently, oil every six months):

Upper and lower wheel bearings;

Table trunnions;

Upper wheel tilt and tension screws;

Blade guide blocks.

CHAPTER 11

The Jig Saw

A jig saw can be utilized for a certain percentage of the work that can be done on the band saw, but it has the added advantage of being able to cut inside curves. Jig saws are used for cutting wood, thin-gauge copper, aluminum, brass, and similar soft metals and plastics. Where delicate scroll work, fretwork, and similar types of ornamental cutting are required, the jig saw is an indispensable tool in the home workshop.

The essential parts of a jig saw are shown in Fig. 1.

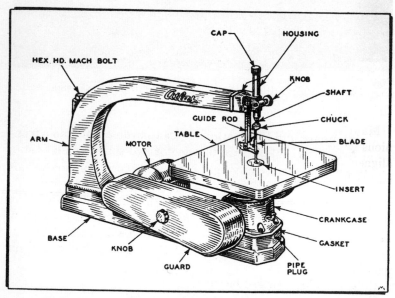

Fig. 1. Parts of a jig saw.

356

Installation of a jig saw. The instructions in this chapter covering installation, adjustment, and operation are for a standard type of jig saw and apply to all of the better makes. Various manufacturers set some of the controls in slightly different positions which may affect to some extent the adjustment of any particular jig saw. Be sure to check these instructions given with manufacturer's directions before proceeding.

The jig saw must be mounted on a sturdy, level bench or stand. The top of the jigsaw table should be slightly lower than the elbows. Be sure that the base of the saw is level before bolting it in place.

With a ⅓ or ½ h.p., 1725 r.p.m. capacitor or repulsion-induction type motor, the average jig saw has four spindle speeds: 570, 858, 1220, and 1658 r.p.m.

To install the motor, slide the jigsaw pulley onto the motor shaft so that the small step of the spindle pulley is next to the motor; tighten the pulley setscrew. Fasten motor to motor base, but do not tighten bolts securely. Place belt around small step of motor pulley and large step of spindle pulley. Shift motor until pulleys are aligned and belt is absolutely straight. Slide the motor base back until belt is tight, and secure in this position. The motor must rotate counterclockwise facing the pulley end. The belt should be just tight enough to prevent slipping and this tension must be maintained at all times.

Controls on the jig saw. The knob at the rear of the saw table controls the *table-tilt lock*. The table can be tilted 15° to the left, and 45° to the right, with the angle shown on the graduated scale. The trunnion support bracket swivels in a complete circle to permit cutting compound angles. In this type of jig saw, a hose carries air from a pump mounted on the drive shaft to a blower nozzle above the table. This blower hose keeps layout lines free of sawdust and visible at all times (Fig. 2).

The *work hold-down* holds the work against the table, enabling one to concentrate on following the layout lines (Fig. 3). The vertical position is controlled by the adjustable sliding bar. To make any adjustments merely loosen the thumbscrew on the left side of the saw arm, place the hold-down against the work, and retighten the screw. The hold-down may be tilted for angular cutting by loosening the machine screw that holds it in place. The hold-down guide bar must always be placed on the right side of the saw arm when the table is swiveled for the full 90° for cutting long pieces of material.

The *lockscrews* in both the upper and lower chucks lock the blade in the chuck jaws. These lockscrews are usually loosened and tightened by an Allen wrench (Fig. 4).

The *blade guide* and the *blade-support wheel*, located directly

Fig. 2. Heavy ribbed table is mounted on two trunnions, graduated to show angle of tilt. Trunnion support bracket swivels in complete circle to allow cutting of compound angles. Hose carries air from pump mounted on drive shaft to blower nozzle above table.

above the work hold-down, support the blade and keep it running true (Fig. 5). Both can be adjusted vertically and horizontally. For vertical adjustment, loosen the thumbscrew on the left side of the saw arm. For horizontal adjustment, loosen the two screws on top of the guide. To adjust the blade guide to accommodate any width of blade, turn the machine screw on the side of the blade guide. Both guide and wheel should be adjusted so that the teeth of the saw blade rub against them lightly. Position the blade guide so that its front edge is even with the bottom of the blade teeth.

The control knob on the right side of saw arm controls the *blade-tension housing* (Fig. 1). Loosen this control to adjust the housing for various lengths of blades.

Selecting and mounting blades. There are two distinct types of blades—the regular jigsaw blade and the Sabre blade. Both come in various sizes. The choice of the type of blade to use depends on the material that is being cut and the circumferences of the curves. A jigsaw blade $\frac{3}{16}''$ wide with eleven teeth to the inch is ideal for general purposes. In addition to this, secure several smaller blades with 12 to 16, and 18 to 20 teeth to the inch. For fine work secure several blades with from 20 to 50 teeth per inch.

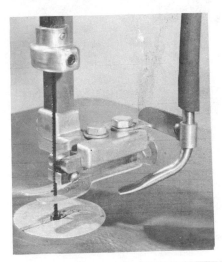

Fig. 3. View showing upper operating shaft, blade-support roller and adjustable blade-guide bar, work holddown, and blower nozzle.

Always use the largest blade with the coarsest teeth that will cut the material cleanly and is able to cut the sharpest curve in any pattern that you are working on. Sabre blades, thicker and wider than ordinary blades, are used for cutting large panels or surfaces. For cutting wood, the thinner and harder it is and the finer the finish desired, the finer the teeth of the blades should be.

The abruptness of the contours to be cut governs the thickness and width of the blade to be used; sharp curves require thin, narrow blades.

Thin-gauge metal can be cut on the jig saw with fine-toothed blades. The width and thickness of metal-cutting blades are governed by the same rules that apply to the selection of wood-cutting blades. To cut plastics, a medium-thin blade with medium teeth is used.

To mount a jigsaw blade insert it approximately $\frac{3}{8}''$ into the

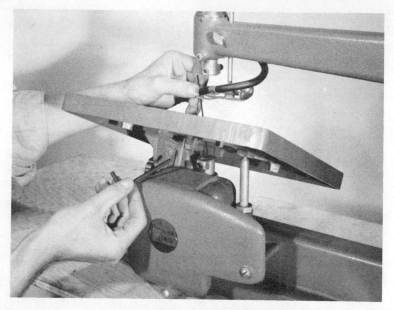

Fig. 4. Inserting blade in jig saw. Blade is first clamped in the lower chuck, then secured in the upper.

Fig. 5. Heavy Sabre blade is held in V jaws of chuck, and guided and braced by a special blade support.

lower chuck with the teeth pointing downward, and tighten the lock screw. Turn the spindle pulley by hand until the blade is at the top of the stroke, loosen the blade-tension knob, set the blade about ⅜″ into the upper chuck and tighten the lockscrew. Release the tension-housing lockknob and raise the housing until the desired blade tension is obtained; tighten the lockknob. Be sure that the blade is perpendicular to the table and that the teeth are pointed downward (Fig. 6).

Rotate the spindle pulley by hand. If further blade tension adjustment is necessary, loosen the tension-housing knob, raise or lower housing, whichever is required, and retighten lockknob.

To mount a Sabre blade, remove the table insert plate. Turn the lower chuck 90° clockwise, by removing lockscrew, which holds it to the lower shaft. Replace lockscrew in hole in front of shaft and lock securely. Place blade in the V jaws of the lower chuck so that it is perpendicular to the table (Fig. 5). Tighten the chuck lockscrew. A Sabre-blade guide attachment should be used with this type of blade. This attachment, mounted on the table trunnion bracket beneath the table, is used as an additional support for the blade. Sabre blades are usually used for cutting large panels with the overarm of the jig saw removed (Fig. 7).

Fig. 6. Correct tooth direction.

OPERATING THE JIG SAW

Before attempting to operate the jig saw fill the crankcase with SAE 30 machine oil. Keep the crankcase filled with this oil at all times to keep drive mechanism properly lubricated.

Before starting the motor always turn pulley by hand to make sure proper blade and chuck clearances have been obtained. Apply

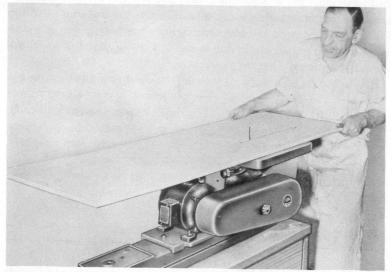

Fig. 7. Sabre blade cutting large panel, with overarm of saw removed.

soap and beeswax to the blade when cutting metal. It assists blade to cut freely and prevents scoring of blade.

Correct speeds. No set rule can be given for speed of operation; the speed used will depend upon the material being cut and the operator's skill. For cutting wood or plastics either of the two medium speeds should be used. For cutting metal the slower speed is employed. Higher speeds result in faster cutting and require more skill. The main objective is to use a speed that will allow easy manipulation and guidance of the work. The faster speeds are usually employed when using Sabre blades. Remembering that a jigsaw blade cuts only on the downward stroke, feed the stock easily and steadily to the saw. After a little practice one can determine quite easily the correct speeds to use.

Cutting to pattern on a jig saw. The jig saw is used principally in the making of small ornamental cutouts such as lawn ornaments, door stops, weather vanes, and similar articles. With this type of work, cutting on the jig saw consists mainly of cutting to a pattern or an outline. Draw the pattern full size on a piece of paper and either trace or paste the paper pattern on the material (Fig. 8). Start the saw at a medium rate of speed, until you have attained a certain amount of dexterity in handling the tool and manipulating the material. When cutting to an outline follow the same procedure as for cutting on the band saw. Never attempt to follow a line continuously from one end to the other. Pick out the most prominent parts of the curve or pattern. First cut these out and then return to the smaller and more intricate

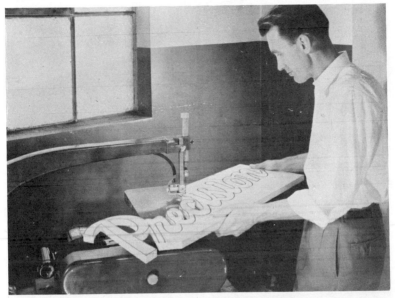

Fig. 8. Cutting along paper pattern pasted on stock.

sections. An inside cut must be started from a hole that has previously been bored by a bit and brace (Fig. 9). Insert the blade in this hole, mount it on the saw, and make the inside cut in the usual manner.

Multiple cutting. Thin material of like size and design can be cut on the jig saw in multiples by fastening the required number of pieces together as described in Chap. 6. When cutting patterns in multiple groups on the jig saw be sure that the saw table is perfectly square with the blade. If the table is not absolutely square the top piece may be perfect, following the outline of the design in every respect, yet the bottom one will be considerably distorted (Fig. 10).

Fig. 9. Sawing a circular ring from 2″ stock. Note hole drilled in stock.

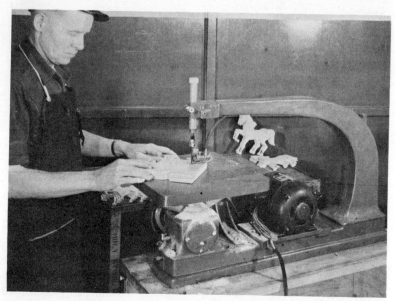

Fig. 10. Multiple cutting on the jig saw.

Lubrication and maintenance. Keep saw crankcase filled with SAE 30 motor oil. Replace oil every month if the saw is used frequently. If it is used infrequently, put new oil in every six months. To drain out old oil, remove drain plug on front of saw base.

The saw table must be covered with a film of oil, when saw is not in use, to keep it from rusting.

Maintain proper belt tension at all times. Keep belt just tight enough to prevent slipping.

Oil the guide-wheel shaft and blade guide occasionally.

Lubricate upper shaft bearing by putting a few drops of SAE 20 machine oil in hole and side, and in top of blade-tension housing at frequent and regular intervals.

CHAPTER 12

The Drill Press

A good drill press can be used for many jobs in the home workshop. In addition to the primary function for which it was originally intended—that of drilling holes in wood and other materials—with inexpensive and efficient accessories now available, a drill press can be used for such intricate procedures as shaping, routing, making mortises and tenons, making dovetail joints, and cutting rabbets and dados. It can also be utilized for making carvings and moldings, and for sanding. The modern drill press can safely be classed with the lathe as being one of the most versatile of the power tools available.

Two types of modern drill presses are shown in Figs. 1 and 2.

Description. A drill press consists of four basic parts, namely, the base, column, table, and head. The head is the term used to designate the entire working mechanism attached to the upper end of the column. The central part of the head is the spindle. The spindle revolves in a vertical position, and is housed in ball bearings at either end of a movable sleeve which is called the quill. The quill and the spindle which it carries, is moved downward by means of a rack-and-pinion gearing, actuated by the feed lever. When the feed lever is released, the quill and spindle is returned to its natural position by means of a coil spring. Adjustments are provided for locking the quill in any desired position by means of the double-acting depth gauge. The same depth gauge allows the operator to preset the depth to which he wishes the quill to travel.

The 14″ drill press is so named, since the diameter of the largest circular piece of work which can be drilled through the center on the drill press table is 14 inches. In other words, the distance from the center of the spindle to the front of the drill press column is 7″. Another indication of the size of a drill press is the distance between the end of the spindle and the table. As can be readily seen this distance is much greater on floor models than on bench model drill presses. In either case, the depth of the hole that can be drilled with one stroke of the feed lever, is approximately 4″.

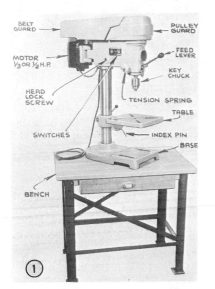

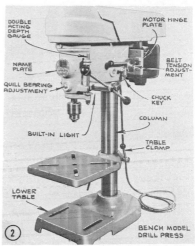

BENCH MODEL DRILL PRESS

Power and speed. The drill press is usually fitted with cone pulleys so that a variety of selective speeds can be obtained. With a 1725 r.p.m. motor and four step pulleys the speed will range from 710 to 4470 revolutions per minute. Since the shaft stands vertical, only a motor designed for vertical mounting, should be used as a power unit. A one-third horsepower motor is sufficient for average work since this is approximately the power required to drill a one-half inch hole through steel.

Spindles. Interchangeable spindles are supplied for most drill presses, thus adapting the machine for a wide variety of work. The standard spindle has a taper which holds a one-half capacity.

Jacobs key chuck (Fig. 3). Other common types of spindles are also shown in the illustration.

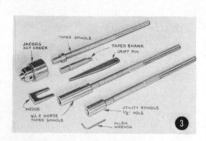

UNPACKING THE DRILL PRESS

A drill press is a precision tool which should be handled with care at all times. It should be carefully unpacked and installed so that all of the fine accuracy built into it by the manufacturer will be retained.

The crate is easily removed from the drill press. Pull out all the nails driven through the sides of the crate into the top and bottom panels. Pull out the nails driven through the side panels into the cross member near the center of the crate. Unhook the looped ends of the binding wires, and lift off the top panel. Unwrap the side panels from the crate. Remove the protective paper, and the bolts which hold the drill press base to the bottom of the crate.

Cleaning the drill press. A cloth soaked in kerosene will remove the heavy grease used to prevent the drill press from rusting in transit. After cleaning, all parts should be wiped thoroughly, and the unpainted surfaces coated with a coat of good machine oil.

INSTALLING THE DRILL PRESS

Mounting the motor. The motor should be unpacked and mounted on the motor hinge plate (Fig. 2) with the cap screws furnished. The hinge plate with motor attached is then mounted on the drill press head between the two cone pivot screws. The screws are then tightened with a screwdriver until play is eliminated, but should be loose enough to allow the bracket to swing freely. The lock nuts on the pivot screws should then be tightened (Fig. 4). Avoid excessive pressure when tightening pivot screws, or the motor base casting may be damaged.

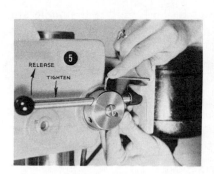 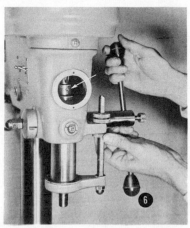

Mount the motor pulley (packed with motor base) on the motor shaft with the small step next to the motor (Fig. 4). Align the motor pulley with the pulley on the drill press spindle, using a good straightedge. Then insert the brass plug and set screw (packed in an envelope with the motor pulley), and tighten set screw to hold the pulley securely.

Next attach the lead wires to the motor. Remove the plate covering the terminals and attach the wires according to the diagram found on the inside of the terminal cover. Replace the cover.

Adjusting belt tension. Place the belt on corresponding steps on both the motor and spindle pulleys. Loosen the belt tightener lock screw (Fig. 5). With the lever in position as shown in Fig. 5; exert enough backward pressure against the motor base until the desired belt tension is obtained. Lock in position by tightening the set screw. The belt should run with a small amount of slack. Adjusting the belt too tight will cause excessive wear on the belt, and also on the motor and spindle bearings. The added friction will absorb power unnecessarily.

Changing spindle speeds. Four direct drive spindle speeds are available, 710 to 4470 r.p.m. being obtained with a 1725 r.p.m. motor. By raising the belt tightener lever (Fig. 5), the motor is allowed to swing forward, releasing the tension on the belt so that it may be shifted to any one of the four pulley steps. Lowering the lever retightens the belt to exactly the same tension on any of the four pulley steps.

Lubrication. The ball bearings on both quill and spindle are of the sealed type, lubricated for life and will require no further attention. The outer shell of the quill should be lubricated occasionally when in the fully lowered position. The splined end of the spindle shaft should also have a few drops of oil at regular intervals depending on use.

Changing spindles. The first step in removing the drill press spindle is to take off the nameplate on the front of the head (Fig. 2). Lower the quill until the top is exposed through the open-

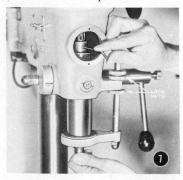

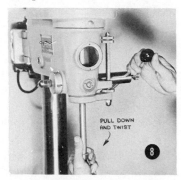

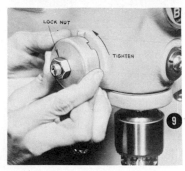

ing as shown in Fig. 6. Tighten the lock nuts on the depth gauge of either side of the head casting lug to hold the quill in this position. With the Allen wrench, remove the small set screw in the spindle lock collar as shown in Fig. 7. Loosen the depth gauge lock nuts and return the quill assembly to its normal position. Gently tap the splined end of the spindle which projects through the upper pulley with a wooden mallet to loosen it from the quill. When the spindle begins to move grasp the lower end (Fig. 8) pulling downward and twisting back and forth until the spindle is completely out of the assembly.

Replacing spindle. To replace a spindle the above process is reversed. Lower and lock the quill in position with the top of the quill exposed through the nameplate opening. Slip the spindle locking collar over the spindle-lock-collar sleeve. Place locking collar and sleeve through the nameplate hole on top of the quill assembly in a vertical position. Insert the spindle in the bottom of the quill and firmly push or lightly tap the spindle in place with "to and fro" twisting motion to aid passage of the spindle through the quill assembly, the locking sleeve and collar, and the splined pulley assembly. With the spindle in place, lower the locking device and firmly seat the spindle locked-collar sleeve against the inner race of the ball bearing in the top of the quill assembly. Make sure the set screw in the spindle collar is 180° from the slot in the spindle lock collar sleeve. With the Allen wrench tighten the set screw (Fig. 7), until firmly seated. Test the spindle with the power "off." There should be no "vertical play," or up and down movement, and the spindle should rotate freely. Unlock the depth gauge lock-nuts and return the spindle assembly to its normal position. Replace the nameplate.

Adjusting spindle return spring. To adjust the return spring, first remove the outer or cap nut entirely and then loosen the second or retaining nut several turns. Grasp the spring housing (Fig. 9) and lift away from the drill press head to disengage the housing notch from the lug on the head casting. Be sure to hold the spring housing firmly to prevent it from unwinding when released from this notch. To increase the tension, turn the housing counterclockwise one-half turn at a time, pushing the housing in at the end of each half turn so that the notch engages the lug. To release the tension, turn the housing by half turns in a clockwise direction, pushing the housing in at the end of each half turn to engage the notch. When proper tension has been obtained, re-tighten the retaining nut and lock with the cap nut which was removed first.

Adjustments. In average drilling operations, the hole in the center of the table should be directly under the drill so that the drill, after going through the work, will enter the hole in the table. Where it is necessary to drill through the stock on which you are working, the feed lever should always be pressed without the work in place to see that the drill enters the table opening. The drill press table may be tilted and locked at any angle, right or left (Figs. 10 and 11). Holes are drilled in the swivel head for the insertion of the knurled index pin when the table is in the horizontal, vertical, or 45° angle position. When it is neces-sary to adjust the table to any intermediate angle, the nut on the swivel screw is tightened to lock the table in the desired

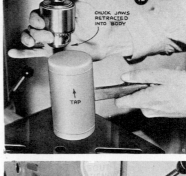

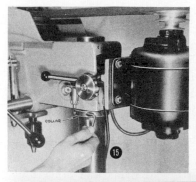

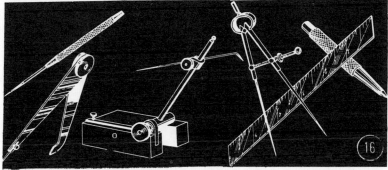

position. When average work requires the setting of the table to a variety of angles, it is advisable to set a scale and adjustable pointer to the under side of the table to locate these positions.

Mounting chuck. Mount the Jacobs key chuck to the taper spindle as shown in Fig. 12. Do not strike the chuck jaws. *Note* that they have been withdrawn into the body of the chuck before it is tapped in place with a wooden mallet or rawhide hammer.

Removing chuck. To remove the chuck from the drill press spindle, insert the slotted steel wedge (Fig. 3), between the shoulder on the spindle, and the top of the chuck, as shown in Fig. 13, and strike the wedge a sharp blow with a hammer. At the same time, hold the chuck with one hand to prevent its falling onto the drill press table when driven off.

Double acting depth gauge. By adjusting and locking the two knurled stop nuts (Fig. 2), depth of the spindle travel can be accurately controlled. By adjusting the lower knurled stop nut, the length of return stroke can be controlled. By tightening both the bottom and top stop nuts, spindle can be securely anchored at any height for routing, shaping, surface grinding or other similar operations which require the vertical movement of the quill to be locked.

Chucking drills. Chucking a drill with a key chuck is easily accomplished as shown in Fig. 14. The drill is usually held in the left hand, while the key is inserted and the jaws tightened with the right. Drills are removed in the same manner, except that the twist on the key is reversed. On no account should the drill be loosened from the chuck unless the hand is in position to prevent it from falling. The insertion of drills and other tools in a spindle which has a hole in the end to receive the shank of the drill is quite simple, the drill being pressed into the hole and the set screws being tightened to hold it. Where taper shank drills are used, the drill is fitted by pressing it into the tapered hole at the end of the spindle, engaging the tang of the drill in the corresponding slot of the spindle. During use the drill becomes tightly wedged in the tapered hole, and must be driven out by the means of a drift key (Fig. 3). One edge of the drift key is flat and the other round. The round edge fits against the upper round part of the slot in the spindle while the flat edge fits against the end of the drill being removed.

OPERATION

The drill press head and work table can be adjusted to various positions on the column. Both are clamped securely in place by double plug binders. The position ·of the work table, being readjusted more frequently than the head, is provided with a quick acting hand lever which will instantly release or tighten the binder, with a quarter turn of the clamp handle (Fig. 2). The double plug binder in the head is released or tightened by a heavy Allen screw wrench. Great care should be used in adjusting the position of the head on the column. It should be well supported when the binder is released to prevent it from dropping and striking the table, and possibly injuring the chuck, the spindle, or other parts of the head. A column collar (available as an accessory) as shown in Fig. 15, should be mounted below the casting of the drill press head. With this collar in place, the head binder may be released and the drill press head swung from side to side with safety. By placing the collar a few inches below the head it will act as a safety stop when raising, lowering, or changing the position of the head.

Laying out the work. Practically every hole that is drilled requires that first of all, a layout mark be made which will locate either its approximate or exact position. Various tools are used in making the layout, ranging from square, hammer, and punch, to expensive instruments essential for very exacting work. A few of the layout tools commonly used are shown in Fig. 16. One of the most useful tools for average work is the combination square. This can be used for center lining, as shown in Fig. 17, in case the work is being done on wood. If the layout work was required

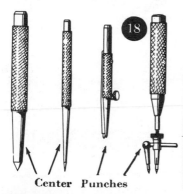

Center Punches

on metal, a scriber or punch would be substituted for the pencil shown in the illustration. Various substances and devices are used to mark on a variety of materials.

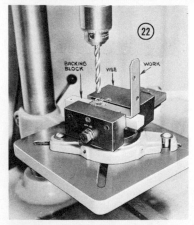

After the scriber or pencil has been used to locate the hole position, it is further necessary to indent this point. This is done with a center punch a few of which are shown in Fig. 18. There are various sizes of center punches, and the size selection will depend upon the work, and the accuracy which is required. Center punching should be done carefully so that the punch mark comes at the exact intersection of the layout lines. Despite the care of laying out and clamping, it will sometimes be found that after the drill has cut a few revolutions into the work, the hole is found to be off center. The drill may be led back to the proper position by cutting from one to three or more grooves with a small round nosed chisel, the grooves being on the side toward which it is desired to draw the hole. When the drill is again started, it should drift over to the correct position. This must be done before the drill starts to cut its full diameter.

DRILL PRESS VISE

The *drill press vise* offers the most practical method of holding small work while being drilled. The base of the vise (Fig. 19) can be clamped to the slotted work table enabling the vise to hold the work rigidly for drilling or reaming. The center tapered pivot on the upper part of the vise fits into the hole in the base and is clamped in place with the set screws as shown in Fig. 20. These set screws, when turned in part way, allow the upper part of the vise to turn freely. When the set screws are tightened, they securely lock the vise at any desired point in the circle. Figure 21 shows a round metal rod clamped in the drill press vise for drilling The long end of the rod is turned over against the drill press column for added support. In this case it would be unnecessary to tighten the set screw securely. Figure 22 shows an angle plate clamped in the drill press vise. A block of hard wood or metal is placed under the work so that the pressure of the drill

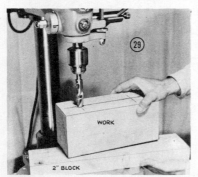

will not loosen or force the work out of line. Figure 23 shows a hollow pipe clamped in the drill press vise. For such drilling operations a good center punch mark is essential to keep the drill point from drifting off of the rounded surface. If the hole in this case is to go completely through the pipe it is advisable to drill first through one side, then turn the work over and drill through the other. This will avoid going through the bottom and drilling into your vise.

The various equipment shown in Figs. 24, 25, and 26 show the surface plate, "V" blocks, and angle plate being used in conjunction with surface gauges for layout and checking of final work.

DRILLING PRACTICE IN WOOD

Speeds. Spur bits in sizes up to approximately $\frac{3}{4}''$ should be worked at speeds between 1800 and 3000 r.p.m.'s. No exact speeds may be given, since this depends to a great extent on the wood, grain, depth of hole, style of bit, etc. Generally speaking, smaller bits can turn faster than larger ones, more speed can be used on soft woods, less speed should be used for deep holes, and more speed can be used for end drilling. Large bits must always be run at a low speed. Multi-spur and expansive bits will burn if worked at greater than 500 r.p.m.

Drilling. The work is properly laid out and the position of the hole marked. The bit is mounted in the chuck. The table should be located so that the bit will pass through the table opening after the hole has been drilled. The drill is forced into the work by pulling on the feed lever. The feed should be slowed down when the operator judges the drill to be almost through the work. The feed should be very slow from this point on to avoid splintering the work as the drill projects through the under side. Most operators prefer to place a scrap block of wood under the work, so that as the drill passes through it meets a solid foundation, and by thus drilling part way into the scrap stock a clean neat hole is left on the under side of the work. In many instances a larger auxiliary wood table is mounted on the regular drill press table to give added support for larger work (Fig. 27).

Drilling to depth. One method of drilling to a specified depth is shown in Fig. 28. The depth of the hole to be drilled is marked on the side of the work. The quill assembly is then lowered with the drill along side the work until it reaches the proper depth, holding it in this position, set the stop nut as shown in the illustration. The quill assembly is then returned to its normal position, the drill is centered on the cross lines of your layout marks and the feed lever is pressed until it is stopped by the lock nuts on the depth gauge. One other method is to bring the point of the drill down against the work and then read the scale on the depth gauge. Then proceed to feed the drill into the work, adding the required depth to the first reading.

Drilling deep holes. One method of increasing the depth over the normal spindle travel is shown in Fig. 29. The first full stroke is made, sinking the drill to a depth of 4″ in the work. The feed handle is then released, and the work lifted with the drill inserted in the hole and a base block is slipped under the work as shown in the illustration. The feed handle can now be pressed again and an additional two inches may be drilled with the same quill travel. In all deep hole drilling, cutting should not continue after the flutes of the bit have passed below the work surface. After this point has been reached, the chips cannot get out, and burning starts immediately. Where it is necessary to go beyond this depth —the bit should be lifted frequently in order to permit clearing the hole of chips.

Drilling large holes. Holes over 1½″ diameter can be classified as large holes. The removal of comparatively large amounts of wood causes considerable strain on the work and it is therefore advisable to use clamps. This applies especially to any kind of bit which has but one cutting edge. Other style cutters of the multi-spur or continuous rim pattern can be operated without clamping. Figure 30 shows a multi-spur bit being used.

Drilling in round work. Various methods are in use for drilling a round stock, however, one of the most common is the use of the "V" block. Figure 31 shows a round metal bar being drilled. If the hole is not too large and the feed is relatively slow, clamps will not be found necessary for a drilling operation of this kind. The pressure of the drill securely seats the bar in the "V" block and little pressure will be found necessary to hold it in position.

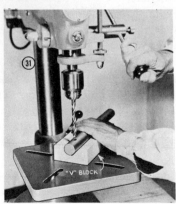 

Figure 32 shows a circular disc of wood being drilled around its edge by means of the "V" block method. In this case the table has been locked in a vertical position and a "V" block clamped to the surface and also resting on the lower surface. The wood disc may be held against the surface easily with one hand while the feed lever is operated with the other.

Another method of drilling round work is shown in Fig. 33. In this case, the table is tilted to 45° and a block of wood is clamped to the table as shown in the illustration. The work is laid in the "V" formed by the table surface and the block. The table may be pivoted back and forth in order to center the drill on the surface of the round work.

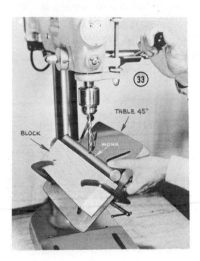
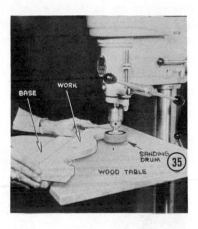

Pivot points. Where the holes are to be drilled around the edge of a circular piece of work as shown in Fig. 34, the work is pivoted on a wood or metal pin which may extend completely through or merely part way from the under side. The use of a pivot pin locates the holes accurately in relation to the center, but does not space them equally around the circle. A jig with a locating pin or indexing head will regulate this part of the work.

MISCELLANEOUS DRILL PRESS OPERATIONS

Grinding. Light surface grinding can be done perfectly on the drill press, using a cup wheel which is mounted on a special spindle. The grit and bond of the wheel should be selected to suit the work, as with any other type of grinding. The speed of the drill press should be about 5000 r.p.m. The work is projected along the drill press table and under the cup wheel, which has been set to take a suitable bite and the quill locked in position. Heavy cuts should be avoided. Good use can be made of a column collar under the drill press head. The work is clamped in place in the vise (Fig. 35), and the drill press head is swung back and forth across the work.

Countersinking. The various types of wood and machine screws are set so that their heads come either flush or below the surface of the work. To make holes for these heads, an ordinary drill of suitable size can be used for average work. For more accurate work, however, regular countersink drills should be used as shown in Fig. 36.

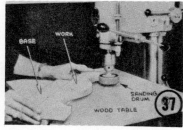

Sanding. Another useful drill press operation is sanding. Sanding drums of various shapes and sizes are available at most machine tool dealers, which will take much of the time consuming work out of hand sanding many of the curved surfaces of your shop projects. A 3″ sanding drum should run at from 1200 to 1500 r.p.m.'s. Smaller sizes should run faster. Drums are used mostly for edge operations, and good use can be made of fences, pivot pins, and other simple jigs to guide the work. Irregular curves are simply fed free hand with a uniform feed and pressure to obtain good work and prevent burning. Figure 37 shows a typical example of free hand edge sanding. The work is supported on the base block in order to center the edge of the sanding drum on the edge of the work.

The main difficulty with free hand edge sanding is that the work must be kept moving at an even pressure against the drum, otherwise a deep cut is made into the work at any place where the operator pauses too long. One way to avoid this fault is to sand with a pattern or against a wood disc exactly the same diameter as the sanding drum, set below the drum and fastened to the table. The pattern is then fastened to the under side of the work and while the pattern rides against the wood disc the work rides against the sanding drum. The same pattern may thus be used to duplicate the first piece as many times as necessary.

CHAPTER **13**

Jointers and Shapers

·
·

JOINTERS

A jointer, sometimes called a jointer planer, is essentially a motorized plane. Its principal function is planing the surface of material as it is passed over a revolving cutting head. This power tool is used mostly for surfacing and planing narrow widths and edges of stock prior to the making of glued joints, and for planing and surfacing the faces of lumber. A jointer can also be utilized for rabbeting, chamfering, and similar operations.

The parts of a well-designed jointer are shown in Fig. 1.

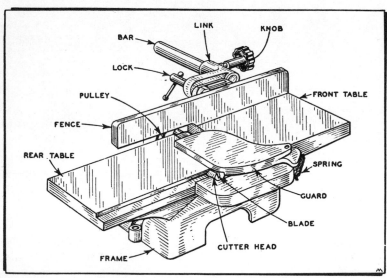

Fig. 1. Typical jointer and its parts.

To do efficient, accurate work the base supporting the tables of the jointer must be sturdy or the cutter heads that rotate at a high speed will not produce an even, smooth surface. The base must be constructed of one piece so that parts cannot work loose or get out of alignment.

A jointer is equipped with two tables: the front or infeed table, and the rear or outfeed table. A control must be provided to raise or lower these tables as required. The tables are accurately machined and are mounted on inclines, so when either raised or lowered they remain level. They should be made of cast iron and preferably ribbed on the underside for additional strength and rigidity. The cutter head of a good jointer is machined out of a solid piece of steel and is the round cutter-head type, sometimes called the safety cutter head. On a round cutter head, the cutting blades or knives project only a slight distance, thus lessening any possibility of injury. These knives should be made of thin, hardened, high-speed steel rather than carbon steel, as the former keep their edges sharp five or six times longer.

The guide or fence should be wide and long, and machined smooth and perfectly straight on the face side. It should be easily adjustable back and forth at any point across the table, and provided with a tilting arrangement combined with a locking device for holding it securely in any desired position.

The jointer shown in Fig. 1 is a standard type and requires a $\frac{1}{3}$ h.p., 1725 r.p.m. repulsion-induction or capacitor motor with a $3\frac{11}{16}''$-diameter pulley.

The jointer is usually operated at speeds ranging from 5000 to 8000 r.p.m.

Installation of the jointer. To assemble a new jointer fasten the fence bracket to the right side of the front table with the cap screws provided by the manufacturer. Put the fence on the fence bracket and tighten the lock. To mount the guard in position put the fiber washer on the guard stud. Fasten the guard spring to the cotter pin in the table of the jointer. Push the stud into the hole in the top of the table. Before mounting the jointer cut a hole in the top of the workbench to facilitate chip removal. Mount the jointer on a level bench or table, but check to make sure that the base rests squarely and solidly on all feet before bolting it down. Uneven mounting will eventually throw the tables out of alignment.

Controls and adjustments. The ball crank handle, beneath the front table of the jointer, controls the depth-of-cut adjustment.

The front table lock control on the right side of the jointer locks the front table in position. Before the table can be adjusted, this lock must be released. The knob beneath the rear table controls rear table elevation. Before adjusting the rear table, loosen the hex capscrew found on right side of jointer frame.

The adjusting knob on the fence slide bracket releases and locks fence, when making necessary adjustments for width of cut. The fence tilt lever locks fence in any required position (Fig. 2).

The top of the rear table must be exactly level with the cutting

Fig. 2. Jointer fence adjustments.

arc of the knives. To align the rear table, loosen the table lock screw on right side of jointer and raise or lower the rear table, until it is level with the cutting edge of any one blade at the highest point in its cutting arc. Check accuracy of alignment by placing a straightedge on the rear table with one end projecting over one of the cutter blades. The blade of the cutter should just touch the straightedge.

Each blade in the cutter head must be the same height and parallel with the rear table. To check and make the necessary adjustment proceed as follows: Remove fence and guard. Place a straightedge on the center of the rear table with one end projecting over the cutter blades. Revolve the cutter head by hand. Adjust blades to touch the straightedge. To adjust the blades, loosen the setscrews which hold them in place in the cutter head. If blade is too high, tap it very lightly with a piece of hardwood. If the blade is low, raise it by inserting a small punch under bottom edge of blade. Repeat these operations, placing straightedge along each side of table, and adjusting the blades if necessary. After all of the blades have been checked and adjusted, place paper or metal shims beneath them so they seat firmly. Tighten the blades securely with the setscrews.

To adjust the table depth gauge, proceed as follows: Place a straightedge on the front table so that one end projects over the cutter blades. Adjust table until blades just touch the straightedge. When table is in this position the depth-gauge pointer should be at the zero reading. If not, loosen setscrew that holds pointer and adjust to zero.

To adjust the fence proceed as follows: Loosen the fence tilt lever (Fig. 2). Using a try square, set the fence perpendicular to the table. Tilt gauge pointer, which should now be at the zero reading. If not, loosen setscrew and adjust pointer to zero.

OPERATING THE JOINTER

In jointing or planing boards, the rear table must always be level with the knives at their highest point. This setting must never be changed except, of course, when operations other than planing are performed. To test the accuracy of the alignment of the rear table with the cutting knives, start the machine and run a test piece of material over the knives for several inches. If the tables are correctly aligned, there will be no space showing between the table and the board as the newly planed surface passes over the rear table. If the rear table is too high there will be a slight raising of the board and the cutters will cut more off the first end of the board than off the rear end. If the rear table has been set too low, light will be visible between the board and the rear table (Fig. 3). When the stock is pushed forward, the front end of the board will eventually drop until it rests on the rear table, causing the blades to cut a notch in the material.

Planing. Wood up to 4½″ wide may be planed or surfaced

on the jointer without removing the guard or fence (Fig. 4). For wider boards it is necessary to remove both the guard and the fence. Boards exceeding 4½″ in width can readily be surfaced by moving the guard and the fence, and taking several thin cuts of approximately the same width on the inside and outside. When jointing or planing a board on a jointer, always cut with

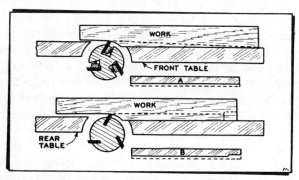

Fig. 3. Top, table set too high; bottom, table set too low.

the grain. If the direction of the grain changes and the jointing is done across or against the grain, feed the stock slowly. Always be sure to examine the material carefully beforehand to make sure that it is free of nails and other obstructions.

Use a wood pusher block when planing boards or strips less than ½″ thick, not only as a safety measure, but to assure accuracy (Fig. 5). It is impossible to hold down thin strips of material with the hand alone and secure a smooth even surface. Material thicker than ½″ can be held down and fed with the hands only. Do not hold the sides or edges of the wood with fingers while the material is passing over the knives.

When it is desired to have the edges square with the surface, set the fence of the jointer to a 90° angle and lay

Fig. 4. Planing boards up to 4½″ wide.

the board on its edge. In feeding the board across the knives, be sure that you hold its entire surface against the fence, exerting as much pressure sideways as down.

Cutting chamfers or bevels. For bevel jointing the same procedure is followed as for planing square edges, except that the fence is adjusted to the correct angle to produce the desired bevel or chamfer. Secure the fence in this position before proceeding to cut the material. Take cuts of medium thickness until the bevel is nearly planed to full shape, then finish with light cuts. Be sure to hold the side of the board in contact with the fence. At the same time hold the board down against the table as you feed it through the machine (Fig. 6).

Fig. 5. Always use a pusher when planing thin stock.

Fig. 6. Angular planing with jointer.

Rabbeting. The rabbeting ledge incorporated in the front table of the jointer is merely an extension of the table that helps support the board being rabbeted. To cut a rabbet, remove the guard and slide the fence toward the left side of the table until it is the same distance from the left end of cutter blades as the desired width of the rabbet. Lower the front table to the required depth of rabbet. If the full depth of the rabbet is within the capacity of the machine, make the rabbet in one cut. If the cut is wider or deeper than the capacity of the machine, make it in several cuts, feeding the work slowly (Fig. 7).

Making moldings. A jointer can make only moldings that have a combination of either flat or beveled surfaces. These various cuts and surfaces can be made at different depths and at varying angles. Attractive moldings can be made by combining these cuts.   Procedure is exactly the same as for conventional cuts (Fig. 8).

Lubrication.   If the machine is used frequently it must be oiled every month.   Use SAE 20 machine oil throughout.   To oil bearings remove pulley and collar next to bearings.   If used

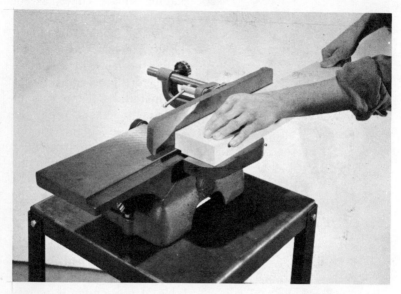

Fig. 7.   Cutting a rabbet.   Note clearance provided by rabbeting ledge.

infrequently oil every six months.   Oil table, frame ways, and all adjusting screws at regular intervals.

Sharpening cutter blades.   When the surface of the planed wood begins to have a fuzzy look, or when the stock being jointed begins to chatter, it is necessary to sharpen the cutter blades.

As a general rule, honing the blades with a flat oilstone or medium-grade slipstone is all that is necessary.   Before honing, check alignment of blades per directions given in this chapter. Then proceed as follows: Adjust and lock front table ⅛″ below cutting edge of blades.   Partly cover sharpening stone with paper to avoid scratching the surface of the table and lay it on the front table.   Turn the cutter head so that the stone is resting flat on the bevel of a blade.   Hold the cutter head in this position.   Rub

Fig. 8. Making moldings. All cuts and surfaces are flat, being made at different depths and angles.

the stone with an even pressure along the length of the blade until the blade is sharp. Treat each blade similarly with exactly the same number of strokes. Readjust the rear table if necessary.

SHAPERS

A shaper is used for straight and irregular shaping, matched shaping, tonguing and grooving, planing, making drop-hinged leaf joints, fluting and reeding, and sanding. It is simple to operate and turns out superior work quickly and accurately. The essential parts of a standard vertical-spindle shaper are shown in Fig. 9. In selecting a shaper be sure that it is sturdy and well constructed. The base should be made of a single casting. All of the controls must be readily accessible. The spindle should preferably be of the stationary type, to insure absolute rigidity at its operating speed of over 10,000 r.p.m. The spindle should be constructed in one piece, of tempered alloy tool steel, and be equipped with a keyed washer and shaft to prevent the cutters from coming loose.

The table must be equipped with a bevel-gear-and-screw mechanism so that it can be moved up and down rapidly. The positioning of the table should be controlled by an easily accessible ball crank and a positive locking device that will clamp the table securely in any desired position (Fig. 10). The bearing

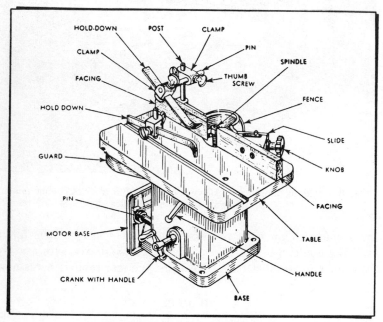

Fig. 9. Parts of a spindle shaper.

ways of the table should be cast integrally with the base for extreme rigidity. The table top should be accurately ground and well finished to facilitate the sliding of the work. Both the table and the base should be made of heavy iron castings, properly braced to minimize vibration and provide the essential rugged support to accomplish smooth finished work.

A well-designed spindle shaper is equipped with an adjustable fence and hold-downs made of adjustable spring-steel clips. These clips are used to maintain a constant even pressure on the work, holding it securely and firmly against the table and the fence during the entire length of the cut. (Fig. 10).

To hold it in the necessary rigid alignment the shaper should be equipped with two large precision ball bearings. These bearings should be permanently sealed against dust and grit and have an additional cover plate for added protection.

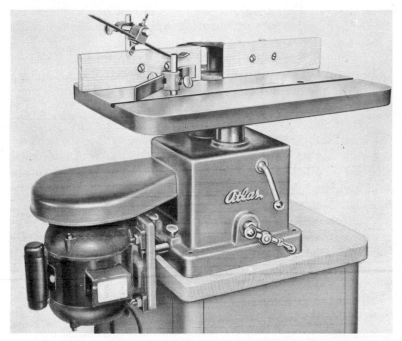

Fig. 10. Spindle shaper, showing motor mounting base and table raising column.

The shaper should be powered with a ⅓ h.p., **3450** r.p.m. capacitor or repulsion-induction type motor and a $3\frac{11}{16}''$-diameter motor pulley to obtain a spindle speed of 10,000 r.p.m. This high speed is necessary for the majority of shaper operations.

Assembling. To assemble the shaper remove the fence from the table. Use a cloth soaked with kerosene to remove the usual rust-preventive coating from the surface of the table. Replace the fence and lock in position with the setscrews and washers. Mount the spring hold-down clips. One of these clips is mounted to the fence and the other to the table (Fig. 10). Fasten the two mounting-bracket pins to the motor mounting bracket with the washers and nuts furnished by the manufacturer. Mount the bracket and the belt guard on the rear of the shaper.

Installing. Bolt the shaper to a sturdy level bench that is high enough so that the top of the shaper table is slightly lower than your elbows. Mount the shaper near the rear of the workbench so the adjustable motor mounting bracket extends below the bench top.

The shaper, if possible, should be set up in a central location in the workshop, as the length of the work that it can handle is limited by the distance from the spindle to the walls of the workshop, or to other machines or workbenches.

To install the motor, mount the pulley on the motor shaft and set the motor on the motor mounting bracket. Place the belt over the pulleys, and shift motor until pulleys are aligned and belt is straight. Pull motor back until belt is just tight enough to prevent slipping. Lock motor mounting bracket securely with the two thumbscrews.

Controls and adjustments. The crank handle or wheel on the front of the shaper is used to adjust the table height. The handle or control directly beneath the table locks it securely in the desired position. Before changing the height of the table always release this lock.

Two capscrews are used to lock the fence to the table. To position or set the entire fence for any required depth of cut, loosen these screws, slide the fence the desired distance from the cutting circle, and retighten these two screws.

The knobbed handle of the fence casting controls the positioning of the right fence for depth-of-cut adjustments on operations where the entire edge of the work is to be removed. Always release table fence lockscrew before positioning the right fence.

On a well-designed shaper a machine bolt is used to lock each facing to the fence. To adjust the opening between the faces, loosen the bolts, push the facings to the required position, and retighten. When making these adjustments be sure that the opening is never larger than will just clear the cut.

The only spindle adjustment ever necessary is one to eliminate end play. To make this adjustment loosen the spindle-pulley setscrew. Press spindle downward and push the pulley tightly against the spacer. Lock pulley in this position.

OPERATING THE SPINDLE SHAPER

Types of cutters used. Two types of cutters are available
for shaper work. One is the loose type mounted on a safety head,
and the other is the solid cutter. The latter is milled from a solid
bar of hardened and properly tempered tool steel, and ground to
the required shape. It is the safest type of cutter to use and is
recommended for the home workshop.

To do creditable work on the spindle shaper, it is not necessary
to have many cutters of different shapes and contours. Many
different types of moldings can be made with comparatively few
cutters (Fig. 11).

Straight shaping. Straight shaping is the process of cutting

Fig. 11. Molding cutters.

a profile or contour on the straight edges of tabletops and bench-
tops, and cutting moldings on straight lumber.

Select the cutter to be used. Hold spindle firmly with wrench
on flat part of the spindle beneath the table. Place the cutter
on the spindle and lock it securely in place with the keyed washer
and hex nut. At this point check to make sure that the cutter
rotates toward the work to be cut. To cut in the desired position
on the work, adjust the table to the correct height. Position
fence for depth of cut desired and move wood facings of fence
just far enough apart to clear the cut. The two fence facings
must be aligned for most straight shaping or molding operations.
To align the fence facings, place a straightedge against the left
one and move the right one up to the straightedge.

Adjust the spring hold-down clips before starting the machine.
These clips are used to hold the work firmly against the fence and
the table. Do not set clips too tightly against the work—just

enough to hold the work down and at the same time permit it to pass the revolving cutters smoothly and evenly. The correct speed to use for straight shaping is about 8000 r.p.m.

Start the machine. Make several trial cuts on pieces of scrap wood to check depth and position of cut before proceeding with the actual work.

Irregular shaping. Irregular shaping is the process of shaping the irregular edges of oval shaped tables, curved legs, chair and table stretchers, and decorative moldings on all types of curved irregular edges (Fig. 12).

For irregular shaping remove the fence and spring hold-down clips and replace with the proper depth collar for the depth of

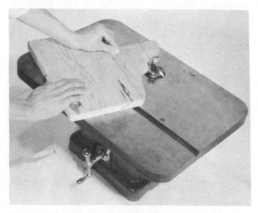

Fig. 12.   Irregular shaping on edge of shelf bracket, using shaping depth collar.

the cut to be made. Depth collars are set above or below the cutter or between two cutters, to prevent cutting beyond a certain depth. When the material is cut until its edge strikes the depth collar, the collar naturally prevents the cut from going any farther. The difference in diameter between the cutter and the collar regulates the width of the cut. Lock the collar and cutter on the spindle.

The two methods used for irregular shaping are called irregular shaping to a finished edge and irregular shaping with a template or pattern.

For irregular shaping to a finished edge, finish the edge of the work to the desired shape and sand smooth. Set the cutter on the spindle with the depth collar above it, and adjust it for the required width.

Use the guide pin furnished with the shaper as a fulcrum to support the work until it has been fed into the collar. Place this guide pin in either of the two holes next to the table opening, the right hole if the cutter rotation is clockwise, the left hole if counterclockwise (Fig. 13). The correct speed to use for irregular shaping is 8000 r.p.m. or faster. It is unnecessary to reverse the direction of cut for irregular shaping. Clean cutting can be accomplished both against and with the grain when the cutters are sharp. When cutting against the grain use a slower speed. Make the cut on the bottom, with the work face down and resting on the surface of the shaper table. Make several trial cuts on

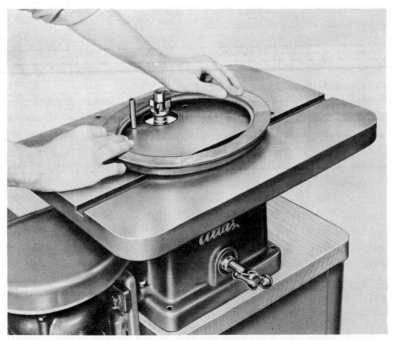

Fig. 13. Irregular shaping. Note use of guide pin and shaping depth collar on spindle below cutter.

pieces of scrap wood to check depth and position of cut before proceeding with the actual work.

The template method is usually employed in doing duplicate and matched irregular shaping. The template should be made of plywood, birch, or similar hardwood. Cut it to conform to outline of the work, sand all edges perfectly smooth, and rub a little paraffin wax into them. Place the work face down on the shaper table. Place the template on the work and drive several small wire nails or brads through it, about $\frac{1}{16}''$ into the work to prevent the template from slipping. Adjust the depth collar and cutter for the desired depth of cut. The shaper collar rests against the finished edge of the template and the cutter can cut into the work only as far as the template will permit. Move the template around the entire circumference of the work, keeping its edge in contact with the collar at all times.

Matched shaping, tonguing, and grooving. Matched shaping, sometimes called coped jointing, is used in the construction of cabinets, interior trim, and similar work. A pair of matched cutters is used: one to cut the female portion of the molding forming the joint, and the other to cut the male portion. Matched shaping or coped joints, and tongue-and-groove joints are similar. The procedure for shaping either is exactly the same.

Select a pair of matched cutters of the required size. The female portion of the joint is cut with a single cutter, from $\frac{1}{8}''$ to $\frac{3}{8}''$ or $\frac{1}{2}''$ in width, depending on the thickness of the material. The two methods of making the male portion of this joint are standard procedures. One method is to use a cutter in which a square recess has been ground that will cut a tongue that is a fairly close fit in the female portion of the joint. The other method is to use two cutters of the same outside diameter, with at least a $\frac{1}{2}''$ face on each, with a collar or a spacer washer inserted between them. This separates the cutters so that they will cut a tongue to make a close fit for the female portion of the joint. The latter method is preferable, since the fit of the tongue into the groove can be controlled by varying the thickness of the collar or the spacer washer used.

In making joints of this type the shaper fence is used to guide the work (Fig. 14). Speed and procedure is the same as for straight shaping.

Making dado cuts. Dado cuts are made on a shaper with a male cutter of the required size from a tongue-and-groove cutter set. The procedure is the same as for straight shaping (Fig. 15).

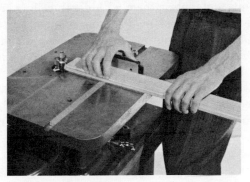

Fig. 14. Matched shaping with the spindle shaper. Cutting tongue for tongue-and-groove joint.

Reeding and fluting. To reed or flute straight or curved irregular work on the shaper, special cutters are required. They are available in a variety of shapes and sizes. The cutting edge

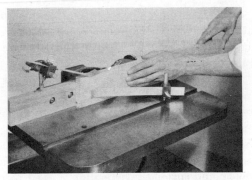

Fig. 15. Cutting a dado with the spindle shaper.

of a reeding cutter consists of two coves coming together in the center of the cutting face. A fluting cutter is the exact opposite and is rounded off on the cutting edge. To save time and to turn out more uniform work when reeding or fluting flat faces, use more than a single cutter. The shaper fence and the hold-down clips are used to guide the work. Procedure is exactly the same as for any other type of straight shaper work.

For curved or irregular work, remove the fence and the spring hold-down clips and replace them with depth collars or a template to gauge the cut. Proceed in the same manner as for irregular shaping. Make a simple jig or template of a piece of wood with a block fastened on each end of the turning. Drive a nail through each of the blocks to act as a center on which to revolve the turning.

Two procedures can be used for gauging the depth of the cut and for guiding the turning against the cutter: one requires the use of depth collars, the other the use of a template. The base board of the jig can be utilized as a template. Where the turning is tapered or curved, it is necessary to taper or curve the edge of the base board to conform.

When the depth collar method is used to determine the depth of the cut, be sure that the collars are of the proper diameter and project beyond the cutter to get a bearing on the turning.

With the template method the cuts may be more accurately gauged and better work accomplished. Cutting is similar to irregular shaping.

Planing. Select a cutter wider than the thickness of the stock. Slide the entire fence to the circumference of the cutting arc. Move the right fence facing back from the left one a distance equal to the depth of cut desired. The left facing acts as a support for the work after it passes the cutter. Move it in and out for planing operations (Fig. 16).

Use the miter gauge attachment to support the work when planing end miter joints.

Drum sanding. Sanding spindles or drums are available for use on the spindle shaper in various types of surfaces graded from rough to fine. With them, irregular shaped pieces of wood are sanded easily and speedily.

To install the sanding drum remove the fence and spring hold-down clips. Set the table slightly above the bottom of the sander, so that all of the wood to be sanded contacts the drum. Install the sanding drum on the spindle (Fig. 17).

For sanding, the spindle speed must be reduced to 1750 r.p.m. A higher speed will burn the wood and glaze the sandpaper.

Fig. 16. Left section of spindle shaper fence moves in and out for planing operations. Graduated scale shows depth of cut. Note large opening in fence casting for chip removal.

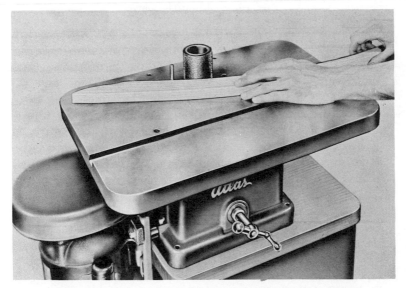

Fig. 17. Using a sanding drum on the vertical shaper.

Lubrication.   Keep shaper clean and free from dust at all times.   Use SAE 20 machine oil and lubricate regularly at all points shown in Fig. 18.   The shaper table should be covered with a film of oil when not in use.   If the machine is used frequently, lubricate all points shown at weekly intervals; otherwise inspect and lubricate monthly.

Sharpening cutters.   Shaper cutters must be kept as sharp

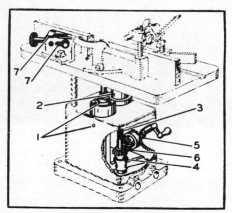

Fig. 18.   Lubrication points.

as possible, with special sharpening stones.   A flat Arkansas oilstone about 2″ by 6″, and a slipstone made of the same material about 4″ long and tapering from ⅛″ to ⅜″ in thickness, with rounded edges, is required.   Also, one about 4″ long and ¼″ square and another 4″ long, 2″ wide, and ½″ thick.   An additional oilstone convenient to have on hand is triangular in section with each face ¹⁄₁₆″ wide and 3″ long.   With these oilstones it is possible to sharpen almost any cutter used on the shaper.

The action of the cutter when shaping wears the cutting edge. To renew this cutting edge, no great amount of metal need ever be removed at any one time.   The cutting angle of the edge must be changed as little as possible.

Select the oilstone that fits the shape or curve of the cutter. Rub the stone lightly, holding it almost flat against the back of the cutting edge.   To remove the wire edge that will result from sharpening, lay the cutter flat on the flat oilstone and rub it with a back-and-forth motion.

CHAPTER 14

Sanders

⁞

Powered sanders are available in both disc and belt types. Portable belt sanders are used for sanding and finishing work that cannot be done in the home workshop. They come with sanding belts ranging from 1½″ to 3″ or 4″ in width. Their utility is limited to sanding flat surfaces, so they are not especially recommended for use in the home workshop where various-shaped parts have to be done.

A more practical and versatile combination disc-and-belt sander now available is designed to do all types of sanding and finishing (Fig. 1).

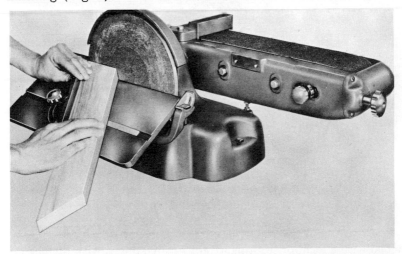

Fig. 1. Disc-and-belt sander for all types of sanding and finishing. Miter gauge on tilted table is used here to finish compound angle with disc sander.

The base and frame of a powered belt-and-disc sander should be constructed of heavy well-braced castings, with the sanding-disc table supported by double trunnions at one end and a single trunnion at the other. To do fine finishing work the belt table must be rigidly braced.

To assure long life and trouble-free performance, both the disc spindle and the belt drums should run on deep-grooved sealed precision ball bearings.

A sanding belt fence should be provided, as it is an essential accessory for all accurate edging operations. The fence should be tiltable 45° both ways from the vertical position with the angle of tilt shown on a graduated scale. To permit duplication of work without necessity of readjustment, a suitable device should be provided to lock the fence in any desired position (Fig. 2).

The disc table should be tiltable 45° up or down, and be pro-

Fig. 2. A sanding belt fence is essential for accurate edging operations. It tilts 45° both ways from vertical. Angle of tilt is shown on graduated segment.

vided with a lock for securing at any desired angle, with the angle shown on a graduated scale. The table unit should be usable in both belt and disc sanding.

The sander shown in Fig. 1 requires a ¼- or ⅓-h.p., 1725-r.p.m.

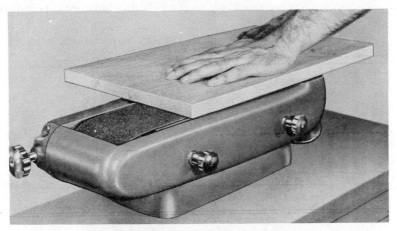

Fig. 3. Using belt sander for finishing the surface of a wide board.

repulsion-induction capacitor motor. This gives it a spindle speed of 1360 r.p.m. and a belt speed of 1150 f.p.m. It is equipped to use a 10" sanding disc and a sanding belt $37^{13}/_{16}$" × 4" wide. Abrasive discs and belts are available in grit sizes ranging from fine to very coarse.

Operation. The belt section of the sander is for sanding wide boards. The disc and guards are easily removable and the belt section of the sander is used as shown in Fig. 3.

To sand concave surfaces remove belt guards and use upper portion of belt (Fig. 4).

To finish a chamfer on the sanding disc, simply tilt table to the required angle and lock in position (Fig. 5).

Fig. 4. Curved pieces may be finished on belt drums when belt guards are removed.

To surface narrow stock, place the belt in a horizontal position (Fig. 6).

To finish the ends of any work to any required angle on the sanding disc, tilt the table up or down (Fig. 7).

Fig. 5. Finishing a chamfer on the sanding disc.

Fig. 6. Surfacing stock on the sanding belt.

To sand the surfaces of small work the belt section is usually used (Fig. 8). Note use of stop fences.

To sand and finish edges of work to any desired angle up to 45° adjust the sanding belt fence to the desired angle and lock it (Fig. 2). Note angle of tilt as shown on graduated segment.

Maintenance. To keep sander in good working condition all parts of the tool must be kept free from all dirt and accumulated sawdust. All moving parts must be lubricated as per lubrication chart furnished with each tool by the manufacturer.

Fig. 7. Finishing the end of a piece of work on the sanding disc.

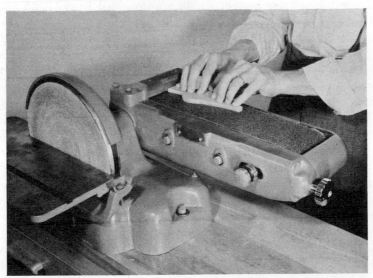

Fig. 8. A stop fence is necessary in sanding small work on the belt.

CHAPTER 15

Selection and Care of Painting Tools and Equipment

—————————— :

Next to the actual paints, brushes are the most important tools used for painting and decorating. Good cheap brushes are non-existent. Cheap brushes will ruin the best painting job. Good-quality brushes, properly taken care of, will ordinarily outlast a half dozen cheap brushes, and in the long run give a great deal more satisfaction and produce cleaner and better work. The cost of the better grade of brushes over a period of time will be considerably less. With few exceptions, all good brushes are made of hog bristles, the best of which are imported from China and Russia. The cheaper, inferior brushes are made of synthetic materials combined with a poor grade of bristle, adulterated with horsehair.

The only type of good brushes made with materials other than bristle are those that are to be used in painting structural iron or steel. Brushes for this purpose can contain a small percentage of horsehair. The paint does not have to be worked into iron or steel surfaces. Horsehair resists abrasion better than hog bristle and a small amount of horsehair will increase the life of a brush used for this purpose. Inferior brushes are cleverly camouflaged and difficult to detect; therefore do not make the mistake of selecting brushes just by appearance. When purchasing brushes select the type best suited for the job. Go to a reliable paint dealer and buy the best brush that he recommends.

All new brushes, no matter how good they are, will probably shed a few bristles. Before putting a brush into paint or varnish

408

rub your hand back and forth across the bristles to work out loose ones.

Even good brushes will sometimes develop defects. All reputable manufacturers guarantee their brushes and will replace any defective brushes returned to them.

CHOOSING THE RIGHT BRUSH FOR THE JOB

Always choose the right type of brush for all painting and decorating work. While there are many types of brushes, you need only purchase from time to time such brushes as are needed.

Descriptions of brushes generally used are as follows:

Flat wall brush. (See Fig. 1.). Flat wall brushes are used for spreading paint on walls and must not be used for applying varnish. They are made of Chinese bristle, vulcanized in rubber, bound in metal, and available in half-inch sizes ranging from 3″ to 5″. A good all-purpose size is one 3½″ or 4″ in width.

Flat woodwork or varnish brush. (See Fig. 2.) Flat woodwork brushes can be used for both paint and varnish. They are

Fig. 1. Flat wall brush.

Fig. 2. Flat woodwork or varnish brush.

made of Chinese or Russian hog bristles and are usually metal-bound and vulcanized in rubber. They come in sizes ranging from 1″ to 3″ in width. For working around glass panes in windows and doors, the smaller sizes are preferable. For painting and varnishing trim and other parts of the house the larger sizes are generally used.

Flat sash brush. (See Fig. 3.) The flat sash brush is similar to the flat varnish brush, but slightly thinner, and is sometimes called a trimming brush. Good-quality sash brushes are vulcanized in rubber and can be used for both paint and varnish. Available in 1″, 1½″, and 2″ widths.

Oval varnish brush. (See Fig. 4.) The oval varnish brush is an excellent brush made of Chinese bristles. It is oval in shape

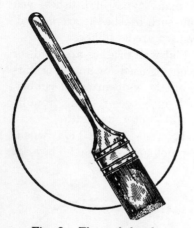

Fig. 3. Flat sash brush.

Fig. 4. Oval varnish brush.

with an open center. It is used only for varnishing and is preferred over the modern flat varnish brush by many painters. It is available in many sizes, which are designated as 1/0 to 10/0. The circumferences of these brushes vary with each manufacturer. The 6/0, a popular size made by a well-known manufacturer, is an oval slightly under 2″ in its greatest width.

Oval sash brush. (See Fig. 5.) The oval sash or trimming brush is made of Chinese bristles and can be used for both paint and varnish. They are available vulcanized in rubber in numbered sizes from 1 to 10. The No. 6 brush of a leading manufacturer is a popular size, with a solid oval 1⅛″ in width.

Flat calcimine brush. (See Fig. 6.) Good calcimine brushes should be made of stiff Russian hard bristle. The Russian variety of bristle is heavier in texture than the Chinese and is preferable for this particular purpose. They are used principally for painting smooth plastered walls with calcimine and should not be used for any other purpose. Flat calcimine brushes, made of either gray or yellow bristle, are available in 6″, 7″, and 8″ widths. The 7″ is the popular all-around size, with bristles 5¼″ in length.

Dutch calcimine brush. (See Fig. 7.) Calcimine brushes of

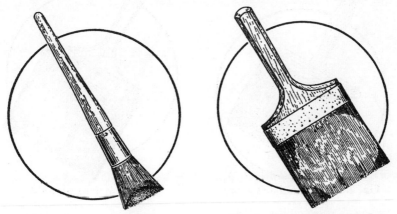

Fig. 5. Oval sash brush.   **Fig. 6.** Flat calcimine brush.

the Dutch type are used for calcimining rough plaster or stucco. They are made of gray Russian bristle, with the bristles set in knots and vulcanized in a solid rubber block, so that they will not pull out. A good general size is 6″ in width with the length of the bristle not exceeding 5″.

Whitewash brush. (See Fig. 8.) Whitewash brushes are usually made of gray and yellow Russian bristles set in cement and leather-bound. They are available in various sizes. The 9″ width is the size generally used. They are used for applying whitewash and exterior cold-water paints.

Duster brush. (See Fig. 9.) The flat type of duster brush is the one most generally used for the removal of dust before painting. The use of a dust brush is essential to clean spots and corners where a cloth will not do an efficient job. There are many types of duster brushes, but the flat variety is more practical. They are made of various kinds of bristles and horsehair and the better types are vulcanized in rubber. It is an inexpensive brush and should be used for dusting only. It is available in one size, 4½″ wide.

Radiator brush.   (See Fig. 10.)   Radiator brushes are made with long handles and a flat, thin structure for painting between

Fig. 7.   Dutch calcimine brush.   **Fig. 8.**   Whitewash brush.

radiator **coils** and unreachable places.   They are made of black Chinese **bristle** from 1″ to 2½″ in width.

Flat artist's brush.   (See Fig. 11.)   The flat artist's brush is made of black or white Chinese bristle, cement-set and metal-

Fig. 9.   Duster brush.   **Fig. 10.**   Radiator brush.

bound. It is designed for painting fine lines and for decorating. Available in widths ranging from ¼″ to 2″.

Roof-painting brush. (See Fig. 12.) The roof-painting brush shown at *A* is made of gray Russian bristle, double-nailed and leather-bound and is used for painting shingles. The brush shown

Fig. 11. Flat artist's brush.   **Fig. 12.** Roof-painting brushes.

at *C* is attached to a long handle and is used in the same manner as a broom, for painting large roof surfaces. The roof-painting brush shown at *B* is made of poorer-quality Russian bristle mixed with a percentage of horsehair. It is less expensive than the type previously described but is adequate for painting smaller metal roofs and for applying tar. It is available in two-, three-, and four-knot sizes with bristles about 3½″ in length.

Stippling brush. (See Fig. 13.) Stippling brushes are used to pound or stipple paint that has previously been applied to a smooth plaster wall, so as to give it a stipple effect. Stippling brushes are usually made of stiff gray Russian bristle.

Flat color brush. (See Fig. 14.) Flat color brushes are made of pure squirrel hair, usually called camel's hair, cement-set and bound in brass. They are usually used for the application of

Japan colors.   Available in half-inch sizes ranging from 1″ to 3″ in width.

Flowing brush.   (See Fig. 15.)   Flowing brushes are usually made of a mixture of badger hair and French bristle with an outer layer of pure badger hair, although various other mixtures of hair and bristle are sometimes used.   The type shown in Fig.

Fig. 13.   Stippling brushes.

Fig. 14.   Flat color brush.

15 is the one most generally used in applying color varnish and finishing coats on automobiles and boats.

Stencil brush.   (See Fig. 16.)   A stencil brush is a stiff, stubby brush used for stenciling.   It is made of tampico or fiber and set in vulcanized rubber.

Waxing brush.   (See Fig. 17.)   Waxing brushes are used for finishing after wax has been applied to floors.   They are equipped with felt protectors, to prevent scarring or marring baseboards. They are made of tampico and fiber, stapled into a solid block 7¼″ × 9¼″.   Available in 15- and 25-pound sizes.

CARE OF BRUSHES

To remove short or loose bristles before using, twirl the brush by rolling the handle between the palms and against the extended fingers of the hand (Fig. 18).

Before using varnish brushes, rinse them in thinner to remove dust.   To keep brushes in good condition never suspend or soak them in water. In addition to making the bristles soft and flabby, water will swell the divider or handle of the brush and will cause the brush to spread out, like a mop, and will sometimes break the ferrule.

Never let a brush rest for any length of time on the ends of the

Fig. 15. Flowing brush.   **Fig. 16.** Stencil brush.

bristles. It will put a kink in them and will ruin the brush.

To keep brushes in good condition when in use, suspend them in the proper thinner with the bristle a short distance from the bottom of the can or paint pot. To suspend a brush properly,

Fig. 17. Waxing brush.   **Fig. 18.** Twirling brush to re-
                                      move loose bristles.

drill a ⅛″ hole through its handle at the proper point so that a stiff wire passing through it and resting upon the upper edge of the can or paint pot will suspend it at the desired height. Several brushes can be hung on the same wire (Fig. 19).

To keep brushes overnight or for several days proceed as follows:

Work out all excess material in the brush on either a board or a newspaper.

If brushes have been used in interior or exterior oil paints they should be suspended in a mixture of two parts of raw linseed oil to one part of a good-quality thinner. While plain turpentine or thinner is often used, it is better to use the thinner specified by the manufacturer of the paint. Before re-using the brush, rinse it in clean thinner.

Brushes that have been used in varnish or enamel should be suspended in a mixture containing equal parts of varnish and turpentine. If pure turpentine is used the brushes may get full of specks. If brushes have been used in synthetic varnishes they must be washed out thoroughly immediately after use, with either the specified thinner or pure turpentine. Synthetic varnishes are labeled as such by all reputable manufacturers.

After using brushes in rubber-base paints, wash them out either in the special thinner recommended for the paint or in lacquer thinner.

Use denatured alcohol to wash out brushes that have been used in shellac. If a shellac brush becomes slightly stiff it will soften when dipped into fresh shellac. Brushes used in water paint must be washed out in warm water and hung up to dry.

Storing brushes. Brushes used in oil paint, varnish, or enamel should be thoroughly washed out in thinner. Use plenty of thinner and then pour the used thinner into a bottle. The color will settle to the bottom and the clear thinner can again be used for cleaning brushes or thinning paint. Follow this cleaning by washing the bristles with hand soap and warm water. Get the suds well into the base of the brush, and rinse. Repeat until no color comes out. Comb bristles straight, shake out all excess water, and lay brush flat. When it is thoroughly dry, wrap it in paper to keep the bristles clean and in shape (Fig. 20).

Other brushes should be treated in the same manner, using for the first cleaning the proper thinner as recommended above.

Do not attempt to clean old brushes with strong soap powders, lye or other detergents, or strong cleaners.

Never leave a brush in benzine or benzine substitutes. The

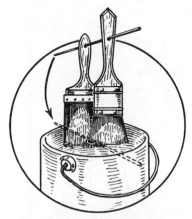

Fig. 19. Supporting brushes in thinner.

Fig. 20. Wrap brushes separately in oiled paper.

brush will become full of hardened specks of paint or varnish which can never be removed.

Never put a brush on a hot radiator to dry. It will take the life out of the bristles and ruin the brush.

OTHER TOOLS

Several ladders, extension brush holders, a putty knife, a scraping knife, and a paint spray gun are additional tools that may be required for painting and decorating work in and around the home.

Stepladders. For interior painting one or two stepladders are necessary. These should be of good, sturdy construction (Fig. 21).

If a scaffold is needed, two sturdy stepladders and a plank approximately 10″ wide, 2″ thick, and as long as required are usually used (Fig. 21).

Long ladders. Long ladders are used for exterior painting.

They are available in lengths of 8′, 10′, 12′, 14′, 16′, 18′, and 20′. The longer lengths are usually adequate for two-story houses. Where areas that are to be painted cannot be reached by the longest of these ladders, an extension ladder is required (Fig. 22).

Extension ladders.   For some exterior jobs extension ladders are necessary.   Of the several types, one generally used is shown

Fig. 21. Two stepladders and a plank used as a scaffold.
Fig. 24. (circle) Wide scraping knife.

in Fig. 22.   Extension ladders consist of several long ladder units plus mechanical devices used to raise, lower, and fasten them. Two-section extension ladders will extend from 20′ to 40′ and each additional section extends the ladder 10′ to 20′.   The limited use that most people have for extension ladders does not warrant purchasing this equipment.   In most localities they can be rented for any length of time for a nominal sum.   Directions for raising and lowering extension ladders vary with the type and are furnished with the equipment.

Fig. 22. Long and extension ladders.

Roof ladder hooks. Roof ladder hooks are safety devices that fasten onto the rungs of the ladder and hook over the ridge of a roof to give a firmer support (Fig. 23).

Steel ladder shoes. These simple little devices should be screwed onto the bottoms of all long ladders to give them a firmer footing.

Putty knife. A putty knife, for applying putty to window sashes, is also a general-utility tool for cleaning and scraping off old paint and dirt prior to painting.

Scraping knife. Scraping knives are available in widths ranging from $2\frac{1}{2}''$ to $4''$. They are used for scraping cracked, scaled, or blistered paint from surfaces before painting (Fig. 24).

Extension brush holders. For painting places that are difficult to reach even with a ladder, an extension brush holder is used. A variety of sizes and lengths can be had (Fig. 25).

SPRAY GUNS AND COMPRESSORS

Extensive exterior painting jobs can be accomplished economically and well with spraying equipment in a fraction of the time required by the use of brushes. Contrary to general belief, even beginners with just a little practice can do a creditable job by this automatic method of paint application. Complete spray-gun equipment, including the necessary compressor, can be rented by the hour or day for a nominal fee.

Spray guns. There are many types and sizes of spray guns, each designed for a specific purpose. A typical general-utility spray gun and its parts is shown in Fig. 26. A paint spray gun is a mechanical means of bringing air and paint together, atomizing the paint stream into a spray of the required size, and ejecting

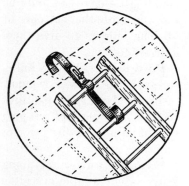

Fig. 23. Roof ladder hook   **Fig. 25.** Extension brush holder.

it by compressed air for the purpose of coating a surface. Each manufacturer furnishes specific directions for the care and the maintenance of his product. While the disassembly, reassembly, and general maintenance directions for each individual type may vary to some extent, the same general technique can be applied to practically all types of spray guns.

The type of gun shown in Fig. 26 has as one of its main features a removable spray head. The advantages of this type of head are: ease of cleaning, and inexpensive replacement in case of damage. If required, extra spray heads can be bought. The method of removing the spray head is shown in Fig. 27.

The principal parts of the spray head are the air cap, fluid tip, fluid needle, baffle, and spray-head barrel (Fig. 28).

The air cap is the part at the front of the gun that directs the compressed air into the paint stream to atomize it and form it into a suitable spray pattern (*A*, Fig. 28).

The fluid tip is another part at the front end of the gun, which meters and directs the material into the air stream. It provides a

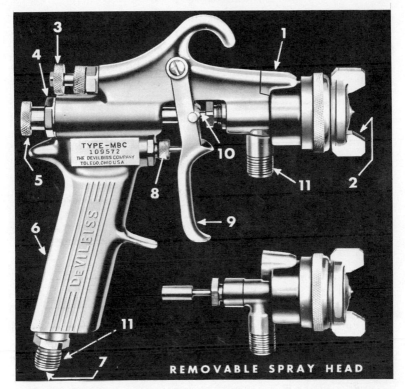

REMOVABLE SPRAY HEAD

Fig. 26. Parts and features of a well-designed, efficient spray gun.

1. Removable spray head. Saves time in changing materials and cleaning.
2. Ball-and-cone principle of nozzle parts assembly. Air-tight seating between air cap and fluid tip assures continuance of correct spray performance.
3. Graduated spray-width adjustment. Easy and instantaneous selection of desired spray width and pattern.
4. Cartridge-type fluid needle adjustment assembly. May be quickly removed and replaced as a unit.
5. Fluid adjustment. Conveniently located for quick, accurate, and easy control of fluid flow.
6. Unbreakable gun body.
7. Large air passage. Affords better atomization at lower air pressure.
8. Cartridge-type air valve. Assures perfect assembly of all parts and economical replacement.
9. Scientifically designed trigger. Gun can be held in all practical spraying positions without fatigue.
10. Stainless-steel fluid needle. Heavy, with large diameter, ground to seat perfectly, and will not rust.
11. Air and fluid connections. A choice of interchangeable thread sizes is available.

self-aligning, concentric seat for the air cap and equalizes the air leaving the center hole of the cap (*B*, Fig. 28). The opening in the fluid tip is called the nozzle. The comparative sizes of fluid tips and standard nozzles are shown in Fig. 29. Standard nozzle sizes are specified as follows: A, C, D, E, FF, FX, F, G. They are, as a

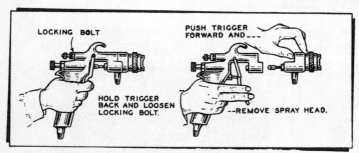

Fig. 27. Removing spray head from gun body.

rule, stamped on the collar of the needle and on the outer edge of the fluid tip.

The sizes in general use are E, FF, FX, and F.

Air compressors. An air compressor is a mechanism designed to supply compressed air continuously at a predetermined maximum pressure and the required minimum volume in cubic feet per minute. There are two general types of air compressors: single-stage and two-stage. For all general house-painting where a maximum pressure not exceeding 100 pounds is required, the single-stage type should be used; this amount of pressure is more than adequate. Two-stage compressor outfits are used principally for various industrial purposes. These two main types of air compressing outfits are further divided into many subtypes. Of these, the two generally used are those powered by either an electric motor or a gas engine. Single-stage compressors with suitable power equipment

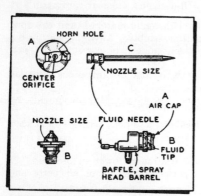

Fig. 28. Parts of spray head.

are available in a self-contained, compact, portable outfit that is equipped with a handle and mounted on wheels so that the compressor can be easily moved to any required spot (Fig. 30). Operation and control of various air compressors differ in detail.

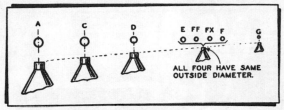

Fig. 29.   Standard comparative nozzle sizes and fluid
tips.

Follow all the directions for operation of any particular type.

Preparing paint for spraying.   Thoroughly mix and stir the paint. If the paint contains any lumps or skins or any foreign matter whatsoever, it must be strained through a fine screen (Fig. 31). Paint that is to be used in a spray gun must be thinned to the consistency specified by the respective manufacturers.

Correct procedure for using spray gun.   A spray gun must at all times be held perpendicular to the surface that is being painted; never hold the gun in any other position (Fig. 32). Hold the gun from 6″ to 8″ from the surface to obtain an even spray. A simple method of determining the proper distance is shown in Fig. 32.

Make the strokes with a free arm motion, keeping the gun the same distance from the surface at all points of the stroke (Fig. 33). The ends of all strokes are feathered out by "triggering" the gun, that is, by beginning the stroke before pulling the trigger and releasing the trigger just before ending the stroke. Arcing the gun will result in uneven application and excessive over-spray at the.ends of each stroke.

At corners, spray within one or two inches of the end of each side (Fig. 34). Then, holding the gun sideways, do both unsprayed sides of the corner with one stroke. Attempting to spray corners by any other method will not only waste material, but will cause an overspray on the adjacent side (Fig. 35).

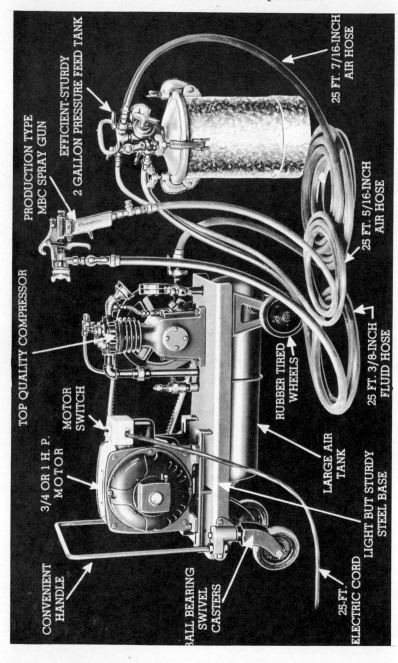

Fig. 30. Portable compressor and additional equipment that can be rented locally.

Fig. 31. Preparing paint.

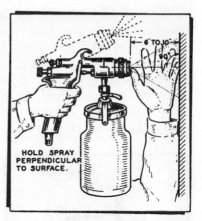

Fig. 32. Using gun, and measuring distance.

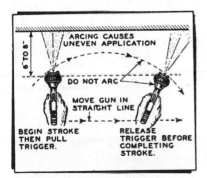

Fig. 33. Correct spray-gun strokes.

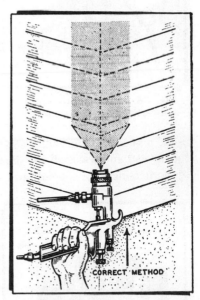

Fig. 34. Corner spraying.

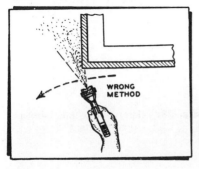

Fig. 35. (left) Incorrect corner spraying causes overspray on adjoining side.

Cleaning and lubricating the gun.   A spray gun is a precision instrument and should never be put away, even for a short time, without cleaning.   The general procedure is as follows: Remove cup from gun.   Hold a cloth over openings in air cap and pull trigger (Fig. 36).   Air diverted into fluid passageways forces paint back into container.   Empty the container of paint and replace with a small quantity of the type of solvent specified by the manufacturer (Fig. 37).   Spray solvent through gun in the

Fig. 36.   Cleaning air cap and diverting fluid into container.

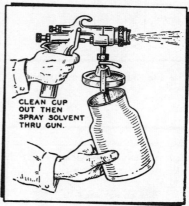

Fig. 37.

usual manner.   This will clean out passageways.   Then remove the air cap and wash off the fluid tip with solvent.   Clean air cap by immersing it in solvent, and replace on gun.   If small holes in

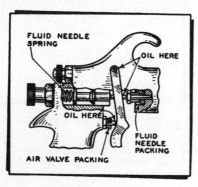

Fig. 38.   (left) Spray gun lubrication points.

air cap become clogged, soak the air cap in the solvent. If reaming of the holes is still necessary after this procedure, use a matchstick, broom straw, or any other soft, thin implement. Do not dig out holes with wires or nails as cap may be permanently damaged by this practice. Note: It is a common practice among some mechanics to clean spray guns by placing the entire gun in solvent. This should never be done, as solvents remove lubricants and eventually dry out packings.

The required points of lubrication in the spray gun are: the fluid-needle packing, air-valve stem, and trigger bearing screw. Apply at these points the lubrication specified by the manufacturer of the gun (Fig. 38).

CHAPTER 16

Paints and Painting, and Finishing Procedures

The various forms of paint, stain, varnish, enamel, etc., are used to protect wood, metal, concrete, and other surfaces from deterioration caused by changes of temperature or by the natural elements. Paint seals the pores of wood, keeps out moisture, prevents rotting to some degree, prevents corrosion of metal surfaces, and helps to preserve the surface of brick, cement, and concrete walls and floors. In addition to the protection of surfaces, paint is used to a great extent for decoration. It can give surfaces varying degrees of glossy or flat finishes, and can be matched to harmonize with any color scheme.

COMPOSITION OF PAINT

Most paints are composed of a pigment material, an oil or vehicle, a thinner, and a drier. The proportion of each of these basic ingredients varies with the quality of the paint and the purpose for which it is to be used.

Types of pigments. The various types of pigments used in paint to give it its covering power, body, and color are: white lead, zinc oxide, lithopone, whiting, red lead, and color pigments. All paints prepared by reputable manufacturers contain one or more of these basic pigments. All paints used for exterior painting should contain a percentage of white lead, which is considered one of the most durable of the white pigments. However, unless it is mixed with at least 15 per cent of zinc oxide it may chalk or powder off under certain climatic conditions.

Zinc oxide is used to a great extent in enamels, which also contain varnish and a small quantity of white lead.

Lithopone is a commercial product. It is a mixture of zinc sulphide and barium sulphate, nonpoisonous, and used principally as a pigment for flat wall paints.

Red lead is used mainly for painting metal surfaces. It is available in both the paste form or prepared ready for use, mixed with linseed oil.

Whiting is used mostly in the making of calcimine.

Types of vehicles, thinners, and driers. Most commercial paints consist of 65 per cent pigment and 35 per cent vehicle and thinner. For exterior painting, the best types of paints consist of a high-grade pigment, linseed oil as a vehicle, and turpentine as a thinner and drier. All reputable paint manufacturers give the ingredients on the label of the container

Turpentine is used as a thinner for either paint or varnish. There are several types of turpentine. The three most commonly used are: gum, wood, and distilled. Gum turpentine is preferable. Turpentine in paint has three distinct functions: it secures penetration of the paint into the pores of the wood, it causes the paint to spread evenly and smoothly, and it speeds up drying.

Benzole is a thin, volatile liquid distilled from coal tar. Because of its ability to penetrate and dissolve the ingredients of varnishes it is used in the manufacture of varnish removers. To prevent the paint from scaling off, in painting wood surfaces that are full of sap gum, a pint of benzole is usually added to a gallon of paint.

Driers usually consist of one or more active natural driers, such as red lead, litharge, lead acetate, manganese, or cobalt, ground in linseed oil and thinned to the required consistency with turpentine. Driers are added to the paint to hasten setting and drying. When a liquid drier contains either a gum or resin it is called Japan drier. Liquid or oil driers, as they are called, or Japan driers, are available prepared and ready for use.

PREPARED PAINTS AND ALLIED PRODUCTS

Paints, enamels, shellacs, and varnishes of various types, prepared for specific purposes, are available ready-mixed, containing the necessary proportion of pigments, oil, turpentine, and drier.

In the best grades of prepared house paints, lead and zinc pigments make up approximately 85 per cent of the total amount of pigment. In the cheaper types of paint these important ingredients vary to as low as 50 per cent. The higher the percentage of white lead, zinc, linseed oil, and turpentine contained in the prepared paint, the more serviceable that paint will be. According to specifications given in Circular No. 89 of the Bureau of Standards, United States Department of Commerce, the standard for ready-mixed paints is as follows: "Ready-mixed paints shall be well ground, shall not settle badly or cake in the container, shall be readily broken up with a paddle to a smooth, uniform paint of good brushing consistency, and shall dry within 18 hours to a full oil gloss, without streaking, running or sagging. The color and hiding power when specified shall equal those of a sample mutually agreed upon by buyer and seller. The weight per gallon shall be not less than 15¾ pounds."

Exterior paint. Exterior paint is available in white and a variety of colors, requiring only to be properly mixed before use. If, after mixing, the paint is too thick, it should be thinned per manufacturer's directions which are usually printed on the label. The first step in preparing paint for use is to shake the can before opening. Then secure a larger empty can or tin bucket and pour the liquid from the top of the can into this receptacle. With a flat paddle stir thoroughly what remains in the bottom of the original can. Pour back a little of the liquid from the second can into the first can and mix. Keep pouring the mixed material back and forth from one container to the other several times. If thinner is required, add the necessary amount, stir with the paddle, and pour the mixed material from one container to the other until mixing is complete. Always prepare enough paint for an entire section of the work. Because of the evaporation of the thinner, the paint may thicken during use. If this occurs add a little more thinner to bring it back to the proper consistency.

Flat wall paint. Many types of prepared flat wall paint are now available. This paint is used only on interior walls. When properly mixed according to the directions given previously it is easy to apply and will dry without luster. Correctly brushed, a good grade of flat wall paint will not show any brush marks. It sets and dries evenly and quickly. Usually two coats are required. If color is to be used on the second coat, a slight amount of the colored paint should be mixed with the white for the first coat. Flat wall paints are available in a great many tints and colors. Most of them can be washed without damaging the finished surface.

Calcimine. Calcimine is used to paint and decorate interior plaster, cement, stone, and masonry walls. Prepared calcimine is now available containing all necessary ingredients in pure white and several tints. It is a dry powder and requires only the addition of a specified amount of water to prepare it for use. As a rule, only one coat of calcimine is necessary to cover a surface satisfactorily.

Water paint. Several types of water paint are now available with all ingredients ready-mixed and requiring only the addition of a specified amount of cold water. Several types of water paints have been specially prepared by various manufacturers for painting previously painted walls quickly and inexpensively; in some cases they can even be used to cover wallpaper. Water paints dry quickly and leave no brush marks.

Wall-size. Wall-size is a thin liquid that is brushed on plaster or stucco walls, wallboard, and muslin- or burlap-covered walls to seal the pores and as a preparation for the application of either paint or wallpaper. Ready-mixed wall-sizes are available.

Cement and concrete paint. Paint specially prepared for cement, concrete, and stucco can be bought in ready-mixed form. Specific directions for the preparation of the surface and the method to be used in applying this paint are usually given in detail on the paint label on the can.

Wood filler. Wood filler is used to fill the grain of the wood and to produce a nonabsorbent surface for finishing or varnishing. The two types usually used are liquid and paste fillers. The paste type is used on oak, ash, chestnut, walnut, mahogany, and other open-grained woods. Liquid fillers are used on gum, maple, birch, pine, and similar close-grained woods. Paste wood fillers are brushed on, allowed to set for several minutes, and then wiped off with a cloth. The filler remaining in the pores of the wood is then allowed to dry before finishing or varnishing. Liquid filler is spread on, allowed to dry, and then lightly sandpapered. Various other types of commercial fillers including crack fillers are available. They are sold under various trade names in powder, liquid, and paste forms. Directions for preparation and use are usually printed on the container.

Paint cleaner. Interior walls must be cleaned of all dust, dirt, and stains before painting. If ordinary soapsuds in warm water will not remove all dirt and stains from a previously painted wall, specially prepared paint cleaners that come in either powder, jelly, or liquid form should be used. Follow directions given by the manufacturer.

Enamel undercoating. A good grade of enamel will cover a surface fairly well with one coat; however, a specially prepared enamel undercoating will ensure a smoother finish coat. Such an undercoating dries nearly flat, and when properly applied shows no brush marks. When it is dry, sandpaper it lightly before applying the finishing enamel coat.

Enamel. Enamels are available in prepared form in white and various colors. They are used only for finishing coats and when properly applied will not show any brush marks. Either high-gloss or matte-finish types are obtainable. Special enamels are available for specific purposes.

Shellac. Shellac is actually a kind of varnish made by dissolving shellac gum in alcohol. There are two types of shellac: orange and white. The orange is the natural shellac, the white is orange shellac bleached. Shellac is quick-drying and transparent. Shellacked surfaces can usually be sandpapered within two hours after application. Shellac is used mainly as a temporary finish on floors and interior woodwork prior to varnishing.

Spar varnish. Spar varnish is a tough, durable finish that can be used on both interior and exterior surfaces that are subjected to changes of temperature and humidity. It was originally used for marine purposes only. Clear spar varnish requires no stirring and should never be shaken. If thinning is required, use pure turpentine only. Follow the manufacturer's specific directions for application of the various types of spar varnish.

Floor varnish. The better grades of floor varnish have all of the qualities of spar varnish plus the fact that they are specially prepared for quick drying. A good floor varnish will resist shocks, dampness, and changes of temperature, does not scratch easily, and will usually be bone dry overnight. Floor varnish is made specifically for varnishing floors and should not be used for any other work.

Cabinet finishing varnish. Cabinet finishing varnish is light in color, dries hard with a high gloss, and does not get sticky or tacky at any time. It is used principally for varnishing furniture and can be rubbed and sandpapered for all types of fine finishing.

Interior finishing varnish. Specially prepared for interior trim, this varnish will dry within twenty-four hours with a fairly good gloss. It should not be used for floors or for any type of exterior work. It is fairly light in color, and once dry does not get sticky.

Other types of varnish. Other varnishes are prepared for specific purposes. The more commonly used are rubbing varnish for finishing automobiles, and polishing varnish used principally for pianos and musical instruments.

Lacquer. Many types of specially prepared lacquers can be bought in a variety of colors and produce a smooth and quick drying finish. They are usually made from nitrocellulose or from cellulose acetate resins and other materials. The composition of lacquer prevents its use over undercoatings of enamel, paint or varnish, as it will act as a softener or remover of any such undercoats. Clear colorless lacquer is used as a tarnish-preventive finish on metalwork. Ready-mixed lacquer in various colors is usually used for painting furniture. Many types of lacquer are sold under various trade names. Manufacturer's directions for mixing, thinning, application, and cleaning brushes must be followed.

Stain. Stains are used to color the grain of wood without covering it. The various types of stain are: oil, water, spirit, shingle, and varnish. All are transparent and come ready-mixed for use.

Oil stain. Oil stain is usually tinted and is made of a base of linseed oil, turpentine, and drier. It is used as a transparent base coat to bring out the grain on a surface that is to be varnished and finished. It is usually applied with a brush and rubbed off with a soft cloth when the required depth of color has been attained.

Water stain. Water stain is made of transparent color dissolved in water to produce the desired tint. It is applied in the same manner as oil stain.

Spirit stain. Spirit stain, also called penetrating stain, is usually used on shingles. It comes in a wide range of colors, and as a rule the coloring is permanent. Its composition is alcohol, benzine, turpentine, and transparent color.

Shingle stain. Shingle stain is usually made of a base of oil or spirit stain, with the addition of creosote. It is available in a variety of colors.

Varnish stain. Varnish stain is, in reality, a combination of varnish and oil stain. It is used to stain and finish a surface in a single coat and is used principally on inexpensive toys and furniture where a certain amount of color is required without covering the grain of the wood.

LATEX OR PLASTIC PAINTS

Latex is a family of paints that are *sometimes* called plastic paints. They are made by mixing or emulsifying various chemicals in numerous formulas with water, instead of dissolving them in solvent such as mineral spirits or turpentine.

All latex paints share the following major characteristics: (1) They dry in less than one hour; (2) they are odor-free; (3) brushes, spray guns, rollers and other tools can be cleaned easily with soap and water, as can spills and splatters; and (4) scratches and high spots can be touched up without brush marks showing.

The mixture of chemicals with water forms the emulsion which looks like the milky latex juice of the rubber tree. This is one of the reasons why these paints are *sometimes* called rubber or rubber-based paints, which they are not, as you will see later in this section. Another reason is that two of the chemicals, which are used in making latexes, are ingredients of synthetic rubber. In fact, it was the research to find a use for the post-war surplus of these two chemicals that led to the development of latex paints. Meanwhile, a similar surplus problem arose in England of a different type of chemical. From this was developed another type of water-emulsion which is generally included in the "rubber-base" or "latex" category.

Still another type has been developed. The chemical used in this is similar to that used in making the clear plastic domes for airplanes. It was found that it could be formulated into an emulsion paint with many desirable characteristics.

Since all three of these substances are also used to make plastics, these paints are *sometimes* called plastic paints. Some paint manufacturers combine more than one of these ingredients in their latex paints.

Procedures. The quick-drying of latex paints permits you to decide to repaint a room in the morning and have it finished and odor-free in time to entertain guests at dinner that same night. If it is necessary to use more than one coat of paint, the second can be applied after an hour or more. Most stains and smears can be washed off after twenty-four hours, although the paint does not reach its maximum toughness for several weeks.

This quick-drying feature of the paint makes it necessary to clean your brushes and other tools immediately after use. If you have spattered some of the paint, wipe it off immediately with a damp cloth.

Most types of latex paint are resistant to alkali. They will not react chemically with fresh plaster, mortar or cement. Therefore, you can paint over these surfaces without using a protective undercoat, and the alkali will not produce staining or blisters.

Latex paints can be used on *interior woodwork,* as well as on *wall surfaces* because of their durability and washability, thus making it easy to have your walls and woodwork match exactly. New woodwork should be first *primed* with an oil paint, because there is sometimes the possibility that the water in the latex paint will raise the grain of the wood.

In addition, latex paints are an ideal decorative and protective coating over *fibre board, gypsum board* and over *wallpaper* which is not loose, or over *old paint* that is not peeling. These paints can also be used over *asphalt roofing.*

At first, all latex paints were flat interior paints. Paint manufacturers now have developed such other finishes as *exterior masonry* and *exterior wood latexes, latex gloss enamels, metal finishing latexes,* and *multi-color latexes.* Some latex paints can be used both indoors and outdoors, others only on interiors.

Before you buy or use a latex paint, be sure to read the label carefully and see what the manufacturer has to say about the uses and limitations of his product and whether it meets your requirements.

Exterior latex paints can solve a decorating problem. They are ideal for painting asbestos shingles and asbestos-cement siding that may have become dull and dirty over the years.

Suggestions. Latex paints do not blend with oil-based paints. *Do not* try to tint a latex with colors in oil. Use colors specifically designed for latex paints.

Do not use latex paints where they will be subjected to water immediately after applying.

Do not use latex paints over calcimine or white-wash without removing the old coating.

Latex paint can be used on woodwork as well as walls. It serves as its own priming coat on plaster and dry wall construction. This paint can be used as a primer for oil paint, and will patch scratches and marks without showing.

SOLVENT-THINNED PAINTS

Vehicles for the solvent-thinned coatings are resins dissolved in solvents. They are neither latexes nor emulsions. The most commonly used resins for masonry coatings are derivatives or modifications of rubber. They have excellent water and alkali resistance and adhere well to masonry surfaces. For many years, paints made with these resins have been used for painting cementitious surfaces such as swimming pools, masonry structures, stucco, and concrete floors. They are suitable for asbestos-cement products.

Application. These rubber resin coatings may be applied as a two-coat painting system in any color desired, directly over the asbestos-cement surfaces.

The advantages of this type of paint are: (1) Extreme water resistance; (2) staining resistance; (3) protection of metal from corrosion (iron nail heads, hinges, etc.); (4) good abrasion resistance; and (5) excellent hiding power.

Solvent type paints will not bond well to damp or wet surfaces. The surface *must* be dry at the time of painting.

Satisfactory results are also obtained by applying a specially formulated rubber resin coating as the *first coat* or *primer* over asbestos-cement shingles or board, followed by conventional oil or alkyd resin *base topcoats*. A number of nationally known paint manufacturers produce and market primers for this use. They are sold under such names as Asbestos Shingle Primer, Alkali Resistant Primer, Brick and Stucco Primer, etc.

OIL VEHICLE MASONRY PAINTS

Oil vehicle masonry paints contain modified linseed or other oils. The modification reduces the alkali sensitivity of such oils. On weathered asbestos-cement siding they will give satisfactory performance, but if there is doubt as to the degree of weathering, a solvent-thinned primer should be applied as a base for oil paint.

Asbestos-cement siding is usually applied on exterior exposures and only paints designed for outdoor surfaces should be used on it.

Since asbestos-cement is not usually factory primed, it should be painted by using any of the previously described painting systems as follows: (1) Two coats of a solvent-thinned resin paint; (2) a solvent-thinned resin-primer, followed by a conventional oil or alkyd resin exterior topcoat; and (3) two coats of exterior latex paint.

If the siding is factory primed, consult your dealer for the manufacturer's specific recommendations for painting.

PAINTING PLASTER WALLS AND CEILINGS

Properly lathed and plastered walls and ceilings present an unbroken sweep or surface and permit a wide range in the choice of decorative coatings. Properly applied plaster offers an ideal decorative base for the application of paint.

Up to a generation ago, a painter would wait from six months to two years after a building was plastered before applying paint. He thought rightly, at that time, that plaster had to be cured for this length of time before paint could be successfully applied. Today, speed of construction, and the need for immediate occupancy of a house make this practice not only impractical but impossible. A shortened waiting period has been made possible by the use of improved paints and plaster materials. However, certain conditions can cause trouble if they are not recognized. If they are recognized and the proper procedures are followed, a completely satisfactory job will result.

INSPECTION OF WALLS

The first step is to learn the condition of the wall. With this information you can decide whether or not it is necessary to apply pretreatment and what types of paint will be satisfactory.

Large volumes of water are necessarily included in wet plaster. Much of this water will not stay in the wall. Some is used in crystallization, but the rest of it will evaporate. The only way the water can evaporate is through the surface of the plaster. If the paint impedes this evaporation, damage to the paint may result. Therefore, it is necessary to know just how dry the wall is.

Drying of plaster. Under normal conditions when the relative humidity is not high, and the temperature is not below 50°, plaster will dry in 3 to 4 weeks on a furred wall. However, if such conditions are not prevalent, longer time is necessary. A special case is one where plaster is applied to an unfurred wall, brick, tile or similar structural material. The solid wall prevents evaporation from the back of the plaster. If only one surface of the plaster is open, the drying time is greatly lengthened.

If it is necessary to paint the plaster while water is still present, the proper selection of paint can minimize the possibility of trouble, but it is wisest to wait until the drying is complete.

Firmness of plaster. The plaster should be examined for firmness. There may be areas which are soft from "sweat-outs" and "dry-outs." Sweat-outs are due to excessive moisture and slow drying. To correct a sweat-out it is necessary to remove the affected area and replaster. Dry-outs are due to the evaporation of the water before the gypsum crystallizes. To correct a dryout it is necessary to spray the affected area with an alum and water solution, about two pounds per gallon. This provides the water necessary for crystallization, and should be done until the affected area has hardened to a condition which will receive paint satisfactorily.

Uniform density of walls. The walls should be examined for uniform density. If the finish trowelling was not uniform over the wall, there may be spots which have non-uniform "suction." They are usually hard, but they have a "dead" appearance. Such spots will cause uneven gloss and color in the paint if this is not prevented. Dead spots can also be caused by lack of thorough mixing of lime and gauging plaster.

If the plaster is uniformly dull, it should be examined for "chalk." This is a white powder which shows on the hand or a rag rubbed over the wall.

Efflorescence. Sometimes an examination will reveal tiny crystals on the wall. The evaporating water brought them to the surface. They are crystals of soluble salts called *efflorescence*, and they are found only infrequently today. If they are found, they should be brushed off repeatedly until no more form. They do not form instantly—time should be allowed after brushing off. *Do not* use water, as it may bring out more crystals from just beneath the plaster surface.

Finally, just prior to painting, the walls must be examined for any grease or oil. If grease or oil are present, they must be removed with a detergent. Allow the wall to dry again after washing.

PAINTING PROCEDURES

Providing sufficient time has elapsed since the plastering so it is reasonably certain that the walls are dry, and if none of the other imperfections discussed previously are present, any of the standard interior wall finishes will give complete satisfaction. The conditions that cause difficulties are abnormal, and the great majority of paint jobs on new plaster present no problem. They will last for years.

When an *oil* or *alkyd primer* is used, it is wise to allow at least a week drying time before the topcoat is applied. Sometimes when the second coat is applied too soon, peeling develops.

If drying has not been completed—if a match will not strike against the wall, and it is necessary to paint, the paint must not prevent further evaporation of water. In addition the pigments must be insensitive to alkali. Some small quantities of alkaline chemical may remain in the plaster wall and if this is in solution in the water, it will react with certain colored pigments.

Latex paints are best for *incompletely dried walls.* These paints have satisfactory adhesion to damp plaster, and if only one coat is used the water can continue to evaporate. One coat is not usually sufficient to achieve complete coverage, but if that is acceptable it will allow evaporation to take place until the wall is in condition to receive permanent decorative finishes.

A *soft area* caused by a sweat-out or a dry-out can sometimes be hardened with a coat of shellac or lacquer if it is not large. If the shellac binds the wall, further finishing can be normal. Otherwise, replace the plaster.

If the wall is not uniform due to the presence of uneven suction, it is essential that the wall be dry before painting begins. Then apply an oil type primer-sealer. After this any desired paint system can be used.

Chalk. Chalky plaster is quite common, and it is a frequent cause of paint peeling. When there is chalk on a plaster wall, it should be removed before painting. Sometimes in subgrade plaster, there may be *loose sand.* This also must be removed before painting. Vigorous brushing will accomplish this, but it sometimes is difficult to be certain that all chalk has been removed. Latex paints will not easily wet chalk, so they should be avoided. Instead, use an alkyd flat or an oil vehicle primer-sealer, or a proprietary surface hardener prior to any paint system.

Furred wall. At times it may be necessary to paint a wall on which there is efflorescence, before it is certain that the crystals have ceased to form. If the plaster is on a furred wall so that it can dry from the back as well as the front, it is usually possible to stop crystal growth on the inside wall. The wall is sealed and crystal formation is transferred to the back of the plaster. The sealing can be accomplished by two coats of a latex paint or any other system that is impervious to water vapor. If the plaster is on a solid wall without furring it should not be sealed before it is dry. As mentioned previously, an unfurred wall requires much more drying time than a furred wall. This should be kept in mind when estimating drying time.

Cracks. In isolated instances very fine, hairline cracks develop in finish plaster. These are hard to detect until the wall is painted. This causes the paint to be mistakenly blamed for the condition. Walls should be inspected by viewing at a low angle (with the eye close to the wall) to determine if cracks are present. If they are, a paint with a little texture is the best solution. The cracks are obscured. An emulsion paint will frequently obscure these cracks.

Whether or not any of the potential sources of trouble mentioned are present, the secret of long time satisfaction lies in good workmanship when the primer is applied to the wall. The bond between the plaster and the first coat of paint determines the adhesion of all future paint coats.

PAINTING HARDBOARD

Hardboard, as previously described in Chapter 3, is reconstituted natural wood and is fabricated by reducing natural wood to fibers and then pressing the fibers together into panels of various thicknesses and surface dimensions. In many respects hardboard resembles natural wood, and possesses many of the characteristics of natural wood. On the other hand, it is without grain and, as a result, has substantially equal strength in all surface directions and has neither knots nor other natural imperfections. Also, any slight dimensional changes would be uniform in all surface directions. These factors are advantages with respect to paint-holding characteristics.

Required coats of paint. The usual practices in painting natural wood are applicable to painting hardboard. For durability, two coats of paint frequently are adequate, but three coats usually are required, particularly on exterior applications. The first, or primer coat, must seal the surface and provide adequate adhesion for succeeding coats. The top coats provide the decorative effects desired and protect the surface against moisture, sun, abrasion, and other deteriorating effects. Top coats which have given good performance on natural wood are, in general, suitable for top coats on hardboard.

INTERIOR PAINTING

Since the painting of interior surfaces is most important from the decorative standpoint, care must be taken that a uniform and smooth surface is obtained. Good sealing by the primer is required to prevent absorption of the top coat.

Primers and sealers. Most latex paints are good sealers, and shellac is often used. Many enamel undercoaters and varnish or alkyd-base primers and sealers are also satisfactory. Flat paints, semi-gloss, or gloss enamels, and similar types of top coats are usually not the best sealers, and should not be used as primers. Sanded areas and areas roughened during transport and handling should, even though previously primed, be given another coat of primer-sealer to assure adequate sealing.

Paints. After the hardboard panel has been properly sealed, the top coat, chosen for protective and decorative needs, is applied. Painting properly sealed hardboard is no different from painting other paintable surfaces. As a general practice, flat paints are used for walls and ceilings, and semi-gloss or gloss enamels for those surfaces where higher resistance to abrasion, washing, or moisture penetration is required. Surfaces in bathrooms, laundry rooms and shower stalls, where prolonged exposure to moisture is expected, are better protected by two coats of the finishing paint which increases moisture resistance.

Procedures. For a good paint job on hardboard, good painting practices must be employed. Surfaces to be painted should be clean and dry. All grease and dirt should be removed with suitable cleaners before painting. Paint should not be applied during low temperatures. Nail heads should be countersunk and puttied, if possible, or else painted with an anticorrosive primer as should other iron or steel surfaces being prepared for painting: This is particularly important when latex paints are to be used, as many of these accelerate corrosion of iron. A smoother and better appearing finish will be obtained if the sealer is lightly sanded before application of the top-coat. The purpose here is to remove irregularities which would spoil the appearance of the top coat. This is especially important when the final coat is a gloss enamel.

Even when hardboard is not painted for decorative purposes, as in work bench tops, it is good practice in many cases to seal it for protection against dirt and grease. Clear finishes, such as penetrating wood sealers, are suitable and are often used for this purpose as they do not build up a surface film which could be scratched or worn away.

EXTERIOR PAINTING

Tempered hardboard is a very satisfactory material of exterior service, but should always be adequately painted. If not, water which may penetrate into the panel will ultimately damage it.

Primer. Here again, the best results in painting exterior hardboard may be expected if the manufacturer's directions are followed in the choice of primer and finish coat. However, excellent performance may be obtained by the use of any good primer followed by a coat of exterior house paint. Exterior house paint primers should be used. All exposed edges should be sealed for better paint adhesion at this critical point.

The use of factory-primed hardboard assures a good sealer and usually has better adhesion and sealing properties than will be emphasized again that all areas where the original primer is damaged or removed in handling or construction must be spot primed.

Paints. Once the hardboard has been well sealed, paints which have given good performance in similar service on natural wood are the logical choice. For siding, and vertical surfaces generally, high-grade exterior house paints give the best service. When high gloss or extreme color retention is desired, and especially when bright colors are called for, exterior trim paints usually are the most satisfactory. Other exterior paints with good durability may also be used.

Where hardboard panels are installed horizontally, or nearly so, there is some likelihood that water or snow may stand in pockets or channels around the ends or edges and a good grade of floor-and-deck enamel should be applied as the top coat. It is formulated for long resistance to penetration by water. Here again a primer must be used.

Procedures. Nearly all of the practices which experience has shown to be necessary or desirable in painting natural wood, whether the painted surface is out-of-doors or indoors, are applicable to hardboard. The most frequent exterior use of hardboard is as house siding and it is important that good construction practices, such as the use of an adequate vapor barrier in exterior walls, which do not allow penetration of moisture behind hardboard be followed. This is an equally good practice regardless of materials used. Moisture absorbed through the back surface is even more destructive to the adhesion of the paint coating on the front than is moisture which penetrates from the front. All holes and cracks should be calked before painting.

Where hardboard is exposed on both sides, as when used for purposes such as fence panels, barbecue-pit windbreaks and sun-screens, all edges and both sides must be carefully sealed against moisture.

REPAINTING HARDBOARD SURFACES

If the old paint is in *good condition,* the same good repainting practices that are satisfactory for natural wood will be satisfactory for repainting hardboard.

Procedure. *For example,* dirt, grease, and loose material should be removed and loose nails reset and puttied or primed. Any areas where the paint film is damaged should be spot primed, and then one or two finish coats applied. No primer is needed when the paint film is in good condition.

If the old paint is *peeling,* it is probably due to moisture. The source of this moisture should be located and eliminated before repainting. All loose paint should be removed and the edges of the areas of good paint should be sanded and feathered-out to assure a smooth overall surface. In these cases it is usually easier to apply primer to the entire surface than it is to spot-prime relatively large areas. A more uniform paint surface will result. *Primer coat* should not be applied until the board is thoroughly dry. *Finish coats* should not be applied until the board is thoroughly dry, and has been thoroughly sealed.

Primer and sealer. In general, while there are many uses for hardboard, painting follows the same pattern—application of a good primer-sealer to protect the material from absorbing moisture and to supply a base for one or more finish coats chosen for the expected exposure. Painting improves the appearance and increases the service life of hardboard and, when properly done, makes it an excellent construction material.

PAINTING PLYWOOD

Fir plywood has a tendency to show grain pattern and to "check" after being painted, but with proper priming or sealing this versatile material can be painted, enameled or varnished as attractively as any other wood surface.

Procedures. The first step, of course, is to prepare the surface which must be smooth, clean and without any traces of oil, grease or laminating glue. Nail holes and wood blemishes should be filled and sanded, and the sandings removed with a cloth dampened with turpentine or odorless solvent.

Paints. For an *opaque finish* which hides the grain completely, the best results are obtained in the following manner:

Brush on a coat of flat oil or alkyd paint, enamel undercoat or penetrating resin sealer. *Do not* use a water-thinned latex paint for this coat, because the water may raise the grain. The flat paint may be thinned slightly as directed on the label to make it more brushable. Sand lightly and dust clean as described.

Then apply a second coat. If the finish coat is to be a gloss enamel, make this second coat a 50-50 mixture of enamel undercoat and the finish coat. When dry, sand lightly. Lastly, apply the top coat as it comes from the can.

If the top coat is to be a latex paint, then the prime coat should be either a clear resin sealer or a flat white oil paint. Finish according to the latex maker's directions for a sealed surface.

For a *clear* or *natural finish* which permits the wood grain to show through, first select plywood with an attractive grain pattern, free of blemishes and insert "plugs." Sand smooth and clean before applying any finish. To retain the completely natural appearance of the wood, first apply a coat of the clear resin sealer. After it has dried, sand to remove gloss and follow with one or two coats of flat varnish or brushing lacquer.

For *blond effects,* brush on a coat of white pigmented resin sealer thinned according to label instruction or use a white interior undercoat thinned 50-50 with turpentine or odorless solvent. After 10 to 15 minutes, dry-brush with the grain or wipe with a dry cloth. This lets the grain show through. After this coat has dried, sand lightly. Then seal with a coat of clear resin sealer, and sand lightly with fine sandpaper when dry.

At this point it is also possible to impart any desired color to the wood. Use tinted interior undercoat, thinned enamel, pigmented resin sealer (or clear sealer tinted with colors in oil) or colors in oil. Light stains may also be used. Sand lightly when dry.

If a *colored grain effect* is desired, some craftsmen do not whiten the wood as a first step. Instead, they tint clear or white resin sealer with the colors in oil to the desired shade, reduced 25 per cent with proper solvent. This is brushed on and allowed to set a few minutes, then rubbed into the pores of the wood and finally wiped off with the grain. After the surface is completely dry, it is sanded smooth and followed with the desired topcoat of varnish or brushing lacquer.

FINISHING FURNITURE AND WOODWORK

Almost every house contains interesting and beautiful pieces of stained and varnished or painted furniture that has seen better days. You may have an antique stored away or a cherished piece that needs its original beauty restored. Perhaps the furniture in everyday use is beginning to show the marks of long service.

Many homes have paneled rooms that have never been finished, or that now need refinishing, where the same knowledge and care required for fine furniture applies.

In either case, it is easy to renew old furniture and woodwork, and actually make it more beautiful than ever, because today's products, designed for finishing furniture and woodwork simplify every operation.

BASIC STEPS TO ACHIEVING A FINE FINISH

While the following are basic steps in obtaining a good finishing job, they are not all necessary for the finishing of every piece of wood: *Sanding* to smooth the wood for a fine finish. *Bleaching* to lighten or to uniform unfinished wood. *Staining* to enhance the grain and to achieve the color you desire. *Filling* required on open-grain woods for smooth surface. *Finish coat* which may be gloss or satin. *Rubbing, buffing, waxing,* and *polishing* are all optional. Use *only* the steps necessary for the type of finish you desire.

You will find it is much easier to work if all hardware and fixtures are removed. Place them in a glass jar or coffee can for safe keeping.

REMOVING THE OLD FINISH

The *old way* was to scrape and sand and to keep on sanding with coarse sandpaper to remove the old stain and varnish coats. On a flat surface, this could be accomplished with a power-sander. But for spindles, crevices, moldings, etc., it was necessary to hand sand, which could take many hours of tedious work.

Today, you can remove the old finish in a new, easy and safe way by using wash-away paint and varnish remover. It is inexpensive, fireproof, and the results are sure and satisfying.

To remove the old finish, flow on a liberal coat of the wash-away remover on an area up to 2′ x 2′ in size (Fig. 1). *Do not* work too large a surface at one time. Let it stand (approximately 10 to 30 minutes) until the old finish is soft.

When the old finish is well-wrinkled or softened (test with putty knife or fingernail), the bulk of the softened old paint or varnish can be scraped or lifted off with a wide scraper or putty knife. Then apply a second coat of the remover and you can quickly clean up the job by washing away the remaining paint or varnish with water and a cloth, or steel wool dipped in exolvent.

For carving, moldings, and other hard to reach places, use a stiff brush such as a toothbrush, and steel wool for the wash-away. A little detergent added to the water will help.

Sand the surface with fine sandpaper after the old finish has been removed down to the bare wood, again using steel wool for carvings, etc., instead of sandpaper. Remove sand dust with a cloth and then gather up any remaining dust with tack rag. Now you are ready to start finishing the furniture as desired.

Note: When finishes are being removed from veneer surfaces that are bonded with water-sensitive adhesives, turpentine or exolvent should be used to wash away the remover, rather than water.

Fig. 1.   Fig. 2.

SANDING

The important step to a smooth finish is to start with a smooth surface obtained by careful and thorough sanding. Otherwise, more coats and more sanding between coats will be required to fill up and level out the roughness.

Unfinished furniture and paneling. On unfinished furniture and paneling that you have made or purchased, the wood has probably already been sanded so that a rather quick additional sanding with medium or fine sandpaper is all that will be necessary. But on old furniture, the finish is most likely in such condition that very thorough sanding will be necessary to remove checks, scratches, and marred spots.

Use medium sandpaper to start with. Finish the sanding with fine sandpaper to remove fine scratches left by the medium paper. Sand with the grain, not across grain. On deep scratches and dents, be careful not to sand through to the bare wood. Sand just enough to remove most of the scratch or dent.

You can clamp the sandpaper in a patented holder to sand large, flat areas. Or, you can make a holder, by tacking sandpaper on a wood block.

Grooves and crevices. For grooves and crevices, fold squares of sandpaper in quarters. Folding the sandpaper over itself keeps it from slipping. It is easy to sand into molded curves, and so on. Some craftsmen prefer to use sandpaper this way for flat surfaces too. On curved and molded areas, fine steel wool can be used, though it has a tendency to discolor some woods.

Fig. 3.   Fig. 4.

Large flat areas. On large flat areas, sand in long sweeping strokes. Be sure you always sand with the grain of the wood. Sanding across the grain results in scratches which require more sanding to remove. Electric sanders may be used, followed by hand sanding, to take care of places impossible to reach with the power sander. Sand until all surface scratches are removed, because they are magnified by the clear finish coat of varnish or shellac.

Deep scratches, cracks, and nailholes. Deep scratches, cracks, and nailholes should be filled with plastic wood (Fig. 2) before the surface is sanded. Apply the plastic wood with a putty knife or small spatula. If you are planning to stain the furniture, you can use plastic wood in a color approximately matching the finish color before staining, although the stain will "take" on the plastic wood.

Thoroughly dust off the sanding dust with a cloth. Use a brush to dust out carvings, moldings, etc. The piece is now ready for staining and finishing.

Old surface. If the old surface is in good condition, it may not be necessary to remove the old finish before applying new varnish. If waxed, remove by wiping with exolvent or turpentine. Sand to a dull, clean surface, to assure adhesion of new finish. Wetting the surface and using wet-or-dry sandpaper is faster. Be careful not to cut through into the bare wood.

BLEACHING

The popularity of very light natural wood finishes for contemporary furniture has increased an interest in bleaches. Bleaches are used to lighten the natural color of woods, to uniform the color of new woods, or to modernize dark furniture by bleaching out much of the old stain to make it light. In this case, the old finish must be removed as previously described, since bleaches are effective only on bare wood.

Types of bleaches. There are several types of bleaches available. Some involve the application of two liquids, a bleach followed by a neutralizer. "Dexall" wood bleach is a simple, effective system using two liquids which are mixed in equal parts at time of use, and applied as a single liquid. Use a glass or porcelain jar for mixing. (Fig. 3).

Applying the bleach. Apply the mixed solution to the bare wood with a synthetic rubber sponge or rag (Fig. 4). Be sure to wear rubber gloves. When bleach is surface dry, sponge off lightly with water to remove any residue. Woods vary in the way they take bleach. If the old stain is very dark, you may have to make several applications of the bleach.

Sanding. Allow 12 hours' drying time after final bleaching. Then sand to a smooth finish with fine or extra fine sandpaper. Be sure to sand it uniformly and carefully. You are now ready for the next step.

STAINING

The natural beauty of wood gives furniture a certain warmth and dignity that can be achieved by no other material. The graceful pattern of the grain, texture and coloring can be enhanced by the use of wood stains.

Oil stains for traditional wood colors and for the beautiful new color tone effects are available at your local stores.

Procedure. *Brush stain on* the surface that has been sanded smooth and is free of dust and dirt. Stir well to bring all of the pigment into suspension. Brush on a good wet coat of stain, applying it with the grain of the wood (Fig. 5).

Fig. 5.

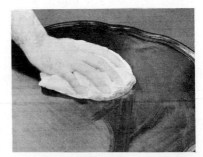

Fig. 6.

Fig. 7.

Fig. 8.

Wipe stain off with a soft, lint-free rag immediately to even the color and pick up excess stain (Fig. 6). The longer the stain remains on the wood without wiping, the more it will strike in, or penetrate and become dark.

Very often a piece of furniture has light or dark areas, or is constructed of two types of wood which may take the stain differently. Control this by wiping the stain almost immediately where it soaks in quickly, and by allowing it to stand longer on other places that resist penetration.

Removing stain. If the stain has "set" too long and is too dark, it can be lightened by wiping with "exolvent" or turpentine (Fig. 7). Allow over-night drying. You are now ready for the next step.

FINISHING OPEN GRAIN WOODS

Open grain woods require a filler before applying varnish or sealer if a smooth finish is desired.

Filler. A paste-wood filler should be used for this purpose. It is not recommended as a crack filler. Other compounds are made for that purpose. This filler comes in semi-paste form and must be thinned to about the consistency of cream with stain, "exolvent" or turpentine. The filler is a light, transparent color suitable for natural light wood finishes. When the wood is naturally dark, or is to be stained dark, the filler should be thinned with stain to darken the light transparent color. *For example,* if the wood is walnut, or is to be stained walnut, thin the filler with walnut stain. This will avoid light filler showing up in undesirable contrast with the dark color of the wood.

Light stain effects. For light stain effects tint and reduce the paste-wood filler with stain. For example, a good light oak effect can be obtained by coloring or thinning the filler with the dark oak stain. Then, as you apply the filler, you also stain the wood in a single operation. Wiping off the filler will lighten the stain to a light oak tone.

Brush on the reduced filler. Apply a liberal quantity (Fig. 8). After a few minutes, the filler will begin to "flatten" or "dull down." The time required for this depends on drying conditions.

Wipe filler off when it begins to dull down or flatten out with a coarse cloth or burlap. Rub across the grain or in a circular motion to force the filler well into the pores of the wood and at the same time, wipe off the excess with a clean cloth so that no filler is left on the surface (Fig. 9).

After the filler has dried overnight, give the surface a quick light sanding with very fine sandpaper. Wipe off sanding dust with a tack rag.

Note: Once the filler hardens, it is very difficult to remove from the surface. Therefore, it is generally advisable to apply filler *only* to a section or area that can be conveniently wiped before the filler hardens. *For example,* when filling a small table—fill the top, then the side pieces, next the legs, etc. A cloth moistened in "exolvent" or turpentine helps soften any filler that has become too hard, but try to avoid this by filling only a small area at a time.

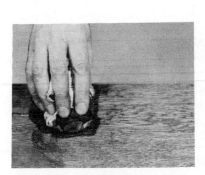

Fig. 9.

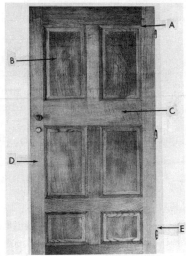

Fig. 10.

THE FINISH COAT

All the following finish coatings are clear, transparent finishes that reveal the full beauty of the grain and the color or staining of the wood. The following finishing instructions will apply for varnish, sealer and shellac.

Applying the finish coat. When applying the finish coat, be sure to use a clean brush. One way to be sure the brush is clean is by putting a small amount of the finish coat in a separate container. Brush several brushfuls from this container across a knife or the edge of another can. Then throw away this small amount of finish coating, which contains the dust and dirt worked out from the brush.

Make sure the surface is clean and dust free. Immediately before applying the finish coat, wipe off the surface (giving special attention to carvings, moldings, crevices, etc.) with a tack rag, to remove any remaining dust specks.

Work in a room as free from dust in the air as possible. The varnish, sealer or shellac brush will pick up every speck of settling dust, which will be magnified in the glass finish. Varnishes and like materials flow better and more easily in room temperatures of about 70°F. or higher.

VARNISH

Use a clear, transparent varnish that intensifies the beautiful grain and color of the wood with a maximum surface coating. It is easy to apply, extremely tough and will last for years, and comes in high gloss and satin finish.

PROCEDURES

New work. By new work is meant unfinished wood (or old furniture from which the old finish has been removed down to the bare wood), which has been properly prepared for the finish coat. (See section on New Work in this Chapter.)

First coat. Use a gloss varnish, reduced 12½ per cent with "exolvent." Brush the varnish on liberally with the grain of the wood, but exercise care to avoid sagging and running. On flat areas, it is well to brush the varnish horizontally and then vertically, repeating the process a couple of times to level out the varnish to a uniform film. This uniformity of film does much to prevent sagging.

Second coat. Allow first coat to dry 24 hours and sand lightly with very fine sandpaper. Wipe with tack rag or cloth dampened in water to remove sanding dust. Apply second coat of gloss varnish just as it comes in the can. This can be the final coat.

An *additional coat* of gloss varnish with a light sanding between coats will give a greater fullness and depth of beauty to the finish.

Hand-rubbed effect. After the first or second coat of gloss varnish has dried, a coat of satin finish varnish will give a beautiful "hand-rubbed effect" without the laborious job of hand-rubbing.

A CLOSE-TO-THE-WOOD FINISH

Both *gloss* and *satin finish* is a new sealer-type finish that penetrates into the wood and seals the pores. This means the finish is actually in the wood instead of on the surface, like a varnish. Many people prefer a close-to-the-wood finish for furniture, woodwork, and wall paneling.

NEW WORK (See Varnish)

First coat. Apply a liberal coat of gloss or satin finish as it comes in the can, brushing with the grain of the wood. Allow 4 hours to dry. Sand lightly. Remove sanding dust with a tack rag, or a cloth dampened with "exolvent" or turpentine.

Second coat. Apply finish as it comes in the can. If it is to be waxed, allow 24 hours for drying. If gloss finish has been used, it is good to sand the surface lightly with finest sandpaper or rub it down with fine steel wool before waxing.

SHELLACS

Shellac is a natural gum dissolved in alcohol. It was at one time very popular as a clear finish, because it dried very hard and very fast. However, it is brittle and so has a tendency to chip, especially when built up to a thick film. Shellac also water-spots rather easily.

Orange shellac is the natural color to be used where it is desired to impart the yellow-orange tint to the finish. It is also used over dark woods or dark stains, or where the natural orange color may enhance the stain.

White shallac is a light yellow-white finish. It can be used for most work, but is especially desirable for light natural finishes.

To reduce heavier shellac. A 4-pound cut can be reduced to approximately a 3-pound cut by adding ½ pint of denatured alcohol to the quart of shellac. To reduce 5-pound cut, add ¾ pint of denatured alcohol to the quart of shellac.

Applying shellac. Apply shellac with a varnish brush. Make sure the brush is clean. Since shellac dries rapidly, it is necessary to work fast—in long strokes with the grain of the wood. Avoid over-brushing.

Coats required. It is better to build up the finish with several thin coats, with a light sanding between coats, rather than one or two heavy coats. The last coat can be rubbed to a dull finish with pumice stone and oil or fine steel wool and oil.

Used as a sealer. Because all the liquid in shellac evaporates and leaves only the gum, it is an excellent sealer over bare wood and over stains to prevent bleeding.

WAX FINISH

For soft, satiny beauty a good quality paste wax, well rubbed on a surface finished in gloss varnish, or shellac not only adds beauty, but helps preserve the finish. Be sure the surface is clean. Apply several thin coats of wax, rather than one or two heavy coats. Polish each coat vigorously to bring out the full lustre of the wax. On curved areas use the "shoeshine" technique to polish.

HAND RUBBING

Today, satin-finished varnish will dry to a subdued satiny finish that eliminates the need for hand rubbing the gloss finish. However, some hobbyists prefer to hand-rub their furniture so as to secure the exact lustre they desire.

When a finish is hand-rubbed, the normal gloss is removed or reduced by using an abrasive. The surface which is to be rubbed should have 3 or 4 coats of varnish to withstand rubbing and the final coat allowed to dry three days or longer. Slow-drying varnishes must be given a longer drying time before rubbing than the faster-drying finishes.

PROCEDURES

Felt-pad and pumice method. Use a felt pad which may be purchased or made by tacking several layers of felt (cut from an old felt hat) to a block of wood. Make sure pad and surface are free of any pieces of sharp grit. Mix pumice and water to a paste consistency. Wet the surface. Dip pad in water and then in pumice paste and rub the surface with the grain of the wood. Use long rubbing strokes with uniformly moderate pressure so that the entire area receives the same amount of rubbing.

On turned areas, use a cloth wet with water. Sprinkle the pumice on the cloth and rub shoeshine fashion. On curved areas, use a toothbrush dipped into a soft paste of pumice and water. Rub until surface is uniformly dulled.

Polish the surface by rubbing with a clean felt pad or soft cloth, using powdered rottenstone and soapy water or rottenstone and rubbing oil. Rubbing oil can be a mixture of light motor oil 1/3 and "exolvent" 2/3. Finish by cleaning the surface with clear water and a soft cloth.

Wet-or-dry sandpaper method. Lubricate the surface with soapy water. Rub (using long strokes) with the grain of the wood, with very fine wet-or-dry sandpaper (grade 360 or 380). When uniformly dulled, polish with a clean soft felt pad or cloth and rottenstone and soap and water. Clean surface with clear water and soft cloth. To clean from carvings and corners, wrap cloth around sharp stick.

Steel wool method. An easier and faster method is to rub the surface with 4/0 steel wool, until uniformly dull. Then apply a coat of paste wax and polish vigorously with a soft cloth or felt pad.

FINISHING A DOOR

The following rotation in finishing a paneled door will give you the best results (Fig 10).

First finish the moldings and beveled edges (A), then finish the panel (B). Complete all the panels, then finish the top, cross rails and bottom (C) and the right and left sides (D). Edges come last (E).

FINISHING NEW AND OLD FLOORS

Finishing new floors. Floor finishing should be the last operation to be performed, after all other interior painting and decorating work has been completed. The first and most important operation connected with the finishing of new floors is scraping or sanding. Hand scraping or sanding, a long and tedious job, has been displaced almost completely by small, compact, easily operated electric scraping and sanding machines (Fig. 11). These machines may be rented from most local hardware dealers.

When sanding a new hardwood floor, go over the floor several times, first across the grain and then with the grain. On the first traverse use No. 2 sandpaper on the machine; switch to No. ½, No. 0 and No. 00 on succeeding traverses. On soft wood floors, however, do not use a finer sandpaper than No. ½. After sanding the floor, sweep it clean and inspect it carefully, looking at it toward the light from a window. Remember that any scratches, undulations, or other blemishes will appear greatly accentuated when the finish is applied.

The newly sanded, clean floor must not be walked on until the first coat of finish has been applied and permitted to dry. Do all finishing work on the floor as soon as possible after sanding. If a floor is to be stained, use a penetrating oil stain at this stage. If floor seal is to be used, however, a stain of the required color can be incorporated in the first coat of floor seal. Some commercial floor seals are now available in colors as well as in the colorless form. Stained floors require careful maintenance to avoid traffic channels in the wood. No stain penetrates very deeply with uniform color, and if a patch becomes light in color through wear it is very difficult to repair it to match in color the unworn areas of the floor. On the other hand, stain may penetrate very deeply in the large pores of some hard woods, so that if the home owner subsequently desires to sand the floor down to get rid of the stain, he may have to sand off a considerable layer of the board. Stain incorporated in a first coat of floor seal is less likely to result in such deep penetration in local spots.

It is necessary to fill oak, chestnut, and other types of hard wood with large pores with paste wood filler before proceeding with the subsequent finishing operations. Maple, birch, pine, and other types of open-grained woods used for floors do not require any fillers. The procedure for the application of fillers has been given previously in this chapter.

The filler used on the floor may be colorless, or a filler containing pigment may be used to bring out the grain of the wood more contrastingly. Paste wood filler is almost always used on oak floors before the application of shellac or varnish coatings. But with floor seals the practice varies. Some manufacturers of seals recommend that a filler be used prior to the application of the floor seal. Others recommend omission of the filler. General directions for the use of floor seals is given later on in this chapter. However, when a filler is used, be sure that all excess filler is wiped off very thoroughly to avoid an uneven, smeared finish.

If the floor is to be finished in its natural color, allow the filler to dry and then sand it lightly. To further protect the surface

Fig. 11.

of a new floor, give it a second coat of filler. After the second coat of filler has dried thoroughly, sand and clean off the surface.

If the floor is to be stained to harmonize with the color scheme of the room, apply the stain before the filler, and color the filler with the stain before applying it to the floor. The procedure for staining floors and the materials and tools used are the same as those described for staining wood trim. If the floor appears to be too dark after staining, continue to wipe it with a cloth to make it lighter before permitting it to dry. Keep wiping the stain evenly all over the floor to assure a uniform color. Let the floor dry thoroughly before shellacking and varnishing.

Shellacking floors. Shellac used for floors should be pure shellac, unadulterated with cheaper resins. It should be purchased in the form of 5-pound cut shellac. Special shellac prepared by reputable manufacturers for use exclusively on floors is available in glass containers. Glass containers are desirable, since shellac that has stood long in contact with metal may contain salts of iron that will discolor oak and similar woods.

The correct thinner for shellac is 188-proof No. 1 denatured alcohol. Before applying the shellac, thin with 1 quart of thinner to each gallon of shellac. Use a brush wide enough to cover three boards of the flooring at a single stroke. Apply the shellac with long, even strokes, taking care to join the laps smoothly. The first coat on bare wood requires from thirty minutes to one hour to dry. When the floor is dry, rub it lightly with No. 00 sandpaper, sweep it clean, and go over the entire floor with a dry, clean cloth. Apply a second coat immediately after cleaning up the floor. Allow the floor to dry from 3 to 5 hours, then sand it, sweep it, and wipe it again with a clean, dry cloth. Immediately after cleaning apply the third and final coat.

If possible, do not use floor until the morning after the final coat. However, if this is not possible, the floor can be walked on about 4 hours after finishing. If wax is to be used, use a paste wax, not a water-emulsion, self-polishing type of wax, since the water in the latter type may turn the shellac white. Wax should not be applied to a shellac floor less than 8 hours after the last coat of shellac and the floor must not be used prior to waxing.

Varnishing floors. Only special floor varnishes should be used for floor finishing; so-called all-purpose varnishes are not durable enough. When varnishing floors, be careful about cleanliness, reasonable control of temperature, and circulation of air. The floor must be absolutely clean and dry when varnish is applied, and the brush used must be kept clean at all times to avoid leaving unsightly grains and lumps in the coating. The room should be kept at 65° F. or warmer, and plenty of fresh air should be provided, since oxygen is taken from the air when varnish dries. Low temperature and a high degree of humidity will greatly retard the drying of varnish. At least two coats of varnish are required over paste filler or over a first coat of shellac, and at least three coats are required when the varnish is applied directly to the bare wood.

The advantage of using varnish on floors over shellac is that varnish does not scratch white or turn white from water stains. The higher cost of varnish is further offset by the fact that it spreads approximately 50 per cent farther than shellac.

Many available types of floor varnishes do not adhere well to shellac. For this reason do not use shellac as a first coat unless the directions of the varnish manufacturer specifically permit it. If you intend to use shellac as a first coat on a floor to be varnished, apply a very thin coat, so that after a light sanding it constitutes more of a filler than a continuous film of shellac.

For varnishing a floor use a good quality, pure-bristle brush from 2½" to 5" in width (See Chapter 15). For the first coat, thin the varnish in accordance with the manufacturer's directions. Apply the varnish with a brush that is well filled. Start varnishing in one corner of the room and coat a strip about 2' wide with rapid strokes running entirely with the grain of the wood for the full length and width of the room. Work back and forth until the entire area of the room has been covered. Plan the work so that the last strokes on the floor will be adjacent to an exit. Do not put on too heavy a coat, but brush the varnish out to a thin coat. Thin coats are more durable and dry quicker.

Permit the first coat of varnish to dry thoroughly. It is good practice to allow at least 12 to 24 hours more than the time specified by the manufacturer of the varnish for thorough drying, and then to rub the floor lightly with very fine sandpaper. After sanding, clean the floor before applying the second coat. If a third coat is to be applied, allow at least 24 hours before sanding the second coat. Permit the final coat to dry thoroughly before waxing.

The use of floor sealers. The use of penetrating floor sealers for finishing floors is becoming increasingly popular. Penetrating floor sealers, as a rule, can be applied only to bare wood or to floors previously finished with a sealer. As its name implies, this material penetrates into the surface of the wood and seals the minute wood fibers into a hard, solid mass. Not being a surface finish, it wears only as the hardened wood itself wears and does not scratch or chip. Floor sealer gives a velvety sheen to the floor, similar to the hand-rubbed finish on old furniture. Floor sealers resist the action of water, soap, and stain. One of the main advantages in the use of floor sealers is that worn spots can be refinished with sealer without showing any laps or contrast; this is impossible with any other type of floor finish.

Manufacturers of penetrating floor sealers give precise and reliable instructions for the proper application of their product. The procedure is usually to brush this material on with a wide

Fig. 12.

brush or applicator (Fig. 12), working first across the grain of the wood and then smoothing it out in the direction of the grain. After an interval of 15 minutes to 2 hours, depending largely upon the type of sealer used, wipe the excess material off with clean cloths or a rubber squeegee (Fig. 13). Then buff the floor with No. 2 steel wool pads attached to the bottom of the same sanding machine as that used for sanding the floors (Fig. 14).

One application of sealer may be sufficient, but as a rule a second application of sealer should be made on new floors or floors that have just been sanded. A correct interval of time between application of the sealer and the buffer is exceedingly important. If the manufacturer of the sealer does not specify the correct interval clearly, the home owner should determine it by making tests in some inconspicuous places where imperfect results will not prove too disappointing.

Waxing floors. Waxing is the most economical and efficient method of maintaining in good condition floors that have been coated with varnish, shellac, enamel, or floor sealer. When waxing a floor for the first time, build up a good foundation with at least two coats of a good type of paste wax. Apply the wax to the floor with an applicator or cloth and permit it to stand until

Fig. 13.

the volatile thinner in the wax evaporates—this usually takes from 15 to 30 minutes. Then polish the floor with an electric floor-polishing machine, which can be rented from a local hardware dealer (Fig. 15). Apply a second coat of wax after polishing the first coat and repeat the process. The floor can thereafter be maintained in good condition with paste wax, liquid wax, or water wax. For those who desire to get along without the use of a polishing machine and are willing to accept a somewhat less attractive and less durable wax finish, there are available various types of so-called no-rub water waxes that are merely mopped on the floor and allowed to dry.

Fig. 14.   Fig. 15.

REFINISHING OLD FLOORS

When floors have become badly discolored and worn by neglect or by improper maintenance, the most practical procedure and often the only one that will restore the floors is to remove the old finish and recondition the entire floor by power sanding. However, where the floors have been reasonably well maintained but the finish has through age and ordinary wear become dingy, refinishing without power sanding may sometimes be practical. The method used for the removal of the old finish will depend upon the kind of finish originally used.

Refinishing floors originally finished with oil. In a great many old houses the floors were originally finished with various oil preparations. These old oil finishes, since they are embedded in the wood, are apt to cause difficulty. If a power-sanding machine is available, it may be possible to clean the floors sufficiently by buffing them with No. 3 steel wool.

If this is not feasible or proves ineffective, a chemical treatment will be necessary. Through the application and action of mild alkalies, the oil that is embedded in the wood can be changed to soap. The alkali used for this purpose may be lye, washing soda, a water solution of trisodium phosphate, or a commercial cleanser available for this purpose. If lye or any commercial cleanser containing lye is used, be sure not to make the solution too strong. Any strong alkali will swell and soften the wood. Note, however, that if the oil that has been originally applied to the old floor contained mineral oil, chemicals cannot be used, since alkalies will not saponify mineral oil. In cases of this type, the only procedure would be to sand the surface of the old floor and refinish it with either paint or enamel.

When applying an alkali solution, use a mop and flood a small area of the floor at a time. Allow the solution to stand for a few minutes and then, with either a stiff brush or a wad of No. 1 steel wool, scrub the wetted area vigorously. Flush the area with clean water and continue scrubbing to remove the soap that has been wormed. Finally, remove as much water as possible with a dry mop and permit the floor to dry thoroughly.

If the floor turns gray as a result of the action of the alkali and water, it may be necessary to bleach it with a saturated solution of oxalic acid in water. When working with oxalic acid wear rubber gloves; this acid is poisonous and must be handled with care. Rinse off the oxalic acid with clean water, mop with a dry mop, and permit the floor to dry thoroughly. Any raised grain or roughening of the surface of the boards as a result of these drastic treatments must be smoothed off with sandpaper or steel wool before the new finish is applied.

A new finish is applied to the floor in the manner previously described for new floors.

Refinishing floors originally finished with varnish, enamel, or similar materials. The easiest and most practical method of removing old, discolored varnish and enamel floor finishes is by power sanding. However, they can also be removed with liquid paint or varnish removers. Alkaline solutions in water and removers that are sold in powder form to be dissolved in water must not be used. The directions for using the suitable liquid removers must be followed carefully. Since some old, discolored varnish remains embedded in the wood, complete restoration of the natural wood color must not be expected, unless the surface of the floor is sanded down for a considerable distance. Traffic channels where the old varnish has long been worn through and dirt has been ground into the wood should be cleaned by either power or hand sanding.

Refinishing floors originally finished with shellac and wax. Old shellac and wax finishes that have merely become soiled by dirt particles ground into the wax coating can be easily cleaned by going over the floor with steel wool saturated with clean turpentine. Any white spots in the shellac that may have been caused by contact with water can be taken out by rubbing the spots lightly with a soft cloth moistened with a solution of equal parts of denatured alcohol and water. This solution must be used with care to avoid cutting the shellac coating. On floors in which the dirt has been ground into the shellac itself or where the white spots penetrate all the way through the shellac coating, more drastic treatment is required. Wash such floors with either a neutral or a mildly alkaline soap solution followed by clear water, using as little water as possible for each of these operations. Then scour the floor with No. 3 steel wool and the denatured alcohol solution. If the floor boards are level and are not warped or cupped, this scouring can easily be done with a floor-polishing machine fitted with a wire brush and a pad of No. 3 steel wool. After the scouring, rinse the floor with a minimum amount of clean water and allow it to dry thoroughly before refinishing.

General floor maintenance procedures. Wood floors on which a great amount of time, labor, and expense have been spent to produce a fine finish must never be scrubbed with water or unnecessarily brought into contact with water except in connection with refinishing operations as previously described. Sweeping or dry mopping should be all that is necessary for routine cleaning. A cotton floor mop kept barely dampened with a mixture of 3 parts of kerosene and 1 part of paraffin oil is excellent for dry mopping. When this dry mop becomes dirty, wash it in hot, soapy water, dry it, and again dampen it with the kerosene and paraffin mixture. Patches of dirt that cannot be removed in this manner can be removed by a light rubbing with fine steel wool moistened with turpentine.

If the finish is a floor seal, badly soiled spots (for example, gray spots where water has been allowed to stand on the floor for a considerable time) can be sanded by hand, patched with seal, and buffed with a pad of steel wool.

Varnish-finished floors, if waxed and kept in good condition, offer excellent protection against water and other stains.

CHAPTER *17*

Woodworking Repairs

—————————⋮—————————————

FLOORS

A familiarity with the general construction of a house floor is essential if you want to make floor repairs in a proper and efficient way. In a well-constructed house the *joists,* or beams which support the flooring, are placed no more than 16″ apart. If the joists exceed a length of 8′, they should be *bridged,* or braced, with strips of wood or nonrusting metal. Bridging prevents joist sway and helps to distribute the stress of additional weight or shock, which would otherwise concentrate on the joists immediately underneath.

There are two kinds of house floors: single and double. The *double* floor is made in two layers. The bottom layer, secured directly to the joists, is called *subflooring* and is made of rough tongue-and-groove lumber laid diagonally, or at right angles to the joists. A layer of building paper separates the subfloor from the finish floor. The *finish* floor, usually of tongue-and-groove hardwood, is laid parallel to one of the walls of the room and is secured to the subfloor with finishing nails. These nails have small heads and must be driven at an angle through the tongue edge of each board so as to conceal them beneath the adjacent board (Figs. 1 and 2).

In old houses, floors may sag because the joists and girders have been weakened by rot or by termites or other insects. In new houses, sagging may result from the use of green lumber or from improper construction.

Repairing a sagging floor. Sagging indicates structural weakness in the floor, serious warping of the joists, or, in severe cases,

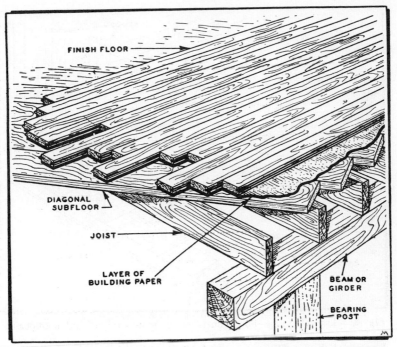

Fig. 1. Typical double-floor construction, with diagonal laid subflooring.

sinking of the foundation. If there is a basement beneath the sagging floor, the sag can be eliminated by using a screw jack of the type shown in Fig. 3 and several lengths of 4″ × 4″ timber.

First, cut one of the timbers 3′ to 5′ in length and lay it on the basement floor, centered beneath the sagging area. (The purpose of this timber is to distribute the strain placed on the basement floor when the sagging area above it is raised.) Next, place the screw jack on top of the timber. Nail another 4″ × 4″ along the sagging joists and measure the distance from it to the top of the jack. Cut a piece of 4″ × 4″ to that length; place it in position as shown in Fig. 3 and raise the jack slightly. Do not attempt complete leveling in one operation. Instead reraise the jack a fraction of an inch each day or so. Check the position of the floor with a level before reraising the jack.

When the floor has been leveled, measure accurately the distance from the horiontal 4″ × 4″ (nailed to the joists) and the

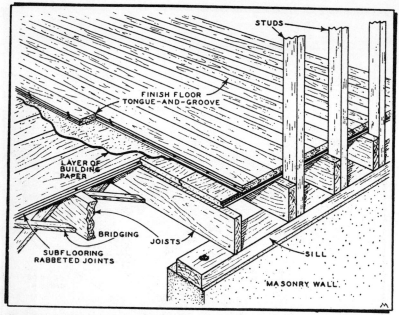

Fig. 2. Typical double-floor construction, with straight laid subflooring.

basement floor. Cut a piece of 4″ × 4″ to that length and raise the jack enough to permit this timber to stand on end under the horizontal 4″ × 4″. After checking to see that the timber is resting firmly and is in vertical alignment, remove the jack and the 4″ × 4″ placed beneath it. When an entire floor sags, it is necessary to use more than one vertical support.

Sagging or weak floors can also be raised or reinforced by using *Teleposts*, which contain built-in screw jacks (Fig. 4). Teleposts are supplied with two plates, one to rest on the basement floor and the other to fit between the top of the post and the bottom of the joist. The jack can adjust the post to any required height. When Teleposts are used, the jack should be reraised only a fraction of an inch every day or so. These posts have two advantages: they become a permanent installation and they eliminate the work required in the use of a screw jack and timbers.

When sagging occurs in an upper floor, where the joists are not exposed, the simplest method for leveling is to take up the finish flooring carefully, following directions given below for repairing

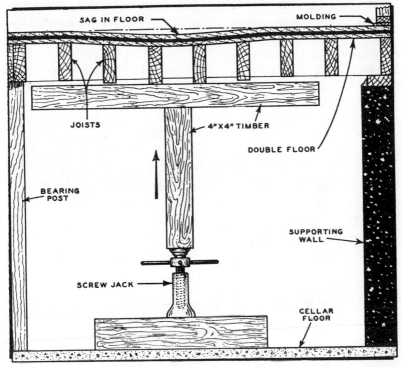

Fig. 3. Repairing a sagging floor.

damaged floors, and then to level the low places in the subfloor with either a filler compound or filler strips.

Filler compound, a commercial product, is a semiplastic material. When using the compound, level it into place on the subflooring with a putty knife and allow it to set for several days before relaying the finish flooring. Then check the floor with a spirit level and, if the floor still sags, apply an additional layer of the compound. *Filler strips* are thin strips of wood cut to compensate for the sag in the floor.

After the floor has been leveled by one of these methods, both of which are shown in Fig. 5, the flooring may be relaid with the use of finishing nails.

Repairing a damaged or worn floor. When floor boards are badly damaged or worn, they should be removed. A brace and bit is used to bore a hole in one of the damaged boards, as near to the joist as possible. If the floor is a single floor, no extra precautions are necessary when boring the hole. A keyhole or compass saw can be used to cut across the first board, thus facilitating its removal. After the first board has been removed, it is a comparatively easy matter to remove the remaining defective boards. If the floor is a double one, bore the hole only to the depth of the top flooring and pry up the board.

When replacing defective boards with new flooring, measure and cut the new boards to the required sizes. Square both ends with a chisel or block plane. Figure 6 shows the method of spacing, or breaking, the joints so that a board which extends over a given joist is next to one that ends on the joist. When

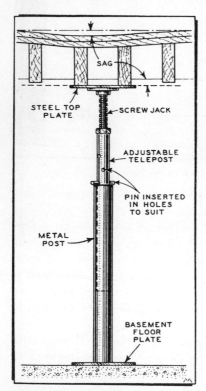

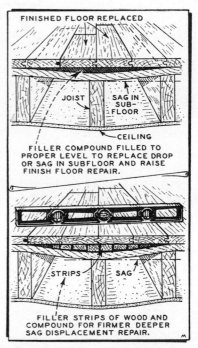

Fig. 4. Using Telepost in basement for permanent repair of sagging floors.

Fig. 5. Using filler compound and strips on upper floor.

the joints are broken in this manner, a strong line of joints running along the same joist is obtained. New boards can also be given additional support by nailing or screwing a small cleat to the side of the joist on which the board is secured (Fig. 6).

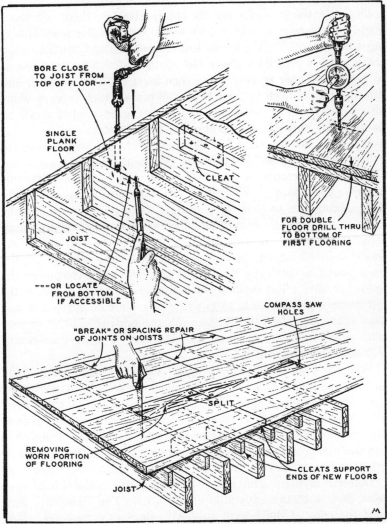

Fig. 6. Repairing worn or damaged floor boards.

Filling cracks in floors. Many older houses have planked floors containing cracks between the boards. There are several commercial plastic fillers that are used to fill cracks, but some are flexible and have a tendency to shrink and crack. Sawdust and wood glue mixed into a paste makes an excellent filler for cracks and is preferable to some commercial fillers.

Do not attempt to fill cracks before cleaning them out thoroughly. Grease or dirt in cracks will keep the filler from adhering to the wood. Use a blunt knife to pack the filler into each crack until it protrudes above the surface of the floor. Allow it to dry and set for several days, then level off with a chisel, and finally sand it down to floor level. When a crack is very wide, glue a thin strip of wood into it and plane or sand it down to floor level. Finish to match the rest of the floor.

Opening the flooring for repairs. When it is necessary to get at heating or plumbing pipes or electrical connections in order to make replacements or repairs, an opening must sometimes be made in the flooring. The procedure for opening up a planked floor is the same as that for repairing damaged or worn boards.

When tongue-and-grooved flooring has been used, the procedure is quite different. In this type of flooring, the *tongue* of one board is fitted into the *groove* of the next. To attempt prying up a board of this type would damage either the tongue or the groove or both. The method for lifting one or more boards without damaging the floor is to cut off the tongue of one board and take crosscuts along the joists. This operation can be accomplished by either a compass or keyhole saw. The three necessary cuts are shown in Fig. 6.

First, bore through the flooring at the tongue side near a joist so that a compass or keyhole saw can be inserted. After boring the hole, saw the tongue along the entire length of the board. Then saw the board at each end, as close to the joist as possible. Remove the first board by sliding a chisel into the lengthwise cut and lifting the board. After removing the first board, remove other boards by sawing each one along the joists.

Before relaying the boards, nail wood cleats to the side of each joist, flush with the underside of the floor. The cleats will support the ends of the boards and will serve as a base on which to nail them. Use finishing nails for this phase of the job and countersink the nailheads below the wood section. Use a commercial filler or a sawdust-glue paste to fill up the holes. Finish to match the rest of the floor.

COVERING FLOORS AND OTHER SURFACES

Two types of linoleum for covering floors and other surfaces are in general use: inlaid and printed. In the better grades of *inlaid* linoleum, both color and pattern go through to the backing, which is usually a specially prepared material. In the cheaper grades of so-called inlaid linoleum, the color and pattern do not go all the way through. In *printed* linoleum, sometimes called "oilcloth," the color and pattern are printed on the surface only. With proper care, a good grade of inlaid linoleum should last a lifetime.

Cleaning linoleum. Linoleum is made of gummed linseed oil mixed with finely ground cork and other materials. Because of the composition of linoleum, harsh caustic soaps and scouring powders eventually destroy the gum that constitutes the major portion of the ingredients. Cleaning should therefore be done with a mop or cloth dampened with pure soap suds. White floating soap or a special linseed-oil soap that can be procured at any paint shop is best for this purpose. The linoleum should then be mopped again with clear water to remove all dirt. Never under any circumstances flood the linoleum with water, because water will work through the joints and eventually soften and loosen the cement. When linoleum is properly treated, it should retain its brightness for a considerable length of time.

Waxing and painting linoleum. To retain its brilliance of color and smooth surface, linoleum should be given, at least once a month, a coat of paste wax or of one of the water-wax emulsions now on the market. The water-wax emulsions dry with a medium glossy finish and do not require rubbing or polishing. They are not so slippery as the paste waxes and are easier to apply. The directions for application furnished by the manufacturer should be followed closely.

If the color or finish of linoleum has worn off, the surface can be painted or lacquered satisfactorily. Neither paint nor lacquer should be applied on waxed linoleum unless all traces of wax have been removed. You may remove the wax by softening the wax coating with benzine, naphtha, or clear gasoline and wiping dry with plenty of clean rags. This job is dangerous and should never be done near a flame; to prevent fire or explosion, make certain that adequate ventilation is provided. After the linoleum has been cleaned thoroughly, allow it to dry overnight. Then apply either lacquer or paint.

Varnish is not recommended as a satisfactory finishing material for linoleum. When it is necessary to remove old and discolored varnish from linoleum before lacquering or painting, use a lukewarm solution of trisodium phosphate, about three pounds to a gallon of water. Allow the solution to remain on the linoleum only long enough to soften the varnish. Work on a small section at a time and do not use too much liquid. After the varnish has been softened, remove it with fine steel wool, thoroughly rinse with clear water, and rub the area dry before proceeding to the next section. This treatment softens the linoleum, which should be allowed to dry for 18 to 24 hours until hard, before wax, lacquer, or paint is applied.

Eliminating bulges. Bulges occur in linoleum if not enough cement was used originally or if the linoleum was not laid properly and was not forced down on the cement. If a bulge appears along a seam, lift the edge of the linoleum and apply linoleum cement to that part of the floor surface directly beneath the bulge. Use a spatula or thin, flat stick to apply the cement, which may be procured at a paint shop. Lay weights on the area to hold the linoleum firmly in place until the cement has hardened and set.

If the bulge is in the center of a strip of linoleum, make a cut with a razor blade or other sharp instrument along the pattern outline of the linoleum where the cut will not show. Press some cement into the opening and spread it with a spatula or flat, thin stick. Press the bulge down and place a weight upon it until the cement has set and hardened.

Patching linoleum. To insert a patch in damaged linoleum, use a piece of linoleum that is large enough to more than cover the damaged area. Lay the new piece on top of the damaged area and with a sharp knife, razor blade, or special linoleum knife cut through both the new and the old linoleum (Fig. 7). Remove the old linoleum and secure the new piece in place with linoleum

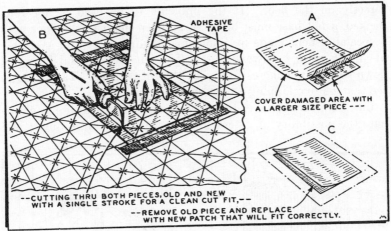

Fig. 7. Patching and matching linoleum.

cement. If you use a matching piece of linoleum, a skilfully applied patch will not be conspicuous. Although it is not always possible to use a matching piece, any piece of linoleum, even one of contrasting color, can be used effectively to form a medallion or design.

Filling holes in linoleum. To fill small holes in linoleum, smooth the edges of the holes with fine steel wool. Crush a small piece of linoleum of the right color into a fine powder. Mix the pulverized linoleum with a sufficient quantity of spar varnish to form a fairly thick paste. Force this paste into the hole as a filler. After the paste has dried, smooth it with No. 000 sandpaper and wax the surface.

Laying linoleum. It is advisable to remove old linoleum before laying new linoleum. Cut any good sections out of the old linoleum and save them for future use. If the floor boards are rough or irregular, plane them smooth. Replace any defective boards. Then wash the entire floor and allow it to dry thoroughly. When a floor is in bad condition and a good quality of inlaid linoleum is to be used, the old floor should be covered with sheets of plywood to insure a smooth, firm base.

Before laying the new linoleum, remove the quarter rounds from the foot of the baseboard (Fig. 8).

The better grades of linoleum are felt-backed and are laid

directly on the floor. If the linoleum to be used is not felt-backed, a felt base must be fitted and cemented to the floor with a special cement made by linoleum manufacturers and available at any paint or hardware store. The felt base should be rolled down so that it adheres firmly to the entire floor. Take care to see that no overlapping or bunching occurs.

Linoleum should never be laid in a cold room. You can eliminate the possibility of its cracking or tearing by unrolling it and

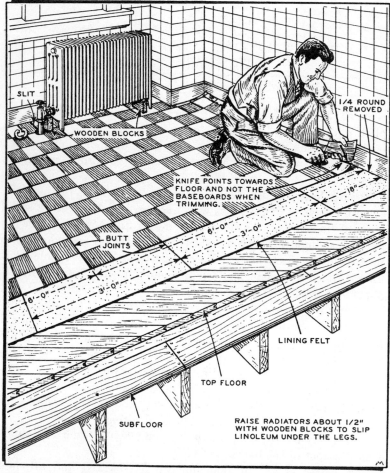

Fig. 8. Laying linoleum on a typical floor.

allowing it to lie flat overnight in a room having a temperature of about 65 degrees.

A linoleum knife should be used to cut linoleum. The inner curved edge, the cutting edge, is sharp enough to cut through the linoleum as the knife is pulled along a line (Fig. 9).

Cutting linoleum to fit along the straight edges of a room presents no problem. Cutting it to fit around doorjambs and so on requires care. The best method is to make an accurate pattern of the irregularity and attach it to the linoleum with a spot of glue, then to mark out the pattern with a piece of chalk or pencil and cut along the marked line.

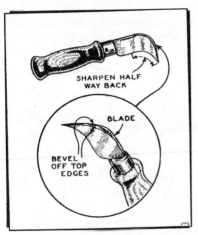 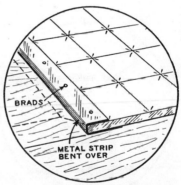

Fig. 9. Linoleum knife and correct sharpening bevel.

Fig. 10. Use of binding at doorways.

After the linoleum has been cut as directed, lay it with linoleum cement. With a cement spreader or putty knife, apply the cement evenly on the floor or on the previously-laid felt base. After spreading the cement over a few square feet (never more), press the linoleum down firmly on the cemented surface. Before proceeding to a new area, make certain that the surface just completed has been covered well with the cement and that the linoleum has adhered firmly to the surface. This is important, since any air bubbles that may be under the linoleum are extremely difficult to remove later. When all the linoleum has been cemented in place, it should be rolled with a heavy roller. A garden roller is satisfactory. Place bricks or other weights on all the seams to prevent them from loosening before the cement is set. Replace the quarter rounds at the foot of the baseboard. Nail them to the baseboard, not to the floor; the linoleum should be free to contract or expand when the room temperature changes.

If the linoleum ends in a doorway, it should be protected by a metal strip (Fig. 10). First nail this strip into place; then lay the linoleum on top of it and trim it to fit under the curved metal edge of the strip. Finally, bend the curved edge over to form a permanent protection for the linoleum edge. Procedures for using other types of metal edgings and bindings are shown in Figs. 11 and 12.

Applying linoleum to sink counters and walls. The methods just described may also be used in laying linoleum on sink

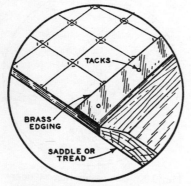 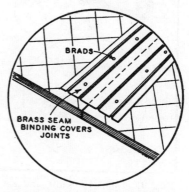

Fig. 11. Use of angle-type metal edging at doorways with treads. **Fig. 12.** Use of brass seam binding at doorways without treads.

counters and plaster walls. Do not, however, lay linoleum over wallpaper. The metal strip described previously can be used on sink counters and walls as well as on floors to protect linoleum edges.

Laying linoleum blocks. Linoleum can be obtained in square blocks as well as in the conventional roll. The floor should be prepared in the same manner as for roll linoleum. It is important, when laying the blocks, to be sure that they are square with the walls and that each block is rolled firmly into place after the cement is applied.

Laying asphalt or cork floor tiles. Asphalt floor tiles can be laid on a wood floor and also on a dry concrete floor. When laying them on a wood floor, first cement down a preliminary felt base. When laying them directly on a concrete floor, coat the concrete first with a special concrete-floor primer. Then spread asphalt tile cement and lay the tiles in the same way as linoleum blocks. Cork tiles are applied in the same manner.

STAIR AND DOOR REPAIRS

Eliminating stair creaking. Stair steps consist of a horizontal board, called a *tread,* and a vertical board at the back, called a *riser* (Fig. 13). Each tread rests on the top edge of the riser of the step below and, as a rule, overhangs it, with the joint between the two covered by a molding strip. When stairs run along a wall, the inner ends of both the treads and the risers are set into grooves in a board attached to the wall and supported by it (Fig. 14). In this type of construction, the treads and risers are secured by wedges glued into the grooves. Because of faulty construction or age and continued use, the wedges may become loose and the treads may spring away from the risers. Then, as the treads are forced down on the risers, the ends of the treads move in the grooves and creaking results.

To eliminate stair creaking, have someone bear down on the tread, forcing it against the riser. Then drive a series of 2″

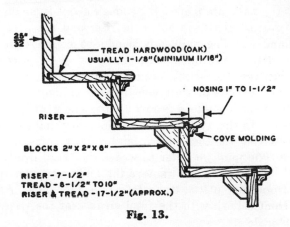

Fig. 13.

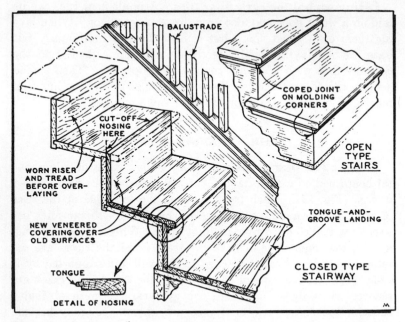

Fig. 14.

finishing nails in pairs—each of the pairs at opposite angles to each other—through the tread and into the riser. Make certain that the nails are driven at opposite angles (Fig. 15). If they are driven straight down, they will eventually work loose. Also be sure that the nails are placed far enough away from the edge of the tread so that they will enter the riser and not pass in front of or behind it. The nailheads should be countersunk with a nail set and the holes filled with plastic wood or other suitable filler. When the filler is set, sand it smooth with the surface.

In the newer type of stair construction, a tongue on the top edge of the riser fits into a groove that is cut in the under edge of the tread. In this type of construction, creaking can be eliminated by driving the thin edge of an ordinary shingle, a wooden wedge, into the joint, in order to wedge the tread firmly against the riser. To do this, first remove the molding under the overhanging front edge of the tread to expose the joint. After cutting the shingle flush with the front surface of the riser, replace the molding.

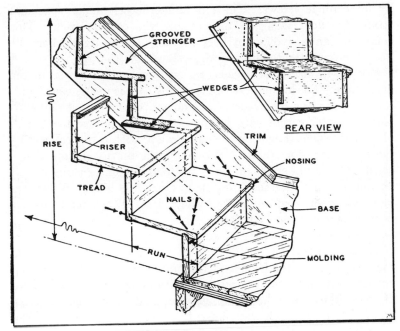

Fig. 15. Procedure for making stair repairs and eliminating creaks.

Replacing worn treads and risers. To replace worn treads or risers proceed as follows: When only the tread is to be replaced, remove it from the stairs. When a riser is to be replaced, riser and tread must be removed. Cut all nails flush with the stringers or side supports of the stairs. Old treads and risers can be used as patterns for cutting the new treads and risers to required size.

When only a tread is to be replaced, place the new tread on top of the stringers and riser. Secure tread onto stringer with finishing nails driven at an angle. Then drive several nails through the top of tread into the lower or supporting riser. When both riser and tread are to be replaced, first secure new riser to stringers; then proceed as previously described for the replacement of stair treads. Be sure to countersink all nails, fill nail holes with filler or plastic wood, and sandpaper flush with the surface.

Eliminating door sticking. Door sticking is usually caused by loose hinge screws. The top hinges loosen under continual strain, the door sags and, as a result, the corners stick. This condition can be avoided by keeping hinge screws tight. Periodic inspection and tightening of hinges should do the job.

Doors will also stick because of swelling and distortion of the doorframe. To eliminate sticking in this case is not so easy, since the door must be removed. To remove a door, open it and support the outer corner with wooden wedges to relieve the hinges of weight. Door hinges are usually made with a pin connecting the two parts of the hinge. Withdraw the pin by pulling it upward. If the pin sticks, drive it by hammering a prying bar at an upward angle against the top knob of the hinge. When removing a door, free the bottom hinge first. When replacing the door, attach the top hinge first.

If door sticking occurs because the front edge of the door is striking the doorframe, and examination shows a space between the rear edge and the frame, set the hinges deeper in the frame by cutting away the wood behind them with an ordinary wood chisel. If there is no space between the front and back edges and the frame, plane the back edge down to a perfect fit. This requires resetting the hinges, a simpler operation than resetting the lock, which would be required if the front edge were planed to fit.

If the latch on a door does not catch, insert a piece of thin plywood or hard cardboard between the hinge leaves on the door and the frame. To do this, the hinges must be unscrewed. When replacing the hinges, use longer screws to make up for the added thickness (Fig. 16).

If the outer bottom corner of a door strikes the sill, a thin wooden wedge placed behind the bottom hinge will tilt the door slightly upward, allowing it to clear the sill. If the outer top corner strikes the frame, the wedge must be placed behind the top hinge. This operation is easier than the alternative one of setting one hinge deeper into the doorframe.

Eliminating door sagging. Heavy garage doors tend to sag if their hinges are not checked and tightened periodically. Usually the bottom strikes the ground so that considerable effort is required to open or close the door.

To fix a sagging garage door, block it up with a wooden wedge. Drive the wedge in at the outer corner, along the bottom edge,

Fig. 16. Repairs to sagging and sticking doors.

so that the door hangs properly and clears without sticking (Fig. 17). Inspect the hinge screws; in nine cases out of ten it will be found that sagging has been caused by a loose hinge. Do not remove the wedge, but proceed to tighten the loose screws with a heavy-duty screwdriver. If the tightened screws appear to be holding the door in place, remove the wedge and the door will clear without sticking.

When the screws can be tightened too easily, they should be replaced with longer screws. In severe cases, the hinges must be removed and reset so that the screws will be held in solid wood. If the door continues to sag and stick, a brace may be used, as shown in Fig. 17. To attach a brace, jack up the door with a wedge until it is hanging straight. Then screw the diagonal brace, or rod, and turnbuckle as shown in Fig. 17.

Correcting door warpage. Outer door and doors between kitchens and passageways are usually subject to warpage, being exposed to dampness on one side and heat on the other. When

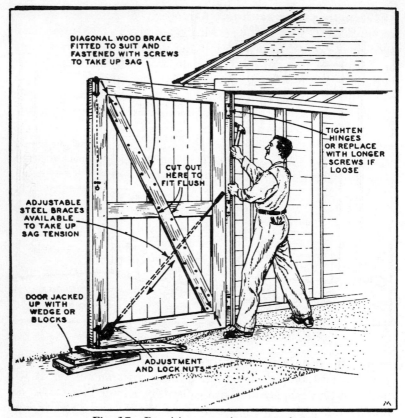

Fig. 17. Repairing a sagging garage door.

warpage occurs, the door must be taken off and laid flat on blocks of wood with the dry or concave side up. If you place heavy weights or bricks on the high end of the warped portions, the door will warp slightly in the opposite direction and, after a few days, will become straight. Before rehanging, paint and varnish the edges to check further absorption of moisture.

Eliminating door creaking. Door creaking is usually caused by rusted hinges. To eliminate this annoyance, first remove the hinge pins; the outer edge of the door should be held securely by an assistant while the pins are being removed. Then with a wad of cotton secured to a stiff wire and dipped in machine oil, swab the length of each pin opening. Then replace the pins.

Eliminating door rattling. A properly fitted doorlatch does not slip into its hole in the striking plate on the doorframe until the door is pressed firmly against the molding in the frame. If the latch does not slip into this hole, the door will rattle. To eliminate rattling, shift the position of the plate slightly by moving it closer to the molding. The plate is usually recessed in the doorframe and moving it will require slight cutting with a chisel or a knife.

Before the plate is placed in its new position, all the old screw holes must be filled with plastic wood or similar wood filler. Then the plate can be set and fastened with screws.

Fitting and hanging doors. Three operations are involved in the fitting and hanging of a door: reducing it to proper size to fit the doorframe, attachment of hinges, and installation of the lock latch assembly and striking plate. The tools required are a jointing plane 18″ or 20″ in length, a ripsaw, and a 1″ chisel.

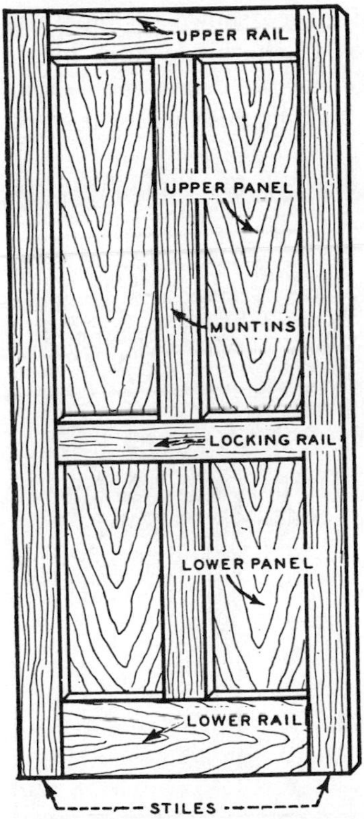

When fitting a panel door, see that the back stile is the same width from top to bottom and of the same width as the front stile when the planing of the edges is completed (Fig. 18).

Bring the door into position with the back stile resting lightly against the edge of the doorframe to which it will be hinged. Hold the door in this position and mark a line down the other stile, using the edge of the jamb as a guide, in order to show the amount of material that will have to be removed before the door will fit between the jambs. Plane the back or hinge edge and square with the face of the door.

UPPER RAIL

UPPER PANEL

MUNTINS

LOCKING RAIL

LOWER PANEL

LOWER RAIL

STILES

DOOR DETAILS

Fig. 18.

To find out the amount of material that must be removed from the rail, hold the door in place between the jambs. Then mark the bottom rail with a line parallel to the threshold or floor. Do not take off all the material from the bottom rail to secure the final fit. Some material must also be removed from the top rail to true up the door. After ascertaining the amount of material to be removed from both the bottom and the top rails, remove the excess material with a saw or plane. Do not plane directly from edge to edge. To avoid splitting, plane halfway in one direction, then plane the remaining half in the opposite direction. Allow $\frac{3}{16}''$ all around the door to afford easy hanging and swinging. If this precaution is taken and the door is properly hinged, it will never bind.

Attaching door hinges. The butt hinge shown in Fig. 19 is the most commonly used hinge. To attach this type of hinge, make undercuts in both the door edge and the door jamb so that the leaves of the hinges are recessed and set flush with the wood of both members.

It is good practice to locate all door hinges throughout the

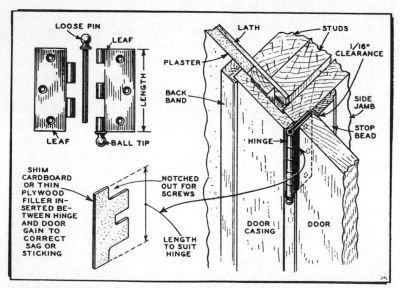

Fig. 19. Attaching butt hinge to eliminate door sag. Parts of hinge are shown (upper left).

house in the same positions. Locate the lower hinge about a foot from the floor, so that the lower edge of the hinge leaf lines up with the upper edge of the lower door rail. Locate the upper hinge about 10″ to 12″ from the top of the door.

Remove the pin from one of the hinges and place the leaf of the hinge on the door edge. Mark around the hinge leaf with a pencil or the point of a knife. On the back edge of the door, mark a line to indicate the width and the thickness or depth of the hinge leaf. Make the necessary undercut on the door edge to fit the leaf of the hinge. With a chisel and hammer, cut along the marked lines on the door edge, as shown in Fig. 20. Continue by making several cuts to approximately the depth of the under-cut, as shown in the same illustration. With a chisel, pare out

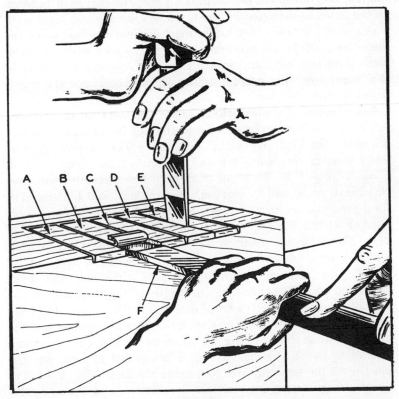

Fig. 20.

the material to be removed, exercising extreme care not to make the undercut too deep. Take light paring cuts with the chisel and from time to time test the depth of the undercut with the hinge leaf. If the undercut is too deep, the door will bind against the jamb and will strain the hinge screws when it is closed. If the undercut is not deep enough, the door will not close properly.

Mark the screw holes in the proper position, drill the holes, and with screws of correct size attach the hinge leaf to the door. Attach the second hinge in the same manner.

Now assemble the leaves of the hinges and insert the pins. Hold the door in position in the doorway and mark the hinge positions on the jamb to correspond with the positions of the hinges on the door. Remove the door and separate the leaves of the hinges by removal of the pins. Place the leaves in position on the jamb, as indicated by the markings just made. Then, with a pencil or the point of a knife, mark around the outline of the hinge leaf. Make the necessary undercut as previously outlined. Drill the screw holes and secure the hinge leaves with screws of the proper size. Place the door in position and fasten the leaves together with the pins.

Installation of door locks. Locks are installed or attached to doors in different ways. The method of installation is determined by the kind or type of lock used. The various types of locks used in the home are fully described and illustrated in Chap. 3 (page 104). In terms of installation, there are four main classifications of locks: mortise, bore-in, rim, and half-mortise. As a general rule, mortise locks, so called because they are mortised or set into the door edge, are used for all outside doors (Fig. 21). To mark the positions of the knob spindle hole, keyhole and lock edge, lay the lock against the side of the door. After making the necessary markings remove the lock and make new markings which must be the width of the thickness of the lock cover plate that is to be placed in the door edge. Drill the necessary holes of adequate size for both the keyhole and the knob spindle as shown in Fig. 21. Extend the lock edge markings around to the door edge. Using a brace and bit, cut out the mortise to the size required to receive the lock (Fig. 22). For directions on cutting out mortises, see Mortise and Tenon Joints, Chap. 3.

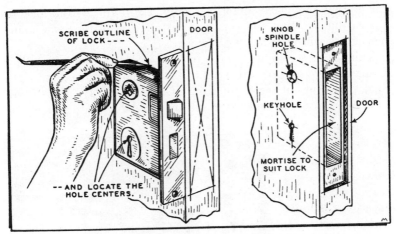

Fig. 21. Locating and installing mortise door lock.

Place the lock into the mortise and, with the point of a knife or pencil, accurately mark around the cover plate. Make the necessary undercut, following the directions just given for the undercuts of hinge leaves. This undercut must be just deep enough to permit the cover plate to fit flush with the door edge (Fig. 22). Install the lock, securing it in place with screws of the proper size and then also attach with screws the keyhole, knobs, and spindle plate.

To determine the position of the striking plate, close the door and operate both the lock and latch so that the jamb can be marked for installation of the plate. Open the door, but hold the plate in place and make a pencil mark around the plate. Make an undercut in the jamb into which the plate will fit. Hold the plate in position in the undercut and mark the jamb for mortising. With a ¼" chisel, make the necessary mortises into the jamb to a depth sufficient for both lock bolt and latch action. Test for proper mortise depth by working the latch and lock, before attaching the striking plate to the jamb with screws of the correct size.

Bore-in locks are generally used for interior doors and are comparatively easy to install. They are installed in two holes, that are bored in the edge and in the stile of the door (Fig. 23). The procedure for cutting the mortise for the lock front is identical to that previously described (Fig. 22). Install the lock in the cut-out mortise, and complete installation in the same manner as described for mortise locks.

Tubular lock sets are a type of bore-in locks, easily installed. Using the template provided with the lock, bore two holes at right angles and cut out recess for front of lock (Fig. 24). This small cross-bore also conserves strength of the door. Adjustment for

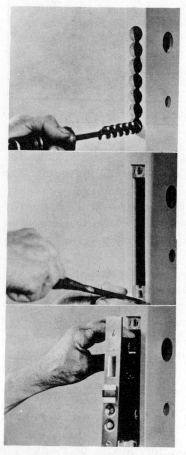 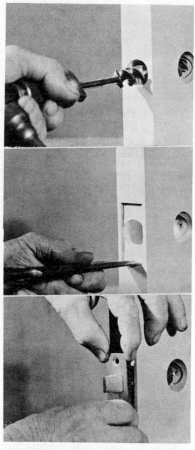

Fig. 22. Installation of a mortise lock: Top, bore holes in edge and stile; center, cut and complete with chisel; bottom, install lock.

Fig. 23. Installation of bore-in lock: Top, bore holes in edge and stile; center, cut mortise for lock front; bottom, install lock.

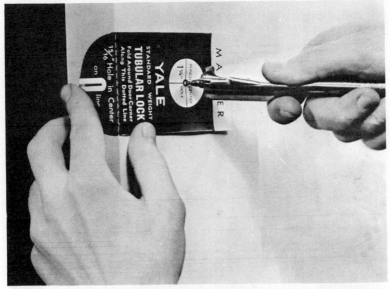

Fig. 24. Using template for locating and boring holes necessary for installation of a tubular lock.

door thickness is made by screwing outside rose to align center of lock with recess in edge of door. The inside springclamp of the locknut compensates for any dimensional changes in the wood. The latchbolt unit is inserted and interlocked with outside knob unit by merely turning the knob. Tighten inside locknut with spanner wrench or screwdriver, snap rose onto springclamp, then snap on inner knob, and the new lockset is durably and securely installed. Fig. 25 shows the four basic steps for the installation of a tubular lock.

Rim locks (copies of colonial box locks) are sometimes chosen for appearances. Night latches are the only rim locks widely used on full-size doors. These locks are placed on the surface of the door and are easily installed by simply boring a hole for the cylinder.

Half-mortise locks are generally used on cabinet doors and drawers. These are installed by cutting a recess on the inside surface of the drawer and boring a hole for the cylinder or tube of the lock.

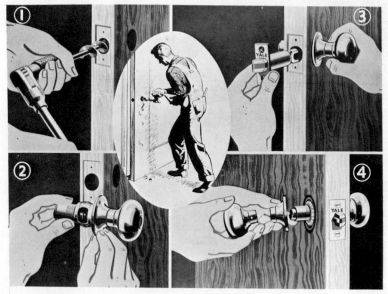

Fig. 25. Progressive steps for the installation of a tubular lock.

WINDOWS

Two kinds of windows are in general use: The casement and the double-hung. The *casement* window consists of one sash, usually metal, which is attached to each side of the window frame with hinges. When this type of window requires adjustment, it is necessary only to tighten or replace the hinge screws.

The *double-hung* window is most commonly used. It consists of two movable sashes, both assembled in the window frame, which is mounted in the wall (Fig. 26). Cords to which weights are attached run over pulleys and down both sides of each sash (Fig. 26). The weights move up and down in pockets on each side of the frame when either or both of the sashes are raised and lowered. A discussion follows of the various adjustments and repairs required by this type of window.

Fixing tight double-hung window sashes. Tight window sashes are caused by hardened paint in one or more of the grooves of the window frame in which the sashes slide, or by shrinkage or

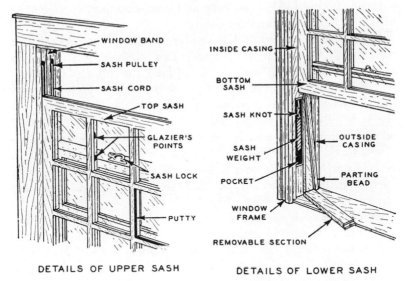

DETAILS OF UPPER SASH   **DETAILS OF LOWER SASH**

Fig. 26. Details of a double-hung window sash.

swelling of the sashes or frame, or by the settling of the walls or foundation of the house.

When paint has worked in and hardened between the edges of a sash and its groove, the molding that forms the front edge of the groove must be removed before the paint can be scraped or sanded off. If the molding is secured by screws, remove the screws, then the molding. If it is nailed, carefully work a putty knife or other thin blade under the molding to pry the nails loose. Pull out the nails with the claw of a tack hammer, using a block of wood under the hammer to prevent marring the surface of the molding. With the putty knife, scrape off the paint and smooth the surface with No. 000 sandpaper. Clean the surface with turpentine and then rub a small quantity of paraffin or wax on the groove. Replace the molding.

Tight window sashes are also caused by a swollen sash or a swollen bead molding, which forms the channel in which the sash slides. To remedy this condition, sand the beading until enough material has been removed to facilitate the sliding of the sash. However, when the condition is too severe, pare the beading with a chisel, taking light, even cuts and removing just enough material so that the sash slides easily.

If both the beading and the sash are swollen, it is necessary to remove the sash from the frame. This procedure is described below; see Replacing sash cords. Plane the sides of the sash with a jointer plane, taking light, even cuts and making careful tests between each cut to avoid removing too much material from the sash. Before replacing the sash, put a thin coat of linseed oil on the edges of the sash and in the grooves of the frame.

The binding or sticking of lower window sashes sometimes can be relieved by pulling on the sash cords and letting them snap back quickly. A few drops of linseed oil poured down the grooves also helps considerably.

Replacing sash cords. The initial step in replacing a broken sash cord is to remove the sash from the window frame. First, detach the molding that is screwed or nailed to the frame. Do this carefully, as described above, to avoid splitting or damaging the finish of the molding. Turn the lower sash partly sideways and remove it from the frame.

If the broken cord is attached to the lower sash, slip the knot on the end of the cord out of the hole in the sash. When doing this, use extreme care to prevent the knot on the good cord from slipping out of the hole, since this would permit the sash weight to drop and possibly snap the good cord when the knot hits the pulley. To remove the upper sash, it is necessary to remove the lower sash first. Then take out the beading strip that separates the two sashes and turn the upper sash partly sideways for removal.

The strip of wood that forms the sash-weight pocket cover in the side of the window frame must be taken out. It usually is found at the lower end of the groove in which the lower sash moves and is held in place by one or more screws. Unscrew and remove this cover to gain access to the sash weights.

Tie a knot in one end of the new cord and, making the necessary allowance for the knot at the other end, measure the correct length for the new sash cord. Thread the unknotted end over the pulley and down into the sash-weight pocket, drawing the cord out through the opening and tying it to the sash weight with a square or bowline knot.

Then bring the sash into position, set the knot into the hole in the sash, and replace the sash in the window frame. Replace the sash-weight pocket cover, beading, and molding in their original positions.

When sash chains are used instead of cord, a link of the chain is opened with a pair of pliers and is secured to the sash weight, then reclosed with the pliers.

Replacing broken windowpanes. Windowpanes are usually held in place with small, three-pointed metal fasteners called *glazier's points* and a triangular beading of putty. These triangular points are available in several sizes, ranging from No. 00, the largest, to No. 3. As a rule, Nos. 1 and 2 are the sizes used. Glazier's putty is available in cans of various sizes.

To replace a broken windowpane, carefully remove all the broken pieces and scrape off the old putty and glazier's points with a scraper. Spread a thin layer of putty on the back of the *rabbet,* or groove (Fig. 27). The thin layer of putty provides a seal between the glass and the inner part of the sash.

With a glass cutter, cut the glass to the required size. (For specific directions on the use of a glass cutter see Chap. 2, page **93.**) Press the new pane of glass firmly into place

Fig. 27. Replacing a windowpane.

against the layer of putty and keep pressing it around the edges until the putty has been spread evenly between the glass and the edge of the rabbet.

Lay the glazier's points against the pane, about 3″ apart, so that the points are toward the wooden sash. With a light tack hammer drive them carefully into the sash to about half their length. Repeat this all around the pane.

Since putty does not adhere to bare wood, apply as preliminary priming a thin coating of linseed oil. Roll some putty between your hands to form a rope approximately ¼″ in diameter. Lay the rope of putty around the edge of the pane. Press it firmly into place with a putty knife to form a neat triangular beading that adheres to both the wood and the pane.

Allow at least a week for the putty to set and dry before painting. When painting putty, allow the paint to overlap about ⅛″ onto the glass pane. Overlapping seals the joint between the glass and the putty and retards the entrance of moisture, which would harden the putty and loosen the seal.

Applying weather stripping. Weather strips are used to close the joints around window sashes and doorframes; efficient weather stripping retains indoor temperature, checks the entrance of air and moisture, and results in a fuel saving of 15 to 25 per cent.

Many kinds of weather stripping are available. Some are flexible; others are rigid. The type commonly used by the home craftsman is a commercial product available at all hardware dealers. Made of a specially treated, flexible felt that is nominal in cost, easily installed, and efficient in operation, it is the most practical kind of stripping to use and, though not permanent, will last for several seasons. It may be attached to window sashes and doorframes with small tacks or brads.

To apply flexible weather stripping on double-hung windows, first close the windows. Fasten to the outside of the window frame, as close as possible to the sash, the weather stripping for the upper, or outer, sash. Then fasten the stripping for the inside of the upper sash on the inside stop-bead molding of the window frame. For the lower, or inner, sash, fasten a piece of stripping to each side and also to the bottom, so that the stripping will fit snugly against the sill of the window. Fasten a final piece of stripping to the top of the lower sash, in order to cover the crack between the upper and the lower sash. The same procedure is followed when using rigid weather stripping.

Rigid weather stripping makes for a more permanent job. It is made of light-gauge metal with a felt interior that projects just far enough to form a tight seal between the sash and the window frame. The manufacturers of rigid weather stripping provide a small cardboard gauge to aid in locating the stripping correctly along the frame and sash before it is nailed in place. The use of this gauge insures a weathertight stripping job and eliminates binding of the sash and damage to the stripping caused by its improper placement.

When applying rigid stripping, miter the corners of the stripping to make effective weathertight joints. All measurements must be absolutely correct before the strips are cut. Miters are cut with a hacksaw and miter box (see Jointing in Chap. 3 for a discussion of this).

Either flexible or rigid weather stripping can be used on steel casement windows. The felt weather stripping must be secured with a special adhesive and the rigid stripping with special clamps available for that purpose. Before using the adhesive, which may be a type of thick shellac, amberoid, or metallic cement called *liquid solder*, make certain that the metal window frames have been thoroughly scraped and cleaned of paint, rust, or corrosion and wiped with benzine. Do not apply the adhesive before the window is completely dry.

A special type of weather stripping is available for metal-framed casement windows. It is made to snap into the grooves along the edges of the sash and is held in position by the springiness of the metal itself. In fitting and securing this type of weather stripping, check all measurements carefully before cutting the material.

Eliminating window-frame leaks. Window frames are tightly fitted to the walls; in houses of good construction, the joints between both the frames and the walls are closed with sheet-metal flashings and building paper along the sides and bottoms. Even with sheet-metal flashings, the shrinkage of the wood sometimes opens the joints between the window frames and the walls, creating cracks that admit air and rain. Leaks of this type result in smudges on the inside wall areas adjacent to the window frames. It is important that such cracks be closed.

In some types of construction, the joints between the window frames and the walls are covered with either moldings or flat strips. To get at window-frame leaks, remove the strips by prying them loose with a prying bar to expose the joints. Then use a flat-ended dowel stick to force tow into the open joints to within approximately ¾" of the surface. *Tow* is a material made of the coarse part of flax or hemp and can be secured at a marine supply house.

Fill the remaining space with a *calking compound*, which can be secured at a hardware or paint store. It has the consistency of soft putty and never becomes quite hard. While a hard skin forms on the surface, the underpart remains pliable enough to take up any subsequent expansion or contraction of wood or other material and thus prevents further leakage. Force the calking compound into the cracks with a putty knife or similar tool, and allow it to set for several days. Then replace the moldings or strips that were removed.

CHAPTER 18

Interior Woodworking Projects

PLANNING THE WORKSHOP

In planning the home workshop consideration must not only be given to present equipment and requirements, but also to proper provision for accommodating any additional tools and equipment that may be added later on.

Generally, space that cannot be utilized for any other purpose in the basement, attic, or garage can be used for the home workshop. This space need not be large. An efficient workshop accommodating a work bench and as many as four power tools (that may be acquired at some future time) will not require a space larger than 4′ × 12′ (Fig. 1).

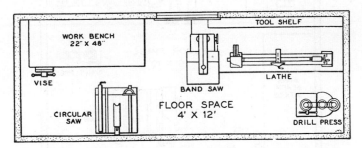

Fig. 1. Floor plan showing arrangement of a small workshop using power tools.

Where a larger space is available and a more elaborate workshop is desired the floor plans shown in Figs. 2 and 3 can be adapted to any particular requirement.

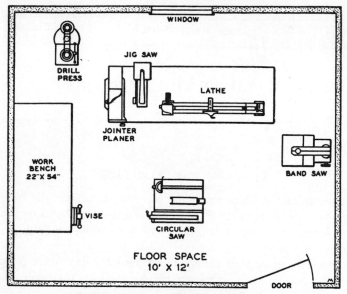

Fig. 2. Efficient workshop floor plan.

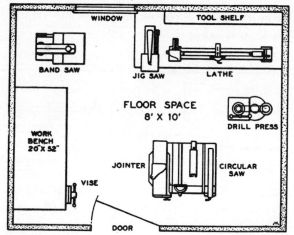

Fig. 3. Another efficient workshop floor plan.

CONSTRUCTING A WORKBENCH AND TOOL RACK

The construction of the woodworking bench and tool rack shown in Fig. 4 is a simple project that requires a minimum

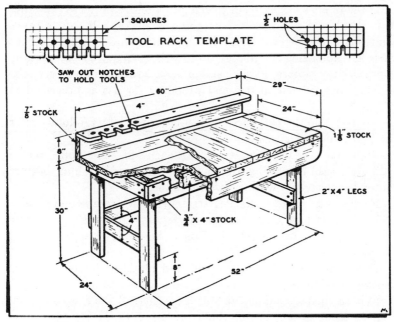

Fig. 4. Working drawings of workbench and tool rack.

amount of tools and material. Workbenches are subjected to hard usage; therefore it is good practice to secure straight, high-grade, kiln-dried birch or pine for the body of the bench, and maple for the working top. Lumber required is as follows:

BILL OF MATERIALS

Pieces	Part	Size		
4	Legs, each	$2''$	$\times 4'$	$\times 30''$
2	Top (inner) leg stretchers	$2''$	$\times 2''$	$\times 16''$
2	Top (inner) leg stretchers	$2''$	$\times 2''$	$\times 48''$
4	Top and bottom (outer) leg stretchers	$\frac{3}{4}'' \times 4''$		$\times 24''$
3	Top and back (outer) leg stretchers	$\frac{3}{4}'' \times 4''$		$\times 53\frac{1}{2}''$
6	Bottom section of top (dressed and matched) each	$\frac{3}{4}'' \times 5''$		$\times 60''$
1	Front apron	$\frac{3}{4}'' \times 6''$		$\times 60''$
1	Back (for tool rack)	$\frac{3}{4}'' \times 7\frac{1}{4}''$		$\times 60''$
1	Tool rack	$\frac{3}{4}'' \times 4''$		$\times 60''$
12	Working top (maple or other hardwood)	$1\frac{1}{8}'' \times 5''$		$\times 24''$

If the lumber has been cut to size, the tools required to construct this bench and tool rack are: a compass or keyhole saw, a brace and bit, and a screwdriver. If the lumber has not been cut to size, the following additional tools will be required: a marking gauge, a try square, a rule, and a saw. In the latter case, the lumber must be cut to size and prepared for use as described in Chap. 3.

To assemble the cut pieces of lumber, proceed as follows (refer to Fig. 4 throughout):

Measure 8″ from bottom of each of the four pieces (2″ × 4″ × 30″) forming the legs and fasten the four bottom outer leg stretchers with screws and glue.

Fasten the four top outer leg stretchers with screws and glue.

Fasten the four top inner leg stretchers with screws and glue to the top outer leg stretchers. Space these screws approximately 4″ apart.

Screw the six pieces of dressed and matched lumber forming bottom section of top of bench onto the frame.

With a chisel round off the bottom corners of the 6′ board forming the front apron. Fasten this front apron to the bottom section of the top. For instructions covering rounding of corners with chisel, see Chap. 2.

With a ⅜″ bit and brace and a ½″ countersink, drill and countersink three holes, 6″ apart, through each of the 12 pieces of maple or hardwood forming the working top of the bench. For directions on drilling and countersinking, see Chap. 2.

With a chisel, cut a bevel on one end of each of these 12 pieces.

Screw the 12 pieces forming the working top onto the bottom section of top.

Fill countersunk screw holes with plastic wood.

Secure the piece forming the back for the tool rack with screws and glue.

Make a template of cardboard to use in marking the holes to be drilled and the notches to be cut out of the tool rack. These notches and holes, spaced at intervals of 4″ to 5″, are used to hold chisels, files and similar tools.

With a ½″ bit and brace drill holes for small tools and cut out notches with a keyhole or compass saw. For directions on the use of compass and keyhole saws see Chap. 2.

Round off two outer corners of the tool rack and fasten it to the back with screws.

Sandpaper entire job.

Suggestions for finishing. The top of the woodworking bench should be finished with linseed oil. Other parts of the bench, including the tool rack, should be oil-stained and varnished.

BOOK AND MAGAZINE TABLE

Low lines, an interesting surfboard shape and a slight tilt to the end panel give this useful book and magazine table character and grace (Fig. 5).

The sturdy, unusual legs can be fabricated easily from aluminum tubing. The plan shown in Fig. 6 gives all the information required. To take care of minor variations in angle and dimensions, you probably will save yourself extra work by having the legs bent before beveling and drilling the bottom shelf, and cutting partition (C) to proper height.

Paint the legs with flat black enamel or in a color to contrast with the shelves.

Cut, rabbet, dado and drill all parts as required. Sand and

SIDE ELEVATION

END ELEVATION

CUTTING DIAGRAM

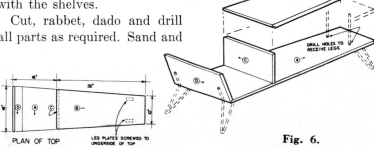

PLAN OF TOP

LEG PLATES SCREWED TO UNDERSIDE OF TOP

Fig. 6.

Fig. 5.

PARTS REQUIRED

CODE	NO. REQ'D	SIZE	PART IDENTIFICATION
A	1	16″x44¾″	Bottom Shelf
B	1	16″x32″	Top Shelf
C	1	7¼″x14″	Divider
D	1	8½″x16″	End
	2 Sets	½″ Diameter	Wrought Iron Legs
	2 Ea.	1″x2½″x⅛″	Leg Plates

Miscellaneous—6d Finish Nails and Glue
1″ No. 8 R. H. Screws as required

fill exposed edges, and fit mating parts together. Glue and nail all the joints.

Fasten end (D) to bottom shelf (A). Nail partition (C) in slot, then support shelf (B) on a block while attaching to (C). Some adjustment for length of legs can be obtained by drilling blind holes underneath top shelf. Plates can be threaded up or down a few turns for positive location.

Install legs after finishing as recommended, making sure the threaded ends of the legs at open end of rack are exactly vertical.

TELEPHONE BENCH

A massive, expensive-looking effect is achieved at little cost in this design of telephone bench, through applying beveled wood molding to the edges of inexpensive fir plywood (Fig. 7).

Take the plan shown in Fig. 8 to any welding or metal work shop to have the steel

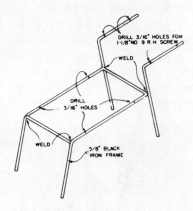

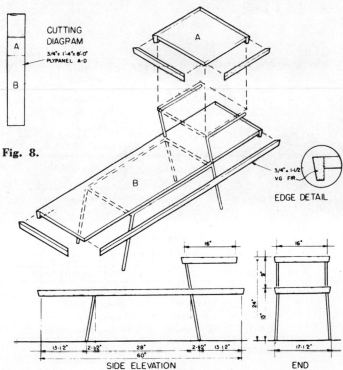

Fig. 8.

frame and legs fabricated, or, if you can, do it yourself. Aluminum tubing can be used for the steel frame and legs, if desired, which is easily formed. Finish in flat black enamel or in a color that contrasts with bench and shelf or in natural aluminum.

Tilt the bench panel and notched edges will fit around frame. Nail and glue molding mitred to fit around plywood panels screwed to frame. Protect the frame with masking tape while finishing as recommended.

Fig. 7.

PARTS REQUIRED

CODE	NO. REQ'D	SIZE	PART IDENTIFICATION
A	1	16"x16"	Top Shelf
B	1	16"x60"	Seat
	16 Lin. Ft.	¾"x1½"	Edging
	1 Only	⅝" Diameter	Wrought Iron Frame

MISCELLANEOUS—6d Finish Nails and Glue
1⅛'' No. 9 R. H. Screws as required
Finishing Materials

BUILT-IN MAGAZINE AND BOOK RACK

Complete flexibility to fit nearly any circumstance features this built-in magazine and book rack (Fig. 9). Contract, lengthen or expand it vertically by changing its dimensions.

Assemble the wall cabinet before hanging on stringers. All joints should be glued and nailed. Cut parts according to the diagrams shown in Fig. 10 and parts list, rabbet ends, dado top and bottom panels for

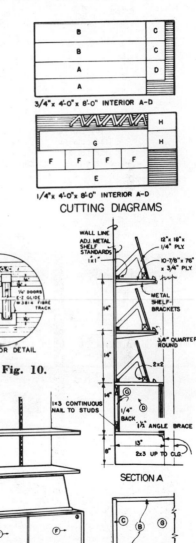

3/4" x 4'-0" x 8'-0" INTERIOR A-D

1/4" x 4'-0" x 8'-0" INTERIOR A-D

CUTTING DIAGRAMS

BRACKET
(MAKE NINE)

SLIDING DOOR DETAIL

Fig. 10.

SECTION A

END DETAIL
FRONT VIEW

PARTS REQUIRED

CODE	NO. REQ'D	SIZE	PART IDENTIFICATION
A	2	10⅞ x 76''	Shelf
B	2	13'' x 76''	Top and Bottom
C	2	13'' x 13¼''	End
D	1	11¾'' x 12½''	Standard
E	1	12'' x 76''	Shelf Back
F	4	12-13/16''x18-13/16''	Sliding Doors
G	1	12½'' x 74½''	Back of Unit
H	2	12'' x 18''	Shelf Back
	9	See Drawing	Bracket
	10½ Lin. Ft.	2'' x 2''	Back Stop
	10½ Lin. Ft.	1'' x 1''	Blocking for Bracket
	13 Lin. Ft.	1'' x 3''	Cabinet Support
	20 Lin. Ft.	¾'' Quarter Round	Magazine Support
	1 Pc.	2'' x 3''—8'-0'' Long	Wood Stanchion
	16 Lin. Ft.	Adjustable	Metal Shelf Standard
	8 Ea.	As Req'd.	Metal Shelf Brackets
	1 Ea.	1½''	Angle Brace

MISCELLANEOUS—4d and 6d finish nails & brads
glue and finishing materials.

Fig. 9.

doors, sand edges and check fit of all mating parts.

Nail ends and divider to top and. bottom and check to be sure cabinet is square.

Nail 1″ x 3″ stringers to wall studs, level with floor. When you apply back (G), heads of large nails will be covered. Leave space for cabinet end, if installing at a corner.

Hang cabinet by nailing through top panel into stringer.

Bandsaw magazine rack brackets to shape, sand edges and nail into ends of 1″ x 1″ and beveled 2″ x 2″ blocking nailed to shelves. Glue and nail sloping racks to blocks and brackets, and install quarter-round along shelf edges.

Use 1½″ angle brace to attach cabinet to post, which should be a snug fit between floor and ceiling.

Finish completely as desired, slip sliding doors in place and install shelves on adjustable brackets at wall stud locations.

ROOM DIVIDER WITH STORAGE SPACE

By using various multiples of individual units as shown in Fig. 11, this room divider fills any space attractively and usefully. Cabinets may be either drawer or door sections, depending on your need and use.

Cutting diagrams (Fig. 12) and the parts list provide four sections as illustrated.

Butt joints in cabinets, which should be glued and nailed, simplify construction.

When parts are cut and fitted for the sections you select, nail sides (E) or (L) to bottoms (B) or (I). Then install backs and tops. Square up each assembly perfectly before driving nails flush.

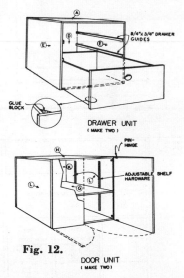

DRAWER UNIT
(MAKE TWO)

Fig. 12.

DOOR UNIT
(MAKE TWO)

Drawer guides can be positioned most easily before assembly.

Nail drawer sides and back to bottom, then install front panel after fitting drawer in place in the cabinet.

Paint cabinets as desired before hanging on partition posts and installing hardware.

Nail 1 x 4 strip to ceiling and nail first dadoed post to wall (at a stud, if possible).

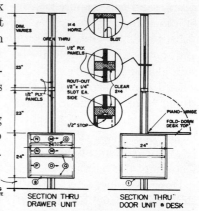

SECTION THRU DRAWER UNIT

SECTION THRU DOOR UNIT & DESK

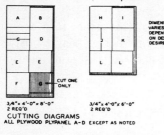

3/4" x 4'-0" x 8'-0"
2 REQ'D

3/4" x 4'-0" x 6'-0"
2 REQ'D

CUTTING DIAGRAMS
ALL PLYWOOD PLYPANEL A-D EXCEPT AS NOTED

DIMENSION VARIES — DEPENDING ON DESK HT DESIRED.

Support cabinet at desired height on blocks and drive screws through side into that post. Slip lower square panel (completely finished) into dadoed slot, with bottom edge resting on cabinet, then toe-nail cross-member to post. Insert top partition panel in slots, fit and position each post, and attach cabinet with screws. Repeat procedure for each section.

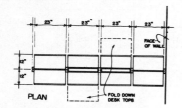

PLAN

FOLD DOWN DESK TOPS

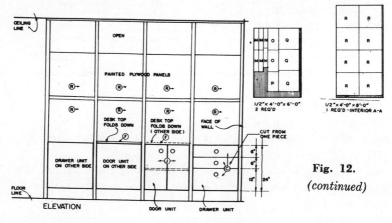

ELEVATION

DOOR UNIT

DRAWER UNIT

1/2" x 4'-0" x 6'-0"
2 REQ'D

1/2" x 4'-0" x 8'-0"
1 REQ'D -INTERIOR A-A

Fig. 12.

(continued)

Fig. 11.

PARTS REQUIRED

CODE	NO. REQ'D	SIZE	PART IDENTIFICATION
A	2	22½'' x 23''	Top of Drawer Unit
B	2	21'' x 23''	Bottom of Drawer Unit
C	2	23'' x 24''	Drawer Fronts
D	2	23'' x 24''	Back of Drawer Unit
E	4	22½'' x 23¼''	Side of Drawer Unit
F	2	23'' x 23''	Desk Top
G	2	21¼'' x 22½''	Adjustable Shelf
H	2	22½'' x 23''	Top of Door Unit
I	2	21'' x 23''	Bottom of Door Unit
J	2	23 ' x 24''	Door
K	2	23'' x 24''	Back of Door Unit
L	4	22½'' x 23¼''	Side of Door Unit
M	8	4¾'' x 22½''	Drawer Side
N	4	4¾'' x 20⅜''	Drawer Back
O	4	10¾'' x 22½''	Drawer Side
P	2	10¾'' x 20⅜''	Drawer Back
Q	6	20⅝'' x 22'	Drawer Bottom
R	8	23¼'' x 23½''	Plywood Panels
	48 L. F.	2'' x 4'' Clear	Partition Framing
	9 L. F.	1'' x 4'' Clear	Nailing Strip
	2 L. F.	2'' x 2'' Cut Diagonally	Glue Block—Drawer
	8 L. F.	¾'' x ¾''	Drawer Guides
	12 Ea.		Door, Drwr. & Desk Top Pulls
	4 Pr.		Pin Hinges
	6 L. F.		Adjustable Shelf Hardware
	6 Ea.		Door & Desk Top Catches
	4 L. F.		Piano Hinge

MISCELLANEOUS—6d and 8d finish nails and glue
finishing materials

RECORD PLAYER AND RADIO CABINET

Figure 13 shows an attractive record player and radio cabinet that can be constructed with simple hand tools.

This plan (Fig. 14) does not give exact dimensions for certain parts because components which may be installed vary greatly. Determine space your equipment requires before laying out plywood.

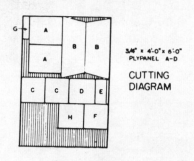

3/4" x 4'-0" x 6'-0"
PLYPANEL A-D

CUTTING
DIAGRAM

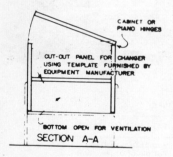

CABINET OR
PIANO HINGES

CUT-OUT PANEL FOR CHANGER
USING TEMPLATE FURNISHED BY
EQUIPMENT MANUFACTURER

BOTTOM OPEN FOR VENTILATION
SECTION A-A

Cut all similar dimensions on mating or related parts without changing saw setting. All joints should be nailed and glued. Drill panels (F) and (H) for equipment before assembly.

First nail two sides (B) to ends (C), (E) to (H), and (D) to (G). Then install the shelves

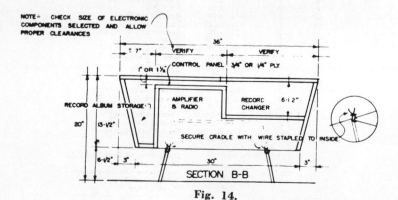

NOTE: CHECK SIZE OF ELECTRONIC COMPONENTS SELECTED AND ALLOW PROPER CLEARANCES

36"

7" VERIFY VERIFY

OR 1½" CONTROL PANEL 3/4" OR 1/4" PLY

RECORD ALBUM STORAGE

AMPLIFIER B RADIO

RECORD CHANGER 6-12"

20" 13-1/2"

SECURE CRADLE WITH WIRE STAPLED TO INSIDE

6-1/2" 5" 30" 3"

SECTION B-B

Fig. 14.

and vertical dividers according to bracing required. Amplifier and radio hang from control panel (F). If this is not practical for the chassis you have, install a half-shelf between the sides, which still will provide ventilation.

Finish completely as desired, attach to welded cradle and install hardware and components. Connect a remote speaker.

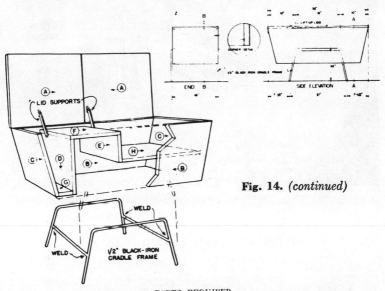

Fig. 14. *(continued)*

PARTS REQUIRED

CODE	NO. REQ'D	SIZE	PART IDENTIFICATION
A	2	16'' x 18''	Lid
B	2	12¾'' x 36''	Side
C	2	13¾'' x 14½''	End
D	1	11'' x 14½''	Vertical Divider
E	1	5½'' x 14½''	Vertical Divider
F	1	* x 14½''	Control Panel
G	1	± 3¼'' x 14½''	Bottom – Record Storage
H	1	* x 14½''	Record Changer Support
	1 Only	½'' Diameter	Wrought Iron Cradle Frame
	2		Metal Lid Supports
	4		Cabinet Hinges

Miscellaneous: 6d finish nails and glue
Screws, wire and staples as required
Finishing materials
* Dimensions vary – see drawings

Fig. 13.

HI-FIDELITY AND TV ROOM DIVIDER

Fig. 15.

Fig. 16.

This handsome music center (Figs. 15, 16, and 17) demonstrates rather dramatically that solutions to requirements of a particular situation or a combination of circumstances create the most successful designs.

In this case, (1) room acoustics dictated a change in speaker location from midpoint on the long living room wall; (2) it was hoped that the TV set could be seen either from the kitchen in one direction or the living room in the other; (3) storage space should be provided for a large number of long play record albums; (4) a room divider was needed between

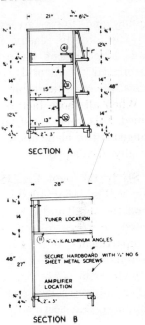

SECTION A

SECTION B

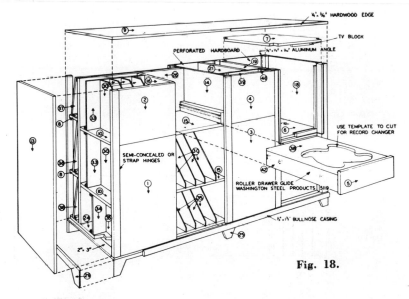

Fig. 18.

dining and living areas; and (5) an orderly, easily accessible arrangement for a large assortment of monthly magazines was most desirable.

When all those factors combined, this very satisfying arrangement of elements just naturally developed.

Study the plan Fig. 18 and you will see that all space behind the left hand door is devoted to three record album compartments only. If that exceeds your needs greatly, or if your room is not big enough for a cabinet seven feet long, eliminate that section.

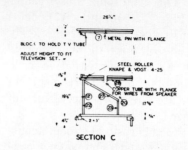

SECTION C

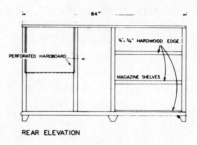

REAR ELEVATION

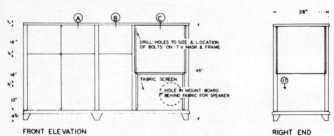

FRONT ELEVATION

RIGHT END

Fig. 18. *(continued)*

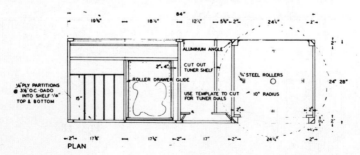

PLAN

Dimensions given make it possible to cut all parts before assembly, but minor variations that generally crop out in a project this large make it advisable to cut and fit as you go. Identical dimensions on mating or matching parts still should be cut at the same time without changing saw setting for perfect fit.

Glue and nail all the joints. Start at the base. Nail the mitred plywood legs to the rabbeted 2″ x 3″ frame. Dado bottom panel 24 for record album partitions and notch edges for 2″ x 2″ posts, 1″ x 2″ stiles and speaker mounting board before nailing to base.

Nail all posts and stiles, divider panels 14 and 20, and ends 13 and 17 in place next. Notice that a diagonal section is removed from the four posts about 18″ above the base. Exact length of these segments depends on the height of the TV chassis your turntable must accommodate, as they are used later for corner posts in the sub-assembly for the TV turntable.

Before installing shelves, construct the air-tight speaker enclosure shown in Section C. Dimensions and form shown were specified for the 10″

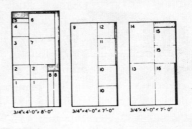

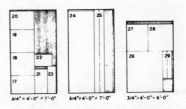

Fig. 18. *(continued)*

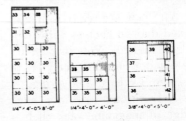

ALL PLYWOOD PLYPANEL A-D
CUTTING DIAGRAMS

speaker used in this installation. To modify for a 12″, 15″ or co-axial speaker, consult your high-fidelity supplier. Line all surfaces of the enclosure completely with 1″ glass fiber sound absorbing blanket, to control resonance.

Fig. 17.

You now are ready to install fixed dadoed shelves with panels 16 and 26. *Note* that an arc is cut out of tuner shelf 11, to let the TV turntable swing.

Nail through 26 into back edge of magazine rack shelves 8. Bevel cleats, magazine rack panels, hardwood edge and ¼-round stop can be installed any time.

Leave space open behind panels 33 and 34, to run wiring. Cut, fit and drill your tuner control panel and install with diagonal masks 40 and partition 21.

Assemble record changer carriage after checking model you

are installing to be sure you allow ample clearance for its enclosed mechanism and to pass center stile, with sliding hardware in place.

Cut, fit, drill and attach fixed shelf 28 below TV turntable. Face the upper surface with a disc of stiff plastic laminate to provide a smooth, hard track for rollers.

As a sub-assembly, join turntable top, bottom and end panels with segments from 2″ x 2″ corner posts, after checking fit in place and notching, drilling, mortising and installing rollers and pivots as shown. Attach strips shown on either side of the picture tube opening and blocks shown above and below. Lift sub-assembly over posts into socket for pivot tube.

Drill socket in underside of top panel 9 for upper turntable pivot and attach top to posts, dividers and end 13. Nail front panel 3 in place; the amplifier can be installed through back before you install corresponding perforated panel.

Using 4d finish nails and glue, attach mitred hardwood edge around top and bullnose casing around base. These do not extend around left end in front elevation, since cabinet was built to project from wall.

Finish unit completely as desired. Slip partitions in place and hinge doors. Move into position and slide TV set into turntable compartment through back. Install and connect speaker, amplifier, tuners and changer. Apply grill cloth with prefinished molding. Attach back panels to aluminum angles for ventilation.

PARTS REQUIRED

CODE	NO. REQ'D	SIZE	PART IDENTIFICATION
1	2	17⅜"x28⅛"	Doors
2	2	17⅜"x14⅜"	Doors
3	1	17"x28⅛"	Doors
4	1	17"x14⅜"	Doors
5	1	4¼"x16¼"	Changer Face
6	1	25⅛"x26¾"	Revolving Shelf
7	1	26¼"x26¾"	Revolving Top
8	2	6"x36¾"	Magazine Shelves
9	1	28"x84"	Top
10	2	18¾"x20¼"	Shelves
11	1	17½"x27"	Tuner Shelf
12	1	17"x17⅝"	Mount Board
13	1	26½"x42½"	End
14	1	26½"x41¾"	Standard
15	2	18⅛"x20¼"	Shelves
16	1	20¼"x41¾"	Standard
17	1	18⅜"x24"	End
18	1	23⅛"x24"	TV End
19	1	23⅛"x24"	TV Standard
20	1	18⅜"x24"	Standard
21	1	14"x24⅝"	Standard
22	1	11¾"x17⅝"	Speaker Frame
23	1	7½"x26¾"	Speaker Back
24	1	27"x82½"	Bottom

CODE	NO. REQ'D	SIZE	PART IDENTIFICATION
25	2	4⅜"x84"	Legs
26	1	36¾"x41¾"	Magazine Back
27	1	22"x26¾"	Speaker Top Enclosure
28	1	25⅞"x26¾"	TV Stationary Shelf
29	1	4⅜"x28"	Legs
30	12	14¼"x15"	Record Partitions
31	1	14"x17¾"	Record Backs
32	1	12¼"x17¾"	Record Backs
33	2	14"x18¼"	Record Backs
34	1	12¼"x18¼"	Record Backs
35	8	12½"x13"	Record Partitions
36	2	14⅝"x36¾"	Magazine Rack
37	1	12½"x36¾"	Magazine Rack
38	1	16"x19¼"	Changer Mount Bd.
39	1	14"x17¼"	Dial Panel
40	2	2½"x14"	Dial Panel Sides
41	1	3⅜"x15"	Changer Back
42	2	3⅜"x19¼"	Changer Sides
	28 Lin. Ft.	¼"x¾"	Hardwood Edging
	17 Lin. Ft.	½"x1½"	Bullnose Casing
	20 Lin. Ft.	2"x3"	Framing
	10 Lin. Ft.	½" Quarter Round	Stops for Magazines
	8 Lin. Ft.	⅝"x¾" net Moulding	For Fabric Screen
	2 Lin. Ft.	¾"x1⅝" net	Bottom Edge Facing—TV Cabinet
	2 Lin. Ft.	½"x1⅛" net	Bot. Edge Support—TV Set
	14 Lin. Ft.	1"x1" Nailer	Back of Record Partitions
	10 Lin. Ft.	¾"x¾" net	Stops and Facing
	1 Pc.	1⅝"x1¾"x6"	Block to Hold TV Tube
	20 Lin. Ft.	¾"x2" net	Stiles
	16 Lin. Ft.	2"x2" net	Vertical Framing
	12 Lin. Ft.	1"x2"	Cleat and Ledger
	2 Lin. Ft.	2"x4"	Blocking for Record Player
	1 Pc.	3/16"x4'-0"x4'-0"	Perforated Hardboard
	1 Ea.	1⅝" Diam.—3" Long	Copper Tube and Flange
	1 Ea.	¼" Dia.	Metal Pin with Flange
	4 Ea.	¾" Diam.	Steel Rollers
	1 Pr.	—	Drawer Guides for Changer
	5 Pr.	H-Type	Wrought-Iron Hinges
	5 Ea.	—	Wrought-Iron Door Pulls
	16 Lin. Ft.	½"x½"	Aluminum Angle

Miscellaneous—4d, 6d and 8d Finish Nails and Glue
F. H. and Sheet Metal Screws as required

PHOTOGRAPHY EQUIPMENT AND PROJECTOR CABINET

Protection for films, slides and equipment replaces possible damage and loss when this projector cabinet is put into use (Fig. 19). Also, it turns disorder and confusion, that so often handicap home film showings, into convenience and a smooth performance.

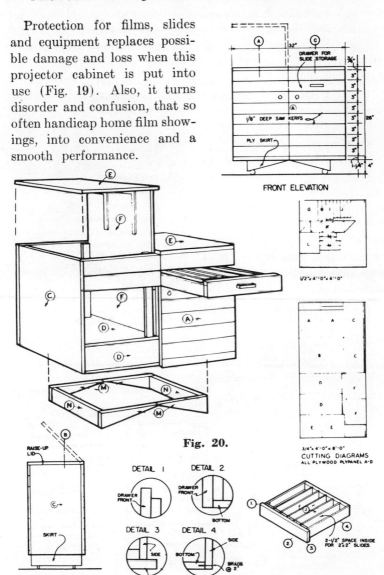

Fig. 20.

Saw framing members and structural plywood parts to exact size, sand edges and check mating parts for fit.

Use the same saw settings to groove panels (A) and (B) and to cut out doors, drawer front and facing strip as diagrammed from (A), to obtain uniform grain pattern (Fig. 20).

Glue and nail all joints.

Since you will not be able to nail through bottom panel (D) into skirt pieces after shelf (D) is in place, first attach skirt to bottom. For the same reason, nail shelf (D) to fixed divider (F) before assembly. Stand this sub-assembly on end to attach back; then fasten sides, storage compartment bottom

(L) and 32″ long facing strip cut from panel (A). It is necessary to nail through shelf into the end of 1″ x 2″ slide track, so that member should be installed before adding the bottom and skirt sub-assembly.

Fig. 19.

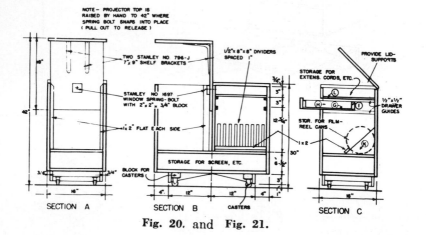

Fig. 20. and **Fig. 21.**

Now hang the doors. All door sliding panel and lid edges should be primed thoroughly after sanding, and it is important to apply equal finish coats to both inner and outer faces. Install drawer guides, film can partitions and lid. Drawer construction is clearly shown in detail in Fig. 20. Assemble sliding panel (F) and cabinet top. Finish as desired. Attach casters and hardware fittings. (See Fig. 21.)

PARTS REQUIRED

CODE	NO. REQ'D	SIZE	PART IDENTIFICATION
A	1	25¼"x32"	Front of Unit
B	1	25¼"x32"	Back of Unit
C	2	14½"x25¼"	Side of Unit
D	2	14½"x30½"	Bottom and Shelf
E	2	16"x16"	Projector Top and Lid
F	2	14½"x18"	Fixed and Sliding Standard
G	1	13⅜"x14½"	Drawer Bottom
H	2	3"x14½"	Drawer Side
I	2	2½"x13⅜"	Drawer Front and Back
J	5	2½"x12½"	Drawer Dividers
K	9	8"x8"	Reel Dividers
L	1	14½"x14½"	Bottom of Compartment
M	4	3"x12"	Skirt Board
N	2	3"x14½"	Skirt Board
	5 Lin. Ft.	¾"x¾"	Drawer Guides
	2½ Lin. Ft.	2"x3"	Caster Blocks
	1 Ea.	2"x2"x¾"	Spring Bolt Block
	4½ Lin. Ft.	1"x2"	Slide Track
	2 Ea.	7"x9"	Metal Shelf Brackets
	1 Only	No. 1697	Window Spring Bolt
	4 Ea.	—	Rubber Wheel Casters
	2 Ea.	—	Door Pulls
	1 Ea.	—	Drawer Pull
	2 Pr.	—	Pin Hinges

Miscellaneous—4d and 6d Finish Nails and Glue

BUILT-IN BAR CABINET

This built-in bar cabinet (Fig. 22) offers one of the best examples of how plywood simplifies and speeds construction. Rigid panels eliminate any need

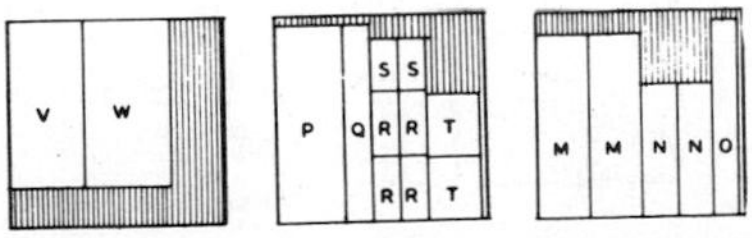

3/4" x 4'-0"x 4'-0"
PLYPANEL A-D

1/2"x 4'-0"x 4'-0"
PLYPANEL A-D

3/4"x 4'-0"x 4'-0"
PLYPANEL A-D

for the framing normally used in cabinets this large.

Cut parts to size, rabbet sides (A) ⅜″ deep for back panel and fit matching pieces together. To sides, join bottom shelf (B), facing strip (O), divider (Q), bottom (P) of light trough and partition (C), being careful to keep entire structure exactly square (Fig. 23). Glue and nail all the joints.

Next, fit and nail the brushed plywood back in place. Nail and glue brushed plywood to back of door material and cut

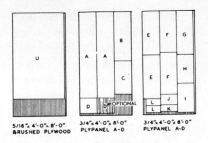

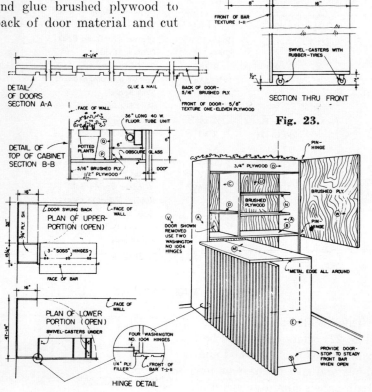

Fig. 23.

to size. Intermediate shelves may be nailed in position, or installed with adjustable shelf supports after finishing.

Before assembling the hinged front bar, notch partitions (F) and (K) for the 1″ x 4″ nailing strip across the top. Because working space is limited, assemble these partitions with fixed top (M), shelves (H), (I), (J), bottom (G) and hinged side (E) before exposed side (E) is installed. Apply texture one-eleven front, hinged top and casters last.

Move cabinet into place against wall and attach doors and hinged front bar after finishing as desired.

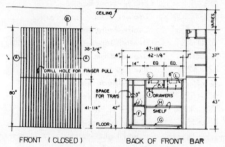

FRONT (CLOSED)   BACK OF FRONT BAR

Fig. 23. *(continued)*

Fig. 22.

PARTS REQUIRED

CODE	NO. REQ'D	SIZE	PART IDENTIFICATION
A	2	16"x80"	Side—Back Bar
B	1	15⅝"x45¾"	Lower Shelf—Back Bar
C	1	15⅝"x30½"	Standard—Back Bar
D	1	14⅛"x15⅝"	Shelf—Back Bar
E	2	15½"x40¾"	Side—Front Bar
F	2	15½"x38½"	Standard—Front Bar
G	1	15½"x40¾"	Bottom Shelf—Front Bar
H	1	15½"x26¾"	Shelf—Front Bar
I	1	15½"x26¾"	Drawer Shelf—Front Bar
J	1	9½"x15½"	Shelf—Front Bar
K	1	6"x15½"	Divider Between Drawers
L	2	6"x13"	Drawer Front
M	2	12"x42¼"	Bar Top
N	2	8"x30⅞"	Shelf—Back Bar
O	1	6"x45¾"	Face of Light Trough
P	1	15⅝"x45¾"	Bottom of Plant Box
Q	1	6"x45¾"	Divider between Plant Box and Light Trough
R	4	5⅞"x14⅜"	Drawer Side *
S	2	5⅞"x12"	Drawer Back *
T	2	12"x13⅞"	Drawer Bottom *
U	1	46½"x80"	Back of Back Bar
V	1	16"x38¾"	Door and Door Backing
W	1	31¼"x38¾"	Door and Door Backing
	3 Pcs.	16"x79½"	2" T 1-11 Doors and Bar Front**
	3½ Lin. Ft.	¼"x1"	Filler
	3½ Lin. Ft.	1"x4"	Bracing
	1 Pc.	5½"x45⅜"	Obscure Glass
	1 Only	40-Watt-36" Long	Fluorescent Tube
	2 Pcs.	12"x42¼"	Plastic Laminate Top
	11½ Lin. Ft.	For ¾" Edge	Metal Edging
	3 Ea.	"Soss"	Bar Top Hinges
	6 Ea.	For ¾" Plywood	Hinges
	2 Ea.	—	Pin Hinges
	3 Ea.	As Required	Rubber-Tired Casters
	1 Ea.	—	Door Stop for Bar

Miscellaneous—4d and 6d Finish Nails and Glue

* Parts not identified on drawings by letters

** Cut from 3—1'-4"x8'-0" Panels of 2" Texture, One-Eleven

DARK-ROOM CABINET

When time for a hobby is limited, organization of working space, equipment and materials is most important. Any photographer will be well repaid for building this darkroom cabinet (Fig. 24), in added convenience and efficiency.

If necessary, adjust any dimensions to your space, then cut parts specified in the diagrams and material list. Nail and glue all joints.

Fig. 24.

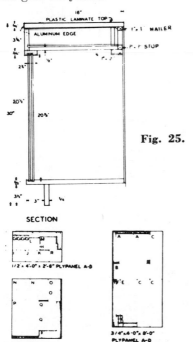

Fig. 25.

Cut toe space, rabbet ends, and dado frame and bottom for doors. Nail ends to bottom and base strip (F), fit and nail back into rabbet, and install 1″ x 2″ framing for drawers.

Construction of drawers according to detail given in Fig. 25, and fitting guides (M) to frame and underside of drawers will be done most easily before nailing top (E) to sides.

Cut and fit sliding doors, sealing all edges carefully and painting inner and outer faces alike.

Apply plastic top, metal edging, and finish completely as required.

When building the paper cabinet shown in Fig. 24, fit all pieces carefully to insure light-tight joints. *Note* that side (R) projects ½″ past front edge of side (J), for hinging. Dado sides for shelves, nail to back and top, and install by nailing up through middle shelf (C). Fit shelves (O), hang door, finish completely and apply felt strips and quarter-round to keep out light. Hang shelves on adjustable standards or fixed brackets, as desired.

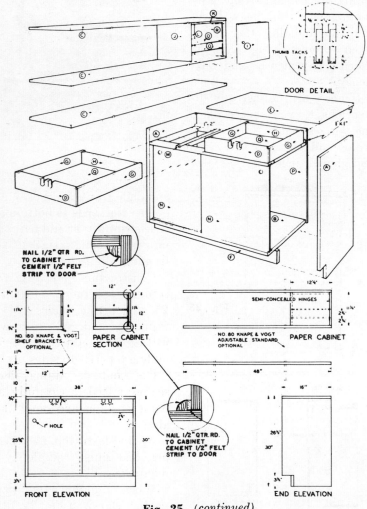

Fig. 25. *(continued)*

PARTS REQUIRED

CODE	NO. REQ'D	SIZE	PART IDENTIFICATION
A	2	16"x29¼"	Ends
B	1	15¾"x34½"	Bottom
C	3	12"x48"	Shelf
D	2	3¾"x17-3/16"	Drawer Front
E	1	16"x36"	Top
F	1	3½"x36"	Base
G	4	3¾"x14⅝"	Drawer Sides
H	2	3"x16"	Drawer Back
I	1	11¼"x12½"	Door—Paper Cabinet
J	1	11¼"x11½"	Side—Paper Cabinet
K	1	11½"x11½"	Top—Paper Cabinet
L	1	10¾"x11½"	Back—Paper Cabinet
M	6	¾"x15¼"	Drawer Guides
N	2	17⅝"x20⅞"	Door
O	2	11"x12"	Shelf—Paper Cabinet
P	1	25¾"x35¼"	Back
Q	2	14⅝"x16"	Drawer Bottom
R	1	11¼"x12"	Side—Paper Cabinet
	14 Lin. Ft.	1"x2"	Framing
	1 Pr.	For ½" Plywood	Semi-Concealed Hinges
	4 Lin. Ft.	—	Felt Strip and Qtr. Round
* {	6 Lin. Ft.	—	Adjustable Shelf Standard
}	6 Ea.	—	Shelf Brackets—12"
	6 Lin. Ft.	1"x1"	Drawer Stop and Nailer

Miscellaneous—4d and 6d Finish Nails
Waterproof Glue
* Optional—Use fixed brackets if desired

MIXING CENTER CABINET

With its companion overhead cabinet, shown in Fig. 26, this mixing center cabinet centralizes food preparation for the oven, range or table in one area.

Accurate measurements are most important before constructing this mixing center cabinet. Any or all of the several parts of the unit may be built, as desired. This flexibility of choice—with the several variable elements shown in Fig. 27—make it possible to fit practically any space available.

Cut structural parts to size after detailed dimensions have been determined, sand edges and fit together. Attach bottom

Fig. 26.

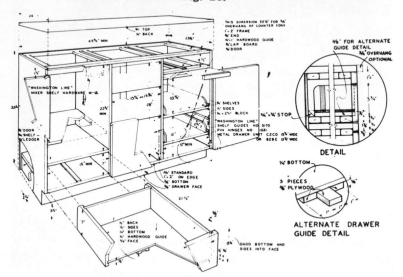

Fig. 27.

to base and ledger strips first. Fasten ends and back in place, then tip forward and install intermediate standards.

Tip back onto base to install fixed shelves, frames for top and lap board and drawer guides.

Use glue and 6d or 8d finish nails at all joints.

Move into position, level up if floor is uneven and nail to floor or wall.

Install facing strip and top, apply surfacing material, band edges and finish plywood as desired. Attach hardware and hang doors, being careful to seal edges thoroughly. Finish doors inside and out equally.

Dimensions for drawers and sliding shelves will be determined by the cabinet sizes you select. Cut all parts to size, dado the joints, sand and assemble with glue and 4d finish nails. Finish as desired.

SLIDING SPICE RACK

Fig. 28.

This unique sliding spice rack and tuckaway shelf put space to maximum use and provide for tall bottles as well as small cans and boxes (Fig. 28). This unit can easily be added to the shelves in an existing cabinet or built into a new overhead cabinet as shown in Fig. 29.

If you are building the complete overhead cabinet, measure the over-all dimensions of your space which fix the size of various parts.

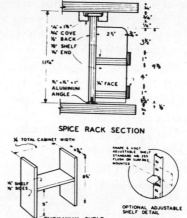

SPICE RACK SECTION

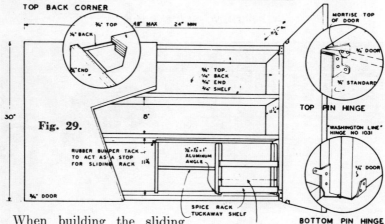

Fig. 29.

When building the sliding rack and tuckaway shelf for an existing cabinet, its size determines the variable width shown.

Cut all parts to size, sand edges and check for proper fit. All joints should be glued and nailed.

Use 6d or 8d finish nails in assembling the cabinet. Fasten the tuckaway shelf to shelves and back with 4d finish nails. Hang cabinet on wall by driving screws through back into wall studs.

Also use 4d finish nails and glue to assemble the sliding spice rack. Install track and hang doors on cabinet. Finish as desired. Be very careful to prime edges of doors and finish both faces alike.

SINK CABINET

Convenience at the sink work center saves hours of time daily, because so much housekeeping revolves around that area. A plywood sink cabinet (Fig. 30) lets you choose any color you want, to match other cabinets and provide relief from the stark monotony of an all-white kitchen.

Adjust any variable dimensions to fit your space and the size of the sink you are installing.

Fig. 30.

Cut all structural panels and frame parts to size (Fig. 31). Use only plywood made with 100% waterproof glue (EXT-DFPA) around locations exposed to moisture or dampness. Sand edges and fit together.

Assemble with waterproof

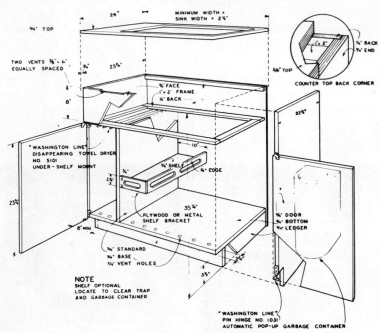

Fig. 31.

glue and 6d or 8d finish nails at all joints. Fasten bottom panel to base and ledger strips first. Then install ends, back and frame.

Tip cabinet forward so you can nail through bottom when installing the intermediate standard. After face, top and shelf are fastened, move cabinet into position and level up to correct any unevenness in the floor.

Fit and hang doors, which should be cut from the same panel as the face to insure matching grain patterns. It is very important to prime edges of doors well and to finish inner and outer faces alike.

Finish the entire cabinet as required, apply surfacing material to counter and install fixtures and accessories desired.

FRUIT-VEGETABLE STORAGE

Fruit and vegetable storage space that is easy to clean and does not collect grime is provided by convenient metal bins as shown in Fig. 32. The entire unit is neatly concealed by a single door beneath the cutting board, so you still have complete freedom in choice of colors for your kitchen.

To facilitate cleaning vegetables, these bins should be situated near the sink. They can be built as a separate unit (Fig. 33), or combined with other base cabinets.

Cut all structural panels and

Fig. 32.

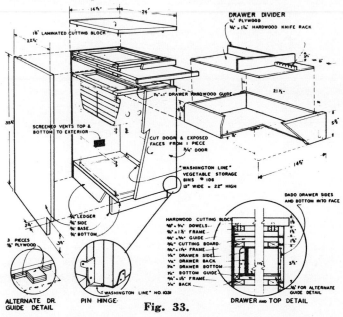

Fig. 33.

frame parts to size, sand edges and fit together.

All joints should be glued and nailed. Fasten bottom to base and ledger strips first, using 6d or 8d finish nails. Then install ends, back and frames. Move cabinet into position and level base if floor is uneven.

Cut door drawer front and face strips from one piece of plywood so grain pattern will match, sand edges and install. Be sure to prime all edges of the door and apply equal finishing coats inside and out.

Cut drawer parts, check in place for fit, sand edges and assemble with 4d or 6d finish nails.

Finish entire cabinet as desired and install cutting block and baskets.

CHAPTER 19

Exterior Woodworking Projects

CONSTRUCTION OF WINDOW, DOOR, AND PORCH SCREENS

While ready-made screens are available in a variety of sizes and shapes to meet almost all requirements, considerably better screens can be constructed at a fraction of the cost.

The screening material used, known as "screen cloth," is available in 14, 16, and 18 mesh openings per inch and in widths ranging from 18″ to 48″. It is made of finely drawn wire so that it will not exclude air and light. Since screens are exposed to all kinds of weather these fine strands of wire will rust if the metal is not corrosion-resistant. A single break in the mesh renders the entire screen useless. Bronze or copper insect-screen cloth have proved to be highly resistant to rust and other forms of corrosion that destroy ordinary screens, and will provide lasting protection.

For the handy man who would like to make his own screens, only a few simple hand tools are necessary. Materials can be readily procured at lumber and hardware dealers. Secure well-seasoned wood that is free from knots. All nails, tacks, and staples used should be of copper, while hinges, screws, handles, and corner pieces should be of brass or bronze. This will assure a rustproof screen that will give satisfactory service over a period of years.

With these materials and a cross-cut saw, a hammer, a square, and a miter box, proceed as follows. Measure each window frame carefully, as they may vary as much as ¼″. Select the type of joint preferred, mark the lumber carefully and cut exactly on the marks to insure a close fit for the finished job.

The *step joint* is the simplest and strongest joint. The upright

539

pieces should be the full height of the frame while the cross members should be cut the width of one side member shorter than the measured width of the frame. Cut square notches, half the width of the side members (*A*, Fig. 1). Stagger the nails and drive them on a slight slant toward the inside so they won't meet and either split the wood, bend, or come out at the side. If the screen is over four feet high, strengthen it with a crosspiece (*B*, Fig. 1). Drawing *C* illustrates another simple joint that may be employed at the corners.

The *mitered joint*, strengthened with a cross-corner brace, is another easily made type (*A*, Fig. 2). Cut the lumber the full size of the openings both ways, then with a miter box saw the ends at a 45° angle. The point of the angle should be exactly on the corner of the piece. Then miter the cross-corner members, also with a 45° angle. Employ plenty of nails and check the alignment with a square as the fastening proceeds. Countersink the nails for a neat appearance. Instead of a cross-corner brace, there are many fastening appliances available at any hardware dealer that may be used in building screens. Shown in Fig. 3 are an angle (*A*), corner brace (*B*), and corrugated fasteners (*C*), all of which will add to the strength of a screen frame.

The *doweled joint* is a mitered joint fastened with two diagonal dowels instead of the corner brace (*B*, Fig. 4). After the lumber has been cut and mitered, fasten with a small nail to keep the joints from slipping; then bore two holes through the corners, insert the dowels, and glue the joint. After it has set, trim the dowels flush with the frame. The square-end doweled joint, similar to the doweled mitered joint, is shown at *C*, Fig. 4.

After sandpapering, give the frames two coats of good paint, permitting each to dry thoroughly. The first step in applying the insert of screen cloth is to lay the frame on a flat surface and place a section of lumber under each end. Then bend the frame down in the center and fasten lightly with a nail or clamp. Trim the screen cloth and tack with 4-oz. copper tacks on both ends. Release the frame and the screen cloth will be stretched tightly. Tack the sides and then cover all edges of the screen cloth with a half-round molding of appropriate size. Put identifying numbers on each screen and the corresponding window frame. When brass or bronze hangers, hinges, and handles are affixed, the screen

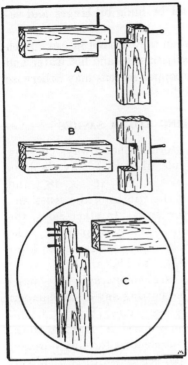

Fig. 1. Two simple types of joints used in the construction of screens.

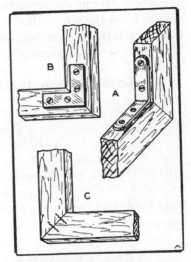

Fig. 3. Metal corner fasteners used in the construction of screens.

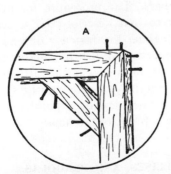

Fig. 2. Method of fastening a mitered joint with a corner brace in constructing all types of screens.

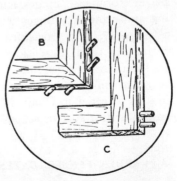

Fig. 4. Two types of doweled joints used in the construction of screens.

is ready for service. Screens should be hung on hinges and secured with hooks and eyes.

Exercise care in storing screens when they are not in use. Each spring, scrub the screens thoroughly with soap and hot water and coat with thinned clear lacquer, as copper screens may otherwise stain a house with white walls.

CONSTRUCTING AND FITTING STORM SASHES

When planning and constructing storm sashes always consider standard glass sizes. As a general rule, glass that is available in standard sizes, such as 8″ × 10″, 12″ × 14″, 16″ × 18″, and other sizes will not have to be cut if the widths of the stiles and rails of the sash are planned in accordance. In other cases, the widths of stiles and rails can be altered slightly by planing. The ideal lumber to use for storm sashes is either straight-grain kiln-dried pine or cypress, usually from 13⁄16″ to 1⅛″ thick.

The procedures for construction are comparatively simple. Measure each window carefully before cutting any of the lumber. Cut rabbets in the stock for the glass panes (Fig. 5; Chap. 3). While miter joints are sometimes used in making storm sashes they are not particularly recommended for this purpose. A stub tenon joint set in a mortise and secured with two nails in addition to the usual gluing is preferable (Fig. 5). For making mortise and tenon joints, see Chap. 3. Hardware dealers stock special storm-sash hinges and fasteners. The procedure for fitting and attaching hinges is similar to that described for doors in Chap. 17. The procedure for attaching the fastener depends on the type used. Directions are usually furnished by the manufacturer. After assembling the frame of the sash and attaching hinges to the frame, proceed to set in place and putty the glass as directed in Chap. 17. Storm sash should be painted to conform with the color scheme of the exterior of the house.

GARDEN FENCES, GATES, TRELLISES, AND PERGOLAS

The construction of these various garden accessories has been simplified to a tremendous degree by the availability of ready-cut lumber for this specific purpose. Since these garden accessories

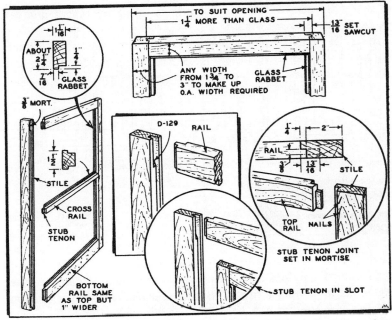

Fig. 5. Procedure details for the construction and fitting of storm sashes.

will be exposed to different weather conditions, an excellent quality of lumber should be used. While pine and cypress are used to some extent, California redwood is really the ideal type for this purpose. Redwood is comparatively inexpensive, is an easy material to either paint or stain, and if left unpainted will acquire a natural weathered effect.

In the construction of any of these projects, preferably set all posts in concrete. Coat the ends of the posts with tar where they will come in contact with the concrete; secure some roofing tar, melt it in a large galvanized pail and dip each post into the melted tar. This acts as a sealer and forms a bond between the wood and the concrete, decreasing any likelihood of moisture collecting there. Use an ordinary concrete mixture, set all posts square, and tamp the concrete well.

Building garden fences. All of the materials required for the construction of the various fences shown are available in ready-

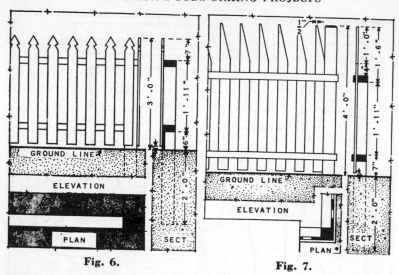

Fig. 6.   Fig. 7.

cut form. Variations of stock picket designs can be made by the ingenious man who desires to have a garden fence individual in design. An angular cut, a design of drilled holes or a silhouette cut out in each of the pickets can be used effectively to produce distinctive patterns. Secure the horizontal rails to the posts with a simple rabbet joint and countersunk screws in all of these designs. Nail the pickets or boards to the rails with galvanized nails. Fig. 6 illustrates a simplified dart motif used for the top of the pickets; a fence of this type is strictly in character with the modern derivatives of English cottage architecture. The decoration at the top of the pickets is made entirely with straight saw cuts, and can be done either at the planing mill before delivery or by the builder on the job. Place posts ten feet apart and space pickets their own width. Each ten feet of this fence will require the following materials:

2 horizontal rails	2″ × 4″ × 10′ 0″
1 post	4″ × 4″ × 6′ 0″
1 board	1″ × 8″ × 10′ 0″
16 pickets	1″ × 4″ × 35″

Fig. 6 shows the fence three feet high. This dimension may be changed to suit the requirements of the site.

By cutting the tops of pickets symmetrically (Fig. 7), it is possible to introduce a feeling of movement into the design of a fence. Be sure to make the angle of the picket face toward the house for the aesthetic purpose of making the house itself the most important part of the landscape design. Notice the extra strips placed outside the row of pickets parallel to the rails. Place posts at ten foot intervals and carry corner posts to the full height of the fence; intermediate posts only as high as upper rail. For each ten feet of fence, the following materials are needed:

2 horizontal rails	....	$2'' \times 4'' \times 10'\ 0''$
2 strips	....	$1'' \times 2'' \times 10'\ 0''$
1 post	....	$4'' \times 4'' \times 7'\ 0''$
20 pickets	....	$1'' \times 4'' \times 47''$

Board fences. By so simple an expedient as notching the sides of the board, it is possible to relieve the monotony usually inherent in a board fence, and give it a very pleasant decorative effect. Rough boards may be used if the paint is to be sprayed on or if the boards are to be dipped before applying. If painted by hand, it will be far easier to use surfaced stock.

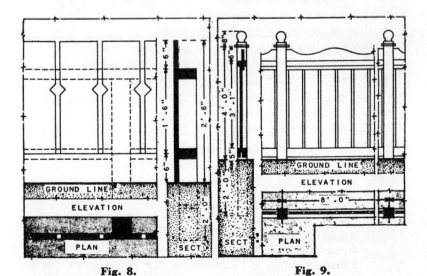

Fig. 8.　　　　　　　Fig. 9.

Such a fence may be of various heights. That shown in Fig. 8 is 2½′ high. Its proportions might be improved by increasing the height somewhat. Note the baseboard which is placed directly against the posts and upon which the vertical boards are set. For each ten feet of fence, the following materials are needed:

2 horizontal rails .... 2″ × 4″ × 10′ 0″
1 vertical post .... 4″ × 4″ × 6′ 0″
14 vertical boards (notched as shown)....... 1″ × 8″ × 2′ 0″
1 baseboard .... 1″ × 6″ × 10′ 0″

Though somewhat more elaborate in structure than other board fences, the design shown in Fig. 9 has the advantage of presenting exactly the same appearance from both sides. There is no "inside" or "outside." Depending upon its height, it may be used to insure privacy from passers-by. It will also serve to keep children and pets from wandering out into the street. The finial shown may, if desired, be eliminated. For each ten feet of fence, the following materials will be needed:

2 horizontal rails .... 2″ × 4″ × 10′ 0″
1 horizontal bottom rail .... 1″ × 4″ × 10′ 0″
1 horizontal top board (cut scalloped top
    as indicated) .... 1″ × 5″ × 10′ 0″
1 post .... 4″ × 4″ × 7′ 0″
1 square molding .... 1″ × 2″ × 10′ 0″
17 vertical boarding .... 1″ × 6″ × 3′ 0″
1 redi-cut turned finial .... 4″ × 4″ × 1′ 0″
1 redi-cut square finial base................ 1″ × 6″ × 0′ 6″

Lattice fencing. Lattice fencing of the type shown in Fig. 10 has become particularly popular because of its double usefulness in the garden: it affords a good-looking windbreak for the plants behind it and can also give support for climbers or espaliers. It is simply constructed of redwood materials obtainable at any lumber yard. Lattice strips need be nailed only to the rails and posts and at their ends. Materials needed for each ten-foot unit of fence are:

2 horizontal rails .... 2″ × 4″   × 10′ 0″
1 post .... 4″ × 4″   × 7′ 0″
35 lattice .... ⁵⁄₁₆″ × 1⅜″ × 10′ 0″

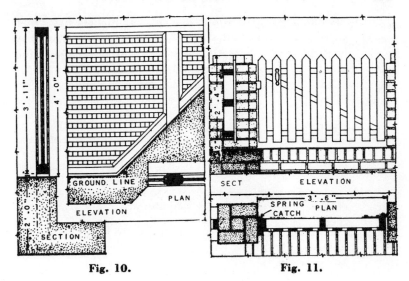

Fig. 10. Fig. 11.

Gates. One of the simplest gates to build is the straight picket gate shown in Fig. 11. The procedures for the construction for this and other gates are similar to that described for fences. The pickets themselves are available in pre-cut redwood. The first step in its construction is to build a simple rectangular frame with a single cross brace of 2 × 4's. The pickets are placed against this, spaced at approximately their own width to fit the opening. Though illustrated as built between brick piers, it is also suitable for use with picket fences.

Note the small stopping block sunk into the brick at the left. This will not be needed if double-swing hinges are used. The materials needed are:

2 horizontal rails	2″ × 3″ × 3′ 6″
1 cross brace	2″ × 3″ × 3′ 6″
9 pickets	1″ × 3″ × 2′ 6″ net 2½″ wide, 35″ long in Picket Pack
1 block gate stop	2″ × 6″ × 3″ cut to form stop as indicated

A slightly more elaborate gate that presents the same appearance from both sides is shown in Fig. 12. The ends of the two side framing members and the top rail may be cut with a bandsaw. In building the gate, place the vertical pickets first, then cut diagonal pieces to fit. Besides their decorative value, they serve as bracing members for the gate to prevent sagging. For each such gate, materials needed are:

2 horizontal rails.................	2″ × 6″ × 3′ 6″ tongue-and-grove and glued to vertical rails
2 vertical rails...................	2″ × 4″ × 2′ 6″ ends cut as shown, grooved to receive tongue of horizontal rails
1 square	1 $^{11}/_{16}$″ × 1 $^{11}/_{16}$″ × 12′ 0″ straight molding No. 1622
1 block gate stop	2″ × 6″ × 3″ cut to form stop as indicated

Pergolas. Pergolas add beauty and utility to a garden and are inexpensive to build. In order to use standard lengths of material and to prevent waste this pergola has been laid out on a two-foot module or unit plant (Figs. 13 and 13A). All dimensions are taken from center line to center line. A dimension less than one module would be one-half module or one foot. Any dimension less than one foot should be used only to space lattice uniformly. One complete unit can be built and another unit added later. The sizes of individual members, such as posts, beams, rafters, and lattice, may be whatever standard size preferred that is procurable. Posts should be constructed of an all-heart grade of lumber.

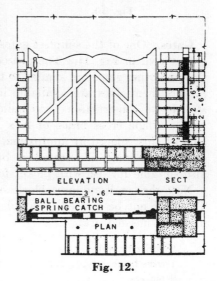

Fig. 12.

The brackets, beam, and rafter end designs can run from the straight line effects to the scroll type. Scroll ends can be cut and shaped by hand tools, if necessary. However, if power equipment is available it can be used to advantage. Materials required are as follows:

Fig. 13. Construction details and completed pergola.

MATERIAL LISTS

Posts Set One Module on Center

4 Posts	....	4″ × 4″ × 10′ 0″
2 Beams	....	4″ × 4″ × 8′ 0″
4 Rafters	....	2″ × 6″ × 10′ 0″
4 Brackets	....	3″ × 6″ × 2′ 0″
2 Bottom rails	....	2″ × 4″ × 2′ 0″
14 Roof lattice	....	5⁄16″ × 1⅝″ × 8′ 0″
4 Side panels	....	5⁄16″ × 1⅝″ × 7′ 0″
16 Side panels	....	5⁄16″ × 1⅝″ × 2′ 0″

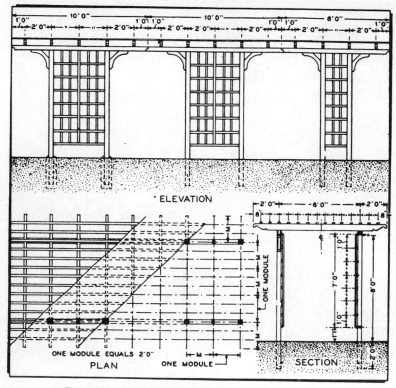

Fig. 13A.   Plan and elevation drawings of a pergola.

Posts Set Two Modules on Center

4 Posts	4″ × 4″ × 10′ 0″
2 Beams	4″ × 4″ × 10′ 0″
5 Rafters	2″ × 6″ × 10′ 0″
4 Brackets	3″ × 6″ × 2′ 0″
2 Bottom rails	2″ × 4″ × 4′ 0″
2 Middle rails	2″ × 4″ × 7′ 0″
14 Roof lattice	5⁄16″ × 1⅝″ × 10′ 0″
8 Side panels	5⁄16″ × 1⅝″ × 7′ 0″
16 Side panels	5⁄16″ × 1⅝″ × 4′ 0″

Trellises.   A number of suggested trellis designs are shown in Fig. 14.   As can be seen, their construction is extremely simple. With a little originality trellises can be built in many pleasing and original designs. Lattice, battens, and lath are available in the following standard sizes:

LATTICE, BATTENS, OR LATH FOR TRELLISES

Type	Thickness in Inches	Width in Inches
Lattice	$\frac{5}{16}$	$1\frac{1}{16}$
Lattice	$\frac{5}{16}$	$1\frac{1}{8}$
Lattice	$\frac{5}{16}$	$1\frac{3}{8}$
Lattice	$\frac{5}{16}$	$1\frac{5}{8}$
Lattice	$\frac{5}{16}$	$1\frac{3}{4}$
Batten	$\frac{3}{8}$	$2\frac{1}{8}$
Batten	$\frac{3}{8}$	$2\frac{1}{4}$
Batten	$\frac{5}{16}$	$2\frac{1}{2}$
Batten	$\frac{3}{8}$	$2\frac{1}{2}$
Batten	$\frac{3}{8}$	$2\frac{3}{4}$
Lath	$\frac{3}{8}$	$1\frac{1}{2}$

Lattice lengths—Standard lengths are 6' and longer in multiples of 1' up to and including 10', and in multiples of 2' from 10' to 20 .

Batten lengths—3' to 10' in 1' multiples, and in multiples of 2' from 10' to 20'.

Lath lengths—4', 6', and 8'. 50 laths per bundle.

The number of lineal feet of lattice required for each design is shown in Fig. 14.

GARDEN FURNITURE

The construction of attractive and serviceable garden furniture presents no special difficulties. The suggested designs shown in Figs. 15 to 21 are simple in construction. If power equipment is not available they can all be constructed with the hand tools generally found in a home tool kit.

Lawn chair. The chair shown in Fig. 15 is a variation of the conventional Adirondack-type chair, featuring folding arm extensions and supports. Cut all parts to sizes and shapes (Fig. 15) from ⅞" clear kiln-dried lumber. The curved members forming the arm rests, the supports, and the chair seat can be cut out on a bandsaw. If a bandsaw is not available, proceed as described in Chap. 2 for cutting convex and concave cuts with a saw and chisel. After cutting all members to size and shaping, assemble with countersunk screws and nails in the following order.

Secure apron to the two front uprights, then attach the side pieces to the uprights. Next, with hinges secure the hinged part of each of the arms. Assemble and secure the back supports to the bottom side members (Fig. 15). Secure the crosspiece forming

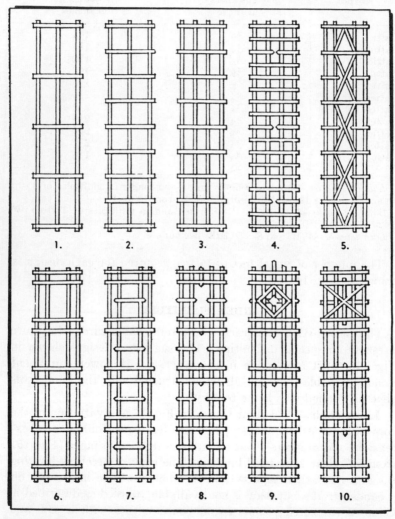

Fig. 14. Suggested trellis designs and material required. (All are 1′ × 6′.) 1. 24 lineal feet; 2. 30 lineal feet; 3. 36 lineal feet; 4. 48 lineal feet; 5. 48 lineal feet; 6. 36 lineal feet; 7. to 10. 42 lineal feet.

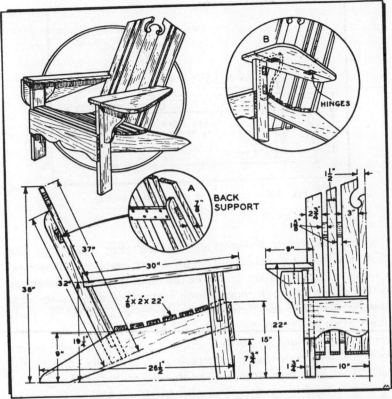

Fig. 15. Construction of lawn chair with folding arms.

the back support (*A*, Fig. 15). Nail pieces forming seat and back members and proceed by securing the arms to the back and the front uprights. Finally, fit and secure the folding arm supports in place with hinges (*B*, Fig. 15). Sand and finish the completely assembled chair.

Roll-away lounge. The comfortable roll-away lounge shown in Fig. 16 is a unique piece of garden furniture that can easily be constructed of 1⅛" kiln-dried clear pine or cypress. While the dimensions given in the drawing will accommodate a 24" × 60" plastic-covered pad of foamite rubber, dimensions can be altered as desired.

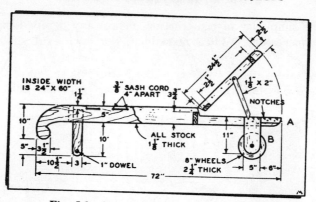

Fig. 16. Constructing a roll-away lounge.

As can be seen in the working drawing (Fig. 16), all of the joints are butted together and secured with countersunk screws. A series of $7/16''$ holes are drilled in the main frame and the hinge section of the lounge, through which is threaded a $3/8''$ sash cord. This cord is laced and forms the necessary support for the padding. Make the entire pad of two thicknesses of $1''$ rubber foam, cement together and cover with one of the many types of waterproof and washable plastic materials now available at local upholstery or hardware stores. The hinged section can be adjusted to several heights by means of the notch supports fastened to the main frame (*A*, Fig. 16). Bandsaw the $8''$ wheels from $2\frac{1}{4}''$ stock or from two thicknesses of $1\frac{1}{8}''$ stock glued together. For a discussion of procedures on gluing and clamping see Chap. 3. Mount the $8''$ wheels on a $1''$ hardwood dowel with $1\frac{1}{4}''$ dowels on the end of the axle to hold them in place (*B*, Fig. 16). Assemble and finish as desired.

Roll-away lawn seat. This lawn seat is a companion piece to the roll-away lounge previously described. The novel feature of this piece of garden furniture is the two removable chairs which can be placed in almost any desired position (Figs. 17 and 18). The seats are perfectly square and are identical with the exception of the arms. One of the seats has the arm on the left, while the other has it on the right. Construction details are shown in Fig. 19. The completeness of this working drawing, combined with the simplicity of construction, makes any detailed instructions unnecessary. When assembled, the lawn seat should be finished.

Lawn tables. The designer of the lawn table shown in Fig. 20 conceived the clever idea of making the tops of these tables from

Fig. 17. Roll-away lawn seat.

Fig. 18. Roll-away lawn seat.

discarded barrel tops. Where barrel tops are not available, cut the table tops from 1⅛″ stock either to the size shown or to any size desired and bevel off the edges on the shaper. Use ¾″ stock for the legs and stretchers of the table and bandsaw them to the required shape. Half-lapped joints are used throughout with the exception of the necessary dado cuts for setting in the legs at the required angle (*A*, Fig. 20). See Chap. 3 for the making of dado joints. Assemble the table with countersunk flathead wood screws. Sand the top smooth and finish natural by

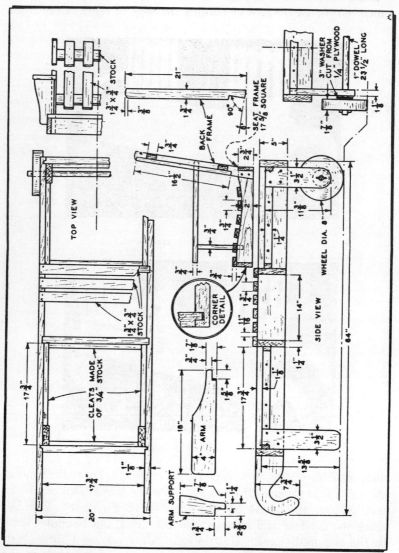

Fig. 19. Construction and details of a roll-away lawn seat.

applying several coats of clear Valspar or similar waterproof varnish. The balance of the table should be either painted or lacquered.

Outdoor gymnasium for the children. The working plans for an outdoor gymnasium of simple yet sturdy construction that can be fitted into a comparatively small space are shown in Fig. 21. This outdoor gym can be assembled with carriage and log bolts to make it easy to take apart and set up in the basement for use during the winter months.

Clear 2″ × 4″ pine or cypress is used for most of the parts. The bottom frame, which comes in contact with the ground, should be given a coat of creosote to prevent the wood from rotting. Assemble the framework of the gym with carriage and log bolts. Make the ladder rungs and the teeter-totter handles from either old broom handles or 1¼″ maple dowels. The teeter-totter is mounted on a piece of ¾″ or 1″ pipe cut to size shown with regular pipe straps for fittings (*A*, Fig. 21). To add rigidity to the entire structure, put metal reinforcement plates on all corners and bracing members (Chap. 3).

Round or break all edges and sharp corners before proceeding with the finishing and painting.

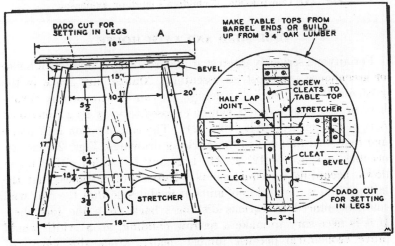

Fig. 20. Lawn table construction and details.

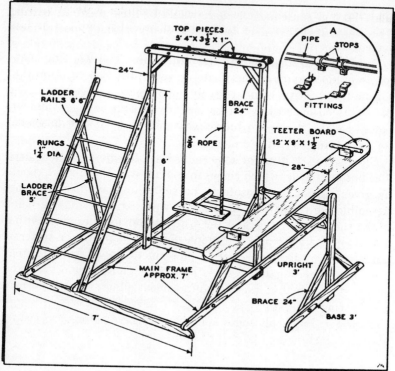

Fig. 21. Construction of children's outdoor gymnasium.

TOOL SHED AND LATH HOUSE

For anyone seriously interested in gardening, a small lath house or greenhouse is almost an essential. Almost any space in the garden will do for such a structure. It can be screened by shrubbery or, if neatly painted, can be exposed to view as a functional part of the garden itself (Fig. 22). The combination lath house and tool shed detailed in the working drawings, Figs. 23 and 24, occupies a space of 12′ × 24′, but may be scaled either up or down, according to requirements. Notice, for instance, that the lath portion is planned in 6′ units or modules so that the rear wall could be placed at various distances back from the tool shed. If it is necessary to make a narrow building, an 8′ width would prove economical because lumber dealers stock this length of material and consequently there would be little waste in cutting. The whole structure may be erected easily without special tools.

Note that the complete bill of materials for the construction of the tool and lath house includes those required for the workbenches and tables (Fig. 25). A notation, such as ⅞′ listed in the column headed "Pieces Required," indicates that seven pieces will be needed, each 8′ long. Because the wood will be exposed to weathering and alternate wetting and drying, a durable species of lumber such as California redwood should be used. All items on the material list are usually carried in stock by lumber dealers.

Fig. 22. Completed tool shed and lath house.

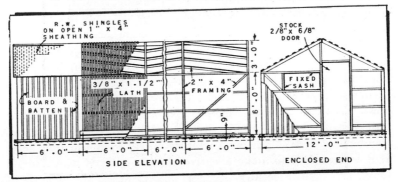

Fig. 23. Elevation details.

Structural details. Notice that roof bracing in the lath house portion of the structure is designed to carry off rainwater. Braces are slanted toward alternate rafters. (Only nailing strips are necessary under the shingled portion of the roof.)

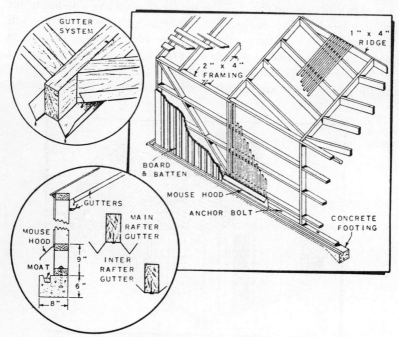

Fig. 24. Structural details.

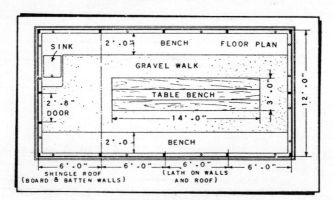

Fig. 25. Floor plan.

LATH HOUSE—MATERIAL LIST

Item	Pieces	Net Length	Pieces Required
Sills			2/10′ 2/12′ 2/14′
Studs	13	5′ 8″	1/6′ 6/12′
Horizontal braces	36	6′ 0″	18/12′
Diagonal braces	21	2′ 4″	7/8′
Plates			6/12′
Rafters	14	6′ 7″	7/14′
Nailing joist	24	6′ 0″	12/12′
Ridge boards	2	12′ 0″	2/12′
Door header	1	2′ 8″ ⎱	1/6′
Window frame	1	1′ 8″ ⎰	
Boards—sides	24	6′ 0″	12/12′
Boards—ends	48		2/6′ 8/8′ 3/14′ 4/18′
Battens			4/18′ 3/6′ 8/8′ 3/14′ 12/12′
Roof sheathing	20	6′ 6″	10/14′
Shingles			1 Square
Side lath			3 Bundles 6′
End lath			1 Bundle 6′
Top lath			3 Bundles 8′
Cornice molding	4	12′ 0″	4/12′
Benches:			
Horizontal supports	13	2′ 0″ ⎱	3/12′
	3	3′ 0″ ⎰	
Legs	18	3′ 0″	9/6′
Top (sides)			8/12′ 1/6′
Top (center)			3/14′

Nail gutters of galvanized metal or copper to the underside of roof members. These may be obtained from a local sheet metal worker.

The necessary concrete foundation can be poured per standard procedures. Other constructional details are shown in Figs. 23 and 24.

The moat in the concrete foundation receives water from the gutter system, so that it may be drained off at a convenient point.

Index